INSIDE THE MIND OF
JOSEPH SMITH

INSIDE THE MIND OF JOSEPH SMITH

PSYCHOBIOGRAPHY AND THE BOOK OF MORMON

ROBERT D. ANDERSON

SIGNATURE BOOKS / SALT LAKE CITY

For Delores

I would wish for every man a wife like she,

for every child a mother like she,

for every grandchild a grandmother like she ...

COVER DESIGN BY BRIAN BEAN

Inside the Mind of Joseph Smith: Psychobiography and The Book of Mormon was printed on acid-free paper and was composed, printed, and bound in the United States of America.

04 03 02 01 2000 99 6 5 4 3 2 1

LIBRARY OF CONGRESS CATALOGING-IN-PUBLICATION DATA

Anderson, Robert D.

Inside the mind of Joseph Smith: psychobiography and the Book of Mormon / by Robert D. Anderson.

p. cm.

Includes bibliographical references and index.

ISBN 1-56085-125-2 (pbk.)

1. Smith, Joseph, 1805-1844—Psychology. 2. Book of Mormon—Criticism, interpretation, etc. 3. Church of Jesus Christ of Latter-day Saints—Presidents—Biography. I. Title.

BX8695.S6A 1999

289.3'092—dc21

[b] 98-46501

CIP

Contents

Preface

This book began more than four decades ago in a challenge to a group of newly "called" missionaries, all of us volunteers, for the Church of Jesus Christ of Latter-day Saints (Mormon). As part of our basic training, we nineteen-year-old males (the women were twenty-one) spent a week at church headquarters in Salt Lake City, Utah, where we were taught that the Book of Mormon would be our main tool in converting individuals who would respond positively to our knock on their door, our street meetings near the center of town, or inquiries in response to various Mormon activities such as the youth movement. The challenge was, simply, to find an alternate explanation to the supernatural origin of the Book of Mormon. As a sincere and earnest young missionary, I was sure that such an explanation could not be found. I now feel differently and have, in fact, tried to articulate such an alternate explanation in the pages that follow.

The Book of Mormon's central role is epitomized in the fact that it provides this religious movement's earliest and most enduring nickname. Near the end of the book, a pre-Columbian American prophet named Moroni urges his readers to pray about the book, promising, "And if ye shall ask with a sincere heart [and] real intent, having faith in Christ, he will manifest the truth of it unto you by the power of the Holy Ghost."[1] It is a scripture memorized by tens of thousands of missionaries every year and is read to every investigator in the first or second meeting. This process of study and prayer while reading the Book of Mormon brings thousands each year into the Mormon church.

My own ancestors were among the hundreds, then thousands, and then tens of thousands of the socially disenfranchised who received religious and economic hope simultaneously of transcending social class discrimination or psychological restrictions. My maternal ancestors came from the slums of Liverpool in the first decade of the twentieth century. My paternal great-grandfather reached America in 1857 from Glasgow. Assigned to help found one of Brigham Young's hundreds of farming towns, he often repeated, "It's good we left Scotland when we did." Both families escalated in status; it is safe to say that I am better off because of, or despite, their beliefs. A century later I returned to Great Britain as a missionary, baptizing two dozen into Mormonism. One of these Scottish converts visited me in the United States almost twenty-five years later. She said, "You know how it goes. It was too late for Davey and me, but our children now have hope. Without the church, they would have been as hopeless as we were." This is the genius of Joseph Smith and the closest thing to a miracle in Mormonism. Today throughout the world, the "miracle" continues among the hopeless.

At the heart of this dynamic, both positive and negative, is the Book of Mormon. According to Joseph Smith, founding prophet and translator of the Book of Mormon, the book was produced by and gains its proofs from supernatural aspects: the visitation of angels, special seer stones through which an ancient script was translated into English, and so forth. Indeed, as we missionaries were told, how else could a semi-educated farm boy from New York produce in three months a 588-page, 275,000-word history covering a thousand years of pre-Columbian history with the detail and complexity of the Book of Mormon?

Yet no one has ever successfully differentiated spiritual experiences from psychological ones, and the existence of a Christian civilization in the pre-Columbian New World, as described in the Book of Mormon, enjoys no support from non-Mormon anthropologists and archaeologists. Naturalistic explanations of the book have come and gone, some more persuasive than others. Beginning with Fawn Brodie's naturalistic biography of Joseph Smith in 1945,[2] and again in 1969, new historical materials and approaches regarding Mormon church founder Joseph Smith have increasingly questioned traditional claims of divine translations and visions. Mormons who believe that Smith's prophetic calling depends on the sum of his miracles often find such modern historical revelations discomfiting.

This new information suggested a progressive reworking of his important "first vision" and evidenced his attempt to rewrite history after the fact, changing dates and years to dramatize his story.[3] Smith's claim to translate ancient Egyptian foundered when the original papyrus resurfaced.[4] These historical advances were troubling to me for they suggested, I believed then and now, misrepresentation on the part of Joseph Smith, with good documentation of such behavior before and after the publication of the Book of Mormon.[5]

This opinion, shared by others, left every claim by him open to question, especially when he emphasized the truth of a happening or incident. Viewing Smith as only partially reliable means that information from others became relatively more important as I pursued my study; the opinions of others, including previously disdained antagonists, took on added weight, especially if their observations fit a consistent pattern, as I believe they do.

This problem of Smith's reliability as a narrator was compounded by a second level of control and modifications of the original history by Mormon leadership since Smith.[6] Much of this new troubling information had come from non-believing Mormons or non-Mormons, which had historically made it easier to dismiss; but some had also been recorded by devout members striving for historical truth. As new information has also become available from a variety of historical sources, including the archives of the Mormon church, it has become clearer that, at least on some issues and in some cases, a history had been created or molded.[7] But what about the Book of Mormon?

Unknown to most Mormons for more than half a century, LDS church leader, theologian, and philosopher Brigham Henry Roberts proposed a compelling alternative explanation for the Book of Mormon in the 1920s. Finally published in 1985 as *Studies of the Book of Mormon,* Roberts's thought-provoking analysis suggested that the book's general outline, as well as every major concept, had come from another book, *A View of the Hebrews,* published a few years earlier and written by Ethan Smith (no relation to Joseph Smith), a knowledgeable theologian of the day.[8] *A View of the Hebrews* subscribed to the popular 400-year-old folk belief that Native Americans descended from the lost Ten Tribes of Israel. Roberts explored the legend in depth, noting the Book of Mormon's potential debt to Ethan Smith and identifying Joseph Smith's New World scripture as the most enduring representative of the theory that Native Americans were Israelites. Earlier in his life, Roberts had vigorously defended the Book of Mormon, but now his private analysis contained fierce irony, evidence of his expanding incredulity. In public he continued to champion the book's ancient historicity.

Even if the Book of Mormon derived its outline and concept from *View of the Hebrews,* what accounted for its detailed stories of miracles, conversions, heroism, visions, wars, prophecies, and teachings? Where did these stories come from? While brief forays into this area have been made by non-Mormons, there has been no comprehensive, consistent answer, despite a growing number of insightful naturalistic studies.[9] One Mormon apostle dismissed such studies: "The practitioners of that approach typically focus on a limited number of issues, like geography or 'horses' or angelic delivery of nineteenth-century language patterns. They ignore or gloss over the incredible complexity of the Book of Mormon record."[10]

By the time Roberts's family published his long-secret manuscript, I no longer participated in Mormon worship but retained an interest in its history, culture, and people. I returned to a serious study of religion and Mormonism after taking practical and theoretical psychoanalytic training and becoming interested in applying psychoanalytic principles to group and national movements, individual leaders, writers, artists, and creative works. I realized during those years that, if the Book of Mormon were not ancient history, Joseph Smith's own world and personal experiences might be discernible in its narrative, thus documenting the development of miracles from fantasy. In other words, the Book of Mormon might make an ideal subject for applied psychoanalysis. Such an approach could provide the framework into which other studies could be woven. Moreover, an analysis of its text might reveal elements of Smith's state of mind and also explain the book's many-faceted aspects, perhaps allowing for a comprehensive psychoanalytic assessment of Smith.

Using the text of the first edition (1830) of the Book of Mormon, I have tried to "listen" to it in the same way I listen to patients. The picture of Smith that emerges for me is fascinating though not always complimentary.

When I began, I did not think of writing a psychoanalytic assessment of Joseph Smith. He was a complex, unusual character of considerable force, and the idea was too daunting. However, as my study of parallels between his life and the Book of Mormon progressed, patterns and themes began to emerge which increased my understanding. The psychoanalytic literature remained consistently useful.

I realize that some Mormons, for whom the Book of Mormon is the primary external evidence for Smith's divine calling, may dismiss my discussion out-of-hand, seeing only a black or white choice. In the words of one Mormon writer: "If the Book of Mormon is true, if it is authentic history brought forth in the last days for the wise purposes of God, then the Saints have good reason for faith and a genuine hope for a trust in God. If the Book of Mormon is the product of a deliberate deception or the sincere psychological delusion caused by severe stress, the Saints have no reason for faith or hope."[11]

I hope this dismal assessment is not true. Both outside of and within Mormonism are people whose belief in God and spiritual experiences are more philosophic than literal but who nonetheless retain ongoing faith in the workings of humankind and hope for continued improvement of our welfare. Mormonism is a growing force within Christianity and continues to double in numbers every seventeen years or so. Indeed some non-Mormon observers predict that the Mormon church will become *the* American religion by the year 2020.[12] I believe that Christianity has played at least an indirect role in the leadership of Western culture. Except for fundamentalistic beliefs that disdain reason and individual democratic rights, much of what remains is uplifting. Historian Michael Grant writes that Christianity is the "only religion to profess and practice total, revolutionary, unrestricted charity, compassion, and consolation."[13] Many in Mormonism who doubt or disbelieve, but who have grown up inculcated in faith by loving parents, remain attached to its history, culture, and idealized Christian beliefs.

I would like to assist in the continued evolution of the Mormon church. Once a cult led by a dynamic charismatic and revolutionary leader, it became a potential enemy of the U.S. government with the immediate goal of forming an independent Mormon empire. For a while the church controlled by intimidation, coercion, and even murder.[14] It was arguably the most hated religion the United States has known. Less than a century later, it has transformed itself into today's international corporate giant of loyal citizens, conservative thinking, and champion of community standards.

Our pluralistic society, awash in social problems of drugs, family disintegration, illegitimacy, violence, and destructive sexual behavior, can use the stabilizing influence of such an institution in promoting family and health values. If this work nudges the Mormon church toward its potential as a world caregiver in a nondoctrinal sense, then I will consider the undertaking worthwhile.

Historian Herbert Butterfield once wrote that a serious "sin in historical composition is the organization of the story in such a way that bias cannot be recognized."[15] In an attempt to avoid such "sin" and for readers who may be curious about my own beliefs, I place on the record the fact that my assumptions informing this discussion of Joseph Smith and the Book of Mormon are explicitly naturalistic. However interested I may be in supernatural phenomenon, such miracles cannot be established as scientific or historical fact. I address this issue—including my own assumptions and methodology—at greater depth in the introduction that follows.

The primary purposes of this book are to investigate the psychology of Joseph Smith, demonstrate the benefits of psychobiography, expand awareness of psychological processes, provide an alternate explanation for at least some supernatural claims, and expand scientific knowledge.

As this work was in final preparation, I became aware of another work on Joseph Smith, entitled *The Sword of Laban: Joseph Smith, Jr., and the Dissociated Mind,* by William D. Morain, a plastic surgeon with connections to the Reorganized Church of Jesus Christ of Latter Day Saints (Washington, DC: American Psychiatric Press, 1998). It is always reassuring when two individuals reach the same conclusions independently, in this case that the character Laban in the Book of Mormon plays a symbolic role associated with young Joseph Smith's traumatic surgery. There is much in Morain's book to recommend it. However, my approach sees the life-determining event of surgery on young Joseph as the beginning of inquiry—for a single event, even an overwhelming one, does not make a prophet. Morain does not attempt to evaluate the personality behind the *voluntary* actions of Smith in his dictation; and if Smith experienced dissociative states while creating the Book of Mormon, they were, in my opinion, limited in degree. Dissociative states require amnesia, significant distress, impairment in functioning, and/or a disruption of the integrative functions of consciousness, memory, and identity. But the Book of Mormon contains integrated careful calculations of fact and date, creating a complex history instead of a disorganized mess. This result suggests either full or nearly full personality function at the time of dictation.

Acknowledgements

I owe a great deal to a number of people who have assisted with this work. These include psychoanalysts: first and foremost, my office partner for many years, Frederick S. Hoedemaker, M.D., and also Drs. Werner S. Schimmelbusch, Edward Freedman, Robert Campbell, and Charles Mangham. JoAnn Campbell, Ph.D., did a very useful child-anthropological review of the book, and Jeanette Dyal, A.R.N.P., M.S.W., and Barbara Milam, M.S.W., made useful comments. Special mention should be made of Jesuit psychoanalyst William W. Meissner, who holds the only chair of psychoanalysis in the United States. His many works—over a dozen books (including a psychobiography of the saint and founder of his priesthood order) and 200 papers—bridging the gap between psychiatry and religion demonstrate what can happen when a religion, even an authoritarian one, protects and encourages its intellectuals. He made extensive comments on the organization of an early draft of the work.

I am grateful to Dan Vogel and H. Michael Marquardt, both experts in early Mormon history, who carefully corrected errors and made useful suggestions. Academic encouragement was given by Brigham D. Madsen, professor emeritus at the University of Utah, and, before his death, by the eminent Mormon philosopher, Sterling M. McMurrin. Both made suggestions and recommendations for early drafts of this work.

From the beginning, this work has been encouraged by Gary James Bergera, who has been a gentle point of stability and knowledge through frustrating times. Susan Staker did a miraculous editing of the first draft to the present size, making it more readable; and the final finishing—with useful challenges—was done by Lavina Fielding Anderson. She not only improved the book's literary style and completeness; but as a knowledgeable devout Mormon, she raised challenges to many points, forcing better documentation and helping me to see biases that could not be sustained. I alone, however, am responsible for factual errors and misjudgments.

Notes

1. *The Book of Mormon* (Palmyra, NY: E. B. Grandin, 1830), 586; now Moro. 10:4.

2. Fawn M. Brodie, *No Man Knows My History: The Life of Joseph Smith* (New York: Alfred A. Knopf, 1945). The second edition, revised and enlarged, was published in 1971.

3. Wesley P. Walters, "The Question of the Palmyra Revival," *Dialogue: A Journal of Mormon Thought* 4 (Spring 1969): 59-81; Brodie, *No Man Knows My His-*

tory, 30-31. I have summarized these arguments in "The Dilemma of the Mormon Rationalist," *Dialogue: A Journal of Mormon Thought* 30 (Winter 1997): 80-84.

4. Klaus J. Hansen, *Mormonism and the American Experience* (Chicago: University of Chicago, 1981), 31-32, 222n39: "A scholarly translation published in 1968 revealed the papyri as rather common funerary documents bearing absolutely no relationship to [the LDS canonized scripture of] the Book of Abraham." See also his "The Joseph Smith Egyptian Papyri: Translations and Interpretations," *Dialogue: A Journal of Mormon Thought* 3 (Summer 1968): 67-105.

5. Brodie, *No Man Knows My History,* 405-6; W. D. Purple, "Joseph Smith, the Originator of Mormonism: Historical Reminiscences of the Town of Afton," *Chenango Union,* 2 May 1977, reprinted in Frances Kirkham, *A New Witness for Christ in America* (Independence, MO: Zion's Printing and Publishing Co., 1951), 2:362-67. The evidence for Smith's disingenuousness has been convincingly summarized in Dan Vogel, "'The Prophet Puzzle' Revisited," *Dialogue: A Journal of Mormon Thought* 31 (Fall 1998): 125-40, and Susan Staker, "The Lord Said, 'Thy Wife Is a Very Fair Woman to Look Upon': The Book of Abraham, Secrets, and Lying for the Lord," 17 Aug. 1996, Sunstone Theological Symposium, Salt Lake City, copy in my possession. For examples of Smith's coercion, manipulation, and disingenuousness after the publication of the Book of Mormon, see Linda King Newell and Valeen Tippetts Avery, *Mormon Enigma: Emma Hale Smith, Prophet's Wife, "Elect Lady," Polygamy's Foe, 1804-1879* (Garden City, NY: Doubleday, 1984), 95-168, and George D. Smith, ed., *An Intimate Chronicle: The Journals of William Clayton* (Salt Lake City: Signature Books in association with Smith Research Associates, 1995), 93-136.

6. Anderson, "The Dilemma of the Mormon Rationalist," 85-87; D. Michael Quinn, *The Mormon Hierarchy: Origins of Power* (Salt Lake City: Signature Books, 1994), 272-75; Brigham D. Madsen, *Against the Grain: Memoirs of a Western Historian* (Salt Lake City: Signature Books, 1998), 358-60.

7. Dean C. Jessee, "The Early Accounts of Joseph Smith's First Vision," *BYU Studies* 9 (Spring 1969): 275-294, esp. 275n2.

8. Brigham H. Roberts, *Studies of the Book of Mormon,* edited and introduced by Brigham D. Madsen, with a biographical essay by Sterling M. McMurrin (Urbana: University of Illinois Press, 1985). Ethan Smith, *A View of the Hebrews* (Poultney, VT: Smith & Shute, 1825).

9. See, for example, the essays in Brent Lee Metcalfe, ed., *New Approaches to the Book of Mormon: Explorations in Critical Methodology* (Salt Lake City: Signature Books, 1993).

10. Dallin H. Oaks, *The Historicity of the Book of Mormon* (Provo, UT: FARMS, 1993), 2.

11. Gary F. Novak, "Naturalistic Assumptions and the Book of Mormon," *BYU Studies* 30 (Summer 1990): 35.

12. Harold Bloom, *The American Religion* (New York: Simon and Schuster, 1992), 89-90.

13. Michael Grant, *Jesus: An Historian's Review of the Gospels* (New York: Macmillan, 1977), 190.

14. See Klaus J. Hansen, *Quest for Empire: The Political Kingdom of God and the Council of Fifty in Mormon History* (East Lansing: Michigan State University Press, 1970); Marvin S. Hill, *Quest for Refuge: The Mormon Flight from American Pluralism* (Salt Lake City: Signature Books, 1989); Quinn, *The Mormon Hierarchy: Origins of*

Power, and Quinn, *The Mormon Hierarchy: Extensions of Power* (Salt Lake City: Signature Books, 1997). The retreat of Mormonism from antagonism and enmity toward the U.S. government began in 1890 under pressure of disenfranchisement, the failure of Jesus to reappear as soon as expected, and the inherent loyalty of the majority of the church members. By 1930 the foundation was in place for Mormonism to become the corporate giant of conservative loyal citizens which it now is. Thomas G. Alexander, *Mormonism in Transition: A History of the Latter-day Saints, 1890-1930* (Urbana: University of Illinois Press, 1986).

15. Herbert Butterfield, "The Whig Interpretation of History," qtd. in Stephen Jay Gould, *An Urchin in the Storm: Essays about Books and Ideas* (New York: W. W. Norton, 1987), 150.

Introduction

Understanding Assumptions

Every writer's assumptions inform his or her observations, analysis, and conclusions and determine the make-up of the audience he or she wishes to address. Nowhere is this truer than in the area of religion and religious belief. For example, during the witch hunts in medieval Western Europe, thousands of people, mostly women, were condemned to death after confessing under torture to supernatural actions involving the devil. Some 350 years later, historian Joseph Hansen wrote a naturalistic analysis of this bizarre phenomenon. He believed that confessions of supernatural activities were the result of coercion, including torture, and that witch/demonic interactions did not really occur. Two years later Catholic cleric Robert Schwickerath responded that the "one-sided *a priori* treatment of the [sixteenth-century Catholic] scholastics was fatal; and it would be well if [Hansen's] book were studied by Professors of Philosophy and Theology." Nevertheless, he thought that the work was "based on a false supposition in denying the existence of evil spirits, and consequently leads to wrong conclusions."[1]

The supernatural assumptions possible in any study of religion or religious personality may be positioned along a continuum and divided into four categories. At one extreme, God determines all motivations and behavior, thus excluding socio-political, economic, or psychological factors as explanations. This position leaves little room for psychobiography. Early Mormon writings emphasized this approach to LDS history; it is still found in some church manuals and appears to be the position of some church leaders.[2] Such biographies of Joseph Smith simply reiterate his official story, along with experiences from his mother, other acquaintances, friends, and enemies, without close scrutiny or analysis. Most non-Mormon historians consider these narratives to be of limited value.[3]

Joseph Smith opened the door to the second consideration when he declared that "a prophet is a prophet only when he is acting as such."[4] This concept allows for a division of analytical approaches. Scholars may largely exempt his revelations and translations from psychological and environmental inquiry, while seeking understanding of his daily life in the shaping forces of the nineteenth-century American frontier and, within limitations, some psychological principles. Such a position is probably shared by most present-day devout Mormon historians, who assume that the psychological forces at work in Smith were mostly healthy and that his underlying motivations were fundamentally charitable. The assumption that he was chosen by God leaves little room for other conclusions.[5] Perhaps these assumptions explain why "there has been little effort to uncover the background modes of thought, the controlling categories and assumptions, of Joseph Smith himself."[6] This second approach excludes Smith's revelations and translations, including the Book of Mormon, from psychological inquiry, holding rather that his personality played no part in revelations or translations and assuming that all supernatural acts were accomplished external to his psyche. In other words, this second approach assumes that Smith was no more than God's tool. Friendly observers David Whitmer and Joseph Knight described the translation of the Book of Mormon in exactly these terms.

Recently, a third type of inquiry has been attempted—namely, seeing the psyche of a saint or prophet as the medium through which God works; his internal conflicts appear not only in his ordinary living but constitute an important element in his visions and spiritual calling. This approach not only acknowledges psychological forces—healthy or pathological—but sees their fusion with spiritual forces; the will of God manifests itself through the resulting struggle for expression.[7] This approach is implied in Mormon and non-Mormon analyses arguing that the Book of Mormon is authentic history to which Smith added elements from his own life and time.[8] Even more naturalistic is the position that the Book of Mormon has no historical validity but that its spiritual values are worthy of study and adoption in behavior and worship.[9] Both orthodox believers and some nonbelievers criticize such devotion, querying why something that is not what it purports to be should be revered.[10]

These three approaches assume that God, supernatural forces, and spiritual experiences exist but are of no interest to the psychobiographer. William W. Meissner, a Catholic psychoanalyst and psychobiographer of Ignatius of Loyola, founder of the Society of Jesus (Jesuits), elaborates:

> The psychoanalyst is concerned with only those aspects of his subject that reflect basically human motivation and the connections of psychic meaning—whether or not the patterns of behavior have religious or spiritual meaning. ...
>
> His method and his perspective do not include the theological nor the spiritual. If he is wise he will leave those considerations to theologians and spiritual writers. The psychoanalyst is in no position to deny or exclude any actions, effects, or purposes of God. He is simply not interested in them since his approach has nothing to say about them.[11]

At first, this approach may seem hair-splitting, but Meissner identifies a significant difference: assuming that God and the supernatural exist (while ignoring them) is not the same as refusing either to assume or deny such sources for visionary, prophetic, inspired translations, statements, and acts. The existence of God lies not only beyond the psychoanalyst's professional interest but, as a scientist, beyond his or her knowledge. This position does not deny the possibility that God could exist and could/would intervene; it simply insists that, given the assumptions of science and history, miracles have not been established as fact and cannot be used as automatic explanations for events. One can acknowledge that the scientist or historian—or anyone, for that matter—may miss vital elements by refusing to acknowledge the spiritual. Perhaps such subjective experiences will forever be outside scientific replication, and science and history may forever miss ultimate causality. Nevertheless, this form of agnosticism is the theoretical position of science and academic history. As a result and on a practical level, science and academic history must not only passively ignore but also actively exclude the supernatural. Michael T. Walton, a historian of science, explains:

> The reason for this aspect of academic history is both clear and persuasive. What sense data exist to reveal God's hand? If such data existed, whose God would it reveal? Because God is not sensible, data dealing with him is nonsense and speculative. Were historians to admit such nonsense data, they would lose much of their shared universe of discourse which allows them to evaluate theories. Personal, inspired speculation with no data would become as valid as hard documents, and chaos would replace orderly criticism.
>
> ... Academic history, like science, has limited its universe of discourse to sense data. God and his action, in history, being non-sensible, therefore, do not fall within the bounds of that universe of discourse. ... Behind this limitation of subject matter was an attempt to facilitate communication among historians. ... Were historians to accept revelations and other metaphysical data, communication would be greatly hindered because individuals from different religious traditions could not agree on which revelations were to be accepted or rejected.
>
> ... Should [the believer] seek evidence of God's action in history, let him turn to his faith, for academic history can never provide proof for something which its methodology excludes.[12]

Walton's explanation presents two reasons for excluding the supernatural from consideration. The first, explicated by Pearl of Great Price scholar Edward H. Ashment, is that historians and scientists must be able to communicate despite differences in their individual belief systems. Otherwise, Mormon historians would be required to accept only

> Mormon Truth claims. In like manner, historians of Catholicism must accept Catholic Truth claims and the Catholic Holy Spirit as a reliable indicator of those claims, which of course would automatically nullify Mormon Truth

> claims. The same must obtain of historians of eastern Orthodoxy, Lutheranism, and the remainder of the almost 21,000 Christian denominations. Since it would not be possible for historians of religion to write about other religions or denominations without accepting *their* Truth claims, no historian of one perspective could critically analyze another perspective with any validity because he or she would have to accept the latter's Truth perspective.[13]

Requiring Mormon scholars not only to include but to give priority to Mormon truth claims results in a circular argument: Not only must the scholar accept God and the supernatural, but he or she must also accept Mormon truth claims about them. The conclusion leads back to the assumptions—accepting the claims of the religion under discussion. There can be no discussion across lines of faith, for different assumptions disallow it.

The second reason for excluding supernatural claims is that they cannot be established as historical fact or replicated scientifically. What is the proof of a spiritual experience? Only another spiritual experience. In all other areas of our lives, we have learned to review critically strong emotional experiences (such as feelings about the "right" marriage partner, the "right" profession, or the "right" investment), looking outside the experience itself for objective correlating evidence. In some fundamentalist religions, this internal assurance is interpreted as evidence—replacing "knowledge"—that the earth is 6,000 years old or, within Mormonism, reading the Book of Mormon as a record of what actually happened in pre-Columbian America. We will not find objective evidence for the visions of Joseph Smith, but his translation of ancient records is another matter. Historians have largely ignored the Book of Mormon because American archaeologists have not found any supporting objective evidence for it.

CURRENT LDS APOLOGETICS

There is a vast and rapidly enlarging literature by the faithful on the Book of Mormon. Many books are written for rank-and-file members of the church in periodicals and newspapers, while more scholarly articles can be found in books and journals published in association with Brigham Young University. These include many papers and journals from the Foundation for Ancient Research and Mormon Studies (FARMS) in Provo, Utah, which has an official connection to the university. In addition to many articles in *BYU Studies,* the *Journal of Book of Mormon Studies,* published by FARMS, contains many relevant articles. Useful on both sides of the question of the origin of the Book of Mormon is FARMS's recent publication of sixteen essays, Noel B. Reynolds, ed., *Book of Mormon Authorship Revisited: The Evidence for Ancient Origins* (Provo, UT: FARMS, 1997). Some scholarly studies by doubters or nonbelievers, demonstrating problems and inconsistencies and suggesting a naturalistic origin for the Book of Mormon, may be found in the ten articles in Brent Lee Metcalfe, ed., *New Approaches to the Book of Mormon* (Salt Lake City: Signature Books, 1993), hostilely reviewed in FARMS's *Review of Books on the Book of Mormon* 6, nos. 1-2 (Provo, UT: FARMS, 1994).

Of special interest in the context of this discussion are studies on American archaeology and the geography of the Book of Mormon. Book of Mormon geography has long been a thorny problem with unsatisfactory answers, despite many attempts at developing an internally consistent picture. The most notable of these attempts is John L. Sorenson, *The Geography of Book of Mormon Events: A Source Book* (Provo, UT: FARMS, 1992), 5-206. Mormons in Joseph Smith's day assumed that the Book of Mormon "land northward" and "land southward," connected by a "narrow neck of land," were the North and South American continents connected by the Isthmus of Panama. Thus, locating the Hill Cumorah, site of the final Nephite/Lamanite battle and burying site of the gold plates, two or three miles from Joseph Smith's home was not unreasonable. In 1887 Baptist minister M. T. Lamb in *The Golden Bible* (New York: Ward and Drummond, 1887), 96-101, emphasized internal inconsistencies in Book of Mormon geography, distances, and migrations. Although Book of Mormon editions to 1920 listed the supposed geographic parallels (and others) in footnotes, the passing decades brought no archaeological or anthropological support for a Book of Mormon culture but rather increasing evidence that the pre-Columbian Native Americans had never developed past a smooth stone culture. In 1973 non-Mormon American archaeologist Michael D. Coe stated bluntly, "The bare facts of the matter are that nothing, absolutely nothing, has shown up in any New World excavation which would suggest to a dispassionate observer that the Book of Mormon, as claimed by Joseph Smith, is a historical document relating to the history of early migrants to our hemisphere."[14]

The continued absence of archaeological evidences resulted in a two-pronged defensive response by the faithful. To replace archaeological evidence, believing Mormons have looked for literary evidence within the Book of Mormon. They have found Old Testament styles of writing/speaking (chiasmus), and "wordprints," complex statistical studies demonstrating that there were different writers, not just Joseph Smith, behind the book's sermons and dialogues.[15] Critics of these approaches have demonstrated possible chiasmus in other writings which do not claim to be ancient Hebrew texts and have challenged the successful use of wordprints with the Book of Mormon.[16]

As my work suggests, Joseph Smith identified with various people, including revivalist ministers, local and traveling, in his area; I argue that, through his fantasy alter egos, they spoke in their own manner and style in Book of Mormon episodes. I also suggest that, to whatever extent chiasmus does or does not exist in the Book of Mormon, Smith may have picked up the style from the ministers who may, in turn, have picked it up as a style learned from their Bible memorizations and training. Naturally, the Bible is also a direct influence on Smith himself.

The second approach by the faithful has been to adjust the geographic and archaeological assumptions about the Book of Mormon. Following the publication of Lamb's book in 1887, certainty in Book of Mormon geography shifted to recommendations by Mormon authorities that it was a mystery best left alone, and then to compromises that crystallized in the 1960s.[17] Orthodox Mormon academicians proposed a restricted site in southern Mexico of less than 400 miles in diameter for the Book of Mormon that may yet prove to contain Nephite artifacts when it is found and properly explored; the theory also includes two Cumorahs, with the New York hill being named by Moroni for the original in Mesoamerica.[18] It is not clear, in this case, why Moroni, in the nine meetings or more that Joseph Smith claimed to have with him, did not inform him of this renaming and spatial shift.

Additional hypotheses suggest that some time before, during, or after Book of Mormon times, Asiatic peoples crossed the Siberian-Alaskan landbridge and intermingled with the surviving Lamanites until no language or Middle Eastern characteristics remain. Unlike the assumptions of Joseph Smith and friends, these theories propose that only a small fraction of Native Americans are remnants of the Book of Mormon peoples. The Book of Mormon does not mention any other peoples in the Americas, although archaeological evidence dates their presence 10,000 years before the Nephites/Lamanites or the Jaredites.[19] Many of these proposals run into difficulties with Book of Mormon statements and contradict the first official account written by Oliver Cowdery with Joseph Smith's help.[20]

John Sorenson suggests the hill Cerro Vigia in Veracruz, Mexico, for the original Hill Cumorah, and Santa Rosa, Chiapas, Mexico, as the site for Zarahemla, the Book of Mormon's major city. The Grijalva and upper Usumacinta rivers in Guatemala and part of Mexico are both candidates for the river Sidon. Sorenson suggests that Joseph Smith may have mistranslated a number of words in the Book of Mormon and that the animals in the text called *cattle* and *oxen* are really deer and bison, that *horses* are tapir or deer, that *swine* refers to the wild pig, that *asses* are tapir, and that a *curelom* may refer to bison or mastodon.[21] This flexible interpretation of the translation/dictation period of the Book of Mormon does not seem to fit the described process and careful evidence from the remaining handwritten manuscript of the Book of Mormon dictation, as I will discuss in chapter 3. I read these proposals as attempts to surmount the absence of hard historical or scientific evidence to support the Book of Mormon and as a search for a workable compromise by believing Mormons with one foot in belief and the other in rationalism. In contrast to these ideas, I will propose a naturalistic explanation for the geography of the Book of Mormon taken from Joseph Smith's life. (See chapter 4.)

HISTORIANS AND THE SUPERNATURAL

The historian or scientist may personally believe in miracles but must exclude them from his or her professional products. This is the reason historian Michael Grant, in his biography of Jesus, wrote, "It is true that words ascribed to the risen Christ are beyond the purview of the historian since the resurrection belongs to a different order of thinking. ... Accordingly, therefore, to the cold standard of humdrum fact, the standard to which the student of history is obliged to limit himself, these nature-reversing miracles did *not* happen."[22]

In contrast to Meissner, who saw the will of God expressed partly through the way in which Ignatius solved internal conflict, or the many Mormon writers on Joseph Smith who separate Smith's problems from his supernatural claims, a writer who takes his or her stance within the perspective of science or academic history cannot simply ignore or exclude supernatural claims. He or she must attempt to explain them by naturalistic methods. With Joseph Smith, this task has been fraught with problems.

Recently, Lawrence Foster, a careful non-Mormon historian, proposed that Smith may have suffered from an unusual form of bipolar affective disorder.[23] While this suggestion has problems, it is worthy of consideration. Yet it is at best a half step, for nothing in the spectrum of manic-depressive illness explains Smith's claims to receive revelations and translate ancient records. Other friendly non-Mormon historians examine wide varieties of Mormon history but avoid explaining Smith's claims.[24] Perhaps any attempt would threaten their friendly status, for Joseph Smith, unlike many other religious figures, presents a special problem in efforts to understand him psychologically, whether these naturalistic forces are understood as separate or as fused with spiritual ones.

A comparison with sixteenth-century Ignatius of Loyola, founder of the Catholic Jesuit order, may clarify the problem. Ignatius was born to a wealthy family. His mother died when he was a child. To outward appearances, he seemed psychologically unaffected by the loss, becoming a heroic soldier in his late twenties. A courageous and aggressive military leader, he was brave to the point of foolhardiness until a cannonball shattered his legs. Without anesthesia, the surgeons' attempts to set the broken bones in a usable manner failed; later they rebroke the bones in an effort to set them properly, but he walked with leg deformities and an obvious limp until his death in 1556, twenty-six years later. The deformity struck him as hard as the surgical trauma, for he had been a wiry, vain courtier, a sword-swinging Spanish *hildago,* ready to pull a knife in defense of honor. Leg surgery was also Joseph Smith's most traumatic physical experience in childhood. Similarly, Loyola's traumatic physical experience, though occurring in adulthood, was a turning point. During his convalescence, he experienced a beatific vision of the Virgin Mary and the Christ Child, redefined himself as a "soldier" of faith on the battlefield of religion, had repeated visions and supernatural "mystical" experiences, faced the Inquisition and prison in 1526, 1530, and 1536 for possible heresy (the Reformation had begun) and preaching without adequate education. He defended himself adequately, gained his master's degree in Paris in 1535, and gathered a core of loyal followers. With them he wrote his "Spiritual Exercises" and "Constitution" for the Society of Jesus (founded 1540). These "Jesuits" would spearhead the Counter-Reformation.

If we strip away the claims of supernatural guidance, Ignatius' behavior can be adequately explained as the result of childhood loss, psychopathological response to adult trauma, upper-class training and education, and, possibly, inborn genetic superiority. His later life was characterized by priestly vows of chastity and poverty. When the wealthy came to him, they found him in a simple house, furnished only with a bed, chair, and desk. He was nearly worshipped by attractive women from all strata of society, yet his comportment was ultra-proper. Funds flowed to his organization. His priest-followers were willing to give their lives to him and his cause in obedience to the pope and church. Only after his death were the Jesuits linked with political intrigue and maneuvering. Today we would despair at his physical self-mortification and vigorously oppose his demand for obedience over reason or anything else,[25] but if we concentrate primarily on his behavior, it is easy to admire many aspects of the man without believing in the supernatural, whether one is a believing Catholic or not.

In contrast, if we strip away Joseph Smith's claims of supernatural guidance, how might his behavior be evaluated? He contracted polygamous marriages, including some with adolescent girls and already-married women.[26] He took the position that all civil marriages were invalid in God's eyes and could therefore be disregarded. He engaged in secret political maneuverings using the Danites and Council of Fifty. He failed to separate his personal finances from those of the church. He made strenuous efforts to create a theocracy that fused church and state. He showed marked aversion to democratic justice systems—although it must be conceded that this aversion was grounded in considerable legal maneuvering on the part of opponents that can be fairly described as harassment. A number of his dealings with others give marked evidence of expediency, deceit, coercion, and manipulation.[27]

If commanded by God, each of these acts could perhaps be justified. But were any of these acts the result of Smith's personality, not God's commands? If we set aside the possibility of supernatural intervention, the image of Joseph Smith is less than morally satisfactory and may actually be part of the reason why his followers so strongly defended and idealized him. (See chapter 7.) Yet, to the faithful, any naturalistic explanation is unacceptable. Any interpretation, whether traditional or innovative, must be drawn from the basic historical documents. Yet control of these documents has become a hotly contested area in Mormon group life. Church officials have taken the explicit position that any criticism of "the Lord's anointed"—usually interpreted to mean the church presidents and/or apostles—will not be tolerated.[28] Such a stance censors nontraditional historical scholarship and seems to include the assumption that the faithful are incapable of recognizing the difference between "office" and "personality."

The task of trying to develop accurate history against this prejudice has somewhat fallen to the so-called "New Mormon Historians" who have, over the past three decades, been attacked by other devout scholars and sometimes officially condemned by their church for presenting evidence of the limitations and failings of church leaders since Joseph Smith. Shortly before his excommunication in September 1993 for not following church counsel in his research and writing, D. Michael Quinn defined his position against "rancorous, paranoid, and deliberately slanderous" personal attacks:

> Even my revisionist examination of the esoteric and occult dimensions on Mormonism's origins affirmed the reality of the metaphysical events in Joseph Smith's experience.
>
> ... New Mormon Historians have criticized *instances* where Traditional Mormon History ... posits that "the hand of God" is the only needful explanation for any event in the Mormon experience. ...
>
> [But] I have always opposed those who present the Mormon past from a perspective that excludes the possibility that there is objective reality to divine revelation, visions, and angelic manifestations.[29]

Attempting to blend the supernatural with the natural leads to a large, poorly defined gray area. Quinn, a believing Mormon both before and after his excommunication, has focused on Joseph Smith and the "metaphysical" world of magic, using hazel rods and seer stones to find buried treasure, etc. Were these experiences "spiritual," "spiritual preparation," deceit of self and others within a context of a dying subculture, or a blend of all three? If the latter, how much of each? Although I respect Quinn's research, I think it also demonstrates the difficulty in finding solutions that merge the supernatural and natural. Even considering the possibility of a mixture raises difficult questions which the church shows no inclination to answer.

Whereas Quinn sometimes finds fault with traditionalists who believe that "the hand of God" is enough explanation for Joseph Smith, he would probably also see my work as limited because it occupies the other end of the spectrum. By using the framework of traditional science and that of the academic historian in this work, I therefore exclude "the hand of God" from consideration. I assume that Joseph Smith composed the Book of Mormon and I read it to understand Smith psychologically. Some may find this approach unacceptable; others might allow it as an hypothesis to be explored.

I wish to be very plain about what I am saying. This book is not about "Did Joseph Smith create the Book of Mormon?" but "How did Joseph Smith create the Book of Mormon." In this case, fortunately, the epistomological position of science and academic history in excluding the supernatural is supported by the evidence of science and academic history.

To summarize: Belief in the Book of Mormon relies on personal, internal, spiritual experiences, supported by wishes, cohesive group pressure, and family/authoritarian demands. In contrast, there is no "hard" evidence from archaeology to support the book, and the vacuum has grown so large that Mormon archaeologists have rewritten Mormon history in a way that would have probably surprised Joseph Smith and his friends. The "soft" literary evidence is questionable and, to whatever extent it exists, can be explained by naturalistic means. In contrast to this "negative" evidence, history of the last fifty years provides some "positive" evidence about Joseph Smith. We can document intentional deceit from courtroom records before the development of the Book of Mormon, and repeated coercion, manipulation, and misrepresentation after the Book of Mormon was published. Every believing Mormon must ignore, rationalize, or justify his or her founding prophet's behavior. With this documentation, all statements by Joseph Smith are suspect, and I will pay increased attention to outside documentation and the voices of others, including antagonists. These will include the townspeople in the Palmyra/Manchester area and his wife's relatives and friends in Pennsylvania. Generally, these voices paint what I see as a consistent picture of a progressively fabricated history, moving from the world of magic to Christianity.

It may be understandable why authorities in the Mormon church place limitations on historical research and have engaged actively in censoring and altering church history, but it is not excusable. They not only remain uncooperative today but also punish those who have not been obedient to their insistence in writing "faith-based" history. Given the resulting level of documentary unreliability, I will sometimes use Brigham Young University historians (who must follow the directions from the Mormon hierarchy), but will, of necessity, pay increased attention to others, nonbelievers included.

The strict naturalistic assumptions that form the basic approach of this book have further consequences. If to a neutral observer I am successful in demonstrating an internally consistent chronological pattern and repetitive psychological style that probably is a reflection of Joseph Smith's personal life, then this work can help fill in gaps and provide depth and consistency to the historical picture. In areas of incomplete history or even controversy, the fantasies in the Book of Mormon may help us evaluate such historical questions, for which answers based on contemporary documentation are currently unavailable. These include: (1) Did Joseph Smith behave inappropriately with a woman during his stay in Pennsylvania with his wife's family? (2) Did his father have alcohol problems? and (3) Were there other problems in the childhood home of young Joseph? I will occasionally use the Book of Mormon to suggest such possibilities. But these evidences, in the reverse direction from the Book of Mormon to Joseph Smith's life, will always be only clues or suggestions. They will never provide historical fact or documentation. No matter what happened factually, we will be looking through the eyes of a child who is constructing a compensatory fantasy. In the final diagnostic chapter, I will propose a theoretical formulation of Joseph Smith's personality, using his mother's biography of her son, Joseph's statements, outside testimony by others (including antagonists), *and* by reading from within the Book of Mormon back into his life.

If, as Mormon general authority B. H. Roberts wondered in the 1920s, Joseph Smith used Ethan Smith's *A View of the Hebrews* in composing the Book of Mormon, it provided only an outline and a concept. Its contribution to the Book of Mormon may be summarized in perhaps half a dozen pages. But the Book of Mormon is not an outline—it is an ongoing narrative covering a thousand years and including detailed personal experiences, religious interactions, conversions, and miracles. Heroes and villains abound, many with distinct personalities. The narrative includes extensive military and governmental activities, some economic and agricultural descriptions, and even an excursion into currencies. As I will discuss later, Smith had the opportunity to prepare these stories by thinking about them and relating them to his family for years. However, when the time was ripe, he apparently dictated virtually the entire book in less than thirteen weeks, a prodigious feat. In my professional opinion, such speed is a characteristic, not of translation, but rather of spontaneous free association; the book's size, from a psychodynamic point of view, thus provides an excellent opportunity to use the techniques of applied psychoanalysis, including simile, allegory, and metaphor.

In this book, I will argue that Joseph Smith, both knowingly and unknowingly, injected his own personality, conflicts, and solutions into the book he was dictating. Thus I hypothesize that the Book of Mormon can be understood as Smith's autobiography, that we can discern repeated psychological patterns in Smith's transformation of his childhood and youth before 1829 into Book of Mormon stories, and that these observations can contribute to a psychological understanding of Smith. With this information, supplemented by his mother's biography and other sources, we can develop a reasonably complete psychoanalytic profile of Joseph Smith.

The Methodology of Psychoanalysis

Psychoanalytic psychotherapy enhances patients' experience of their feelings and fantasies and can help their therapists better understand their patients and their psychological defenses. There is little external stimulus to stir the conversation; the therapist says little but listens much. Over time and often indirectly, the patient articulates feelings and fantasies that both approach and avoid areas of potential psychological conflict in endless cycles. Many of these come from childhood; the patient's discourse—such as talking about work or spouse—takes on stronger and stronger coloring from childhood. Fantasies spring from nowhere and may become elaborate yet disturbing to their creator. These fantasies may contain childlike conquering compensations and solutions, grand and impossible in scope. Interestingly, some of the physical arrangements employed during the dictation/translation of the Book of Mormon mirror psychotherapeutic settings. (See chapter 5.)

Psychiatry is a branch of medicine dealing with the diagnosis and treatment of mental dysfunction; psychiatry is a medical specialty. Psychology is not a medical field or specialty, even though its areas of interest overlap significantly with those of psychiatry. The area of psychiatry (and psychology) that focuses on a person's mental forces, such as sexual and aggressive impulses, drives toward self-fulfillment, achievement of core identity and self-esteem, etc., and his or her conscious or unconscious efforts to modify these forces to permit successful social adaptation, is a subspecialty generally referred to as "(psycho)dynamic psychiatry." Its most intense form is psychoanalysis, or the process of collecting knowledge and a body of theory, as well as a specific form of treatment for some patients.

Classical psychoanalysis began with Sigmund Freud around 1900 and, for sixty years, dominated psychiatry. In the absence of other theories or knowledge, it overextended itself into the treatment of severe psychotic mental illnesses now known to be partly, or largely, genetically determined. In the last thirty years, psychoanalysis has yielded leadership in the field to technical laboratory methods and their results in the burgeoning fields of neurophysiology and psychopharmacology. This development has allowed psychiatrists to modify, but not cure, the most severe forms of mental illness by administering medications. The next fifty years hold promise that the study of the mental drives will unite with technical studies of brain chemistry, and we will be able to give reasons, in neurophysiologic terms, why a mother's death when a child is two may result in certain types of adult mental disturbance. This goal is one of the presently stated objectives of research at the National Institutes of Mental Health. Freud foresaw this development,[30] and today some "psychoanalysts" are active in laboratory research.

The term *psychoanalyst* is not legally regulated in most states, with the result that anyone in those areas may claim the title, including the uneducated and charlatans. Technically, however, in the United States, it is usually reserved for the 10 percent of psychiatrists and, more recently, psychologists and social workers, who have completed a minimum of four to six years of advanced training at the various psychoanalytic institutes recognized by the American Psychoanalytic Association. Others who use the title are expected (but not required) to explain that their use of the term is not the usual or standard definition.

The American Psychoanalytic Association, founded in 1911, and its member psychoanalysts exercise a major influence on all areas of the knowledge and treatment of the mentally ill. The body of knowledge they have accumulated over the last ninety years has filtered beyond the boundaries of mental health professionals into the lives of ordinary citizens. Every modern government has "think tanks" of professionals who use psychoanalytic knowledge to understand the actions of other governments and to evaluate their leaders. Psychoanalytic knowledge is imparted in our high schools; both Hollywood and Madison Avenue have people knowledgeable in psychodynamic understanding and manipulation who use these techniques successfully and without moral compunction. Some of its techniques, modified over decades of practice, appear in the treatment of all mentally disturbed patients. Its classic treatment, using a couch and free association in frequent sessions extending over years, continues to be the treatment of choice for a small percentage of patients.

One division of psychoanalytic thinking, applied psychoanalysis, does not deal with theory or the treatment of patients but instead focuses on culture, art, history, politics, and literature. Attempts to enhance our understanding of individuals by their writings or personal histories is termed psychobiography. Freud's first attempts to apply psychoanalytic concepts outside of the psychoanalytic treatment of patients began as early as 1897. He made additions to these studies in 1900, 1907, 1910, and 1911, attempting to understand unconscious conflicts and processes in artists and writers hidden in their works.[31] Others also realized the potential fruitfulness of such applications. Artistic creativity has been studied, although most of the focus has been on the personalities of artists, including Jonathan Swift, Lewis Carroll, Ludwig Van Beethoven, and William Shakespeare.[32] Ernst Jones in 1951 adapted applied psychoanalysis to studying mass cultural movements, arguing that the historical belief in witches and vampires reflected sexual frustration, a topic that was something of a preoccupation with Freudian thought.[33] Two religious figures who have received attention are Martin Luther and Gandhi.[34] The analysis of fairy tales is helpful to every parent.[35] Applied psychoanalytic literature is now vast.

The greatest contributions of psychobiography have been to expand our ideas about the personality of writers. Besides the contributions of psychiatrists, important contributions have also been made by psychologists, sociologists, political scientists, and historians.[36] Difficulties and potential pitfalls in such endeavors have been carefully reviewed,[37] and two of Freud's works are now considered unfortunate setbacks.[38] However, carefully done psychoanalytical studies open the door to understanding the unconscious processes and motivations among fictional characters, such as Hamlet and his stepfather, or in the Book of Mormon between Moroni and his archenemy Amalickiah. (See chapter 5.) They fit into the object-relations theory of development which presently dominates psychoanalytic discussions.[39] It is a general truism that the first artistic creation of an artist or writer is usually most revealing of his personality, for it is hoped that the artist's work will also be psychotherapeutic work and contribute to resolving original conflicts and problems. When this happens, the artist not only improves in technical quality, but his or her work demonstrates maturation.[40] I spoke with four psychoanalysts who write psychobiography and in applied psychoanalysis, asking for their views. All four agreed with the statement but noted that artists may continue to reflect their stresses in their work throughout their lives. If the creative work of the artist or author is psychotherapeutic (as one hopes it will be and does sometimes seem to occur), then subsequent work will become more and more removed from the original conflicts and struggles. I believe that this same phenomenon applies to the Book of Mormon and will help us understand Joseph Smith.

The interface between psychoanalysis and history is often controversial. In 1958 William Langer, president of the American Historical Association, challenged colleagues to seek deeper psychological meaning in their studies.[41] The response varied from mixed to hostile. Historians emphasize that there is no such thing as completely objective history, but the facts of documented historical events mean that the foundations of their analyses are not subjective. In contrast, psychodynamic psychiatry is a world of feelings, thoughts, misrememberings, forgettings, fantasy, analogy, allegory, and metaphor. No wonder some historians give little credence to attempts to make sense out of ephemeral mental material which does not seem to be connected.[42] In 1930 Freud himself warned that, in applied psychoanalysis, "we should have to be very cautious and not forget that, after all, we are only dealing with analogies and that it is dangerous, not only with men but also with concepts, to tear them from the sphere in which they have originated and been evolved."[43] Analogy is not a good way to establish historical fact, and history cannot be reduced to psychological explanation. Western historian Bernard DeVoto pointed out: "Psycho-analysis has no value whatever as a method of arriving at facts in biography." Rather, he asserted, the first condition of biography must be "absolute, unvarying, unremitted accuracy."[44] Still, psychoanalytic application and attention to factual detail *are* compatible; psychoanalytic interpretation and understanding may add texture to the historical picture, fill in aspects of personal meaning and motive, and provide continuity to a history that has gaps even though the distinction between "fact" and conjecture drawn from those facts must be clear to both the writer and the reader. DeVoto found little value in applied psychoanalysis except in the "consulting room, where it belongs, and to the literary speakeasy." As a result of this refusal to consider psychological implications in coming to terms with Joseph Smith, he dismissed the Book of Mormon as "a yeasty fermentation, formless, aimless and inconceivably absurd ... a disintegration." He later added that the book had "neither form nor structure of any kind, its imagination is worse than commonplace, it is squalid, and the prose is lethal."[45] In my opinion, he seriously misunderstands the work.

The psychiatrist enters the world of history without a historian's tools. He or she is trained to interact with a live and reactive patient, not someone distant or dead for 150 years. The interaction between therapist and patient is the central focus and will be the means of, if not curing, then improving the patient's condition. The work of repeated clarification, confrontation, and interpretation describes the observable process. It is speculative work, gaining assurance only over time and during the interaction itself. Every therapist with psychodynamic experience has had the experience of proposing a painful interpretation, only to have the patient exclaim, "No!", break into sobs, and correct the therapist with even a more painful truth, newly discovered by the therapist's near-miss. It is this interplay that we cannot have in applied psychoanalysis of a dead writer. It is not possible to explore the Book of Mormon as Joseph Smith's autobiography without making errors. Smith is not here to correct or modify our interpretations, and, if he were, we might doubt his cooperation. No live patient fits into any mold, and sooner or later will bristle if he or she senses that the therapist is attempting to fit the full richness of his or her life into a particular psychodynamic model. Such an approach always fails to explain important parts of that life. Because the historical subject cannot challenge, correct, and change this tendency to simplify, it is inevitable that psychobiography will lack some of the complexity and development available to a live interaction.

Furthermore, the psychiatrist must not only understand the patient's personal and familial development, but also the influences of time, place, ethnicity, religion, and culture. A psychiatrist working with a historical personage but not an expert in that person's historical milieu will inevitably make contextual errors of interpretation. Granted, no author has direct first-hand experience with a culture from the past, but a historian's training is designed to compensate, at least partially, for this deficiency while a psychiatrist's is not.

Furthermore, human nature in general, and the inner wellsprings of a particular person's emotions and thought, always contain mysteries. Time veils memories and reshapes interpretations; even with a patient's full cooperation, some aspects of his or her life will never be understood. These difficulties tempt a psychohistorian to become reductionistic, drawing final conclusions where only incomplete information and partial solutions are available. There is a necessary tension and balance between the historical view and the psychological view. If this latter view becomes too strong, then "psychopathology becomes a substitute for the psychohistorical interface. ... The psychopathological idiom for individual development ... [replaces] the idiom for history, or psychohistory. When this happens there is, once more, no history."[46]

And, finally, psychoanalysis as a treatment is not universally successful. Freud affirmed that all patients appropriate for psychoanalysis used "neurotic" psychological defenses such as repression (pushing conflicts behind a screen where they do not seem to exist), obsessive-compulsive styles of thinking (binding conflict and emotion into structured and rigid mental organization), and sublimation (turning conflict into socially productive behavior). However, some patients went beyond these "ordinary" defenses to denial (a more vigorous repudiation of fact or emotion), splitting (seeing the world in polarized opposites of good/bad, right/wrong, us/them), and projection (ignoring troubling qualities in oneself while imagining, observing, and criticizing similar qualities in other people).[47] In contrast, healthier defenses would be altruism (vicarious and constructive service to others) and sublimation (gratification of an impulse by changing the method and goal from a socially objectionable one to a socially valued one).

I have been candid about the dangers of a psychoanalytical approach both to educate the reader and also to assure the reader that I myself am aware of those risks. The potential achievement is still worth the risk, however, for if a balance is maintained, then looking at symptomatic or general behaviors can be productive. The psychodynamic perspective gives valid reasons for believing that all of us derive part of our motives and uniqueness from psychologically meaningful events in our past, most strongly and enduringly from our childhoods. I believe that it is also true for a prophet and that such considerations add depth to our understanding.

If the absence of a live patient is the weakness of psychobiography, its strengths are two areas of collective knowledge and known experience. First, the patterns of style, and, second, overdetermination. "Style" means that we can expect that the mental maneuvers, styles, and defenses of a writer will be represented in his work. As I have already noted, this characteristic is truest if the work was his first or earliest work, for we suspect that the artist has begun an attempt to resolve his conflicts through his work. If successful with this "therapy," his artistry will take on a life of its own, farther and farther removed from the conflict. His personality style will be more apparent if the work was "spontaneous," and if the circumstances surrounding its creation were close to the therapeutic process of free association, as was the case I believe with Smith's creation of the Book of Mormon. The techniques used in applied psychoanalytic investigation are adapted from the techniques of psychoanalytic treatment. If Smith were in dynamic psychotherapy, he could begin the sessions anywhere, under the guide of free association—that is, say anything and everything that came to mind with no editing—while the therapist's job would be to follow, understand, decipher, confront, and clarify. Patients tell their life story, repeatedly emphasizing problem areas in treatment. But some areas of conflict are too painful to discuss and feel directly, so patients use a number of methods, both conscious and unconscious, to modify their pain. They may talk about a friend with similar problems or discuss a movie or book that contains problems similar to their own. They may divide their history into two or more parts, discussing some segments one day and filling in the remaining segments on other days. The more painful the segment, the more repetitious they will be in "working through" the problem. If the pain of sadness is too much on one day, they may reverse it into an inappropriate euphoria that breaks down in the next days or weeks. Their dreams will repeat their life stories and conflicts, disguised by exaggeration, displacement, reversal, projection onto others, condensation, combining of stories, and so forth. Their mental fantasies repeat their problems and frequently show dramatic wished-for solutions and compensations, some reasonable and some impossible.

Over time the psychotherapist begins to know the life story very well, and becomes acquainted with the patient's psychological defenses. What becomes increasingly important is not the life story but its modifications—exaggerations, similarities, aversions, combinings, reversals, eliminations, projections, forgettings, denials, imagined compensations, division of the story into two or more parts, etc. These patterns help the psychiatrist understand the patient and help him face his pain and make a more successful adaptation to life. "No single fact or connection will validate the hypothesis," observed Meissner, "but it begins to take on meaning and consistency in the light of the total complex of facts, data, and their integrating interpretations."[48]

The second principle is overdetermination. Bruce Mazlish explains: "The problem of determinism in psycho-analysis is a point that bothers unsympathetic critics of psycho-analysis. Freud insisted that strict determinism prevailed in respect of psychic acts; there are no 'accidents.' For example, 'free association,' the basis of dream analysis and of therapy, is 'free' only in the sense that it is not hampered by the censorship of 'logical,' 'rational' thought and *mores*. It is not, however, undetermined."[49]

Overdetermination comes in two forms: (1) The same word or symbol usually refers to many elements in the unconscious thought process. (2) A single unconscious drive or pattern of behavior will manifest itself in innumerable different conscious manifestations. These multiple manifestations make the evidence abundant and self-confirming. If we are able to reinforce this information with observations from others who know the individual, it seems both reasonable and possible to complete the historian's tasks of reconciling, interpreting, and confirming evidence, as well as the psychohistorian's task of psychological explaining.

After the review of the Book of Mormon described above, I will discuss Joseph Smith's personality by using five elements of psychodynamic theory: the narcissistic personality, the antisocial personality, pseudological phantastica, the act of imposturing, and his enhancement by his followers through the mechanism of projective identification. However, the last four elements are variations on or additions and modifications to the first.

The concept of the narcissistic personality has developed by a historically complicated process, for it entailed understanding new types of psychological defenses, necessitated a rewriting of theory, and required identifying constellations of personality symptoms ("syndromes").[50]

In 1900 Freud borrowed the Oedipal "complex" from various poets, playwrights, and philosophers dating back to the classic Greeks and put it into a framework of mental health. The name is taken from the drama *Oedipus Rex* by the ancient Greek playright Sophocles, in which a fatally proud king kills his father and marries the queen, only to discover later that he has committed both patricide and incest. According to Freud, this period, which lasts from about age three to six, is crucial in the healthy development of male children. The son becomes aware of his own sexual anatomy, feels sexual attractions for his mother, but fears bodily injury by his stronger and frightening father, with whom he must establish a male-to-male relationship. Basic to Freud's thinking of psychological development was the "libido theory," a concept of sexual instinct found in children as well as adults and emphasized during the Oedipal period. Each child had to find some resolution to the unacceptable, impossible, and threatening sexual wishes. The majority of children, he believed, found resolution in a psychological identification with the parent of the same sex, and part of that identification would have profound influences on personality and character, including the major imprint for his future moral values: the child's future conscience. Freud believed that each individual had a fixed quantity of libido which, in healthy individuals, was balanced between being attached to oneself, thus providing self-love and self-esteem, and being attached to others, thus providing friendships and romantic love.

In addition, following his early experiences with hypnosis, Freud believed that a very large part of our mental and emotional processes go on outside of our awareness—in our unconscious—into which are pushed some forbidden impulses as a way of mentally refusing to admit that they exist. The process of keeping them in the unconscious was termed repression, and successful repression was important for healthy living. During stress, or because the impulses or conflicts were too large, evidence of the impulse might break through into conscious awareness in such things as disturbing dreams or slips of the tongue and pen, producing anxiety and depression.

Despite this contribution, Freud's Oedipal theory suffers from incompleteness in two ways that prevented it from fully articulating the concept of the narcissistic personality. First, he defined Oedipal conflicts as existing only in children ages three to six, hypothesizing that human beings were largely a product of genetically determined sexual and aggressive drives. According to this view, human beings relate to other people only when driven by the necessity of satisfying these drives. Such a closed psychological system *may* be true of adults, and (less likely) even of children ages three to six, but it does not explain the infant-mother dyad, in which the child is "fused" with the mother who fills both physical and psychological needs for the child.

Second, as Freud considered libido to be something of a fixed quantity, the logical consequences of this theory of libido were unsatisfactory. He hypothesized that if an individual did not form an attachment to another person, then his libinal attachment was to himself. Such "narcissistic" personalities were "richer" in libido because none of it was attached to anyone else. While Freud's theory is logically consistent, few of us would argue that a person incapable of loving anyone but himself is healthier or has "more" love than someone who can form attachments to others.[51]

Increasing dissatisfaction with the flaws in Freud's articulation of the narcissistic personality prompted the formation of the "object-relations" theory of human development in Great Britain, beginning in the 1940s.[52] According to this theory, human beings have an inborn primary drive to relate.[53] Thus the healthy infant begins in almost total "fusion" with the mother, internalizes that relationship, next establishes a relationship with the father and internalizes the more complex triangular relationship, and continues to internalize other relationships, even in healthy adulthood, though to a much smaller degree. Children who are deprived of healthy caring relationships or whose needs are repeatedly frustrated very early in life (for example, through neglect, abuse, the death of a parent—particularly a mother—or other traumatic events) frequently have stronger defenses than the "ordinary" neurotic patient, including denial, splitting, and projection.

Another interesting development in the history of psychoanalytic development was the concept of the "false self," developed during the 1940s and 1950s, also in Great Britain.[54] Some patients, whose initial appearance suggested smooth and effective social functioning, revealed during therapy that this apparently successful personality had been artificially created. It was disconnected from core feelings and limited in style. It hid difficult problems. This superficial personality could not be analyzed. The "deeper" personality was a poorly developed self with immature feelings and mental styles, easily threatened self-esteem, no long-range goals, and a weak sense of purpose. Despite the usual smooth functioning, at times the immature shadow became evident. Acquaintances might view such a person in two different ways, depending on which "personality" they saw.

Some very self-centered (narcissistic) patients had the characteristics of a false self. They were frustrating to treat. They did not see the therapist as a person in his or her own right, but only as an agent to serve the patient. These individuals were different from more ordinary "neurotic" patients who wanted the therapist to be different or more fulfilling in some way. Rather, narcissistic patients typically employed conscious and unconscious coercion and manipulation, as if the patient owned the therapist. It was a baffling paradox: the patient, who appeared self-sufficient and even socially successful, would treat the therapist as useless, demanding that the therapist fill a vital psychological function which the patient could not do for himself. If the therapist was unwittingly coerced into this function, then he or she was supporting the patient's "false self." If the therapist refused to act as an extension of the patient's psyche, confronted the manipulation, and attempted to clarify what was happening, the patient would frequently terminate therapy and seek a more compliant therapist. If the patient stayed, however, the poorly defined personality eventually began to reveal itself, along with a profound vulnerability and low self-esteem.

Some of the most historically interesting cases lasted for years. Over time, these patients could go through a period of rage approaching paranoia, then depression as they realized their need for the therapist. As their shadow self expressed itself and matured in therapy, the person became more appreciative of their friends and acquaintances, could deal more quickly with the therapeutic tasks, and could achieve resolution and termination of therapy.

In the larger society these patients used and manipulated other people: spouses, families, acquaintances, followers, congregations. They were sensitive to minor slights and rebuffs from others and could not deal with shame and humiliation. While they might appear unaffected, they seethed in fury. They compensated by fantasies of themselves as conquerors. Some could not stand routine or boredom; while others found situations comfortable, they purposely created dramas and crises. Some patients who functioned by the use of a "false self" had a particular and remarkable degree of artificial self-inflation. The false self of these individuals was given the name "grandiose self." These "grandiose" personalities attracted others who felt their own esteem and importance elevated by the contact and who supported the "charisma" of such individuals. For personal emotional gain, whether consciously or unconsciously, they supported the grandiose false self of the narcissist.

These personality types received a great deal of attention during this period; the study of narcissicism resulted in the identification of new types of defenses, new personality constellations, and new refinements to psychoanalytic theory. The two most important books dealing with psychoanalytic theory during the 1970s were Heinz Kohut's *The Analysis of the Self* (New York: International Universities Press, 1971) and Otto Kernberg's *Borderline Conditions and Pathological Narcissism* (New York: Jason Aronson, 1975). Each described slightly different patient populations, and each proposed different theories and treatment strategies.[55] The vigorous debate that resulted was not acrimonious, for most parties understood the purpose of theory and used the debate to enhance knowledge and the effective treatment of patients. The narcissistic personality became a formal classification in the American Psychiatric Association's taxonomy of mental pathology in 1980:

> A pervasive pattern of grandiosity (in fantasy or behavior), need for admiration, and lack of empathy, beginning by early adulthood and present in a variety of contexts, as indicated by five (or more) of the following:
>
> (1) has a grandiose sense of self-importance (e.g., exaggerates achievements and talents, expects to be recognized as superior without commensurate achievements)
>
> (2) is preoccupied with fantasies of unlimited success, power, brilliance, beauty, or ideal love
>
> (3) believes that he or she is "special" and unique and can only be understood by, or should associate with, other special or high-status people (or institutions)
>
> (4) requires excessive admiration
>
> (5) has a sense of entitlement, i.e., unreasonable expectations of especially favorable treatment or automatic compliance with his or her expectations
>
> (6) is interpersonally exploitative, i.e., takes advantage of others to achieve his or her own ends
>
> (7) lacks empathy: is unwilling to recognize or identify with the feelings and needs of others
>
> (8) is often envious of others or believes that others are envious of him or her
>
> (9) shows arrogant, haughty behavior or attitudes.[56]

There is nothing criminal in the APA description of narcissism. Such a person would not end up in jail, although his or her chances of being involved in civil suits or divorce are high.[57] But if such a person also had elements of the antisocial personality—had moral lapses, made fraudulent claims, and deceived others—then he or she would impose a falsely created image on society and would attempt to manipulate it to his or her personal, financial, and/or social advantage.

Joseph Smith and Narcissism

It is in the light of these criteria that I would like to examine Joseph Smith as a narcissistic personality and how he used the Book of Mormon to express those tendencies. As I read the Book of Mormon, Smith tells his life story in allegorical form at least four times in its pages. The first version—broad, sweeping, and expansive with many diversions and variations—commences at the start and continues to p. 370 in the first edition (1 Ne. 1-Alma 51). Almost one-third of the Book of Mormon is an expanded fantasy of the years 1824-28, ending with the point at which Smith begins dictating the Book of Mormon. He then begins his life story again—pp. 375-451 of the first edition (Alma 53-Hel. 16). The third version covers pages 457-518 (3 Ne. 3-4 Ne.). His fourth and final variation occurs within the single book of Mormon (pp. 518-38). This version corresponds to events in his life when he was ten and a half, rapidly becomes fragmentary, and disintegrates in the carnage and devastation of the Nephite people. All of these variations end at the point where he begins dictating the Book of Mormon. One purpose of the book of Ether is to tell us, yet avoid telling us, about the period of actually dictating the Book of Mormon.

I will not follow the four versions sequentially but will first concentrate on clarifying the story. (See chapter 1.) Chapter 2 reviews Smith's life to about age seventeen, followed by the reasonably clear parallel in 1 and 2 Nephi through chapter 5 or, in the first edition, to p. 73. Chapter 3 completes the life story of Smith to age twenty-four when he begins dictating the Book of Mormon. I then turn to the parallels in 3 and 4 Nephi, which briskly review his life but focus mainly on Smith's life from age ten through his twenties. I then return to 2 Nephi and, in chapters 4 and 5, discuss the autobiographical parallels in the rest of the Book of Mormon except for Mormon, Ether, and Moroni. Chapter 6 summarizes these final three books, with particular attention to Ether.

For example, this book discusses Smith's traumatic leg surgery when he was five or seven. Comprising agonizing suffering before surgery and two surgeries without anesthetic, it was certainly the most physically painful experience of his youth. We could reasonably expect to see post-traumatic stress symptoms, for a time in his childhood, but later in his life such symptoms were not apparent. His surgical experience, instead of being distressing with attempts to avoid the memory, was actively being used for personal reasons. (See chapter 5.)

As another example, at age twenty, Smith experienced shame and humiliation when he was put on trial for being a "disorderly person and impostor."[58] He does not mention this trial in any of his historical or autobiographical writings, but I argue that it appears in the Book of Mormon in the trial of Alma and Amulek, while Smith's intense emotions of humiliation and rejection take the form of devastating cataclysms at the time of Christ's crucifixion.

My technique in dealing with the Book of Mormon as Smith's autobiography is to metaphorically "listen," as I would literally listen to a living patient, until it becomes clear to me that I am hearing major life incidents told allegorically, metaphorically, and in fantasy. After numerous reiterations, an internally consistent chronological pattern and repetitive psychological style emerges. However, of greater interest is how Smith transforms his real-life events into Book of Mormon narratives, for when we start to discern such patterns we begin to better understand him and his motives.

What might the reader expect as Smith alters his personal life into fantasy? Forty years ago, the eminent psychoanalyst Phyllis Greenacre took a personal interest in the study of artists:

> In using the term *artist* I designate the creative individual ... whose work-product shows ... unusual capacity for imaginative creation, original thought, invention or discovery [and] would ... include those prophets, religious leaders and scientists whose philosophies and discoveries have influenced the course of their times and left an imprint on history.
>
> After reading a great many accounts of artists, I was struck with the prominence of the family romance in their lives. The germ of the family romance is ubiquitous in the hankering of growing children for a return to the real or fancied conditions at or before the dawn of conscious memory when adults were Olympians.[59]

The reader should be prepared to see Smith's personal life not only turned to fantasy, but to a fantastic fantasy where the heroes and villains are larger than life. Greenacre's comment is particularly relevant in the analysis of Ether and the final diagnostic assessment in chapter 7.

There are currently dozens of works on Joseph Smith and early Mormonism that demonstrate extensive research, with references numbering into the hundreds and even thousands. I rely on these works for the historical facts of Joseph Smith's life.[60] The contribution of my own work is not new facts *per se,* but rather new ways of seeing the available documentary information.

Conclusion

My assessment argues the advantages of giving psychoanalysis serious weight because of its rationality and explanatory power. The only basis for believing that the Book of Mormon has supernatural origins lies in the individual, personal, internal experience of the believer; yet this reason is the same one cited by every believer regardless of the particular faith. As a matter of logic, the faith claims of the LDS or RLDS believer in the Book of Mormon cannot be placed ahead of the spiritual experiences of all other religious beliefs, especially because they all contradict each other. Little evidence acceptable to scientific or historical scholars supports the historical claims within the Book of Mormon. Ever since Galileo demonstrated that a literal interpretation of the Bible conflicted with the actual functioning of astronomical bodies in the seventeenth century, those in Western civilization have gradually but decisively given priority to naturalistic explanations instead of supernatural ones. An open mind not only allows naturalistic argument, it gives it serious consideration.

Notes

1. Joseph Hansen, *Zauberwahn, Inquisition and Hexenprozess im Mittelalter* (Munich, 1900), and Robert Schwickerath, S.J., "Attitude of the Jesuits in the Trials for Witchcraft," *American Catholic Quarterly Review* 27 (1902): 475-516. For a brief overview of the witch trials, see H. R. Trevor-Roper, *The European Witch-Craze of the Sixteenth and Seventeenth Centuries and Other Essays* (New York: Harper & Row, 1967), 90-192; R. H. Robbins, *The Encyclopedia of Witchcraft and Demonology* (New York: Crown Publishers, 1965); and Robert D. Anderson, "The History of Witchcraft: A Review with Some Psychiatric Comments," *American Journal of Psychiatry* 126 (June 1970): 1727-35.

2. Ezra Taft Benson, *The Gospel Teacher and His Message* (Salt Lake City: LDS Church Educational System, 1976), 11-12, qtd. in D. Michael Quinn, "On Being a Mormon Historian (and Its Aftermath)," in George D. Smith, ed., *Faithful History: Essays on Writing Mormon History* (Salt Lake City: Signature Books, 1992), 69-111.

3. Lawrence Foster, "New Perspectives on the Mormon Past: Reflections of a Non-Mormon Historian," in Smith, *Faithful History*, 113.

4. Joseph Smith, Jr., et al., *History of the Church of Jesus Christ of Latter-day Saints*, 7 vols., ed. Brigham H. Roberts (Salt Lake City: Deseret Book Co., 1951 printing), 5:265.

5. The possibility that Smith may have had an internal conflict between two systems of morality was proposed by Mormon Jungian psychoanalyst C. Jess Groesbeck, "Joseph Smith and His Path of Individuation: A Psychoanalytical Exploration in Mormonism," Sunstone Symposium, August 1986, audiocassette #86319-720. Mormon psychiatrist James Morgan in responding to Groesbeck's presentation emphasized that a prophet's dreams cannot be evaluated by psychological means since such dreams may contain supernatural elements, i.e., prophecy. Morgan obviously excluded even day-to-day mundane mental functions from consideration.

6. Gary F. Novak, "Naturalistic Assumptions and the Book of Mormon," *BYU Studies* 30 (Summer 1990): 23-40.

7. William W. Meissner, S.J., "Psychoanalytic Hagiography: The Case of Ignatius of Loyola," *Theological Studies* 52 (1991): 3-33, esp. 32-33; and his *Ignatius of*

Loyola: The Psychology of a Saint (New Haven, CT: Yale University Press, 1992), xv-xix, 346-58.

8. See, for example, Blake T. Ostler, "The Book of Mormon as a Modern Expansion of an Ancient Source," *Dialogue: A Journal of Mormon Thought* 20 (Spring 1987): 66-123; Robert N. Hullinger, *Joseph Smith's Response to Skepticism* (Salt Lake City: Signature Books, 1992), 1-8, 153-60.

9. See Mark Thomas, "Lehi's Doctrine of Opposition in Its Nineteenth and Twentieth Century Contexts," *Sunstone* 13 (Jan. 1989): 52, his "The Meaning of Revival Language in the Book of Mormon," *Sunstone* 8 (May-June 1983): 19-25; and William D. Russell, "A Further Inquiry into the Historicity of the Book of Mormon," *Sunstone* 7 (Sept.-Oct. 1982): 20-24. Thomas is LDS, Russell RLDS.

10. See Brent Lee Metcalfe, ed., *New Approaches to the Book of Mormon: Explorations in Critical Methodology* (Salt Lake City: Signature Books, 1993), x.

11. Meissner, "Psychoanalytic Hagiography," 3-33. When he rewrote these paragraphs for his later expanded book, *Ignatius of Loyola,* 346-58, he eliminated: "If he is wise he will leave those considerations to theologians and spiritual writers."

12. This quotation is a composite of two letters from Walton, *Sunstone* 8 (Nov.-Dec. 1983): 2 ("Whose God in History?"), and 11 (Jan. 1987): 6 ("God in History, Not History Books").

13. Ashment, "Historiography of the Canon," in Smith, *Faithful History,* 292.

14. Michael D. Coe, "Mormons and Archaeology: An Outside View," *Dialogue: A Journal of Mormon Thought* 8 (Summer 1974), 40-48. When an eminent nonbelieving Mormon historian recently wrote a scholarly yet kindly review of the archaeological evidence in a liberal Mormon periodical, the response was immoderate and hostile. Brigham D. Madsen, "Reflections on LDS Disbelief in the Book of Mormon as History," *Dialogue: A Journal of Mormon Thought* 30 (Fall 1997): 87-97. Four letters of response were published in *Dialogue* 31 (Summer 1998): iv-xv.

15. John W. Welch, "Chiasmus in the Book of Mormon," *BYU Studies* 10 (1969): 69-84, and "What Does Chiasmus in the Book of Mormon Prove?" in *Book of Mormon Authorship Revisited,* 199-224; Wayne Larsen et al., "Who Wrote the Book of Mormon? An Analysis of Wordprints," *BYU Studies* 20 (Spring 1980): 225-51, and John L Hilton, "On Verifying Wordprint Studies: Book of Mormon Authorship," in *Book of Mormon Authorship Revisited,* 225-53.

16. Edward H. Ashment, "'A Record in the Language of My Father': Evidence of Ancient Egyptian and Hebrew in the Book of Mormon," in Metcalfe, *New Approaches to the Book of Mormon,* 329-93, and Brent Lee Metcalfe, "Apologetic and Critical Assumptions about Book of Mormon Historicity," *Dialogue: A Journal of Mormon Thought* 26 (Fall 1993): 153-86.

17. Sorenson, *The Geography of Book of Mormon Events: A Source Book* (Provo, UT: Foundation for Ancient Research and Mormon Studies [hereafter FARMS], 1992), 371-97.

18. Sidney B. Sperry, "Were There Two Cumorahs?" (Provo, UT: FARMS, 1984); John L. Sorenson, *An Ancient American Setting for the Book of Mormon* (Salt Lake City: Deseret Book, 1985, 26, 44-45), criticized in Deanne G. Matheny, "Does the Shoe Fit? A Critique of the Limited Tehuantepec Geography," in Metcalfe, *New Approaches to the Book of Mormon,* 269-328; also Dan Vogel, "The New Theory

of Book of Mormon Geography: A Preliminary Examination," 1985, privately circulated.

19. Matheny, "Does the Shoe Fit?" 281.

20. *Messenger and Advocate* 1 (Nov. 1834): 13, and 10 (July 1835): 156-59.

21. Sorenson, *An Ancient American Setting for the Book of Mormon*, 191-276, 299.

22. Grant, *Jesus*, 13, 39. He emphasizes this required position throughout his writings, as, for example, *Saint Peter: A Biography* (New York: Barnes & Noble, 1994), 4-5: "Students of history ... are not able to take these miraculous happenings into consideration. They can believe in such stories, if they wish, but do so as a matter of faith and not as historians. Or they can dismiss them as they prefer. In either case, it is their duty to attempt to find out what happened, within the realms of historical fact and possibility." Hugh Nibley, "Phase One: Discussion of the Joseph Smith Egyptian Papyri," *Dialogue: A Journal of Mormon Thought* 3 (Summer 1968): 99, writes in agreement, "The problem of Joseph Smith as an inspired prophet never enters into the discussion at all, since that lies entirely beyond the province of scholarship: the experts must judge him as a translator or not at all."

23. Lawrence Foster, "The Psychology of Religious Genius: Joseph Smith and the Origins of New Religious Movements," *Dialogue: A Journal of Mormon Thought* 26 (Winter 1993): 1-22, with my response, "Toward an Introduction to a Psychobiography of Joseph Smith," *Dialogue: A Journal of Mormon Thought* 27 (Fall 1994): 268-72.

24. Jan Shipps, "The Prophet Puzzle: Suggestions Leading Toward a More Comprehensive Interpretation of Joseph Smith," *Journal of Mormon History* 1 (1974): 3-20.

25. Ignatius of Loyola, *The Spiritual Exercises*, trans. by Louis J. Puhl, S.J. (Chicago: Loyola University Press, 1951), 157-60, esp. paras. 353, 361-62, 364-65; Meissner, *Ignatius of Loyola*, 230-37, 405-16; Jean Lacouture, *Jesuits: A Multibiography*, trans. by J. Leggatt (Washington, D.C.: Counterpoint, 1995), esp. 75-97.

26. George D. Smith, "Nauvoo Roots of Mormon Polygamy, 1841-46: A Preliminary Demographic Report," *Dialogue: A Journal of Mormon Thought* 27 (Spring 1994): 1-72; Richard S. Van Wagoner, *Mormon Polygamy: A History* (Salt Lake City: Signature Books, 1986), 1-70; Linda King Newell and Valeen Tippets Avery, *Mormon Enigma: Emma Hale Smith; Prophet's Wife, "Elect Lady," Polygamy's Foe* (Garden City, NY: Doubleday & Co., 1984), 65, 100-101, 146-47.

27. Van Wagoner, *Mormon Polygamy*, 7-8, 38, 43-46; Hansen, *Quest for Empire;* Hill, *Quest for Refuge;* Quinn, *The Mormon Hierarchy: Origins of Power;* Quinn, *The Mormon Hierarchy: Extensions of Power;* Richard S. Van Wagoner, *Sidney Rigdon: A Portrait of Religious Excess* (Salt Lake City: Signature Books, 1994), 211ff; George D. Smith, ed., *An Intimate Chronicle: The Journals of William Clayton* (Salt Lake City: Signature Books in association with Smith Research Associates, 1995), 93-198.

28. Lavina Fielding Anderson, "The LDS Intellectual Community and Church Leadership: Contemporary Chronology," *Dialogue: A Journal of Mormon Thought* 26 (Spring 1993); and D. Michael Quinn, "On Being a Mormon Historian (and Its Aftermath)," in George D. Smith, ed., *Faithful History* (Salt Lake City: Signature Books, 1992), 69-112. These two articles document repeated demands by church authorities that only "faith-promoting" history be written. When the authors of *Mormon Enigma* were censored and forbidden to speak in LDS ward sacrament meetings, one (Linda King Newell) met with Apostle Dallin H. Oaks

about the ban. Oaks was a former Utah Supreme Court justice and past president of Brigham Young University, but his response demonstrates the support of dogma over the search for truth. He said, "My duty as a member of the Council of the Twelve is to protect what is most unique about the LDS church, namely the authority of priesthood, testimony regarding the restoration of the gospel, and the divine mission of the Savior. Everything else may be sacrificed in order to maintain the integrity of those essential facts. Thus, if *Mormon Enigma* reveals information that is detrimental to the reputation of Joseph Smith, then it is necessary to try to limit its influence and that of its authors." Linda King Newell, "The Biography of Emma Hale Smith," 1992 Pacific Northwest Sunstone Symposium, audiotape #J976.

29. Quinn, "New Mormon Hysteria," *Sunstone* 16 (Mar. 1993): 4-5. It is important to note that Quinn, in making these comments, alerts his readers that he is stepping outside the role of academic historian in his acceptance of the metaphysical.

30. See S. Freud, "The Claims of Psycho-Analysis to Scientific Interest. Part II (C)," (1913) *Psychological Works of Sigmund Freud* (hereafter *Standard Edition*), James Strachey, ed. (London: Hogarth Press, 1955), 13:181-82; see also 18:7-64, 20:231.

31. See Freud, *Standard Edition*, Letter #71 (17 Oct. 1897), 1:265-66; "The Interpretation of Dreams," 4:263-66; "Delusion and Dreams in Jensen's *Gravida*," 9:3-95; "Leonardo da Vinci and a Memory of his Childhood," 11:59-137; and "Psychoanalytic Notes on an Autobiographical Account of a Case of Paranoia," 12:9-82.

32. P. Greenacre, *Swift and Carroll: A Psychoanalytic Study of Two Lives* (New York: International Universities Press, 1955); E. Sterba and R. Sterba, *Beethoven and His Nephew: A Psychoanalytic Study of Their Relationship* (New York: Pantheon, 1954); Ernst Kris, *Psychoanalytic Explorations in Art* (New York: Schocken 1971); M. D. Faber, *The Design Within: Psychoanalytic Approaches to Shakespeare* (New York: Science House, 1970).

33. Ernst Jones, *On the Nightmare* (New York: Liverright, 1951).

34. E. H. Erikson, *Young Man Luther: A Study in Psychoanalysis and History* (New York: W. W. Norton, 1958), and *Gandhi's Truth: On the Origins of Militant Nonviolence* (New York: W. W. Norton, 1969).

35. Bruno Bettelheim, *The Uses of Enchantment: The Meaning and Importance of Fairy Tales* (New York: Alfred A. Knopf, 1976).

36. See the twelve essays in Bruce Mazlich, ed., *Psychoanalysis and History* (New York: Grosset and Dunlap, 1971).

37. Heinz Kohut, "Beyond the Bounds of the Basic Rule," *Journal of the American Psychoanalytic Association* 19 (1960): 143-79; John E. Mack, "Psychoanalysis and Historical Biography," *Journal of the American Psychoanalytic Association* 31 (1971), 1:143-49; Harry Trosman, *Freud and the Imaginative World* (Hillsdale, NJ: The Analytic Press, 1985); Fritz Schmidl, *Applied Psychoanalysis* (New York: Philosophical Library, 1981).

38. Freud, "Leonardo da Vinci," and Bullitt and Freud, *Thomas Woodrow Wilson*; Alan C. Elms, *Uncovering Lives: The Uneasy Alliance of Biography and Psychology* (New York: Oxford Press, 1994), 1-50.

39. Healthy people develop through life relatively stable ways of mentally representing themselves and others in interactions. These mental representations

are known as internal objects and form layer upon layer of experiences. Composed of thoughts, ideals, and fantasies mixed with daily reality, they form our outline and guide in living day-to-day. Object relations theory is based on our daily interactions with others, mixed with our ongoing interactions between the mental representations of ourselves and others. We do not just relate to the strict reality of another person but modify such reality by our past experiences with others.

40. Kris, *Psychoanalytic Explorations in Art*, 35, and passim.

41. W. D. Langer, "The Next Assignment," *American Historical Review* 63 (1958): 283-304.

42. See Elms, *Uncovering Lives*, 4.

43. Freud, "Civilization and Its Discontents," *Standard Edition*, 21:144.

44. Bernard DeVoto, "The Skeptical Biographer," *Harper's Magazine* 166 (1933): 181-92.

45. Bernard DeVoto, "The Centennial of Mormonism," *American Mercury*, Jan. 1930, 1, as qtd. in Francis W. Kirkham, ed., *A New Witness for Christ in America* (Independence, MO: Zion's Printing Press, 1951), 1:352; and as quoted in Lavina Fielding Anderson, "Literary Style in *No Man Knows My History:* An Analysis," in *Reconsidering* No Man Knows My History: *Fawn M. Brodie and Joseph Smith in Retrospect*, Newell G. Bringhurst, ed. (Logan: Utah State University Press, 1996), 152n4.

46. Robert J. Lifton, "On Psychohistory," in *Explorations in Psychohistory: The Wellfleet Papers*, eds. R. J. Lifton and E. Olson (New York: Simon and Schuster, 1974), 25.

47. See the hierarchy of defense mechanisms from narcissistic to mature in W. W. Meissner, et al., "Classical Psychoanalysis," in *Comprehensive Textbook of Psychiatry*, Alfred M. Freedman, Harold I. Kaplan, and Benjamin J. Sadock, eds., 2d ed. (Baltimore: Williams and Williams Co., 1975), 1:535-37.

48. Meissner, *Ignatius of Loyola*, xiv.

49. Bruce Mazlish, "Clio on the Couch," *Encounter*, Sept. 1968, 52.

50. The literature on the narcissistic personality is vast. For a comprehensive introduction, see Peter Buckley, ed., *Essential Papers of Object Relations* (New York: New York Universities Press, 1986); Andrew P. Morrison, ed., *Essential Papers on Narcissism* (New York: New York Universities Press, 1986); and Jay R. Greenberg and Stephen A. Mitchell, *Object Relations in Psychoanalytic Theory* (Cambridge, MA: Harvard University Press, 1983). This latter work is an excellent encyclopedic review of psychoanalytic psychology from the time of Freud, suggesting how important object-relations theory has become. The work would make difficult reading for those not in the mental health field, but the last chapter is poetically written. For an example of how Freud's original theories have been changed or altered, and replaced with ideas that more accurately fit newer understandings of developmental knowledge, see Theo. L. Dorpat and Michael L. Miller, *Clinical Interaction and the Analysis of Meaning: A New Psychoanalytic Theory* (Hillsdale, NJ: Analytic Press, 1992).

51. See Clara Thompson, *Psychoanalysis: Evolution and Development: A Review of Theory and Therapy* (New York: Grove Press, 1957), 44-46, see also 7-8, 19-58.

52. Greenberg and Mitchell, *Object Relations in Psychoanalytic Theory*, 100-105, 383-408.

53. See Manfred F. R. Kets de Vries and Danny Miller, "Narcissism and Leadership: An Object Relations Perspective," *Human Relations* 38 (1985): 583-601.

54. Donald Winnicott, *Maturational Processes and the Facilitating Environment* (New York: International Universities Press, 1965).

55. See Kets de Vries and Miller, "Narcissism and Leadership," 587.

56. "Diagnostic Criteria for 301.81 Narcissistic Disorder," *Diagnostic and Statistical Manual of Mental Disorders, 4th Edition* (Washington, D.C.: American Psychiatric Association, 1994), 661.

57. The defining of narcissism, describing its characteristics, and proposing etiologies and theories represents a very fine hour of psychoanalysis. Most have viewed the narcissistic personality as the severest form of character pathology that may not have a significant genetic component and is potentially treatable. Various treatment strategies have been proposed, and treatment failures are common. The psychoanalytic treatment is extensive and requires modification to standard treatment; I know of no statistics of treatment outcomes. Family statisticians have recently proposed that narcissism may be a variant of Bipolar Affective Disorder (Manic-Depressive Illness), thus implying a large genetic component. If this diagnosis fits some percentage of patients with narcissism, it requires a rewriting of the major characteristic of both illnesses: in narcissism, vigorous energy (hypomania) must replace self-centeredness; and in bipolar affective disorder, a steady-state condition must replace periodicity. See the discussion and references in my "Toward an Introduction to a Psychobiography of Joseph Smith," *Dialogue: A Journal of Mormon Thought* 27 (Fall 1994): 268-72. For more recent papers pressuring for the same idea, see Hagop S. Akiskal, "Dysthymic and Cyclothymic Depressions: Therapeutic Considerations," *Journal of Clinical Psychiatry* 55, suppl. (Apr. 1994): 46-52, and "The Prevalent Clinical Spectrum of Bipolar Disorders: Beyond DSM-IV," *Journal of Clinical Psychopharmacology* 16 (1996), supplement 1:4s-14s.

58. Purple, "Joseph Smith, the Originator of Mormonism," 2:362-67.

59. Phyllis Greenacre, "The Family Romance of the Artist," The Psychoanalytic Study of the Child, Vol. 13 (New York: International Universities Press, Inc., 1958), 10.

60. Although some discussion of the Book of Mormon's theology will be inevitable in discussing certain passages, it is not the focus of this book. For scholarly and sometimes nontraditional analyses, see the essays in Gary James Bergera, ed., *Line Upon Line: Essays on Mormon Doctrine* (Salt Lake City: Signature Books, 1989); Dan Vogel, ed., *The Word of God: Essays on Mormon Scripture* (Salt Lake City: Signature Books, 1990); Metcalfe, *New Approaches to the Book of Mormon.* For excellent specific investigations, see Stan Larson, "The Historicity of the Matthean Sermon on the Mount in 3 Nephi," *New Approaches,* 115-64, and Ronald V. Huggins, "Did the Author of 3 Nephi Know the Gospel of Matthew?" *Dialogue: A Journal of Mormon Thought* 30 (Fall 1997): 137-50. Mormon apologists vigorously countered *New Approaches to the Book of Mormon* in thirteen separate essays in Daniel C. Peterson, ed., *Review of Books on the Book of Mormon* (Provo, UT: FARMS, 1994), Vol. 6.

Ellen G White

November 26, 1827 to July 16, 19[illegible]5

age 87

Born in Gorham, Main

Died in St. Helena, California

Joseph Smith

December 23, 1805 to June 27, 1844

Born in Sharon, Vermont

Died in Carthage, Illinois

CHAPTER 1

Prolegomenon to a Biography of the Child Joseph

One challenge in approaching Joseph Smith's childhood and adolescence is the scarcity of primary sources for his early life. A little over six years before his murder in mid-1844, Smith began "writing a history of this Church from the earliest period of its exist[e]nce up to this date"[1] of April 1838. That manuscript, copied in 1839, is known as the Manuscript History of the Church, Book A-1. This is Smith's official version of his story. It was first printed in the church newspaper in Nauvoo, Illinois, in 1842[2] and, after his death, excerpted in the 1851 booklet *The Pearl of Great Price,* which contained other material as well. This history was canonized as scripture by the LDS church's general conference of October 1880.

In it Smith documents his birth date (23 December 1805) and place (Sharon, Vermont), then goes directly to his family's move from Vermont to Palmyra in upstate New York when "I was in my tenth year." About four years later, the family moved two miles south into Manchester township "in the same county." He lists eleven family members. Elsewhere he notes a childhood surgery and briefly describes the move to New York.[3] In short, it is nearly impossible to form an image of Smith's childhood based solely on his own writings. Even if one adds all of the known statements by Smith's siblings, official census records, and comments by neighbors, this compilation leaves the period before Smith turned about fourteen comparatively blank and makes any effort to evaluate his adult life and accomplishments in the light of his childhood tenuous.

Fortunately, Joseph's mother, Lucy Mack Smith, dictated a biography of her famous son in 1844-45, within a year after his death. She explained to her only surviving son, William, on 23 June 1845, almost exactly a year after the double murder of Joseph and his older brother Hyrum:

> People are often inquiring of me the particulars of Joseph's getting the plates, seeing the angels at first, and many other things which Joseph never wrote or published. I have told over many things pertaining to these matters to different persons to gratify their curiosity, indeed have almost destroyed my lungs giving these recitals to those who felt anxious to hear them. I have now concluded to write down every particular as far as possible.[4]

Apparently she had already begun the task during the previous autumn by dictating her reminiscences to Martha Jane Knowlton Coray, a Nauvoo schoolteacher who described herself as a good note-taker. Coray was aided by her husband Howard, who at one time assisted in compiling the official church history. "I wrote the book and my statements were faithful and true as far as I could learn at that time," Martha later stated.[5]

The first draft was apparently finished by early 1845, then edited and polished between March and July 1845, probably by the Corays who added about 25 percent and deleted 10 percent.[6] It is not clear to what degree Lucy assisted in these silent modifications. A copy of this enlarged modified history was made. At a church conference on 8 October 1845, Lucy "gave notice that she had written her history, and wished it printed."[7] Lucy was then seventy years old, in mourning from a series of family deaths, in frail health, and, sometimes of faulty memory.

One of two final copies, a "beautifully written, leather-bound" volume, was taken to Salt Lake City with the Mormon pioneer trek that began in 1847 and remains in the church's archives. The other, which Lucy retained, came into possession of her son-in-law, passed through two other sets of hands, and was finally purchased by Mormon apostle Orson Pratt who, with Lucy's permission, published it in Liverpool, England, in 1853.[8] The present location of this manuscript is unknown and it may have been destroyed. From England the published book was transported to Utah where it was used as a school textbook. By 1865 Brigham Young, in frequent disagreement with Pratt and dissatisfied with "inaccuracies" in the biography that tended to favor Joseph's younger brother William (who was making claim to church authority), suppressed it. Various versions have been published subsequently by both Mormon and non-Mormon groups and individuals.

The original unmodified preliminary draft was uncovered in the church archives in the late 1960s. Excerpts, sometimes lengthy, have since appeared in print, and Dan Vogel published the New York and Ohio portions of this memoir in 1996, side-by-side with the corresponding 1853 published version, with careful editing and annotations.[9] This published comparison is my main reference for Joseph Smith's early life.

In this book, I examine Lucy's biography of her son, the Book of Mormon, and Joseph Smith's life to age twenty-four, raising questions, examining discrepancies, and offering interpretations. This chapter summarizes the traditional account of Joseph's early life. The first part condenses his mother's history,[10] and then, beginning with the age of fourteen, Smith's own story.

Joseph Smith's Childhood and Youth

Joseph Smith was born into a poor family living in Vermont on 23 December 1805. He was the fourth living child, and his mother delivered six more children after him, one of whom died shortly after birth. Both parents came from good New England stock and were clearly religious, but dissatisfied and troubled. Joseph's mother had been raised in a family with some religious dissension. Her mother was a staunch Congregationalist, but her father, although raised by a Congregational minister, believed in a more kindly "Universalism" which taught about a God of love and grace "who will finally restore the whole family of mankind to holiness and happiness."[11] Solomon Mack, Joseph's maternal grandfather, converted to a more orthodox form of Protestantism shortly before his death. In a personal history, published and distributed at his own expense, he described his conversion.[12] He saw a bright light he could not account for and heard someone call his name. He imagined Jesus weeping for Jerusalem. This conversion probably decreased religious tension in the home.

Lucy was the last-born of his eight children. In 1796 at age twenty-one, she married Joseph Smith, Sr., then twenty-four. Joseph's father, Asael Smith, had refused to join any church "because he could not reconcile their teachings with the scriptures and his reason." Asael otherwise encouraged his children to "S[e]arch the Sciptures."[13] Thus both of the future prophet's parents grew up in families with unanswered religious questions. Both parents had been stirred by the idea that the early "primitive" Christian church had been lost, and they were now "seeking" after it. Some seekers expected only "the restoration of God's spirit and power among the true believers"; or, in other words, an idealized group of people who lived with Christian charity and the Holy Spirit in their lives. Others looked for a restoration of a literal ecclesiastic organization, doctrinal accuracy that agreed with the New Testament, and perhaps even apostles bearing the authority of Christ. How such a church might be found was never clear.[14]

Despite Joseph Sr.'s years of religious wandering, he did not subscribe to any particular church or faith. Within the family, his nighttime dreams were seen as inspired by God, and he looked to God to direct his life. Lucy attended various Protestant meetings but ended up believing that "there was not then upon the earth the religion which I sought." The family was hardworking but plagued by misfortune and economic setbacks, not uncommon in those days for New England.[15] Because of such financial woes, the family lost early possessions including a farm and had to move frequently.

Sometime between 1811 and 1813, while they were living in New Hampshire, misfortune struck again, this time when all of the children became ill with typhoid.[16] One daughter nearly died; but the dedication and perseverance of the family pulled them through, even when the doctor abandoned hope. Apparently no one suffered permanent effects except Joseph, then between five and seven years old. (Lucy does not date the epidemic.) He developed a severe typhoid infection in his leg bones, a condition which often required amputation. Providentially, his family was near the fledgling Dartmouth Medical School, whose founder, Nathan Smith, was preeminent in the surgical treatment of typhoid osteomyelitis.[17]

The strength of both the family and young Joseph was demonstrated during this awful surgery, for Joseph reportedly refused alcohol as an anesthetic and also refused to be tied to the bed. Instead he resolved to bear the operation if his father would hold him during the procedure. The surgeon cut open his bone, to expose the trapped infection and allow the area to heal from within. The operation was a success and amputation was avoided.[18] Joseph healed successfully at home for some time, then spent several months in Salem, Massachusetts, at the home of a paternal uncle, in hopes that the sea air would be ameliorative. While Joseph, as a youth and an adult, became a strong wrestler, could run without difficulty, and engaged in the hard physical labor of farming, clearing land, etc., he retained a slight limp.

When crop failures occurred for the following two years, the family's economic situation slipped to what must have been day-to-day hunger. Joseph Sr. determined to leave New England for more promising farm country in upstate New York if the crops failed again. On the other side of the world in 1815, a volcanic explosion, Tambora in Indonesia, sent a cloud of ash circling the globe, affecting solar radiation for over a year.[19] That year, 1816, is now remembered in New England history as the "year without a summer." Joseph Sr. moved to the small town of Palmyra (pop. 3,500) in upstate New York in late 1816, sending for the family when he had located a residence. Joseph Jr., then about ten and a half years old, was still lame from his surgery although he was able to walk for hours as they made their way west.

In Palmyra, Joseph Sr. and his two older sons, Alvin and Hyrum, immediately hired out as farm laborers, while Lucy painted oilcloth and, with her daughters, made and sold pies, cakes, and rootbeer at public events.[20] They lived in the village itself for a few years, then moved a few miles south where they rented or squatted in a small log cabin. As things improved, they moved again only some yards away, but over the line into Manchester township, began the purchase of land, probably built another log cabin, and started to build a farm house.[21] During Joseph's early adolescence, his mother describes him as a child of few words who "always seemed to reflect more deeply than common persons of his age upon everything of a religious nature."[22]

Although Lucy does not comment on religion, the family had moved into an area of religious turbulence. Beginning around 1800 and extending through this period, the country was aflame with the peculiar religious revivalism referred to as "the Second Great Awakening." Religious enthusiasms swept back and forth across upper New York, centered around Palmyra, until the area was called "the Burned-over District."[23] The revivalism reached its zenith during the period of our interest, 1820-30, and continued to 1850.

Joseph states, "Sometime in the second year after our removal to Manchester, there was in the place where we lived an unusual excitement on the subject of religion," adding that he was "at this time in my fifteenth year."[24] The "unusual excitement" began with the Methodists, then involved other sects, notably Baptists and Presbyterians. Four members of Joseph's family, including his mother, joined the Presbyterian church, while Joseph was partial to Methodism. He tells us that as converts filed off to different churches, bad feelings and confusion resulted among the denominations and religious leaders, destroying "good feelings one for another, (if they ever had any)." Because of feelings of "great uneasiness ... confusion [from this] ... strife [and] ... tumult of opinions," he was laboring under extreme difficulties. "Who of all these parties are right?" He read in the Bible that if anyone lacked wisdom, "let him ask of God, that giveth to all men liberally, and upbraideth not; and it shall be given him." Joseph was struck by the importance of this invitation from God, for "how to act I did not know and unless I could get more wisdom than I then had would never know, for the teachers of religion of the different sects understood the same passage of scripture so differently as /to/[25] destroy all confidence in settling the question by an appeal to the Bible." He decided to ask God which church to join.

Visible from the porch of the restored Smith farm house is a grove of trees on the far side of a small field. Tradition identifies this grove as the site of Joseph's prayer, which he tells us in his official history took place "on the morning of a beautiful clear day early in the spring of Eighteen hundred and twenty." When he began to pray, he was seized by a dark power "which entirely overcame me, and had such an astonishing influence over me as to bind my tongue so that I could not speak." He believed he was

> doomed to sudden destruction. But, exerting all my powers to call upon God to deliver me out of the power of this enemy which had seized upon me ... not to an imaginary ruin, but to the power of some actual being from the unseen world. ... Just at this moment of great alarm, I saw a pillar /of/ light exactly over my head, above the brightness of the sun, which descended gradually until it fell upon me. It no sooner appeared than I found myself delivered from the enemy which held me bound. When the light rested upon me, I saw two Personages (whose brightness and glory defy all description) standing above me in the air. One of /them/ spake unto me calling me by name and said (pointing to the other) "This is my beloved Son. Hear him."

Joseph asked

> which sect was right, (for at this time it had never entered into my heart that all were wrong) and which I should join. I was answered that I must join

> none of them, for they were all wrong, and the Personage who addressed me said that all their Creeds were an abomination in his sight; that those professors were all corrupt. ... He again forbade me to join with any of them. ... When I came to myself again, I found myself lying on /my/ back, looking up into heaven.

Relating this experience to a Methodist minister, Joseph was surprised to receive a disdainful response:

> It has often caused me serious reflection both then and since, how very strange it was that an obscure boy of a little over fourteen years of age and one who was doomed to the necessity of obtaining a scanty maintenance by his daily labor, should be thought a character of sufficient importance to attract the attention of the great ones of the most popular sects of the day, and in a manner to create in them a spirit of the most bitter persecution and reviling. But strange or not, so it was, and was often the cause of great sorrow to myself.

Joseph compared himself to the apostle Paul who had also seen a vision and was ridiculed.

> So it was with me, I had actually seen a light, and in the midst of that light I saw two Personages, and they did in reality speak /un/to me, or one of them did. And though I was hated and persecuted for saying that I had seen a vision, yet it was true. ... "[W]ho am I that I can withstand God" or why does the world think to make me deny what I have actually seen, for I had seen a vision, I knew it, and I knew that God knew it, and I could not deny it, neither dare I do it, at least I knew that by so doing /I/ would offend God and come under condemnation.

Devout Mormons believe that this singular event was the most important moment in the history of humanity since the Resurrection, for it inaugurated the restoration of God's only true church to the earth before the Second Coming. Joseph would be the man, under divine command and authority, to found the church his parents had been seeking. He would hardly be able to understand his calling at this young age, but his accomplishments before his death would, in the eyes of his followers, make him the third most important man who ever walked the earth, after Jesus and, perhaps, father Adam. The LDS church after his martyrdom would make the official declaration: "Joseph Smith, the Prophet and Seer of the Lord, has done more, save Jesus only, for the salvation of men in this world, than any other man that ever lived in it" (LDS D&C 135:3).

However, at this youthful moment Joseph knew only that he should not join any church but must await further heavenly instruction. He continued the "common avocations in life" for the next three years, acknowledging his susceptibility to "temptations ... many foolish errors ... weakness of youth, and the [corruption][26] /foibles/ of human nature." "In making this confession," he later clarified,

> no one need suppose me guilty of any great or malignant sins: a disposition to commit such was never in my nature; but I was guilty of Levity, & sometimes associated with Jovial company, &c, not consistent with that character which ought to be maintained by one who was called of God as I had been; but this will not seem very strange to any one who recollects my youth, & is acqu/aint/ed with my native cheery Temperament. In consequence of these things I often felt condemned for my weakness and imperfections.

On 21 September 1823, about three and a half years after his first vision, Joseph knelt in prayer in his room to ask "forgiveness of all my sins and follies" with full confidence that God would respond. "While I was thus in the act of calling upon God, I discovered a light appearing in my room which continued to increase until the room was lighter than at noonday /when/ immediately a personage /appeared/ at my bedside standing in the air for his feet did not touch the floor." Joseph described this figure with precision, including the exquisite whiteness of his loose robe and his naked hands, arms, and bosom. "[H]is whole person was glorious beyond description, and his countenance truly like lightning." The heavenly being told Joseph that he was Nephi,[27] a messenger from God, and that God had work for Joseph to do. Nearby was "deposited" a book written on golden plates that told of the "former inhabitants of this continent and the source from whence they sprang." The messenger also said that the book contained "the fullness of the everlasting Gospel ... as delivered by the Savior to the ancient inhabitants." Buried with the book were two (transparent) "stones in silver bows ... /fastened/ to a breast plate" so that the book could be translated when Joseph looked through them. "The possession of these stones" made one a "seer" in ancient times. The angel quoted Bible verses from Joel, Isaiah, the Acts of the Apostles, and, with minor variations, Malachi. He warned Joseph of punishment if he did not keep these things hidden from others. "While he was conversing with me about the plates the vision was opened to my mind that I could see the place where the plates were deposited and that so clearly and distinctly that I knew the place again when I visited it."

The angel disappeared, then reappeared twice more, each time repeating his message "without the least variation," warned Joseph to be prepared for temptations, and specifically warned him against using this information for wealth. Joseph must have no "other object in view in getting the plates but to glorify God, and must not be influenced by any other motive than that of building his kingdom." These visitations took the whole night. When the exhausted Joseph tried to work in the field the next day, his strength failed him and he fell unconscious while climbing a fence to go home. "The first thing that I can recollect was a voice speaking unto me calling me by name." The angel had reappeared and told Joseph to tell his father about this visitation. Joseph Sr. immediately believed his son's report and declared that his experience was of God. Joseph left the field to go where "the plates were deposited, and owing to the distinctness of the vision which I had had concerning it, I knew the place the instant that I arrived there."

Joseph met the angel at a hill two to three miles from his home. "On the west side of this hill, not far from the top, under a stone of considerable size, lay the plates, deposited in a stone box." In this stone box were also "other things," which included the two "seer" stones attached by silver bows to the breastplate. He was not allowed to take the plates but was commanded to meet the angel in precisely one year and each year thereafter "until four years from that time."

During these four years, Joseph worked as a common farm laborer, but rumors spread that he had found something valuable through the means of folk magic. Employed by a wealthy farmer, he left Manchester and traveled 120 miles southeast to the border of Pennsylvania where he tried to help his employer find a lost Spanish treasure reportedly buried in the earth. He finally "prevailed with the old gentleman to cease digging after it. Hence arose the very prevalent story of my having been a money-digger." While in that area he met his future wife, Emma Hale, and asked her father for her hand in marriage. Isaac Hale refused, believing that Joseph deceived people in his activities as a money-digger. As both young people were of age, Joseph, who did have his parents' blessing, and Emma eloped and were married on 27 January 1827. They moved into his family home in Manchester. On the night of 22 September 1827, the angel let him take the plates, again warning him that he would be held responsible for their care until this angel/messenger "should call for them." Immediately

> the most strenuous exertions were used to get them from me. Every stratagem that could be invented was resorted to for that purpose. The persecution became more bitter and severe than before ... but by the wisdom of God they remained safe in my hands until I had accomplished by them what was required at my hand, when according to arrangements the messenger called for them, I delivered them up to him and he has them in his charge until this day [1838].

Because of this "persecution," Joseph had to leave the family home and with his wife traveled back to her home in Pennsylvania. While he was there, his family in Manchester took in as a boarder a young schoolteacher named Oliver Cowdery. When the Smith family told this young man about Joseph's discovery, he became intrigued. As soon as school ended in late March 1829, Oliver walked the 120 miles to Joseph's residence and within two days began to act as scribe while Joseph dictated the Book of Mormon, using the miraculous means that God had provided. The majority of the translation took place between April and July 1829, a prodigious accomplishment.

Joseph tells us little about this period. Two years later his older brother Hyrum suggested he tell a group of Mormons about the "coming forth" of the Book of Mormon. Joseph responded that "it was not intended to tell the world all the particulars of the coming forth of the Book of Mormon; and [he] also said that it was not expedient for him to relate these things."[28] The printing of the book in Palmyra took about eight months, and was advertised for sale on 26 March 1830. The Book of Mormon was to be a "second witness" (after the New Testament) that "Jesus is the CHRIST, the ETERNAL GOD, manifesting Himself unto all nations."[29]

To believing Mormons, the book represents the most objective evidence for Joseph's divine mission and remains a major force in their lives, resisting attacks intended to diminish the "work of God." Those who have tried to demonstrate the book as human-made run into the issue of Joseph's semi-illiteracy and simple background in contrast to the size and complexity of the book. Joseph's new Church of Christ, quickly nicknamed Mormon, was founded on 6 April 1830, less than two weeks after the Book of Mormon appeared.

Joseph tells this detailed and dramatic story of his early life with certainty. But despite this assurance, its details are not internally consistent. In this 1838 canonized version, Joseph said that he moved to Palmyra in his "tenth year," which would be 1815, but in the 1842 version, he says he was "ten years old," which would make it 1816. He adds that they moved from Palmyra to Manchester "about four years" later and that the revival connected with his first vision occurred "in the second year" after moving. These years add up to 1821 or 1822 at the earliest, and he would have been in his sixteenth or seventeenth year. Yet he announces without ambiguity that the revival and first vision were "early in the spring of Eighteen hundred and twenty" when he was in his "fifteenth year."[30]

This problem was recognized as early as 1842, and Willard Richards added the qualifying phrase "or thereabouts" to these dates.[31] But we can date the Smith family move to Palmyra and then to Manchester with some precision from road tax rolls, his mother's biography, and other evidences. They probably arrived in Palmyra in late 1816 and appear on the road tax rolls for the first time in early 1817. These rolls and other evidences confirm their move to Manchester in 1822.[32] The revival "in the second year" after this move would then have occurred in 1824, not 1820. There was no significant revival in or around Palmyra in 1820, nor in any year between 1818 and 1823.[33]

A Synopsis of the Book of Mormon

The Book of Mormon claims to be a divinely written historical document that begins during the Old Testament period when Jeremiah was prophesying in Jerusalem about 600 B.C.E. There another prophet named

Lehi (never mentioned in the Old Testament, although the word appears as a place name in Judges 15:19) is warned by God of the impending Babylonian captivity of the Jews (around 600 B.C.E.) and is commanded to leave Jerusalem with his family of four sons and an unspecified number (probably two) of daughters, taking along another family with five marriageable daughters and two sons. Lehi's family is also commanded to take with them the "brass plates," or scriptures containing what Joseph Smith apparently viewed as the Old Testament up to 600 B.C.E. plus a family genealogy.

For eight years this tribal group wandered in the "wilderness" near the Red Sea, experiencing numerous miracles, then settled on the shores of a "sea [of] many waters." Here they built a boat in which they sailed across the Pacific to the Americas. But Lehi had a troubled family. His oldest two sons, Laman and Lemuel, were hostile, rebellious, and disobedient. His younger two sons, Sam and Nephi, were righteous. Even at this point, Nephi was becoming a great prophet, superseding his father. It is Nephi who narrates this first part of the Book of Mormon. After their arrival in America, the family tenuously remained together until the aged Lehi's death, then the smoldering sibling rivalry broke out into murderous hatred. Nephi took his group away into the wilderness and founded a higher, complex civilization with metallurgy, art, culture, and true Christian worship. Laman and Lemuel established the opposing "Lamanite" nation that degenerated quickly into barbaric savagery. God cursed this group with a "skin of blackness," thus explaining the origin of the Native Americans, and told Nephi that they would be a "scourge" to his descendants whenever these "Nephites" fell into sin. Furthermore, if the Nephites became too evil, the Lamanites would be allowed to destroy them.

After this detailed beginning, the generations pass more quickly. As these two nations expand over the next 600 years, the historical account is filled with wars, heroism, miracles, prophets, visions, martyrdoms, and so forth. This "Old Testament" section of the Book of Mormon differs from the Bible in an important way; during this time, the prophets preached an explicit belief in the yet-to-be-born Jesus, a Christology similar to the salvationist Christianity of Joseph Smith's day.[34] The Nephites formed Christian communities, were baptized, received the "Holy Spirit," and undertook extensive missionary work among the infidel Lamanites. The wars, during one period, became extreme, then miraculously stopped; then the Nephite nation became corrupt, thanks to an evil secret brotherhood of robbers and murderers.

As the time of Jesus' birth in Bethlehem approached, yet another prophet, warning the Nephites to repent, promised them dramatic signs: At Jesus' birth, they would see a new star; the sun would set one night but there would be no darkness. This prophet also told them that, at Jesus' crucifixion, they would be punished for their sins with natural catastrophes.

The Book of Mormon describes both the night without darkness at the birth and a gigantic geophysical holocaust at the death which convulses the land with earthquakes, fire, tidal waves, and lightnings. Many cities and "great cities" with their inhabitants were destroyed, leaving only a small percentage of the "more righteous." A few days later, Jesus, now resurrected, appeared in the sky, cataloged the destruction, acknowledged that he had caused it, then descended to preach his gospel of love and kindness, including his Sermon on the Mount. He visited the survivors repeatedly over the next three days and established his church with twelve disciples.

For the next two centuries, these severely chastened people lived in complete harmony and happiness, integrated into one people (rather than Nephites/Lamanites). Then envy and unrighteousness returned, the people again divided into white Nephites and dark Lamanites, the Nephites refused to repent, and the next two centuries passed in fighting off, with increasingly less success, repeated short and sharp destructive attacks from the Lamanites. Hatred reigned supreme. God commanded the last great righteous prophet, Mormon, also an army general, to review the records of this 1,000-year civilization and summarize it into a single book. He obeyed, inscribing his summary on metal plates. Then Mormon, along with 240,000 Nephite soldiers and their families, fought and lost a last genocidal battle at a hill called "Cumorah." All were killed except for Mormon's son, Moroni, who recorded this terrible scene and spent the next twenty years in hiding to avoid being killed. Completing his father's record, he buried the "gold plates" in the hill Cumorah in what is now upstate New York, around 421 C.E. Fourteen centuries later, he reappeared as the angelic messenger who announced to Joseph Smith that he had been chosen to unearth and translate this record.

Joseph was then a seventeen-year-old uneducated and inexperienced farm boy living two or three miles from this hill. As already narrated, the angel met Joseph yearly for four years, then gave him the book in September 1827. Various impediments delayed work on the book until the spring of 1829, but it was printed by March 1830 and the Mormon church was founded less than two weeks later.

Naturally, this overview has omitted some elements important for this psychoanalytic study. While the history of the Nephites and Lamanites takes up 95 percent of the Book of Mormon, the book actually recounts three migrations from the Middle East to the New World, not just one. Around 200 B.C.E., the Nephites, migrating to avoid warfare with the Lamanites, encountered a second group (the Mulekites) who had also come from Jerusalem around 600 B.C.E. These people had failed to bring a copy of their scriptures with them and, as a result, were sliding into illiteracy, atheism, and savagery. The good king Mosiah of the Nephites taught these people to read, told them their sacred history, became their king, and merged them with his own Nephites. As a separate group, they disappeared, and their story takes up only a few verses. However, they reported to the Nephites that, only a few months earlier, they had taken in a wanderer who was the last king of a gigantic civilization (the Jaredites). He had died "nine moons" later. This earlier civilization had left a record on its final battlefield where its two final factions had exterminated each other. A group of Nephite explorers soon discovered this record, described as twenty-four gold plates. Translated miraculously by King Mosiah, it revealed the history of a group who had come to the promised land of America at the time of the Tower of Babel, prospered and grew, passed through cycles of righteousness and sin, and utterly destroyed each other in hand-to-hand combat. Their final battle, in which 2 million soldiers died, ended a 2,000-year-old civilization (ca. 2500-600 B.C.E.) of probably 10-15 million people.[35] It also occurred at Cumorah. Moroni abridged this already abridged record as the book of Ether (Ether was their last surviving prophet). It takes up about 5 percent of the current Book of Mormon. These two "extra" migrations provide tantalizing clues to the psychological makeup of Joseph Smith.

Notes

1. Manuscript, the Scriptory Book of Joseph Smith, Jr., 34, in Dean C. Jessee, ed., *The Papers of Joseph Smith* (Salt Lake City: Deseret Book Co., 1992), 2:233.

2. *Times and Seasons* 3 (beginning 15 Mar. 1842): 726.

3. Dean C. Jessee, ed., *The Papers of Joseph Smith* (Salt Lake City: Deseret Book Co., 1989), 1:230-31, 265-302, esp. 268-69.

4. Lucy Smith to William Smith, in Richard L. Anderson, "Circumstantial Confirmation of the First Vision Through Reminiscences," *BYU Studies* 9 (Spring 1969): 387.

5. M. J. Coray to Brigham Young, 13 June 1865, in Dan Vogel, ed., *Early Mormon Documents* (Salt Lake City: Signature Books, 1996), 1:228, hereafter cited as Vogel, Lucy Smith History.

6. See Richard L. Anderson, "The Reliability of the Early History of Lucy and Joseph Smith," *Dialogue: A Journal of Mormon Thought* 4 (Summer 1969): 13-28; Jan Shipps, *Mormonism: The Story of a New Religious Tradition* (Urbana: University of Illinois Press, 1985), 87-107, esp. 95; Shipps references the Anderson paper but it does not give the percentages. Anderson may have made them in personal communication. These are rough percentages, for the preliminary draft may be incomplete.

7. Address, 8 Oct. 1845, *Times and Seasons* 6 (1 Nov. 1845): 1014, in Anderson, "Circumstantial Confirmation," 387. Vogel, Lucy Smith History, 229-30.

8. Lucy Smith, *Biographical Sketches of Joseph Smith the Prophet, and His Progenitors for Many Generations* (Liverpool: S. W. Richards, 1853).

9. "Lucy Smith History, 1845," in Vogel, Lucy Smith History, 227-450. Most of the changes in the 1853 published version were critical in eliminating discrepancies between Joseph Smith's own published history and evidences from other sources. This makes the "preliminary dictated manuscript" one of the most accu-

rate sources for Joseph's early life. It provides enough raw material to begin a psychobiography and, in this case, correlation of Joseph's life with the origin of the Book of Mormon.

10. Vogel, Lucy Smith History, 231-339.

11. Dan Vogel, *Religious Seekers and the Advent of Mormonism* (Salt Lake City: Signature Books, 1986), 25, quoting Russell E. Miller, *The Larger Hope: The First Century of the Universalist Church in America, 1770-1870* (Boston: Unitarian Universalist, 1979), 45-46. See also Richard S. Van Wagoner, *Sidney Rigdon: A Portrait of Religious Excess* (Salt Lake City: Signature Books, 1994), 1-70.

12. Solomon Mack, *A Narraitive of the Life of Solomon Mack* (Windsor: Printed at the expense of the author[, 1811]), 19-21, reprinted in Richard L. Anderson, *Joseph Smith's New England Heritage* (Salt Lake City: Deseret Book Co., 1971).

13. Anderson, *Joseph Smith's New England,* 124-40, and Vogel, *Religious Seekers,* 26.

14. Vogel, *Religious Seekers,* 10-11; Van Wagoner, *Sidney Rigdon,* 1-70.

15. Vogel, Lucy Smith History, 241-46.

16. Ibid., 247-60.

17. LeRoy S. Wirthlin, "Nathan Smith (1762-1828) Surgical Consultant to Joseph Smith," *BYU Studies* 17 (Spring 1977): 310-35, and "Joseph Smith's Boyhood Operation: An 1813 Surgical Success," *BYU Studies* 21 (Spring 1981): 131-54; Reed C. Durham, Jr., "Joseph Smith's Own Story of a Serious Childhood Illness," *BYU Studies* 10 (Autumn 1970): 480-82; Jessee, *Papers of Joseph Smith,* 1:268-69n1.

18. Vogel, Lucy Smith History, 260-69.

19. Ibid., 269-70. Henry and Elizabeth Stommel, "The Year Without a Summer," *Scientific American* 240 (June 1979): 176-86.

20. Pomeroy Tucker, *Origin, Rise, and Progress of Mormonism* (New York: D. Appleton, 1867), 12-18.

21. H. Michael Marquardt and Wesley P. Walters, *Inventing Mormonism: Tradition and the Historical Record* (San Francisco: Smith Research Associates, 1994), 1-14.

22. Vogel, Lucy Smith History, 289, 286-87. The 1853 published version adds that he was a "remarkably quiet, well-disposed child."

23. Whitney R. Cross, *The Burned-Over District: The Social and Intellectual History of Enthusiastic Religion in Western New York, 1800-1850* (Ithaca, NY: Cornell University Press, 1950), 3-151; Van Wagoner, *Sidney Rigdon;* Robert N. Hullinger, *Joseph Smith's Response to Skepticism* (Salt Lake City: Signature Books, 1992), 1-48.

24. Jessee, *Papers of Joseph Smith,* 1:265-82.

25. Slashes indicate interlinear insertions.

26. "Corruption" crossed out.

27. Moroni is the name of the angel according to present-day Mormon belief, but "Nephi" appears in the original manuscript and first printed version, *Times and Seasons* 3 (15 Apr. 1842): 753, and also according to his mother's account in Vogel, Lucy Smith History, 63-64. Unlike most of the editing between the 1844 and the 1853 versions, this change is important. Mary Musser Whitmer, mother of five of the eleven signatories attesting to the physical existence of the Book of Mormon gold plates, identified the angel as Nephi. "I have heard my grandmother (Mary M. Whitmer) say on several occasions that she was shown the plates of the Book of Mormon by an holy angel, whom she always called brother Nephi." John C. Whitmer, Statement, qtd. in "The Eight Witnesses," *Historical Re-*

cord 7 (Oct. 1888), 621, qtd. in D. Michael Quinn, *Early Mormonism and the Magic World View* (Salt Lake City: Signature Books, 1987), 157. The name was changed to Moroni in the 1878 edition of the *Pearl of Great Price* and in the 1902 edition of the *History of the Church* to fit other statements by Joseph Smith. Jessee, *Papers of Joseph Smith,* 1:277n1, ascribes "Nephi" to a clerical error, but Quinn, *Early Mormonism,* 156-57, observes that this explanation is inadequate given the published versions which Joseph Smith did not correct.

28. Donald Q. Cannon and Lyndon W. Cook, eds., *Far West Record: Minutes of the Church of Jesus Christ of Latter-day Saints, 1830-1844* (Salt Lake City: Deseret Book Co., 1983); and Joseph Smith, Jr., et al., *History of the Church of Jesus Christ of Latter-day Saints,* 2d ed. rev., 7 vols., ed. B. H. Roberts (Salt Lake City: Deseret Book Co., 1951 printing), 1:219n.

29. *The Book of Mormon* (Palmyra, NY: E. B. Grandin, 1830), title page.

30. Jessee, *Papers of Joseph Smith,* for ten years old, 429; for 1820 revival and "fifteenth year," 269-72.

31. Ibid., 1:269n2, 274n1; Marquardt and Walters, *Inventing Mormonism,* 9n1.

32. Marquardt and Walters, *Inventing Mormonism,* 3-8.

33. Ibid., 15-41. Mormon historian Marvin S. Hill acknowledges the 1824 date in "The First Vision Controversy: A Critique and Reconciliation," *Dialogue: A Journal of Mormon Thought* 15 (Summer 1982): 31-47. Although Mormon apologetics continue to assert an 1820 Palmyra revival, there is simply no historical evidence to support it.

34. See, for example, Susan Curtis, "Early Nineteenth-Century America and the Book of Mormon," 81-96, and Melodie Moench Charles, "The Mormon Christianizing of the Old Testament," 131-42, both in Dan Vogel, ed., *The Word of God: Essays on Mormon Scriptures* (Salt Lake City: Signature Books, 1990); Dan Vogel, "The Earliest Mormon Concept of God," in *Line upon Line: Essays on Mormon Doctrine,* Gary J. Bergera, ed. (Salt Lake City: Signature Books, 1989), 17-34; B. H. Roberts, *Studies of the Book of Mormon,* Brigham D. Madsen, ed. (Urbana: University of Illinois Press, 1984), 284-316.

35. As estimated by Mormon theologian and apostle Orson Pratt, Book of Mormon, 1914 ed., Ether 15, footnote "b," as qtd. in Roberts, *Studies of the Book of Mormon,* 164.

CHAPTER 2

Joseph and the Sword of Laban

Using psychoanalytic perspectives and tools, I argue that certain themes and incidents from the childhood of Joseph Smith, Jr., repeat themselves in disguise within the Book of Mormon narrative. All scholars who accept naturalistic premises expect that the vocabulary, incidents, and stories within the Book of Mormon are circumscribed by Smith's personal experience, events in his town and environs, ideas from his readings, and political issues of moment in the United States, but few have looked for the sources of his main themes within his personal and family life.[1] Often these events are reworked within the text with a remarkably strict chronological ordering. For this reason, I will begin with an examination of Smith's childhood that emphasizes incidents and themes that will repeat themselves within the confines of his first artistic creation, the Book of Mormon. The creative artist may reveal aspects of his life throughout his works, but it is hoped that the artistic work will be therapeutic and maturational for the artist. When this is so, the first work of the artist is usually most revealing of his personality, and the problems or conflicts most transparent. With resolution of conflicts and problems by his "art therapy," the artist's work becomes more and more removed from the original life problems.[2] I will later use this Book of Mormon material in forming a psychological profile of Joseph Smith, an approach that also requires a review of the observations and opinions of those around Smith and his family. For the first decade of his life, his mother's manuscript biography is almost our sole reference.

The portrait of Smith's childhood in the Book of Mormon emphasizes its difficulties and traumas, and also events and attitudes within both his extended and immediate families. Like all of us, he was greatly influenced by the cultural and psychological inheritance of his family. One important historical incident occurred over 120 years before his birth. During the Salem witch trials, his great-great-grandfather, Samuell Smith, and Samuell Smith's father-in-law, John Gould, accused two women of acts of witchcraft. Both women were hanged on the basis of those accusations. In the annals of witchcraft, the 1692 Salem trials were unlike the many trials occurring in Europe, for these American trials were quickly recognized as the result of a group and cultural delusion, and both official and unofficial amends began within four years.

Our psychoanalysis of Joseph Smith as a member of this family can properly include the question, "Did an unusually strong belief in supernatural evil, in the form of magic and witchcraft, pass down through the generations in the Smith family partly as a defense against the guilt Samuell and his father-in-law felt in causing the deaths of these two innocent women?" We do not know the answer to this question. No known document created by the Smith family dating from Joseph Smith's time refers to Samuell or to the Salem witch trials. We do not know if it was a guilty and shameful secret that Joseph Sr. tried to keep from his wife and children, whether it was a half-fantastical piece of family lore related at the comfortable fireside, or even whether the knowledge had already died out of the Smith family's conscious knowledge in the four generations before Joseph Jr. was born. Still, Joseph Smith, Sr., believed in witchcraft and taught magic to his children, and both magic and witchcraft would appear in the Book of Mormon, while his brother Jesse was contemptuous of the practice and belief.[3]

As we shall see, however, a constellation of family problems may very well have contributed to a world view in which evil forces played an active role. As I read the scanty records describing the early years of Joseph Sr.'s and Lucy's marriage, I see an almost-dysfunctional family, overwhelmed by the threat of economic failure, a tendency toward drink on the part of Joseph Smith, Sr., that, in my opinion, approached or reached actual alcoholism,[4] episodes of short rations that almost certainly produced times of hunger, and two episodes of depression on Lucy's part—one before her marriage in association with the deaths of her sisters and one afterward following the birth of her third child. This suggests a possible pattern of periodic depression and emotional withdrawal. Belief in magic was both a cause and result of this family devastation.

Dysfunction in the Smith Family

The marriage between Joseph Smith, Sr., and Lucy Mack on 24 January 1796 had begun on an economically sound footing, for Joseph's father, Asael Smith, gave them a farm valued at $1,500 as a wedding gift.[5] Lucy's elder brother, Stephen, and his business partner gave Lucy a thousand dollars as a wedding present. Furthermore, Lucy tells us that she had enough money of her own, without touching this gift, to purchase furniture.[6]

Lucy also brought with her a psychological inheritance of visions in her family and an important family record. Her father, Solomon Mack (1735-1820), had published his autobiography in a forty-eight-page chapbook when he was seventy-six. He related his participation in the French and Indian wars and the American Revolution, his long history of poverty and physical accidents, and a striking religious conversion experienced in the year he wrote his autobiography. Previously, he declared that he would not "hearken" to God, but "had practically said unto God, depart from me. It seemed to me that I saw a bright light in a dark night when contemplating on my bed, which I could not account for—" he wrote, "but I thought I heard a voice calling to me again. ... Sleep departed from my eyes; and I literally watered by pillow with tears." He prayed to have his eyes opened, and Christ's lamentations over the future of Jerusalem came forcefully to his mind. "[G]od did appear for me and took me out of the horrible pit and mirey clay, and set my feet on the rock of Christ Jesus."[7] This chapbook set the Mack family apart from others and gave them a quiet prestige, according to biographer Fawn M. Brodie.[8] I hypothesize that this chapbook appears in the Book of Mormon as the brass plates, a critical family record whose possession is a matter of life and death—even justifying murder.

As Lucy reports her own childhood, she seems to have had a tendency to depression and other psychological and physical complaints. Lucy, the last of eight children, had become grief-stricken after the deaths of two older sisters from tuberculosis, and "for months after this I did not feel as though life was worth seeking after." This language suggests a depression that had approached suicidal proportions. Depression is a recurring illness, sometimes with symptoms of exhaustion, physical complaints, and religious preoccupation. Stephen, in an attempt to distract her, brought her to his home eighty miles away in Tunbridge, Vermont; here, at age nineteen, she first met Joseph Smith and his family.

After several months, she returned to her parents' home; but Stephen again returned and made an "urgent request" that she return to Tunbridge with him. She did. On 24 January 1796, she and Joseph, ages twenty-one and twenty-four respectively, were married.[9] Her account is not sufficiently precise to let us determine the dates of her visit, but there is at least a possibility that she was pregnant when they married. About fifty years later on 9 December 1834, Joseph Sr., who became terminally ill in 1839 and died in 1842, recorded in introductory remarks for his five volumes of patriarchal blessings: "The Lord, in his just providence has taken from me at an untimely birth, a son: this has been a matter of affliction; but the Lord's ways are just. ... My next son, Alvin ... was taken ..." His youngest son, Don Carlos, wrote in his family record at some point before his own death in 1841 that Joseph and Lucy's "first Born died soon after it was Born and was not named amongst the living." This information is not conclusive. Lucy never mentioned the birth and death of a first son;[10] however, in her 1853 published biography, she gives Alvin's birthdate as 1799, three years after the marriage, while the town records date his birth at 11 February 1798, two years after the marriage.[11] From a psychoanalytic perspective, we may ask if there had been another birth date she was unconsciously trying to change. Alvin's birth was followed by those of ten more children, all but one of whom survived to adulthood.

The next child was Hyrum, born 9 February 1800. Between 1796 and 1802, Joseph and Lucy farmed the land Asael Smith had given them in Tunbridge.[12] In 1802 they rented the farm and moved to Randolph, population 1,800, where Joseph opened a general store, but moved back to Tunbridge where Sophronia was born 17 May 1803.[13] During the pregnancy or immediately after the birth, Lucy developed a cold and cough with heavy fever, which was diagnosed as "confirmed consumption." Tuberculosis is unlikely, since no one else, including the children, seems to have been infected, and her unlikely recovery would have taken many years. Pneumonia seems much more likely. This illness brought Lucy close to death and left her debilitated. Attended by her mother, she became so nervous that she could not tolerate any noise above a whisper. She covenanted with God that if he would let her live, she would seek the true religion. A voice spoke to her, saying, "Seek and ye shall find ..."

Naturally concerned for her two toddlers and her newborn, Lucy would have been very anxious about her health, especially as she had seen two sisters die of the disease that she was now diagnosed with, whether correctly or not. It seems likely that her earlier depression returned, perhaps masked by religious zeal, somatic concerns, and exhaustion, and perhaps exacerbated by post-partum depression. Although she regained her health, she became preoccupied with Bible reading and concerns about her salvation that continued through the next two crucial decades. She expressed disappointment in the various ministers she heard preach, returning from one sermon in "total despair and with a greaved and troubled spirit ... saying in my heart there is not on Earth the religion which I seek."[14]

This period of stress on Lucy's mental and physical health coincided with stress on the family's economic well-being. Her husband's quest for wealth or "treasure" had already begun to take its toll on the family's finances, and the financial disaster which now occurred explains their return to their farm. Joseph Sr. had been selling mercantile goods at their store on credit, accepting promises of commodities at harvest; as a result, he was in debt to his Boston suppliers. Presumably already over-extended, he decided to process ginseng root, which grew wild in Vermont, and export it to China, where it was prized for curing plague, increasing virility, and prolonging life. The enterprise required getting the root from farmers, crystallizing it, and then shipping it.

Another merchant, whom Lucy identifies as Stevens of Royalton, offered Smith $3,000 for his considerable store, but Smith turned down the offer and made arrangements in New York City to ship the root, expecting to earn $4,500. According to Lucy, Stevens sent his son on the same ship with another small store of ginseng; once in China, young Stevens, rather than the ship's captain, sold the ginseng, then told Smith the trip had been a failure. However, he set up to process more ginseng and, while drunk, showed a trunk full of gold and silver to Stephen Mack, bragging that it was the money he had cheated Joseph Smith out of. Stephen immediately came to Randolph to tell Joseph; but by the time Joseph reached Randolph, Stevens had fled to Canada with the money.[15] Joseph, his mercantile debt compounded by the ginseng failure, was financially ruined. The family would not be in comfortable circumstances for the next twenty-seven years.

Joseph and Lucy moved back to the farm, sold it for half its value, according to Lucy, and used Lucy's wedding gift of a thousand dollars to pay off the last of their debts. Including their original move to the Tunbridge farm as newlyweds, they moved at least ten times in sixteen years. After selling the Tunbridge farm, they moved to nearby Royalton for a few months, and relocated in Sharon, Vermont, where Joseph Smith, Jr., was born on 23 December 1805. Three years later, the fifth child, Samuel Harrison, was born on 13 March 1808. By this time, the family had moved back to Tunbridge.

Joseph Smith Sr.'s lost trunk of gold and silver, viewed by Stephen Mack, must have taken on increasing meaning during these stressful years. According to a later unfriendly account, by 1808 Joseph Smith, Sr., had begun searching for buried treasure or "money digging," using magic rituals to guide him, and would continue this practice for over thirty years.[16] The search for buried treasure and the use of magic is now considered merely a cultural delusion by most educated Americans, with the exception of Wiccans who have revived white witchcraft as an alternative religion. However, it is so important in the creation of the Book of Mormon and subsequent Mormon beliefs that some background is necessary.

Nineteenth-century Magical Practices

Much of what we would now call magic was integrated into or manifested as part of religious practices, apparently from Babylonian times at over two millennia B.C.E. The Old Testament condemns magic, thus providing evidence that it coexisted at the same time. In fact, at least some Old Testament practices would probably be considered magical if they were in current use. The New Testament also records and condemns specific magical incidents. In Western culture, the legend of King Arthur embodies the splitting off from pagan to Christian magic; before Merlin were the Celtic curses of Modred and Morgan le Fay, and after Merlin came the search for the Holy Grail. The Catholic church incorporated enough similarities to magic in the miraculous relics of the saints and in its rituals (the Mass) and talisman (the rosary) to satisfy the common folk. The church provided both umbrella for and boundary between magic and miracle. From a magical perspective, the priest was a magician whose incantation, "Hoc ist Corpus Meum," literally—magically—transubstantiated the sacrament wafer and wine to the body and blood of Christ.

The Reformation made a deliberate attempt to exclude Catholic "paganistic" relics with supernatural powers from Protestantism, thus having the effect, during the sixteenth and seventeenth centuries, of splitting magic and Christianity once more. But in those centuries of wider literacy, magic developed its own voluminous literature.[17]

Magic came with the pilgrims to the colonies. In England it may have reached its zenith around the time Reginald Scott published his works of *Devils and Spirits* (1665) and the *Discoveries of Witchcraft* (five editions 1584-1665). Queen Elizabeth had her own magician, John Dee.[18] In the Salem witch trials of 1692, Tituba, a black Caribbean servant, played a key role. During the Enlightenment in Europe and America, the importance of magic withered under the glare of rationalism as education spread farther. While belief in magic continued to exist through all socio-economic strata during the 1800-30 period, it was most often found and performed by the uneducated. Rather than being a high art or a complex discipline, it had deteriorated into a passion that focused on the here and now, was frequently motivated by a get-rich-quick mentality, and required both credulity and superstition.

For example, folk-magic practitioners of Joseph Smith's time and place believed that the divining rod, when taken from certain "magical" trees such as the witch hazel, and held in the right way, with the question whispered to it, would bend in the direction of lost animals or a desired object such as water or a lost needle. But sometimes, when the goal was more momentous—the quest for a gold mine or for buried treasure, for instance—the rituals grew complex, required precise performance, and included astrological elements such as a reading of the stars, working at the correct phase of the moon, or attention to the seasons of the sun. Sometimes these rituals demanded working at night with a lantern, always in a group of two, three, or more, drawing circles on the ground with a ceremonial knife, burying sticks, repeating incantory phrases while one participant walked three times in a circle, sacrificing a sheep or other animal, and so forth. Numbers were important, especially the number three or three repetitions. Such ventures contained an element of danger, for each treasure was guarded by a spirit who would move the treasure in the earth, even while one dug. Silence and precise performance of the ritual were imperative to "chain" this spirit. Believers in magic imagined that fabulous treasures in large numbers approached the surface of the earth and descended again in regular cycles. These treasures could be a vein of gold but were more commonly conceived of as chests of gold coin buried by sea pirates, left behind by traveling Spaniards, or abandoned by a lost Indian tribe.[19]

During this period, magic belief existed in islands: in New England, especially Vermont, in some sections of New York, and in some parts of Ohio.[20] By 1850 this subculture was gone, except in parts of African American culture, the Mormons, the Pennsylvania Dutch and in such fragmentary forms as New Age crystals and psychic readings. Not only gone, but forgotten. Comments in American diaries seemed puzzling until researchers began to revive the history in the early 1970s.[21]

During its heyday, however, belief in buried treasure accessible only through magic was a vigorous delusion. In the 1820s a sympathetic Vermont paper stated that at least 500 respectable citizens were involved in digging for money.[22] Most articles deplored the wasted energy and credulity. It was not a reputable occupation, although some respected citizens might quietly hire a known money-digger.

Other aspects of folk magic practiced in Joseph Smith's area during the first third of the nineteenth century of particular relevance to this story are necromancy (communication with the dead called up by ritual) and the use of a stone with which to locate desired objects. These natural stones might be found anywhere. Sometimes the stone had some special quality—transparency or translucence, a special design, remarkable colors or shapes, etc. The stone would be placed in a hat, and the seer would bury his face in the hat, pulling up the sides to exclude all light. He could then see the location of the desired object. The process was called scrying and the worker was a scryer, a seer, or, more commonly, a peeper using a peep stone.[23]

Using magic placed one outside of, and frequently in opposition to, mainstream Protestantism, which defined attendant spirits or guardians as evil spirits. This attitude is still much the same on the part of today's fundamental Protestants explaining magic and spiritualism. In rural areas and with spontaneous churches or groups, as in Joseph Smith's day, religion frequently included visions and trances, but attempted to keep itself apart from magic.

A Period of Poverty

With this brief review, we can now return to the story of the Smith family, for Joseph Smith's father, almost certainly spurred on by hopes of improving the family finances, began working in magic around the time he was born or very shortly thereafter. Even if Joseph Sr.'s claim to have been a money-digger for thirty years was a slightly exaggerated boast, he was certainly involved in this practice by 1819, according to many reports from his Palmyra neighbors, even after making due allowances for bias.[24] Thus Joseph Jr.'s parents were spiritually divided in significant ways. Lucy was seeking for a Protestant church that had New Testament characteristics and considered magical practices evil, while Joseph Sr. was not only a practitioner of these arts but also trained at least two sons in their practice.[25] Yet it is not accurate to see a sharp and absolute boundary, for Joseph Sr. attended Protestant meetings with Lucy at least a few times, and Lucy did not seem to be alarmed by magical practices in her family.[26] Mormonism combined these two opposing worlds; and even though it steadily diminished the magical elements, magic practices continued in Utah with the first generation of Mormons and is retained in the title of the church president as prophet, *seer,* and revelator.[27] Joseph Smith, Jr., became a user of divining rods by about age thirteen, and then, around age sixteen, began using a seer stone to seek buried treasure.[28]

On a psychoanalytical note, involvement in such non-rational systems is not a good way to solve financial family distress. While the hope embodied in magic rituals no doubt relieved their immediate feelings of despair, the practice almost certainly contributed to the cycle of impoverishment and despair, as delusional practice replaced productive work and drained off such resources as time, energy, and creative thought that could have been devoted to profitable entrepreneurship. Further, the practice requires self-deception and training in deceiving both the self and others within the believing family or group of practitioners.

About a year before Joseph's birth, the family rented a farm in Sharon, Vermont, from Lucy's father where Joseph Sr. farmed in the summer and taught school in "the winter," which helped the family financially. He apparently continued this practice for a few years until the family became "quite comfortable."[29]

This period of time is crucial to our thinking about the psychology of the young prophet. The family history shows two serious financial losses and moves, a mother's apparent depression, and five pregnancies. We must contemplate his mother's psychological strength, question her emotional availability to her children, and ponder the possibility of irritability—a common symptom in depressed people. She has numerous children to feed, warm, and clothe; possibly her husband was indulging himself in drink during this period. The coming years will almost certainly add more burdens. She will participate in the cultural delusion of "digging for money." The major psychological defenses Joseph will articulate by the shape he gives Book of Mormon narratives suggest unresolved conflict throughout these very early years, which he may have dealt with by the childish devices of magic and omnipotence, beliefs which Joseph Sr., to the extent that he participated in magic, must have reinforced.

The family moved back to Royalton, where the sixth child, Ephraim, was born on 13 March 1810. He died eleven days later, and unlike the living children does not have a representative in the Book of Mormon stories (discussed below).[30] Exactly one year later William was born. The family then moved to Lebanon, New Hampshire, and the children attended school on a street still remembered as "poverty lane."[31] Hyrum, now around twelve, began school at Moore's Charity Academy in nearby Hanover, perhaps as one of their charity students. During this time, family conditions improved. Lucy's preliminary manuscript documents that they lacked nothing to make the children "perfectly comfortable both for food and raiment ... and respectable appearance in society." They planned for the long-term future and old age, and "met with success on every hand."[32] Another child, Catherine, was born to Lucy and Joseph Sr. on 8 July 1812.

At the time of this birth, Joseph Jr. was about six and a half, and the next family catastrophe would fall upon him—the typhus (typhoid) that settled in the bone of his leg. Lucy does not date the typhiod epidemic that afflicted all of the children, and Joseph later recalled his age as "five years old or thereabouts."[33] This typhoid epidemic raged throughout 1812 and 1813, killing 5 percent of the people living in nearby Hanover.[34] I accept as probable that Joseph was seven years old because Nathan Smith, the doctor who operated on his diseased leg, had been in Hanover, Vermont, since 1798 where he headed the medical school at Dartmouth. He had accepted direction of the Yale Medical School in New Haven, Connecticut, and should have been there in January 1813; however, his own family had contracted typhus and he was detained in Hanover until at least March 1813. We do not know the exact date for the surgery. Cyrus Perkins had treated fifty cases in the fall of 1812, but the epidemic in 1813 was larger. Using metaphor, allegory, and simile, and reading from the Book of Mormon back into Joseph's life, Joseph "remembers" his age during this event as five. The precise chronology within the Book of Mormon of the cataclysm at the time of Christ's resurrection provides extremely suggestive support for Joseph's memory. (See chapter 3.) From a psychoanalytic perspective, this cosmic cataclysm is one of the manifestations of young Joseph's personal cataclysm—the barely-averted amputation of his leg and ensuing bloody operation at the hands of a group of surgeons—that replays itself obsessively within the Book of Mormon.

If my reconstruction of the chronology is correct, the epidemic struck the Smith family during the fall and winter of 1812. Joseph turned seven in late December. All of the Smith children became ill. Sophronia, aged nine, was infected first, probably in the early fall, and lay dangerously ill for over three months. After eighty-nine days of constant attendance, the physician admitted that his medicine was useless. Sophronia seemed to be in a final coma, eyes open and fixed and apparently not breathing. After her parents' fervent prayers at her bedside, Lucy picked her up, wrapped her in a blanket, and began pacing the floor, continuing her prayers. Eventually Sophronia caught her breath, sobbed, and began breathing normally.

All of the Smith children recovered uneventfully, except Joseph. He developed a pain in his shoulder, which the local physician misdiagnosed as a sprain even though young Joseph insisted he had not injured himself. The physician anointed the shoulder with bone liniment. Called back two weeks later, he made the proper diagnosis: a large "fever sore" (abscess) between his breast and shoulder. Joseph states it was under the shoulder, making it an abscess in the axilla or armpit. But in lancing or squeezing the abscess to remove the large quantity of pus, the physician apparently seeded the bacteria into the bloodstream. Joseph recalled that the wound "discharged freely, after which the disease removed and descended into my left leg and ancle and terminated in a fever sore of the worst kind." According to his mother, "As soon as this sore had discharged itself the pain left it shooting like lightning as he said down his side into the marrow of his leg on the same side, the boy almost in total despair."[35] Typhoid osteomyelitis frequently settled in the long leg bones of younger people.[36]

Young Joseph had now developed a severe illness, which was possibly physician-caused ("iatrogenic"). Surely both Joseph and the family viewed the physician with suspicion. The pain was excruciating and relentless. Lucy carried him in her arms, the motion soothing his pain, for two weeks until she collapsed; ten-year-old Hyrum took over the task of comforting the suffering Joseph.

The doctor returned a week later and made an eight-inch incision in the front of the tibia between Joseph's knee and ankle. This procedure was done without anesthesia, before bacterial contamination was understood, and probably with little concern for sterility or even cleanliness. The operation opened the infection to the outside, relieved the pressure, and brought immediate, but temporary, relief. As the wound healed, the infection was again sealed inside, and the pain and swelling returned. Two weeks later the doctor returned and again cut down to Joseph's bone. Immediate relief was followed by the wound's healing which again sealed the infection inside his bone, and the terrible pain returned.

At this point, some time between January and March 1813, a council of surgeons was called—the mother remembers seven, Joseph eleven. The only physician whom Lucy identifies by name is a "Dr. Stone"; however, the chief surgical consultant was Nathan Smith (1762-1828), and the coincidence that he shared a surname (though not kinship) with the family may be reflected in the story of Nephi and Laban. Nathan Smith was Harvard Medical School's fifth graduate in 1790, then trained in Edinburgh and London, returning to Dartmouth College in Hanover where he, in 1798, singlehandedly founded Dartmouth Medical School. In 1812 he was joined by Dr. Cyrus Perkins who collaborated in the Joseph Smith consultation along with medical students from Dartmouth Medical School.[37] This council of surgeons decided amputation was necessary to save his life, the standard treatment of the day.

After typhoid infected the bone, pressure from the infection on the outside of the shaft (under the periosteum) as well as inside the shaft cut off the blood supply, necrotizing the bone. New bone attempted to grow over this infected dead bone, sealing in the infection and continuing the problem. In 1798 Nathan Smith innovated the surgical procedure of operating directly on osteomyelitis to drain the wound. He would drill four holes in the bone shaft, then cut a large window out from between these four corners by chipping or sawing. He could then begin pulling out the internal infected dead bone (the sequestrum); this procedure might extend over days to weeks while the bone healed from inside. Lucy mentions a drill and "forceps or pincers." She does not describe the knife, but the image of today's small scalpel is probably inadequate. Nathan Smith, despite his European training, was a frontier surgeon, for whom speed—being able to amputate a man's leg in one or two minutes—was a sign of excellence. William D. Morain, a plastic surgeon writing about Joseph's surgery, describes the frontier surgeon's instrument as an "amputation knife, that foot-long, sword-like instrument whose design had not appreciably changed in the hundreds of years since the primitive barber-surgeons."[38] Nathan Smith's surviving papers provide no record of this incident. We do know that his usual charge for osteomyelitis surgery was $11.[39]

From a psychoanalytic perspective, so critical is this terrible incident in the life of little Joseph that its variations begin and end the Book of Mormon, and shadings of it are found throughout its stories. In preparation for understanding Joseph's experience, later altered into fantasy and then conquering miracle, we must understand the story in as much detail as possible. I accept Lucy's detailed account as authentic. She

> invited them [the doctors] into another room apart from where Joseph lay[.] Now said I gentlemen (for there were seven of them) What can you do to save my boys leg[.] They answered we can do nothing we have cut it open to the bone 2 [times] and find the bone so affected that it is incurable but this was like a thunderbolt to me. I appealed to the principle Surgeon present. Said I Doctor Stone, can you not try once more by cutting round the bone and taking out the affected part there may be a part of the bone that is sound which will heal over and thus you may save the leg you will [not] take off the leg till you try once more. I will [not] consent to your entering his room till you promise this.
>
> They agreed to this after a short consultation; then we went to the invalid:—the Doctor said, my poor boy, we have come again. "Yes," said Joseph, "I see you have; but you have not come to take off my leg, have you sir?" No, said the surgeon, "it is your mothers request, that we should make one more effort; and that is what we have now come for.["] My husband, who was constantly with the child, seemed for a moment to contemplate my countenance; then turning his eyes upon his boy, at once all his sufferings, together with my intense anxiety rushed upon his mind; and he burst into a flood of tears, and sobbed like a child.

The surgeons immediately ordered cords to be brought to bind the patient fast to the bedstead; but [Joseph] objected and when the doctor insisted that he must be confined he said decidedly, "No, Doctor I will not be bound. I can bear the process better unconfined." "Then," said Dr. Stone, "will you drink some brandy."

"No," said the child, "not one drop."

Then said the Dr., "will you take some wine? You must take something, or you never can endure the severe operation to which you must be subjected. "No, answered the boy, "I will not touch one particle of liquor; neither will I be tied down: but I will tell you what I will do, I will have my Father sit on the bed close by me; and then I will do whatever is necessary to be done, in order to have the bone taken out. But Mother, I want you to leave the room, I know that you cannot endure to see me suffer so. Father can bear it. But you have carr[i]ed me so much, and watched over me so long, you are almost worn out. Then looking up into my face his eyes swimming with tears, he said beseechingly; Now Mother, promise me you will not stay, will you? The Lord will help me so that I shall get through with it; so do you leave me and go away off till they get through with it.

To this I consented; so, after bringing a number of folded sheets to lay under his leg, I left him, going some hundred yards from the house.

The surgeons began by boring into the bone, first on one side of the affected part, then on the othe[r] after which, they broke it loose with a pair of forceps or pincers: thus, they took away, 3 large pieces of the bone. When they broke off the first piece, he screamed so loud with the pain of his leg, that I could not repress my desire of going to him but as soon as I entered the room he cried out Oh! Mother! go back! go back! I do not want you to come in I will tough it if you will go. When the 3rd fracture [third piece] was taken away I burst into the room again and Oh! my God what a spectacle for a Mothers eye[.] the wound torn open to view[,] My boy and the bed on which he [lay] covered with the blood which that was still gushing from the wound[.] He was pale as a corpse and the big drops of sweat were rolling down his face every feature of which depicted agony that cannot be described.

I was forced from the room and detained till they finished the operation and after placing him upon a clean bed with fresh clothing clearing the room from every appearance of blood and any apparatus used in the extraction I was permitte[d] to enter.[40]

As a psychiatrist, I find something troubling in this description of the surgery and the interactions between little Joseph and his parents. The father, overwhelmed with anxiety, burst into tears and "sobbed like a child." This was not a helpful response at a time of crisis. What the child needed at this moment was not childlike instability in his father, but stability and effectiveness; Joseph seemed to be taking care of his father. Child psychotherapists know this pattern well—"a reversal of generations"—when parents are emotional labile or dysfunctional. Joseph does the same thing with his mother: "Go back!" Mormon writers have used this story to suggest how good this future prophet was even as a child, and how much his parents cared. In therapeutic terms, this incident is not a commendable one. Joseph was a young child, possibly five, no more than seven, desperately protecting the emotional state of his parents even while he was undergoing a life-threatening crisis and extreme physical pain. The implication is that they were unstable and that, even at this early age, he has learned that his security depends on providing security for them.

Lucy has emphasized three themes in telling this awful event. She has told of her own role in forcing the doctors to the better of two terrible choices (either attempts for curative surgery or amputation); the encouragement of alcohol as an anesthetic, in the form of wine or brandy, which Joseph refuses; and then the vivid glimpses of the agonizing, bloody operation. I will show how Joseph, like Lucy, emphasizes the same themes in the Book of Mormon, as he unsuccessfully attempts to overcome this determining episode in his life.

Almost certainly our human reaction is pity and horror as this young, already suffering child is subjected to such a tortuous procedure. Our natural sympathy for the weeping father, the courageous child, and the heart-stricken mother are our strongest emotional reactions. Yet the psychiatric task is something like the surgeon's, requiring that we proceed despite our natural feelings. The surgeon's goal is the patient's physical health; the psychiatrist's is understanding the mental and emotional processes. It requires us to analyze even painful aspects of this incident and bring to bear upon it psychiatric and psychological knowledge.

Such an ordeal would have been traumatic for anyone. I argue that it was one of the determining events in Joseph's life for two reasons. First, it came at a stressful point in an already stressful family history. Second, about age seven is a crucial point in the developmental history of growing boys.

As for the first reason, even though the move to Lebanon apparently signalled relief from the most pressing financial burdens and Lucy describes them as having, by their "exertions," achieved "prosperity," it is easy to identify a number of stressors. After having been reduced to poverty once, Lucy and Joseph would have been on the alert to avoid a recurrence; apparently they were united in this goal but possibly not in the means for achieving it. If Joseph Sr.'s statement about money-digging for thirty years is correct, then he had begun his explorations into magic about four years earlier. Furthermore, I would suggest that he had drunk to excess on at least enough occasions by this point that it had become a source of conflict between Lucy and Joseph. Where else but in family arguments would seven-year-old Joseph have learned to avoid alcohol, even as an emergency medication, so adamantly? The family was still dealing with the major stress caused by the near-simultaneous illness of all seven children, during which Sophronia had nearly died. Lucy was nursing a new baby. The death of Ephraim was not quite three years in the past. She had moved six times and had experienced eight, possibly nine, pregnancies. She must have been chronically exhausted—physically and mentally. She was certainly physically exhausted during this time period since she had been nursing her sick children for so long that she had become ill herself. Did she resent her husband? Was she continuing to deal with recurring or chronic depression? How available was she to her children?

As for the second reason, Joseph's developmental stage, he was in the late Oedipal period. In contrast to the younger child's total involvement with the mother—which had probably been abbreviated by the births of three children after himself—Joseph had the developmental task of dealing consciously with the "triangular" relationship of his mother, father, and himself. At this stage, the young boy becomes aware of his body, including his sexual resemblances to his powerful father; he fears that his body will be damaged or injured, especially by an angry father; and he dreads his father's punishment because he also desires total ownership of his mother. Successful passage through this period of triangular relationships requires abandoning extreme childhood fantasies of power and developing increased respect for the wishes and thinking of others. Resolution of these struggles is believed to occur with most children by identification with both parents, but especially with the parent of the same sex. Such identification includes accepting their values and results in the final major imprint for his future conscience. This stage prepares the boy for the world outside the family. When boys have completed this task, we feel free to send them to school to learn to master the environment and begin the relationships with others that will eventually lead to their own families.

But successful passage requires that infancy and young childhood have been secure and safe, so that a solid, stable core identity had already begun. If this environment is unstable and conflicted, as I argue was the case for the Smith family, if only some of the time, then the boy's core identity remains undeveloped and immature even if the Oedipal period is not environmentally turbulent. But Joseph, at this vulnerable stage, was also experiencing the trauma of prolonged physical suffering, threats of amputation/mutilation, and a three-times-repeated operation that inflicted purposeful suffering on him. From a psychoanalytic perspective, a boy in these circumstances simply cannot handle the complexities of the Oedipal triangle and nightmare fears which have now become reality. He regresses backward to the defenses of infancy. I argue that Joseph used the Book of Mormon as a narrative stage on which he obsessively replayed his surgery in various forms; present psychodynamic thought suggests that his failure to resolve and settle the trauma of surgery occurred because the family's unstable background left him not fully capable of dealing with such a harsh crisis.[41]

We are turning a page in the history of the Smith family, and it may be useful to reflect on what we know and do not know. The diagnosis of a narcissistic personality is made from symptomatic behavior manifest in the adult. Joseph Smith will manifest at least some of those characteristics. The *psychoanalytic theoretical explanation* for the adult personality, gathered from long-term intensive treatment of adults, is of significant disturbance and deprivation in the child's very early home environment. Such evidence comes from the controlled emotional regression that occurs during treatment and consists of the reexperiencing of early childhood feelings by the patient, mixed with memories. I know of no statistics that correlate early childhood deprivation and later adult pathological narcissism. I doubt such studies can be done, for it would require following a large number of individuals over twenty or more years. (The prevalence of adult pathological narcissism in general society is estimated at less than 1 percent, with males being overrepresented.[42]) Further, the presence of an observer during infancy and childhood would alter parent/child interactions; and if the observer saw depriving behavior, medical ethics would require intervention. Sometimes there is outside confirmation of such disturbance; most of the time there is not, and the family history just reviewed does not provide the kind of information that can be considered conclusive. The evidence, as it is in any family or individual case study of early childhood, is incomplete, and, in this case, contradictory. The mother has emphasized that the family had recovered from financial loss, was comfortable in life, that the needs of the children were provided for, and that the parents were making long-range and clearly prudent plans. The father had worked at farming in the summer and taught school in the winter.

However, sources of negative impact include Joseph Sr.'s business misjudgments and loss of their farm, the death of the baby Ephraim, and six moves throughout New England over a brief span. We know the mother had at least one, and probably two, bouts of what I consider mental illness—probably depression—by the birth of the third child. If, over the years, problems expand and are more observable by outsiders, then it seems probable that the father's drinking may have begun, and we may wonder if he had already begun experimenting with magical practices by way of compensation for personal inadequacies. If not, we might contemplate what kind of self-deceptive thinking—"modes of thought and background assumptions"—at the back of his mind and possibly manifest in family discussions—would later allow him to accept such a cultural delusion.

In writing this summary, I recall certain teenagers admitted to a psychiatric unit under my care. Interviews with the parents revealed little to account for their child's destructive behavior or mental illness. Under such circumstances, I would give more weight to the possible genetics of the problem. However, in a number of cases, I would receive a telephone call from an older sibling, saying, "My brother and I want to talk with you and tell you what it was like growing up in this family." This conversation would make the reason for the problem clearer. "They didn't tell you about the drinking and the physical fights, did they?" The Smith family records do not provide complete information on the family dynamic, leaving us with unanswered questions: What were the emotional interactions between the parents at times of stress? How did they discipline the children? What were the attitudes, thinking, and feeling that governed the atmosphere in the home? How did the mother relate to her children when they were infants and small toddlers, especially during her depression?

I believe we are justified in questioning Lucy Mack Smith's continued positive descriptions of her family. She dictated her history forty years after these events to followers who wanted a heroic view of their martyred prophet. Further, already in this chapter, and again in the next, we have seen her distort reality to a significant degree. Note how she changes the ordinary dreams of her husband into "visions," and how she supports the delusional belief that her husband and sons—before the advent of Mormonism—have supernatural, magical abilities. She is saved from the severe psychiatric label of psychosis (or its legal counterpart, insanity) because her beliefs are part of group belief, albeit a dying subculture. Nietzsche's well-known dictum applies here: "With individuals, insanity is the exception; with groups, it is the rule." We must ask if Lucy is capable of seeing or describing serious dysfuntion within her own family.

As a psychiatrist I would describe the movement of the Smith family as being downhill for the next four to five years. The surgery, by itself, would be enough to regress any child for a period of time, perhaps for life; but I am proposing, in addition, that Joseph remained fixated at this earlier period characterized by magical thinking and powerful images because of the difficulties the family had before and after the surgery in providing a supportive environment. Further, the Book of Mormon provides episodes that strongly suggest physical hunger and psychological inconsistency within the family. The testimony of their later neighbors in Palmyra, whose objectivity is quite naturally challenged by the Mormon faithful, was of a deplorable family but it cannot be dismissed out of hand. I will examine it in this and the next chapter. What were the antecedents to these negative comments? Before the production of the Book of Mormon, we can document deceit by Joseph Smith, Jr., from courtroom documents (see chapter 3) and in personal interactions later in his life. Perhaps the most important question is how little Joseph experienced his family history. I see provocative, though inconclusive, suggestions in the Book of Mormon that all was not well in the Smith household.

Many orthodox Mormons believe that by the sheer force and righteousness of his personality, Joseph remained unscarred by these events.

I think it is more profitable in understanding Joseph Smith to weigh the potential damage from his surgery, combined with a family background that contained multiple moves, past financial loss, and emotional distress. Some astute Mormons will recognize occasional reflections of these events in Joseph's later personal life,[43] but this study is restricted to the Book of Mormon as a manifestation of how he handled these events psychologically.

The Book of Mormon is dyadic in its tensions, focused on struggles between two men, two nations, or two sides of moral conflict within a man, men, or nations. With one possible exception,[44] it makes no use of the equally timeless triangle relationship. Psychoanalytic theory would propose that young Joseph had "regressed to" and/or remained "fixated at" a pre-Oedipal emotional stage of development.

The illness of all of the children, requiring the parents' care, medical attention, and perhaps even hired nurses (Lucy mentions the presence of other adults during Sophronia's crisis), and capped by Joseph's illness and repeated operations obviously had a depleting effect on the family's emotional and financial status. According to Lucy, "sickness with all its attendant expenses ... reduced us so that we were now compelled to make arrangements for going into some kind of business to provide for present wants rather than future prospects as we had previously contemplated."[45] If they were able to pay their debts, which seems doubtful, although Lucy does not discuss this point, there was certainly nothing left over. Joseph's perception, as captured in Book of Mormon narratives, was that the family was virtually bankrupt.

In an act of mixed benefit, Joseph Sr. and Lucy sent Joseph to live with his uncle Jesse Smith in Salem, Massachusetts, probably during the summer of 1813, in hopes that the "sea breezes" would restore his health. We know nothing of Jesse's home arrangements, whether his wife was kindly and welcoming to this young invalid, or how Joseph fit into Jesse's family. Presumably they treated him well, but Jesse certainly seemed to have had no hesitancy in causing turmoil among his brothers and sisters if his open quarreling and fits of temper when brothers Joseph and John visited him later with the Book of Mormon are any indication.[46] It seems plausible that he would have expected Joseph Jr. to conform to the household rather than being accommodated by it and that Joseph would have been afraid of his uncle's temper; furthermore, a normal seven-year-old living apart from his family for several months would quite naturally experience intense loneliness, feelings of abandonment, and insecurity. We do not, in fact, know that he had such feelings. He never comments on that time at Uncle Jesse's and neither does Lucy. But if Joseph experienced such feelings, he may have coped with them by private and comforting fantasies of power and a sense that he should not become too attached or dependent on anyone lest similar abandonment occur. And if so, the separation would have added to the "fixation" of his regressed state. Joseph apparently returned home in a matter of months, for the mother states that "after one whole year of affliction we were able once more to look upon our children and each other in health."[47]

Difficult Times in Vermont

The Smith family's partial solution to its financial difficulties was to move to Norwich, Vermont, probably in early 1814. Were they fleeing creditors? Lucy does not comment which, in itself, is in striking contrast to her detailed description of her strenuous (and successful) efforts to pay off all creditors, even double-paying some, when the family moved from Vermont to Palmyra, New York. They rented a farm and planted crops, but what followed brought their already precarious finances even lower in a period that Joseph, I will argue, recreated repeatedly in the Book of Mormon as a time of privation and repeated hunger.

The first year the Smiths' crops failed. "We bought our bread with the proceeds of the orchard and our own industry," Lucy summarized. Surely there were days of actual scarcity, especially during the winter of 1814-15, followed by hope in the spring as they planted again. The season must have already contained disturbing signs, for Joseph Sr. determined to move to New York state "where the farmers raise wheat in abundance" if the crops failed again.[48] In April 1815, however, the volcano Tambora in Indonesia erupted. If the Smith family read of the event a year later, I doubt they realized its effect on their lives. It killed 50,000 and displaced 35,000 more. Its plume was 150 times the size of the Mount St. Helen's explosion in 1980, and its aerosol of sulfuric acid and other materials began to circle the globe. This veil over the earth caused a European famine and actual starvation in New England, where 1816 was "the year without summer." The *Norwich Courier,* 19 June 1816, reported: "We hear of severe frosts from almost every quarters. In some places north considerable snow has fallen. Vegetation has suffered very much. ... [W]e have seen the streams frozen and the hills white with snow, when ... summer should have been in its flower and prime." Prices for food soared, and "there was great destitution among the [New England] people the next winter and spring. The farmers in some instances were reduced to the last extremity, and many cattle died. The poorer men could not buy corn at the exorbitant prices." There were unconfirmed reports of people hanging themselves after they had slaughtered their flocks. At Plymouth, Connecticut, it snowed for an hour on 10 June.[49]

This experience confirmed Joseph Sr.'s decision to move. Lucy, pregnant that winter, gave birth to Don Carlos, her youngest son and eighth living child on 25 March 1816. Joseph Sr. left, apparently in late spring or early summer; and reached Palmyra, a town of 3,500, in upstate New York. If his antagonistic brother Jesse can be believed, he claimed that he chose Palmyra through magical direction.[50] Lucy explains that Joseph Sr. had settled all of his debts before leaving Norwich; however, when he sent for his family, creditors reportedly descended on Lucy and her eight children and took $150, leaving her with $60 to $80 for the wagon trip to New York.

The family reached New York, probably in the late fall of 1816 and through some snow of that volcanic "winter." This move was another traumatic and humiliating experience for Joseph Jr., who would turn eleven just before Christmas. I argue that versions of this journey also appear, imaginatively reworked into narratives, in the Book of Mormon. (See below.) Caleb Howard, Joseph Sr.'s agent to help the family move, was, according to Lucy, an "unprincipled unfeeling wretch by the manner he handled my goods and money as well as his treatment of my children, especially Joseph who was still somewhat lame. This child was compelled by Mr. Howard to travel for miles [at a] time on foot."[51] Twenty-two years later, Joseph recorded this account of the journey:

> After he [Howard] had started on the journey with my mother and family spent the money he had received of my father by drinking and gambling, etc.—We fell in with a family by the name of Gates who were traveling West and Howard drove me from the wagon and made me travel in my weak state through the snow forty miles per day for several days, during which time I suffered the most excruciating weariness and pain, and all this that Mr. Howard might enjoy the society of two of Mr. Gates daughters which he took on the wagon where I should h[a]ve rode, and thus he continued to do day after day through the Journey and when my brothers remonstrated with Mr. Howard for his treatment of me, he would knock them down with the butt of his whipp.[52]

By this time, the Smith family was so destitute that they were renting sleeping rooms in taverns with articles of clothing.[53] Near Utica, New York, Howard dumped the goods off the wagon, claimed that all the money was gone, and started to drive away. Lucy confronted Howard at a tavern, fired him, and repossessed horses and wagon—"her property." Joseph Jr. was assigned to ride in one of the sleighs of the accompanying Gates family but was "knocked down by the driver, one of Gate's sons, and left to wallow in my blood until a stranger came along, picked me up, and carried me to the town of Palmyra."[54] After traveling some three or four weeks, the family finally arrived in Palmyra with only a few pennies. The reunion scene with the father was moving and tender.

Settling in Palmyra

In Palmyra life began to improve, and the seven to eight years of absolute desolation that began with the death of the baby Ephraim in March

1810 were almost over. Neighbors recalled that the family rented a small house on Main Street near the edge of Palmyra village for about three years.[55] Lucy painted and sold oilcloth coverings for tables, while Joseph Sr. and the older boys hired out for farming, gardening, and well-digging. According to Pomeroy Tucker, a young newspaperman who later turned historian, Joseph Sr. also opened a "cake and [root]beer shop," selling gingerbread, pies, boiled eggs, and such, and peddling them from a hand-cart during civic celebrations. The family lived as common laborers by "the chopping and retailing of cordwood, the raising and bartering of small crops of agricultural products and garden vegetables, the manufacture and sale of black-ash baskets and birch brooms, the making of maple sugar and molasses in the season for that work, and in the continued business of peddling cake and beer."[56]

By their united exertions, the Smiths climbed above destitution. By April 1819, they had moved two miles south of the village, renting or squatting on land owned by one Samuel Jennings, and barely within the Palmyra "township." Here their last child, Lucy, was born 18 July 1821. Joseph Jr. was fifteen and a half. The description of this first Smith family dwelling is brief: "a rude log house, with but a small spot underbrushed around it."[57] They lived here, probably, until the summer of 1822. Lucy summarized that "in two years from the time we entered Palmyra ... we were able to settle ourselves upon our own land in a snug comfortable though humble habitation built and neatly furnished by our own industry."[58]

Lucy tells us little about young Joseph's early adolescence. Nothing unusual happened until he was fourteen. Joseph "reflect[ed] more deeply than common persons ... upon everything of a religious nature," and was a "remarkably quiet, well-disposed child."[59] Despite this inoffensive presentation, someone fired two bullets at him one evening at dusk as he crossed the yard toward the house, returning home from an unspecified errand.[60] Lucy professes herself baffled, but we might note that about this time he had begun his practice of magic.[61]

During this period, Lucy describes none of Joseph Jr.'s activities except for work on the family farm and hired labor for others. He had recovered from his surgery except for a slight permanent limp. Physically he grew tall (over six feet) and muscular (over 200 pounds), and became a strong wrestler—but on at least one later occasion, he teased Howard Coray, who weighed 130 pounds to Joseph's 212, into a wrestling match so strenuous that he broke Coray's leg. Although he seemed remorseful and personally nursed Coray, it was not enough to keep him from doing it again when he walked into his Nauvoo store, where "the diminutive [James] Monroe was clerking. Joseph put his large leg on Monroe's shoulder, and commented, 'You are stouter than I thought.'" He then wrestled him and broke his leg also. As a psychiatrist, I consider these incidents a clue that Joseph may have never completely resolved his leg surgery and that he could find reassurance from his surgical experience by reversing his "passive helplessness" into "active conquest" at the expense of his followers.[62] This theme will reappear in the first story in the Book of Mormon.

While still living in this rude cabin, probably in the late summer of 1820, the Smiths purchased 100 acres sixty feet south of their cabin, a location which was across the boundary in Farmington township. (In March 1821 it was renamed Manchester township; the village of Manchester was five miles farther south.) Their financial arrangement required beginning, middle, and end payments, two years of hard work in clearing and cultivating the land, and the loss of everything if they defaulted at any time.[63] On this property they eventually constructed a "small, one story, smoky log-house," then moved into it. They had also cleared thirty acres. "This house was divided into two rooms, on the ground-floor, and had a low garret, in two apartments."[64] The date of this move was not earlier than July 1821 and probably not until after the last half of 1822.[65] Later a bedroom wing of sawed slabs was added to accommodate the eleven-member family. The clearing of the 100 acres was done by burning.[66] But by August 1821, only a month after daughter Lucy's birth, family finances were already so precarious that the Smiths were about to lose their land. Lucy recorded, "But the second payment was now coming due and no means as yet of meeting it." To make the second payment (and the remainder of the first), the oldest "serious and industrious" son, Alvin, left home, worked elsewhere, and by "persevering industry [and] after much labor Suffering and fatigue" returned with enough money for the second of three payments.[67] At this moment of financial crisis, Alvin is clearly the hero. What would have happened to this ill-prepared family without their industrious son? Pomeroy Tucker noted the problem when he described the daytime activities of the Smiths:

> The larger proportion of the time of the Smiths, however, was spent in hunting and fishing, trapping muskrats ("mushrats" was the word they used), digging out woodchucks from their holes, and idly lounging around the stores and shops in the village. Joseph generally took the leading direction of the rural enterprises mentioned, instead of going to school like other boys—though he was seldom known personally to participate in the practical work involved in these or any other pursuits.[68]

This cabin would be used as home, barn, and then home again over an eight-year period between about 1822 and 1830. The most complete description by Tucker is not complimentary. Looking back forty years later, he said, "But little improvement was made upon this land by the Smith family in the way of clearing, fencing, or tillage. Their farm-work was done in a slovenly half-way, profitless manner."[69]

According to Tucker, nighttime thefts were occurring in the neighborhood and with "inadequate visible means or habits of profitable industry [of the Smith family] the suspicions of some good people in the community were apt to be turned toward them." People watched their "hencoops, smoke-houses, and pork-barrels" more carefully, but no conclusive evidence was found.[70] Tucker's reports, which he admits were unsupported by facts, seem like malicious gossip. Furthermore, they are inconsistent with Lucy's, for, in addition to Alvin's energy, Lucy reports that they made a thousand pounds of "Mapel sugar" each year, and cultivated thirty acres of crops. One neighbor stated that the Smiths were known for their sugar production.[71] Reading with caution from the Book of Mormon back into the Smith family, we might wonder if the inconsistency of the Book of Mormon peoples was a characteristic of the Smith family. The negative view of some neighbors was probably intensified by the family's involvement in money-digging instead of usual work.

I have used a number of these specific testimonies about the Smith family and their involvement in magic. Traditional Mormonism usually discredits these testimonies on the basis of bias in collection methods and intent by a disgruntled disfellowshipped Mormon; a frequent and plausible opinion holds that Joseph's spirituality stirred the kind of antagonism received by ancient prophets. Yet while it is not impossible that some of these reports were, in fact, prompted by malice or a desire to impress the listener or even to have retrospective "reasons" for disliking the Smiths who had certainly disrupted the community, others were willing to sign sworn statements about similar views of the Smith family.[72]

The last payment was due about the time the Smiths moved onto the property in late 1822; but they received a type of temporary reprieve when the land agent died in July. This family, so child-like in their magic beliefs and money-digging, either did not have the money or did not save it for the eventual payment. Tucker explains: "Shortly before quitting the premises they erected a small frame-house thereon, partly enclosed, and never finished by them, in which they lived for the remainder of their time there, using their original log hut for a barn. This property, finally vacated by the Smiths in 1831, is now included in the well-organized farm of Mr. Seth T. Chapman."[73]

In the fall of 1823, according to Lucy, "we ... began to make preparations for building a house[.] We also planted a large orchard and made every possible preparation for ease ~~as~~ when advanced age should deprive us of the ability to make those physical exertions which we were then capable of."[74] Two years later, the house was still not complete; and then, even with the extra year for saving, they were not prepared when payment was finally demanded, and lost it. Lucy tells a complicated story about the house's carpenter who, with at least two other men, told the new land agent lies about the family's care of the property, made the final payment to him, received title to the land, but were shamed into selling it to a Quaker friend who allowed the family to live in the house for another two years. In contrast, William Smith, Joseph's last surviving brother, made a statement fifty years later about the expense of building the two houses that suggests the Smiths had used the money for the final land payment to build the house.[75] By the time Seth T. Chapman bought and completed the frame house in 1860, "it had changed hands many times, and had also been considerably enlarged."[76] This farm house is now a Mormon shrine, seen as evidence of the Smith family's industry. Even in its incomplete form, it was the highest aspiration and achievement of this sad family and the loss of house and farm was undoubtedly the single largest material setback to the family during the life of young Joseph.

Tucker describes the Smith family as "an illiterate, whiskey-drinking, shiftless, irreligious race of people," with the adolescent Joseph

> being unanimously voted the laziest and most worthless of the generation. From the age of twelve to twenty years he is distinctly remembered as a dull-eyed, flaxen-haired, prevaricating boy—noted only for his indolent and vagabondish character, and his habits of exaggeration and untruthfulness. ... He could utter the most palpable exaggeration or marvelous absurdity with the utmost apparent gravity. ... He was, however, proverbially good-natured, very rarely if ever indulging in any combative spirit toward any one, whatever might be the provocation, and yet was never known to laugh. Albeit, he seemed to be the pride of his indulgent father, who has been heard to boast of him as the "*genus* of the family," quoting his own expression.[77]

Such extreme statements need to be taken cautiously, but Tucker's perhaps malicious comments are supported by another historian, Orsamus Turner (discussed below). I wish Tucker had provided specific examples, but after the Smith family had left the area, over fifty townspeople signed affidavits accusing them of laziness, low morals, and shiftlessness.[78] Determining the degree of dysfunction in a family is problematic. We have later reports of the father's drinking, reports that are contradictory or revealing of inconsistency in the work habits of the family, their increasing involvement in the subculture of magic, the mother's apparent depressions, and increasing economic and religious contentions. Mormon psychiatrist C. Jess Groesbeck believed the family was "stressed."[79] Dan Vogel, a historian, argues that the Smith family was dysfunctional and that the parents were stressed because of Lucy's periodic depressions and Joseph Sr.'s alcoholism, as well as by conflict over religion and economic conditions. I believe that Vogel's historical evidence for both Lucy's depression and Joseph Sr.'s alcoholism, though not conclusive, is persuasive. Although not a psychologist, Vogel uses "family systems" thinking to suggest that the children were drawn into the conflict, with the oldest son, Alvin—as assigned in family systems—designated to manage the family's productivity and emulate the family's dominant values and themes. It seems indisputably clear that the family would have lost the farm earlier except for Alvin's industry. With Alvin's death, Vogel proposes, the family experienced psychological disequilibrium which lasted a number of years. Within thirty months of his death, the family experienced an economic crisis with the loss of their farm, a religious crisis with the division of the family during the 1824-25 Palmyra revival, and a legal crisis with Joseph Jr.'s public humiliation at an 1826 trial for "glass-looking." Joseph Jr. then picked up the assignment of saving the family. (The fourth child in family systems theory often carries the assignment of catching and collecting unresolved family tensions). Joseph Jr. stated as much in an 1835 angry response to his brother, William: "I brought salvation to my father's house, as an instrument in the hands of God when they were in a miserable situation."[80]

The economic difficulties of the Smith family did not end with the publication of the Book of Mormon. Joseph Smith, Sr., went to jail for thirty days for nonpayment of a debt in late 1830, and his son Hyrum escaped jail time when the whole family left the Palmyra/Manchester area.

As a psychiatrist, I observe these descriptions of idleness and indolence. I wonder if it is possible that Joseph Jr. suffered from "identity diffusion"—problems with identity and an absence of life direction. I hypothesize that he may have developed a narcissistic "false self" to meet the public, behind which remained an undeveloped true self. Joseph's aversion to direct competition may have resulted from his surgery. If he felt handicapped, it is possible that he used indirect, more subtle methods to achieve his ends, thus reducing the threat of another physical attack.

From a professional perspective, the overall impact of this dysfunctional family on young Joseph remains suspect. Psychologically speaking, Joseph's self-esteem must have been low; he had to deal with a lifestyle of moves, intermittent failures, and the amiable contempt of others. If Tucker is accurately reporting Joseph's exaggerations and palpable absurdities—and for the purposes of my diagnosis I am assuming that he is—then Joseph was probably engaging in a fantasy compensation for personal inferiority, for his family's low social importance, and his own unpromising future. Such a possibility is compatible with a developing narcissistic personality.

Joseph read avidly and assiduously, according to Tucker, far in advance of others in the family, including a book about an imposter.[81] He also read the Bible and could discuss its teachings with assurance. According to Tucker, "The Prophecies and Revelations were his special forte. His interpretations of scriptural passages were always original and unique, and his deductions and conclusions often disgustingly blasphemous, according to the common apprehensions of Christian people."[82] The Book of Mormon would later manifest Joseph's firm grasp of Old and New Testament language and events; but he expands and embellishes biblical miracles.

Joseph also decided against affiliating himself with more orthodox religion. Tucker states that young Joseph "joined the probationary class of the Methodist church in Palmyra and made some active demonstrations of engagedness" but withdrew, announcing that both churches and the Bible were fables. In 1832, shortly after the Book of Mormon was published, Joseph himself stated: "At about the age of twelve years my mind became seriously imprest with regard to the all important concerns for the wellfare of my immortal Soul which led me to searching the Scriptures believeing as I was taught, that they contained the word of God."[83]

At least some of Tucker's negative statements have one sophisticated supporter. Another newspaperman-turned-historian, Orsamus Turner, lived in Palmyra until Joseph was sixteen and a half. Thirty-five years later he described Joseph Sr. as "a great babbler, credulous, not especially industrious, a money-digger, prone to the marvelous; and withal, a little given to difficulties with neighbors, and petty law suits." Lucy Smith impressed him as "a woman of strong uncultivated intellect; artful and cunning; imbued with an illy regulated religious enthusiasm." Notably missing from this portrait is any suggestion of the depression that I have hypothesized afflicted Lucy at least periodically. In this portrait she comes across as sharp, perhaps unpredictable, and wily.[84]

Turner describes the future creator of the Book of Mormon as without direction but much involved in religion and political debate:

> Joseph Smith Jr. ... was lounging, idle; ... and possessed of less than ordinary intellect. The author's own recollections of him are distinct ones. He used to come into the village of Palmyra with little jags of wood from his backwoods home; sometimes patronizing a village grocery too freely; sometimes find an odd job to do about the store of Seymour Scovall; and once a week he would stroll into the office of the old Palmyra Register, for his father's paper. How impious, in us young "dare *Devils*" to once in a while blacken the face of the then meddling inquisitive lounger—but afterwards Prophet, with the old fashioned [ink] balls, when he used to put himself in the way of the working of the old fashioned ramage press! ...
>
> But Joseph had a little ambition; and some very laudable aspirations; the mother's intellect occasionally shone out in him feebly, especially when he used to help us solve some portentous questions of moral or political ethics, in our juvenile debating club, which we moved down to the old red school house on Durfee street, to get rid of the annoyance of critics that used to drop in upon us in the village; and subsequently, [when he was between fifteen and a half and sixteen and a half][85] after catching a spark of Methodism in the camp meeting, away down in the woods, on the Vienna road, he was a very passable exhorter in the evening meetings.

This description invites three clarifying remarks. The blackening of his face by printer's balls would not, in my opinion, have been friendly boyhood teasing between peers but a humiliating insult, since Joseph knew his family had a poor reputation. The term "exhorter" in the evening meetings was a formal designation of a young man with some ability at speaking who was urged to "exercise his gifts." At that time Methodist preachers traveled in circuits, meeting at convenient temporary places such as in the woods, or at a tavern, and established local "classes" under a "class leader." Both Orsamus Turner and Pomeroy Tucker have described Joseph's idleness and aversion to school. Here is Joseph's description of his education:

> and being in indigent circumstances were obliged to labour hard for the support of a large Family having nine children. As it required the exertions of all that were able to render any assistance for the support of the Family therefore we were deprived of the bennifit of an education Suffice it to say I was mearly instructid in reading and writing and the ground /rules/ of Arithmatic which constuted my whole literary acquirements.[86]

It is not surprising that a family with so little material success would place their hopes elsewhere—in the supernatural and the occult, a generally ineffective way to improve their material circumstances. Lucy's account, by recounting dreams of her husband and referring to them as "visions," decades after they occurred, makes it clear that the family valued dreams as a channel to supernatural power.

D. Michael Quinn summarizes evidence suggesting that, during Joseph's mid-teens, he began to follow his father into occult practices, taking up the use of the divining rod, then seer stones, as aids in his money-digging projects. The evidence of these activities comes from both Palmyra/Manchester and near Harmony, Pennsylvania, and is extensive.[87] As the Smiths became involved in Palmyra's religious revivals of 1824-25, their language of dreams and magic became progressively embellished by the language of Christianity. The beginnings of the Mormon story, Joseph's encounter with the angel, and his possession of the golden plates take place mostly contemporaneously with his heaviest emphasis on dreams and magic. He first tells the story of the gold book and its guardian within this context. Over time, however, his story becomes more in keeping with biblical angels and messengers, and the story takes on a Christian refinement. The strict guardian of the book becomes a firm, warning angel.

In her history Lucy Mack Smith reported one of her own dreams dating from 1803. She had remembered this dream for more than forty years, suggesting the immense significance she attached to it. She also reported five dreams that Joseph Sr. had between 1811 and 1819 and mentioned two more that she did not remember in enough detail to recount.[88] In the first, Joseph Sr. is traveling in a barren wasteland, accompanied by a guide—an "attendant spirit"—who tells him that the desolation is because the world is without the true religion. The spirit promises Joseph that he will find a box on a log, the contents of which will bring him wisdom. When he forces open the box, terrifying animals rise up around him. He drops the box and flees in terror, awaking trembling but happy.

The second dream reappears as a Book of Mormon narrative. Joseph Sr. is again traveling in a barren and desolate land, urged on by his spiritual guide. He follows a narrow path to a beautiful stream of water with a rope along the bank, and a handsome tree adorned with dazzlingly white fruit. This tree excites his wonder and admiration, and its fruit tasted "delicious beyond description." He brought his wife and seven children to join him at the tree, and all were inexpressibly happy as they ate the delicious fruit. Then he saw a large building, its doors and windows filled with well-dressed people who were mocking the family and pointing fingers at them while they continued to partake of the fruit. Observing their scorn and contempt, Joseph Sr. asks the guide for an explanation. The building represents "Babylon ... and the inhabitants thereof, who scorn and despise the Saints of God, because of their humility." The fruit represents "the pure love of God, shed abroad in the hearts of all those who love him." The guide also draws his attention to his "other" children, two small youngsters whom he also brings to the tree and feeds with the fruit. Psychologically speaking, these children may represent the dead firstborn son and infant Ephraim. Again Joseph Sr. awoke, so filled with happiness that he clapped his hands.

In the third dream, he is again walking despite severe lameness. His guide directs him to a garden where twelve wooden images, lined up on either side of the walkway, bow to him as he passes. He is then made well. In the fourth dream, unaccompanied by a guide, he is making his way toward a meetinghouse where the Judgement will occur. To his distress, he arrives too late and is locked out; his body wastes away until the porter reminds him to call on Jesus. He does so and is made whole. In the last recorded dream, a peddlar recognizes his honesty but informs him that he lacks one thing for salvation. The peddler will write down the necessary item; but in his anxiety, Joseph Sr. wakes prematurely.

Lucy recorded these dreams in detail twenty-five years after they occurred. But to her and the family, they had the status of visions. He had a "vision," she said of the 1811 dream, "which I shall relate in his own words." He had another "singular dream," followed by "another vision," "one more," "two more visions," "a sixth," and finally "the seventh and last vision my husband had was in 1819." Almost certainly, Joseph or Lucy or both would have told these supernatural visions repeatedly to their children and discussed them during Joseph's youth, ages six to fourteen and beyond. The interchangeablity of dreaming and visions is also an element of Book of Mormon narratives. (See below.)

This biographical outline of Joseph Smith Jr.'s life brings us to about age seventeen, immediately before the appearance of the gold treasure book with its guardian spirit, and probably, I hypothesize, just after he advanced from using a divining rod to being a seer.[89] I have naturally focused on biographical elements that will help us understand his disguised autobiography in the Book of Mormon. My goal is not just to parallel these stories of fact and fantasy to see how he transforms his life story into religious narrative, but also to fit the Book of Mormon into a more comprehensive psychological evaluation of him.

Although we need to examine the crucial events surrounding the coming forth of the Book of Mormon itself, it will be helpful, I feel, to interrupt this historical narrative to compare Joseph's historical autobiography to what I call the "first story" in the Book of Mormon—the flight from Jerusalem, obtaining possession of the brass plates, wanderings in the wilderness, and arriving in the promised land. As background, however, I wish to emphasize the importance of this initial Nephi story. I compare it to the first hour of a patient who has just started intensive psychotherapy. Like other psychotherapists, I try to make detailed notes during that first hour, for my experience tells me that it contains in condensed, symbolic form the main problems to be discussed in the next months.

The Nephi-Laban conflict is the first creative story in Joseph's first creation. It is perhaps more precise to say that this story is the first *surviving* creative story, since we know that he told his family numerous stories from the Book of Mormon before he received it and also because the first dictation of 116 pages was destroyed. The first dictated version would have made a fascinating and significant comparison with the account in 1 Nephi, but the retelling keeps within the first version's story frame.

As we follow the progressive change of the guardian of the treasure with his ritualistic behavior to a firm biblical angel warning of the dangers of disobedience, it is reasonable to suppose that the first dictated version had less Christianity and more magic in it. It is also reasonable to hypothesize that when he again started dictation with his new scribe, Oliver Cowdery, something had changed and that the emphasis shifted toward Christianity. There is good evidence that Smith did not immediately restart his dictation at the beginning of the Book of Mormon but continued on toward the end. (See chapter 3.) I believe he completed his dictation through the small book of Mormon within the Book of Mormon, then returned to the beginning and redid the destroyed 116 pages. Then he dictated the book of Ether, for I will propose that the book of Ether was dictated to tell us (and not tell us) about the period of dictation of the majority of the Book of Mormon. He then dictated the book of Moroni which contains material suggesting that he is getting ready to start a church.

This sequence, if correct, makes this first story nearly the last in his dictation, but the story is so central to the rest of the book, so dramatic and concise, and reflected so thoroughly throughout the rest of the stories, that

I think we are looking at a refined story that had been repeated numerous times and that he had told for the first time in the lost 116 pages. The major differences are that the second version is probably more spiritual and personal in nature, since it is Nephi's private autobiography, rather than being a third-person abridgement of official records made by Mormon, the last great prophet-general. From a psychological and naturalistic viewpoint, I think we gained more than we lost.

From that same perspective, it is important for us to pay attention to one more item. After the guardian spirit showed him the book in its buried stone box, Joseph told his family and a number of other people that the box contained not only the gold plates and spectacle-shaped objects that would enable him to translate the plates, but also a sword. I argue that the sword represents Nathan Smith's scalpel, and serves as a signal that this narrative is about the surgery, and, in fact, was created to deal with the surgery.[90]

Conquest of Surgery: 1 Nephi and the Sword of Laban

> Early frustrations ... lead to reparative attempts to maintain omnipotent fantasies, despite the helpless rage experienced by the infant in the course of ordinary failures of maternal care. One of these defensive efforts involves the attempt to master feelings of rage, frustration, and helplessness by the intrapsychic shift from pride in providing one's self with satisfactions to pride in the fantasy of control over ... one who is responsible for the frustrations.[91]

> Individuals with this disorder [of narcissistic personality] have a grandiose sense of self-importance. ... They routinely overestimate their abilities and inflate their accomplishments, often appearing boastful and pretentious. They may blithely assume that others attribute the same value to their efforts and may be surprised when the praise they expect and feel they deserve is not forthcoming. Often implicit in the inflated judgments of their own accomplishments is an underestimation (devaluation) of the contributions of others. They are often preoccupied with fantasies of unlimited success, power, brilliance, beauty, or ideal love. ... They may ruminate about "long overdue" admiration and privilege and compare themselves favorably with famous or privileged people.
>
> Individuals with Narcissistic Personality Disorder believe that they are superior, special, or unique and expect others to recognize them as such. ... They may feel that they can only be understood by, and should only associate with, other people who are special or of high status and may attribute "unique," "perfect," or "gifted" qualities to those with whom they associate. Individuals with this disorder believe that their needs are special and beyond the ken of ordinary people. Their own self-esteem is enhanced (i.e., "mirrored") by the idealized value that they assign to those with whom they associate. They are likely to insist on having only the "top" person (doctor, lawyer, hairdresser, instructor) or being affiliated with the "best" institutions, but may devalue the credentials of those who disappoint them.[92]

Joseph Smith's associates are none other than the prophets and apostles of the Bible. He brings this fantasy of importance and power into being through his alter ego, Nephi, in the Book of Mormon. The first story in the Book of Mormon is a narrative told by the fourth child of a father with supernatural powers. Joseph Smith, Jr., was also the fourth child of such a father; in both families this child is following in his father's supernatural footsteps. Not surprisingly, given the Smith family's history, Lehi's family's major task is to change locales. The Book of Mormon father, Lehi, a prophet during the time of Jeremiah, receives divine instructions to remove his family from Jerusalem. Jeremiah, Lehi's contemporary, was warning the Jews about their impending captivity by the Babylonians shortly before 600 B.C.E. They reject his message and persecute him; Lehi preaches a similar message of repentance and his life is in danger.

The tale of the fourth son parallels Joseph Smith's autobiography, presenting in disguised form but remarkably precise chronological order the story of Joseph Smith's early years, his traumatic surgery, his family's losing struggles in New England, their difficult journey to New York, and the relative peace and prosperity of their early years in Palmyra. The shared patterns between Smith's story and Nephi's story also preview major patterns repeated four times as the Book of Mormon continues.

In Nephi's story the three older siblings are all brothers—Laman, Lemuel, and Sam. I argue that they correspond to Joseph's three older siblings: Alvin, Hyrum, and Sophronia. Despite the shift in gender, an obvious disguise, Sophronia and Sam share the qualities of being cooperative and quiet, and their names begin with the same letter. (For other examples of Joseph/Book of Mormon characters with similar first letters in names, see chapter 5.) The Book of Mormon siblings are symmetrical opponents: Laman and Lemuel consistently oppose Sam and Nephi. Almost nothing is known about the relationships among the brothers and sisters in the Smith family as children; while Joseph's account mentions both Alvin and Hyrum in glowing terms and Hyrum was inseparable from him as an adult, Joseph barely mentions Sophronia. Is this paired configuration wholly fictional? Perhaps, but it is also possible to hypothesize that the children formed alliances to deal with the family poverty, possible episodes of hunger while they were living "day to day," the stress of repeated moves, and Lucy's frequent pregnancies, perhaps accompanied by depression. The Book of Mormon from the beginning presents a picture of family rivalries and power struggles which will become increasingly difficult to ignore.

In the Book of Mormon, if this hypothesis is accurate, Joseph experienced the headiness of fantasy's power by changing a hard-working brother (Alvin) into an unbelieving reprobate, hostile and defiant (Laman); and he quickly expanded this method by changing a decent, caring human being—his surgeon—into a drunken thieving murderer. Within this context, a passage such as the following in the early pages of the book seems suggestive. The Lord confirms to Nephi a message which had earlier been given to his father: "And inasmuch as thy brethren shall rebel against thee they shall be cut off from the presence of the Lord. And inasmuch as thou shalt keep my commandments, thou shalt be made a ruler and a teacher over thy brethren. For behold, in that day that they shall rebel against me, I will curse them even with a sore curse and they shall have no power over thy seed except they shall rebel against me also. And ... if so ... [the seed of Laman and Lemuel] shall be a scourge unto thy seed, to stir them up in the ways of remembrance" (BM 9; 1 Ne. 2:20-24). Such a passage seems to suggest that Joseph's (Nephi's) parents used the older children to discipline the younger ones. Further, such action by God is at cross-purposes with himself, for he will use extreme physical punishment to teach obedience but at the same time create psychological conflict in his Nephite children. The parents' aggression pressures the child toward conscious submission out of fear and simultaneously toward an unconscious identification with the parents' aggressive behavior. Children of violence often become violent parents. Is this a report of Joseph's experiences with his parents? While no evidence has survived of Joseph Sr.'s and Lucy's parenting practices with Joseph before age seven, such a hypothesis would partially account for what I will argue are Joseph Jr.'s persistent fantasies of power.

Nephi's first independent action—taking the plates from the Jerusalem ruler who holds them (1 Ne. 3-4)—presents a version of what must have been Joseph's most traumatic memory—the bloody surgery on his leg. The Book of Mormon version exaggerates, intensifies, and also reverses the autobiography, a pattern that I will also argue is typical of how Joseph used the Book of Mormon. When Nephi takes the plates by trickery, killing their guardian, he completes a pattern of reversal and compensation; thus a humiliating occasion in real life becomes one of domination in the Book of Mormon, an occasion of sadness becomes one of elation, and so on.

Soon after Lehi removes his family from Jerusalem, God orders him to send his four sons back to the city to obtain the "brass plates" from a wealthy and powerful Jew named Laban. These plates contain two records, "the history of the Jews" (the Bible) and a family genealogy (which may correspond psychologically to Solomon Mack's autobiography). Laban, the possessor of the family history, is thus identified as a relative.[93] I see Laban as the earliest version of surgeon Nathan Smith in the Book of Mormon, a prototype of the killing physician who will make several reappearances in the narrative. Laban shares a number of characteristics with Nathan Smith. Laban is a relative; although Nathan Smith was not, the shared surname would easily lead a child aged five to seven to believe that he was. Nathan Smith has killing power, thanks to his profession, and took the leadership in the council of surgeons. Laban is a man who can "slay fifty ... or command fifty" and then (exaggeratedly) "or even ... tens of thousands." He takes the family's wealth, is associated with alcohol, and carries a sword. Nathan Smith charges a high fee for his services, offers young Joseph alcohol, and carries his surgeon's knife.

The four sons collectively make their first visit to Laban, without success. They then choose Laman to make a second attempt, but Laban calls him a robber and orders his servants to kill him. Nathan Smith, a decent and honorable man as far as is known, has, in Joseph's fantasy of power, become a dishonest drunken would-be murderer. For the third attempt, the four brothers gather the family treasure and offer it in exchange for the plates. Laban takes their possessions but orders his servants to kill them. They flee into the wilderness for safety. Alvin/Laman and Hyrum/Lemuel beat Joseph/Nephi for endangering them; an angel not only stops them but tells them Joseph/Nephi will be a ruler over them. Joseph/Nephi, still determined to carry out the commandments of God despite Laman's and Lemuel's hostility and Sam's passivity, returns to Jerusalem after dark to face his "relative" again as Joseph did in real life. He finds Laban/Nathan Smith "fallen to earth before me, for he was drunken with wine." The surgeon, who offered Joseph brandy or wine is now inebriated. In fantasy, Smith has turned the tables on him by the psychiatric process of "changing passive helplessness into active conquest." He describes the "foot-long" surgeon's knife as it might have seemed to a child: "And I beheld his sword, and I drew it forth from the sheath thereof; and the hilt thereof was of pure gold, and the workmanship was exceedingly fine, and I saw the blade thereof was of the most precious steel."

Joseph/Nephi is commanded "by the spirit" to kill Laban. At first he shrinks but then comes up with four reasons for killing him: "Behold the Lord hath delivered him into my hands. Yea, and I also knew that he had sought to take away mine own life; yea, and he would not harken unto the commandments of the Lord; and he had also taken away our property." This list is a classic presentation of rationalization. If a patient gave such reasons, a therapist's response might be, "You give me one reason after another. I wonder which one is the real one? Or perhaps none of them is? Perhaps there is a reason behind all of them that is the real one, and you haven't told it to me—or, perhaps, even to yourself." What might this "real" reason be? I suggest that it is simple revenge. Laban/Nathan Smith has caused Joseph/Nephi more fear and pain than he had ever before known in his life, in a manner that emphasized his smallness and helplessness; Joseph/Nephi wants to kill him.

And he does: "Therefore I did obey the voice of the spirit and took Laban by the hair of the head, and I smote off his head with his own sword" (BM 13; 1 Ne. 4:18). The retaliation against the surgeon is complete. I see in this early use of rationalization the beginning of a pattern that Joseph Smith will use when he performs other deeds of questionable morality when the "commandments" of God become his reason for later breaking the laws in the United States.[94] Joseph/Nephi's next action is striking: "I took the garments of Laban and put them upon my own body; yea, every whit; and I did gird on his armour about my loins" (BM 13; 1 Ne. 4:19). From a psychoanalytic perspective, this statement may be among the most important in the Book of Mormon. Joseph announces that he will assume someone else's personality and authority (develop an alter ego), and that the process either began or was intensified by the surgery.

As a psychiatrist, I also observe that the real Nathan Smith was a decent man performing a painful but life-saving duty for Joseph Smith. In Smith's later life, when decent men attempt to accomplish tasks which threaten Joseph Smith, he likewise defines them as evil and attacks to avoid the helplessness he felt before Laban/the surgeon.[95] This story establishes a crucial pattern which repeats itself again and again in the Book of Mormon. Joseph Smith compensates for a terrible real-life experience by displacing it with a conquering fantasy.

In this and chapter 3, I will continue to review the misfortunes and tragedies in Joseph Smith's life. In each case, he resolves these issues by a fantasy conquest, the solution he "learned" from his surgical experience. I argue that it set the pattern by which he deals with problems. In the Book of Mormon, I will try to demonstrate, Joseph conquers and solves each real-life dilemma. His next humiliation will be on the wagon journey from Vermont to New York, when mean-spirited Caleb Howard purposely ignores and increases Joseph's exhaustion and pain. How does he compensate for this humiliation?

The Book of Mormon episodes which follow Laban's death confirm the power of disguise. Dressed as Laban, Nephi/Joseph goes to Laban's treasury, mimics Laban's voice, obtains possession of the records, and tricks Zoram, Laban's servant, into following him outside the city where Laman/Alvin, Lemuel/Hyrum, and Sam/Sophronia are waiting. They are also fooled by the disguise and flee until Nephi calls them back in his own voice. Taking alarm, Zoram tries to flee: "And now I, Nephi, being a man large in stature, and also having received much strength of the Lord, therefore I did seize upon the servant of Laban" (BM 13-14; 1 Ne. 4:20-38). This scene can be read psychologically as a fantasy reversal of Joseph's helplessness during the surgery, introducing the theme of Joseph's search for power over others.[96] Zoram is only the first person in the Book of Mormon who comes under Nephi/Joseph's control; psychologically, the first person the child Joseph could control would be his next younger sibling, Samuel Harrison, born in 1808. According to the scenario I am proposing, the Book of Mormon narrative now contains representations of Joseph's parents and the first five living children.

Lehi's family then sojourns "in the wilderness for the space of ... eight years" (BM 42; 1 Ne. 17:1-4), ending with their arrival in the promised land. In Joseph's autobiography, this period begins after the surgery and ends when the family reaches Palmyra, a period that lasted somewhere between three and one-half and five years. In two additional retellings of this story as a Book of Mormon narrative, Joseph makes this period last both seven and four years. Perhaps expanding their duration emphasizes how terrible those years were. My own belief is that, in this version, he dates the Smith family desolation from Ephraim's death in March 1810 to settling in the cabin in Palmyra in comfort around 1818.

Joseph Smith also modifies these early childhood experiences from the age of five—the age he gives himself for his surgery—to eleven or so by interweaving a section of his later life—his marriage—into the story. God commands Lehi to send his sons back to Jerusalem once more to bring out Ishmael, his wife, five daughters, and two sons, so they can marry. They succeed with relative ease. Two of the daughters immediately pair up with Alvin/Laman and Hyrum/Lemuel and become rebellious, desiring to return to Jerusalem. This story contains parallels of Joseph's marriage to Emma Hale (see chapter 3); and the first time Joseph dictated this story, he was living near his in-laws. Isaac Hale, a hardworking and prosperous farmer, refused Joseph's first request for Emma's hand, was distraught when they eloped, and testified against his new son-in-law in a sworn newspaper affidavit six years after their marriage.

Smith apparently did not handle this antagonism well. Several years of confrontation and conflict, interspersed with periods of peace, ended with a breach so irrevocable that Emma never saw her parents again. In fantasy, Joseph eliminates Isaac by having Ishmael die in the wilderness, the only casualty in the party in the Old World. In real life Smith originally brought Emma first to live with his own family in Manchester. Lorenzo Saunders reported, "Joseph's wife was a pretty woman, just as pretty a woman as I ever saw. When she came to the Smith's she was disappointed and used to come down to our house and sit down and cry. Said she was deceived and got into a hard place."[97] Perhaps her bitterness at being separated from her family and her disappointment at her situation (I read Saunders's statement to mean that Joseph had misrepresented the comforts of his parental home) can be heard in the cries of the daughters of Ishmael who "did mourn exceedingly, because of the loss of their father ... saying: Our father is dead ... and they did murmur against me" (BM 41; 1 Ne. 16:35).

As Lucy considered Joseph Sr.'s dreams to be visions, so does the Book of Mormon. Lehi states: "I have dreamed a dream; or, in other words, I have seen a vision." Joseph Sr.'s dream of the first tree, which occurred in 1811 when Joseph was five, reemerges in the Book of Mormon, motivating Nephi to heroic faithfulness. Significantly, Nephi had prayed to have the same dream as his father. In the Book of Mormon version of this dream, a guide "dressed in a white robe" leads Lehi through a dreary wasteland to a tree standing by a river with an iron rod running along the bank. The fruit, which represents the "pure love of God," is "most sweet ... and white" and it "filled my soul with exceeding great joy." Lehi persuades most of the family to join him, but Laman and Lemuel refuse. A spacious building is filled with worldly people who scorn the family eating from the tree representing the "pure love of God" (BM 19-26; 1 Ne. 8-11).

The parallels between Lehi's and Joseph Sr.'s dreams were discovered by non-Mormons as early as 1902.[98] The orthodox Mormon explanation is that Lucy, grief-stricken and then seventy, was influenced by the Book of Mormon and included details from Lehi's dream in her record.[99] Fawn Brodie had earlier countered this argument by pointing out that such reverse borrowing was unlikely since Lucy also remembered and recounted four other dreams in great detail. In my proposal, this dream/vision takes its proper place in the chronology of Joseph Smith's life.[100]

In the wilderness, Lehi and his family turn, as did the Smith family, to magic. Though interpreted as miraculous by the orthodox, the compass called the "Liahona" is best interpreted, in my opinion, as a divining rod, and functions as a magic tool which, under the influence of faithfulness, guides Lehi's family to the "more fertile parts of the wilderness." This instrument appears quite magically on the ground in the front of the tent one morning, "a ball of curious workmanship ... Within the ball were two spindles; and the one pointed the way whither we should go into the wilderness" (BM 39; 1 Ne. 16:10). Other improbable aspects of the story, in which gaps in logic are made up for by magical qualities, are that Nephi/Joseph breaks his "steel" bow and replaces it with a child's bow made of a straight stick. In the Book of Mormon, the families are fatigued and beginning to starve. The story reminds us that in the middle of those years of hardship (1810-18) the Smith family was living day-to-day; this fantasy supports the idea that he experienced hunger. But the fantasy is an exaggeration, and we cannot tell how much the hunger is exaggerated. Using the magical compass, Joseph/Nephi finds food and saves his family. From a psychoanalytic perspective, Joseph is dealing with a real-life misfortune by a compensating fantasy. Now the Book of Mormon provides some evidence of sibling squabbles in the Smith home and envy over Joseph's ascendancy as the developing supernatural seer. (See chapter 3.) The ascension of Nephi as an even greater prophet than his father will be paralleled by Joseph Smith's ascension over his own father as a magician. "And Laman said ... let us slay our father, and also our brother Nephi who has taken it upon himself to be our ruler and our teacher. ... We know he lies ... and he worketh many things by his cunning arts ... to make himself a king and a ruler over us, that he may do with us according to his will and pleasure" (BM 1 Ne. 16:38.)

I hypothesize that the Smiths experienced almost a decade of desolation (1810-18), during which two more sons were born: William in 1811 and Don Carlos in 1816. Similarly Lehi "begat two sons in the wilderness; the elder was called Jacob and the younger Joseph." In the Smith home the crops were failing for the third year when young Don Carlos was born. In the Book of Mormon this situation is also described: "While we did live upon raw meat in the wilderness, our women did give plenty of suck for their children, and were strong yea, even like unto men" (BM 42; 1 Ne. 17:1.) Again this description can be seen as a compensating fantasy for the Smith family's situation and supports the hypothesis that they experienced episodes of hunger.

In the Book of Mormon, after wandering in the "wilderness," Lehi's family reaches the seashore at a place they name "Bountiful" near a sea "of many waters" where they build a boat in which to travel to their promised land. Food is available in abundance. However, Laman's and Lemuel's rebelliousness hinders the construction of the ship. In this struggle the narrative focuses clearly on what I think we must understand as Joseph's ultimate goal: power. Nephi/Joseph has been arguing with his brothers over ship-building. When the brothers become so angry at Nephi's lecturing that they attack him, he responds impressively, "In the name of the Almighty God, I command you that ye touch me not, for I am filled with the power of God ... and whoso shall lay his hands upon me shall wither even as a dry reed." This power lasts a number of days. God commands Nephi/Joseph to demonstrate this power by touching. The shock makes them "[fall] down before me."

As I have noted, I interpret the Smiths' "promised land" to be Palmyra, New York. I think this ship-building episode is best explained as the construction of the rough log cabins, first on the Jennings property and then on their own. If we accept as accurate the descriptions by Orsamus Turner and Pomeroy Tucker concerning Joseph's indolent nature and recognize through Lucy's biography the "serious and industrious" nature of the oldest son, Alvin/Laman, then Joseph has simply reversed the sequence, just as he reversed the family's disadvantages.

In the description of the sea voyage itself can be seen the Smith family's struggle with the harsh and selfish driver, Caleb Howard, and his flirtations with the Gates daughters: "My brethren and the Sons of Ishmael and also their wives began to make themselves merry, insomuch that they began to dance, and to sing, and speak with much rudeness ... yea ... exceeding rudeness" (BM 48: 1 Ne. 18:1-9). Howard had spent the family money on drinking and gambling, had made a little lame boy walk through the snow, and had allowed another driver to knock him down in the mud. This traumatic experience, I suggest, emerges as Laman's and Lemuel's attack on Nephi. They "did bind me with cords, and they did treat me with much harshness." His wrists and ankles "had swollen exceedingly" from the tight cords, "and great was the soreness thereof" (BM 48: 1 Ne. 18:10-13). They repent only when God frightens them with a terrible storm. Nephi, who has remained firmly faithful during the days of ill treatment, guides the ship using the magic compass, and the ship reaches the promised land safely. Again Smith has reversed his helpless humiliation and pain on that trip of his childhood and has become the one in control.

After this difficult crossing, Lehi and his extended family arrive in the promised land, a rich wilderness supporting a dense population of cows, "oxen," asses, "horses," and wild goats (BM 49-50; 1 Ne. 18:25). Joseph Sr. had chosen Palmyra as the site for his next move because it was rich: farmers there raised "wheat in abundance." The Book of Mormon land was immediately fertile: "We did begin to till the earth, and we began to plant seeds; yea, we did put all our seeds into the earth, which we had brought from the land of Jerusalem. And it came to pass that they did grow abundantly" (BM 49-50; 1 Ne. 18:25). The promised land can thus be seen as the first version of the Smith family's early years of relative peace and prosperity after arriving in New York.

In the Book of Mormon, Joseph/Nephi gives a lengthy series of sermons and transcribes Isaiah's prophecies for a number of chapters. Lehi dies after pronouncing his last exhortations, blessings, and prophecies. Immediately sibling rivalry flares into murderous hatred, and God warns Joseph/Nephi to move away from them. After this time Laman, Lemuel, and their descendants ("Lamanites") "were cut off from [God's] presence ... [and he] did cause a skin of blackness [redness] to come upon them. ... They shall be loathsome ... idle, full of mischief and subtlety, and did seek in the wilderness for beasts of prey." These Lamanites, the ancestors of the American Indians, were assigned by God (without knowing it) to be a scourge to Nephi's followers ("Nephites"), and to whip them to repentance whenever they fall into sin, and, if the Nephites become too evil, to destroy them completely. The family is now split into two opposing national factions as God had warned, setting the stage for the dyadic physical and moral contention in the rest of the book.

By now I propose that we have identified the following Smith family members in the Book of Mormon: Joseph Sr./Lehi, Lucy/Sariah, Alvin/Laman, Hyrum/Lemuel, Sophronia/Sam, Joseph/Nephi, Samuel Harrison/Zoram, William/Jacob, and Don Carlos/Joseph. Women are significantly unrepresented throughout the Book of Mormon, but I suggest that Joseph's two younger sisters, Catherine (b. 1812) and Lucy (b. 1821) crop up in Nephi's almost parenthetical statement that, when he moved his people into the wilderness away from the Lamanites, the group included "also my sisters" (BM 71; 2 Ne. 5:6). It is the only mention of sisters, but I suggest they are there because Joseph wanted to assure Catherine and Lucy a place with his family in the promised land. Although Nephi does not specify a number, I believe that Joseph had two sisters in mind because Ishmael's family included two sons, obviously to make symmetrical matches.[101] After Lehi's family's eight years in the wilderness, Book of Mormon scholar John Sorenson estimates that forty-three may have entered the boat. After the division, B. H. Roberts estimated that the original Nephite group numbered under 100, and many of these would have been children.[102]

The accomplishments of Lehi's family during these first years in the promised land are, even in fantasy, exaggerated. Nephi's group includes two elderly widows, three young married couples (probably with children), two young men, and two young women. It is hard to imagine that this group numbered over thirty. He gives a report twenty-two years later when "thirty years had passed away since from the time we left Jerusalem." By this time, the group cannot number many more than a hundred, and probably a majority would be young children; but they have created a major civilization. Instead of dealing with the normal frontier concerns about growing crops, building homes, fighting illness, adapting to the country, defending themselves against predators, and hunting meat, while maintaining a lookout for the Lamanites, the record recounts that they have developed a foundry in which Nephi forges steel swords based on the model of Laban's sword. He has also taught them "to build buildings, and to work in all manner of wood, and of iron, and of copper, and of brass, and of steel, and of gold, and of silver, and of precious ores, which were in great abundance" (BM 72; 2 Ne. 5:7-15). Even more impressively, this small group has built a temple "after the manner of the Temple of Solomon save it were not built of so many precious things; for they were not to be found upon the land. ... But the manner of construction was like unto the temple of Solomon and the workmanship was exceeding fine" (BM 72; 2 Ne. 5:16).

This description is more like a frontier tall tale than a plausible history. The temple of Solomon in Jerusalem was the glory of two nations, built by more than 150,000 workers over a period of seven years. Anti-Mormon E. D. Howe, writing four years after the Book of Mormon was published, was the first to point out the inconsistency of Nephi's temple. B. H. Roberts, an early twentieth-century Mormon general authority, also elaborated on these implausibilities in his review of Book of Mormon problems.[103]

However, questions of plausibility are relevant to this analysis only as they shed light on Joseph Smith's underlying psychological state. When the Book of Mormon is seen as a repetitive tale of wish fulfillment and compensation, then the exaggerations only underscore the intensity of Joseph's need to succeed. When Nephi makes swords using the model of Laban's dreaded sword, Joseph is again controlling and reversing the meaning of the surgeon's feared knife. When the Nephite temple replicates Solomon's, I see it as a fantasy structure compensating for the one building that the Smiths could contemplate with some measure of pride—the "small frame house" on their farm in Manchester. This building's existence psychologically wipes out the series of rented cabins they have lived in for the past decade, corresponding to Lehi's tent. Again the Book of Mormon fantasy compensates for real-life incompleteness and loss.

To summarize: I argue that these chapters of the Book of Mormon take us through Joseph Smith's disguised autobiography from birth to about seventeen—his surgery, moves, years of desolation, the births of his brothers, the painful and humiliating trip to Palmyra, the building of the cabin, and the construction of the farmhouse. He has modified the statistics of his real wanderings by exaggerating the number of years in the wilderness, inserting his marriage out of order, and finding some relief from hunger before the trip to the promised land/Palmyra. The outline of the story paralleling his life is reasonably clear, and the major revelation is his technique of fantasy compensation. However, I have here presented only an outline of complex stories with all sorts of overdetermined connections to episodes in the life of Joseph Smith. For example, in these chapters Nephi is bound with cords, or beaten, or threatened with beating by his brothers and others at least three times, only to be rescued by God. How helpless Joseph must have felt when the surgeons proposed binding him to the bedstead. Another unexplored possibility is that Nephi's discovery of gold, silver, steel, copper, iron, and brass is the lavish wish-fulfillment of at least eighteen unproductive attempts to find buried treasure.[104]

When Nephi dies, the eulogy recorded in the Book of Mormon states that the people loved him "exceedingly, he having been a great protector for them, having wielded the sword of Laban in their defense" (BM 124; Jacob 1:9-10). We might think it strange that this sword would become a symbol of righteous strength in a book meant to be another witness of Jesus Christ, for it was a tool of war and death, still known by the name of its original possessor, who is otherwise remembered for his wealth, greed, corruption, and being murdered while drunk. Furthermore, Nephi took it from him in a morally ambiguous episode that combines heroism, cowardice, and rationalization.

The sword is mentioned twice more in the Book of Mormon. Four hundred years after Nephi's death, righteous King Benjamin wielded it against an invading Lamanite army: "he did fight with the strength of his own arm, with the sword of Laban" (BM 152; Words of Mormon 13). It is last mentioned when Benjamin turns the kingdom over to his son: "And moreover, he also gave him charge concerning the records which were engraven on the plates of brass; and also the plates of Nephi; and also, the sword of Laban, and the ball or director, which led our fathers through the wilderness" (BM 155; Mosiah 1:15-16). At this point, Nathan Smith's "foot-long" scalpel, now a symbol of compensatory power, disappears from the Book of Mormon. However, it reemerges in Mormon legend. For the fiftieth anniversary of Smith's receiving the gold plates and thirteen years after his murder, Brigham Young told a group of Saints in Farmington, Utah:

> I believe I will take the liberty to tell you of another circumstance that will be as marvelous as anything can be. This is an incident in the life of [Joseph Smith's scribe] Oliver Cowdery, but he did not take the liberty of telling such things in meeting as I take. I tell these things to you, and I have a motive for doing so. I want to carry them to the ears of my brethren and sisters, and to the children also, that they may grow to an understanding of some things that seem to be entirely hidden from the human family. Oliver Cowdery went with the Prophet Joseph when he deposited these plates. Joseph did not translate all of the plates; there was a portion of them sealed, which you can learn from the Book of Doctrine and Covenants. When Joseph got the plates, the angel instructed him to carry them back to the hill Cumorah, which he did. Oliver says that when Joseph and Oliver went there, the hill opened, and they walked into a cave, in which there was a large and spacious room. He says he did not think, at the time, whether they had the light of the sun or artificial light; but that it was just as light as day. They laid the plates on a table; it was a large table that stood in the room. Under this table there was a pile of plates as much as two feet high, and there were altogether in this room more plates than probably many wagon loads; they were piled up in the corner and along the walls. The first time they went there the sword of Laban hung upon the wall; but when they went again it had been taken down and laid upon the table across the gold plates; it was unsheathed, and on it was written these words; "This sword will never be sheathed again until the kingdoms of this world become the kingdom of our God and his Christ."[105]

Notes

1. Those who have approached the Book of Mormon naturalistically have commented on its reflection of Joseph Smith's life and environment. Most of these comments have been brief, introductory, or general; or, after noting a few parallels with his life, they have turned to parallels with the happenings in the United States or upstate New York. I. Woodbridge Riley, *The Founder of Mormonism: A Psychological Study of Joseph Smith Jr.* (New York: Dodd Mead & Co., 1902), 26, 113-30; Walter F. Prince, "Psychological Tests for the Authorship of the Book of Mormon," *American Journal of Psychology* 28 (July 1917): 375; Fawn Brodie, *No Man Knows My History*, 2d ed., rev. and enl. (New York: Alfred Knopf, 1971), 50-66. The closest approach to seeing the book as a reflection of Smith's personal life to date—although still flawed, in my opinion—is William D. Morain, *The Sword of Laban: Joseph Smith, Jr. and the Dissociated Mind* (Washington, DC: American Psychiatric Press, 1998). See my discussion of Morain in the preface.

2. Ernst Kris, *Psychoanalytic Explorations in Art* (New York: Schocken Books, 1971), 35, and passim.

3. D. Michael Quinn, *Early Mormonism and the Magic World View* (Salt Lake

City: Signature Books, 1987), 28. In the Salem trials nineteen were found guilty and hanged, one was pressed to death, one was murdered in prison, and five adults and two infants died in prison. See Enders A. Robinson, *The Devil Discovered* (New York: Hippocrene Books, 1991), 204-50, 362-64. Mary Esty, accused of witchcraft by Samuell Smith and John Gould, left written testimony and a moving appeal to avoid the gallows. It concludes, "The Lord alone, who is the searcher of all hearts, knows that as I shall answer it at the Tribunal Seat, that I know not the least thing of Witchcraft, therefore I cannot, I durst not belye my own Soul. I beg your Honours not to deny this my humble Petition, from a poor dying Innocent person, and I question not but the Lord will give a blessing to your Endeavours." Her appeal was rejected. R. Calef, *More Wonders of the Invisible World* (London, 1700); reprinted in George L. Burr, ed., *Narrative of the Witchcraft Cases, 1648-1706* (New York: Barnes and Noble, 1966), 38-369. Quinn, *Early Mormonism and the Magic World View,* 28-30, provides four references to the Smith-Esty trial. Palmyra neighbor Fayette Lapham wrote that "Joseph Smith, Senior, we soon learned, from his own lips, was a firm believer in witchcraft and other supernatural things; had brought up his family in the same belief." Quoted by Quinn and in Francis W. Kirkham, *A New Witness for Christ in America* (Independence, MO; Zion's Printing and Publishing Co., 1951), 2:526. Jesse's contemptuous letter (which possibly implies his brother used magic to leave Vermont) is quoted by Quinn and Richard L. Anderson, "The Mature Joseph Smith and Treasure Searching," *BYU Studies* 24 (Fall 1984): 526. Mentions of witchcraft and magic appear in the Book of Mormon, first ed., [BM] 520-21 (Morm. 1:19, 2:10).

4. The degree of Joseph Sr.'s drinking is impossible to ascertain absolutely, requiring the historian to estimate his drinking. The strongest evidence that he did drink to some degree appears in a patriarchal blessing that Joseph Sr. gave his son Hyrum in 1834, praising Hyrum's respect for his father: "Though he [referring to himself] has been out of way through wine, thou hast never forsaken him nor laughed him to scorn." Richard L. Bushman, *Joseph Smith and the Beginnings of Mormonism* (Urbana: University of Illinois Press, 1988), 208n55. The wording implies serious repetitive drinking. In a healthy family, one episode of a father being drunk will be remembered with humor, a few with mounting apprehension, and many with scorn and contempt. Arguments that the degree of drinking would have been understated are the well-known tendency of the drinking individual and his family to minimize or hide the problem, compounded by the strong possibility of censored history by the Mormon church. Symptoms of alcoholism include hangovers, blackouts, interference with work, requests by others to desist, unsuccessful attempts to stop, drinking alone, hiding the alcohol, and, as with any addiction, continued behavior despite its destructive effects. In a personal communication with orthodox Mormon and Jungian analyst C. Jess Groesbeck, Mormon historian Marvin Hill commented that Joseph Sr.'s drinking was seldom talked about and may be one reason why he has been left in the shadows historically. Groesbeck opined that Joseph Sr. "habitually and chronically abused alcohol, which must have had a shattering effect on the family." That is a good definition of alcoholism. C. Jess Groesbeck, "The Smiths and Their Dreams and Visions," *Sunstone* 12 (Mar. 1988): 24. Indirect evidence for the father's drinking is Isaac Hale's observing Joseph Jr.'s "insolent and saucy" behavior toward his father, followed by sobbing relief when his father was baptized into Mormonism. Hale qtd. in E. D. Howe, *Mormonism Unvailed* (Painesville, OH:

Author, 1834), 263; Dean C. Jessee, "Joseph Knight's Recollection of Early Mormon History," *BYU Studies* 17 (Fall 1976), 37. Pomeroy Tucker, *The Origin, Rise, and Progress of Mormonism* (New York: D. Appleton & Co., 1867), 16, stated that the Smiths "were popularly regarded as an illiterate, whiskey-drinking, shiftless, irreligious race of people."

Dan Vogel, in a review of dysfunction in the Smith family, concurs that Joseph Sr. suffered from severe alcoholism and provides statements about his "intemperance" (along with other members of the Smith family) from neighbors David and Barton Stafford, and another eleven men. Quoting Howe's *Mormonism Unvailed*, 249-51, 262, and a reference fifty years later from Lorenzo Saunders as interviewed by William H. Kelley, 17 September 1884, E. L. Kelley Papers, RLDS Church Library-Archives, Independence, Missouri. See Dan Vogel, "Joseph Smith's Family Dynamics," Salt Lake Sunstone Symposium, August 1998, with agreement in response by psychiatrist C. Jess Groesbeck, audiocassette #SL98, 112, tape and paper in my possession. See other references in Dan Vogel, ed., *Early Mormon Documents* (Salt Lake City: Signature Books, 1996), 1:470n11, hereafter cited as Vogel, Lucy Smith History.

5. Lucy Smith, *Biographical Sketches of Joseph Smith, the Prophet, and His Progenitors for Many Generations* (Liverpool: S. W. Richards, 1853), 51. Not in the surviving preliminary manuscript, published as "Lucy Smith History, 1845," with extensive annotations and side-by-side comparison with the 1853 published version in Vogel, Lucy Smith History, 227-450.

6. Vogel, Lucy Smith History, 236-37.

7. Richard L. Anderson, *Joseph Smith's New England Heritage* (Salt Lake City: Deseret Book Co., 1971), 52-57.

8. Brodie, *No Man Knows My History*, 3.

9. Vogel, Lucy Smith History, 233-37.

10. Joseph Smith, Sr., Introductory Comments: Patriarchal Blessing book 1:1-2, Historical Department Archives, Church of Jesus Christ of Latter-day Saints, Salt Lake City, Utah (hereafter LDS Archives); "Copy of Don Carlos Smith's family record written by his own hand," ca. 1839-40, 7; Bushman, *Joseph Smith and the Beginnings of Mormonism*, 198n65.

11. Larry C. Porter, "A Study of the Origins of the Church of Jesus Christ of Latter-day Saints in the States of New York and Pennsylvania, 1816-1831," Ph.D. diss., Brigham Young University, 1971, 14; Vogel, Lucy Smith History, 242-43n33.

12. Vogel, Lucy Smith History, 236-38.

13. Ibid., 238-43. Lucy gives the birth date as 18 May 1803 (*Biographical Sketches*, 40); Tunbridge town records show 17 May.

14. Vogel, Lucy Smith History, 238-44.

15. Ibid., 243-47.

16. James Colin Brewster, *Very Important! To the Mormon Money Diggers* (Springfield, IL: Brewster, 1843), 2-4, quoted Joseph Smith, Sr., as saying in Ohio, sometime between 1831 and 1838: "I know more about money digging than any man in this generation, for I have been in the business more than thirty years." Qtd. in Jerald and Sandra Tanner, *Mormonism, Magic, and Masonry* (Salt Lake City: Utah Lighthouse Ministry, 1988), 19. Marvin S. Hill, "Money-Digging Folklore and the Beginnings of Mormonism: An Interpretive Suggestion," *BYU Studies* 24 (Fall 1984): 473-88, also uses Brewster's statement as an indication of Joseph Sr.'s long-standing interest in money-digging. Brewster had claimed to receive revela-

tions and once translated a lost book of the Bible. Joseph read his manuscript and stated the book was "not true" and that "God never gave revelations to that Brewster." *History of the Church*, 5:214-15. Brewster was disfellowshipped in 1837.

17. In this discussion, and in the history of magic in the next chapter, I have relied heavily on Quinn's *Early Mormonism and the Magic World View*. He discusses the magic-religious problem in his introduction but would probably agree only with the first paragraph in this summary of my position.

According to many Bible theologians, magic differs from religious miracles in three ways: its philosophy is unsophisticated with limited concepts of God and morality; the motive for magic is usually some immediate gain; and the results are guaranteed if the controlling rituals are performed accurately, i.e., the ritual compels God. Religious miracles, in contrast, usually result from moral behavior without guaranteed results despite correct performance of the ritual, emphasize the moral long-range intent of God, and are contained within a religious philosophy. In sum, the province of magic is to meet immediate goals without further moral obligations. If a believer in magic had "ethics," it was not for a moral position as part of a group, but because his or her religious "purification" increased the chances of accomplishing a successful ritual.

Yet some magic beliefs, such as voodoo in Haiti, *do* contain philosophical thinking. Furthermore, while most prudent magicians would not guarantee results, some aspects of religions do offer guarantees, such as the certainty, for the believer, that the wine and wafer of the Catholic mass become the body and blood of Christ and, within Mormonism, some of the temple ceremonies that are guaranteed except under exceptional circumstances.

In short, how does one distinguish between religious miracles and magic, symbolically represented by the miracle-producing phrase, "Hoc ist Corpus Meum" and its corrupted "magical" counterpart, "Hocus pocus"? For a concise summary, see John Dominic Crossan, *The Historical Jesus* (San Francisco: Harper Collins, 1991), 303-11, who, with other Bible historians, believes that the single decisive factor is that a miracle is performed within an established religion while magic is performed by fringe groups. This view establishes both Joseph Smith and Jesus in his day as magicians. The distinction lies not between the rituals or results, but between the orientation of the viewing groups.

As one historian has written, "'Jesus the magician' was the figure seen by most ancient opponents of Jesus; 'Jesus the Son of God' was the figure seen by that party of his followers which eventually triumphed; the real Jesus was the man whose words and actions gave rise to these contradictory interpretations. 'Jesus the Son of God' is pictured in the gospels; the works that pictured 'Jesus the magician' were destroyed in antiquity after Christians got control of the Roman empire. We know the lost works only from fragments and references, mostly in the works of Christian authors." Also: "Such private dealings with supernatural beings make up most of what we call 'magic' as well as what we call 'private religion.' There is no clear line between the two. ... For instance, spells for destruction of an enemy are commonly supposed to be magical, but there are many in the Psalms. The cliché, that the religious man petitions the gods while the magician tries to compel them, is simply false." See Morton Smith, *Jesus the Magician* (New York: Barnes and Noble, 1978), vii, 69, also 83-84, 91-92.

18. Peter French, *John Dee: The World of an Elizabethan Magus* (New York: Dorset Press, 1972).

19. Quinn, *Magic World View,* 1-26.

20. Ibid.; Keith Thomas, *Religion and the Decline of Magic* (New York: Charles Scribner's Sons, 1971), 253-79.

21. Thomas, *Religion and the Decline of Magic,* ix.

22. Ibid., 253-79; Quinn, *Magic World View,* 22-26.

23. Quinn, *Magic World View,* index entries under *scrying* and *peeper.*

24. Ibid., 27-122.

25. Hyrum was "rarely" involved in digging. Ibid., 58.

26. Ibid., 42-58; Vogel, Lucy Smith History, 285.

27. Quinn, *Magic World View,* 193-224.

28. Ibid., 38-40.

29. Vogel, Lucy Smith History, 253, and "Miscellaneous Document of Uncertain Origin," 646-47. Reference has already been made to Joseph Sr.'s 1834 patriarchal blessing to his son, Hyrum, and its allusion to his heavy drinking. Lorenzo Saunders, a Palmyra neighbor, remembered as an elderly man that, when he was a teenager, "the old man would go to turkey shoots and get tight." Lorenzo's brother, Orlando, reported seeing Joseph Smith, Sr., dressed in the "raggedest and dirtiest shirt and all full of holes." Quoted in Bushman, *Joseph Smith and the Beginnings of Mormonism,* 208n55, and Marvin S. Hill, *Quest for Refuge: The Mormon Flight from American Pluralism* (Salt Lake City: Signature Books, 1989), 190n5.

30. In a psychoanalytic review of an earlier draft of this work, anthropologist JoAnn Campbell of the University of Washington, in a personal communication, speculated that this dead infant was the incipient psychological origin for the angel Moroni/Nephi.

31. Porter, "A Study of the Origins of the Church of Jesus Christ," 25-26.

32. Vogel, Lucy Smith History, 259-60.

33. Joseph Smith "History" Book A-1, 131-32, LDS Archives, qtd. in Reed C. Durham, Jr., "Joseph Smith's Own Story of a Serious Childhood Illness," *BYU Studies* 10 (Summer 1970): 480-82, and in Dean C. Jessee, ed., *The Papers of Joseph Smith* (Salt Lake City: Deseret Book Co., 1989), 1:268n1.

34. The figure is surgeon Nathan Smith's estimate. LeRoy S. Wirthlin, "Nathan Smith (1762-1828), Surgical Consultant to Joseph Smith," *BYU Studies* 17 (Spring 1977): 326.

35. Vogel, Lucy Smith History, 262-63.

36. Jessee, *Papers of Joseph Smith,* 1:268n1; LeRoy S. Wirthlin, "Joseph Smith's Boyhood Operation: An 1813 Surgical Success," *BYU Studies* 21 (Spring 1981): 131-54.

37. Ibid., 263-65.

38. Morain, *Sword of Laban,* 19.

39. Wirthlin, "Nathan Smith," 319-35, and his "Joseph Smith's Boyhood Operation," 131-54. In these otherwise excellent reviews, Wirthlin does not discuss the possibility that the osteomyelitis was iatrogenic. Ten to fifteen years after operating on Joseph Smith, Nathan Smith published two works describing his surgical procedure: *Practical Essay on Typhous Fever* (New York: E. Bliss and E. White, 1824) and "Observations on the Pathology and Treatment of Necrosis," *Philadelphia Monthly Journal of Medicine and Surgery,* 1827, 11-19, 66-75.

40. Ibid., 263-69. Three sources exist about this surgical procedure. One is Nathan Smith's own professional writings, describing his treatment of osteomyelitis. The second is Lucy's preliminary manuscript, which the 1853 pub-

lished version follows without significant variation. The third is Joseph Smith's account, dictated when he was thirty-three and published in 1970 for the first time in Jessee, *Papers of Joseph Smith,* 1:268n1: "When I was five years old or thereabouts I was attacked with the Typhus [typhoid] Fever, and at one time, during my sickness, my father dispaired of my life. The doctors broke the fever, after which it settled under my shoulder, and Dr. Parker called it a sprained shoulder and anointed it with bone ointment, and freely applied the hot shovel, when it proved to be a swelling under the arm which was opened, and discharged freely, after which the disease removed and descended into my left leg and ancle and terminated in a fever sore of the worst kind, and I endured the most acute suffering for a long time under the care of Drs. Smith, Stone and Perkins, of Hanover. At one time eleven Doctors came from Dartmouth Medical College, at Hanover, New Hampshire, for the purpose of amputation, but, young as I was, I utterly refused to give my assent to the operation, but consented to their trying an experiment by removing a large portion of the bone from my left leg, which they did, and fourteen additional pieces of bone afterwards worked out before my leg healed, during which time I was reduced so very low that my mother could carry me with ease."

41. "Psychoanalytic case histories tended to emphasize certain dramatic incidents, certain grossly traumatic events—from the child's witnessing the 'primal scene' to the loss of a parent in childhood. But we have come to incline to the opinion that such traumatic events may be no more than clues that point to the truly pathogenic factors, the unwholesome atmosphere to which the child was exposed during the years when his self was established. Taken by themselves, in other words, these events leave fewer serious disturbances in their wake than the chronic ambience created by the deep-rooted attitudes of the self objects [parents], since even the still vulnerable self, in the process of formation, can cope with serious traumata if it is embedded in a healthily supportive milieu. The essence of the healthy matrix for the growing self of the child is a mature, cohesive parental self that is in tune with the changing needs of the child. ... Some parents, however, are not adequately sensitive to the needs of the child but will instead respond to the needs of their own insecurely established self." Heinz Kohut and Ernest S. Wolf, "The Disorders of the Self and Their Treatment: An Outline," *International Journal of Psycho-Analysis* 59 (1978): 417.

42. *Diagnostic and Statistical Manual of Mental Disorders,* 4th ed. (Washington, D.C.: American Psychiatric Association, 1994), 660 (hereafter DSM4).

43. Morain, *Sword of Laban,* 167-238, sees evidence of trauma from Joseph's surgery in his later sexual life and within the temple ceremonies.

44. See the discussion of Amalakiah in chapter 5.

45. Vogel, Lucy Smith History, 269.

46. Jesse's method of disagreeing with Joseph Sr.'s religious beliefs was to open the door of Lucy's home and "throw" in a copy of Thomas Paine's *The Age of Reason.* He forbade his visiting brother his house and threatened to put him out "with an axe." Vogel, Lucy Smith History, 250.

47. Vogel, Lucy Smith History, 268-69.

48. Ibid., 268-70.

49. Henry Stommel and Elizabeth Stommel, "The Year without a Summer," *Scientific American* 240 (June 1979): 180-81; "Volcano," Public Broadcasting System, *Nova,* 1990. The *Courier* report was shown close-up in the video.

50. In a letter referring to Joseph Sr.'s belief in magic, Jesse scornfully quoted Joseph Sr. as saying, "This is my god which brought me out of the land of Vermont." Jesse Smith, Letter to Hyrum Smith, 17 June 1829, Stockholm, New York, Hyrum Smith, Letterbook 2 (1837-43), 59, qtd. in Richard L. Anderson, "The Mature Joseph Smith and Treasure Seeking," *BYU Studies* 24 (Fall 1984): 526.

51. Vogel, Lucy Smith History, 270-75.

52. Joseph Smith, "History" Book A-1, 131-32, qtd. in Durham, "Joseph Smith's Own Story of a Serious Childhood Illness," 480-82; Jessee, *Papers of Joseph Smith,* 268n1.

53. Jessee, *Papers of Joseph Smith.*

54. Ibid.

55. H. Michael Marquardt and Wesley P. Walters, *Inventing Mormonism: Tradition and the Historical Record* (San Francisco: Smith Research Associates, 1994), 3-4. I follow their careful detective work on the Palmyra area homes of the Smith family.

56. Tucker, *Origin, Rise and Progress of Mormonism,* 12, 14.

57. Orsamus Turner, *History of the Pioneer Settlement of Phelps and Gorham's Purchase* (Rochester, NY: William Alling, 1851), 213-15, 400.

58. Vogel, Lucy Smith History, 276-77, 280.

59. Ibid., 286, 289; the first quotation is not in the preliminary manuscript, the second not in the 1853 published version.

60. Vogel, Lucy Smith History, 287, 323-24.

61. Quinn, *Magic World View,* 38-40.

62. Truman G. Madsen, *Joseph Smith the Prophet* (Salt Lake City: Bookcraft, 1989), 31, 144n60; Hill, *Quest for Refuge,* 196n16.

63. Marquardt and Walters, *Inventing Mormonism,* 4-6. The purchasing method seems typical for that time and place. Frequently the first payment was made over the first few months of the first year, the second on the first anniversary of the agreement, and the third at the end of two years. The seller may have required them to build a cabin, make other improvements, etc. The buyer paid the taxes during the purchase period. Lucy states, "In one year's time we made nearly all of the first payment. The Agent adivised us to build a log house on the land and commence clearing it, we did so. It was not long till we had 30 acres ready for cultivation." Vogel, Lucy Smith History, 277-78.

64. This quotation and most of the information in the discussion that follows, unless otherwise noted, are from Tucker, *Origin, Rise and Progress of Mormonism,* 12-18.

65. Marquardt and Walters, *Inventing Mormonism,* 3-8; Vogel, Lucy Smith History, 280n80. Richard L. Bushman argues that this second log cabin exists on paper only and was a result of an error in finding the township line in the middle of a woods. See his "Just the Facts Please," Review of *Inventing Mormonism,* in *Review of Books on the Book of Mormon* 6 (1994): 122-33. Possibly they may have moved the cabin log by log onto "their" property; but this solution seems unlikely since Peter Ingersoll moved onto the Jennings property in 1822 and most likely used the cabin in which the Smiths had first lived. Dan Vogel, personal communication, 1996.

66. William Smith, Joseph's younger brother, describes it as "mostly done in the form of fire." "Notes Written on 'Chamber's Life of Joseph Smith,' by William

Smith," about 1875, typescript, 20, LDS Archives, qtd. by Marquardt and Walters, *Inventing Mormonism,* 13n24.

67. Vogel, Lucy Smith History, 280; Marquardt and Walters, *Inventing Mormonism,* 6.

68. Tucker, *Origin, Rise and Progress of Mormonism,* 14-15.

69. Ibid., 13.

70. Ibid., 15.

71. Vogel, Lucy Smith History, 284-85, n82.

72. For example, David Stafford stated that Joseph Smith, Sr., was a "drunkard and a liar ... and his boys were truly a lazy set of fellows. ... It was well known, that the general employment of the Smith family was money digging and fortune-telling." Barton Stafford testified that "Joseph Smith, Sen. was a noted drunkard, and most of the family followed his example" and gave an example of drunkenness in Joseph Smith Jr. G. W. Stoddard and Richard H. Ford testified, "The Smith family never made any pretentions to respectability," and fifty signed the statement describing that the family as "destitute of that moral character, which ought to entitle them to the confidence of any community. They were particularly famous for visionary projects, spent much of their time in digging for money which they pretended was hid in the earth; and to this day, large excavations may be seen in the earth, not far from their residence, where they used to spend their time in digging for hidden treasures." Eleven men said they "were not only a lazy, indolent set of men, but also intemperate; and their word was not to be depended upon." See Howe, *Mormonism Unvailed,* 249, 250-51, 261-62. Defense by the Mormon faithful against these testimonies may be found in Richard L. Anderson, "Joseph Smith's New York Reputation Reappraised," *BYU Studies* 10 (Spring 1970): 283-314; Anderson, "Reliability of the Early History of Lucy and Joseph Smith," *Dialogue: A Journal of Mormon Thought* 4 (Summer 1969): 13-28, while affirmation of these statements may be found in Rodger I. Anderson, *Joseph Smith's New York Reputation Reexamined* (Salt Lake City: Signature Books, 1990).

73. Tucker, *Origin, Rise and Progress of Mormonism,* 13.

74. Vogel, Lucy Smith History, 284-85.

75. "The improvements made on this farm was first commenced by building a log house at no small expense, and at a later date a frame house at a cost of several hundred dollars." From "Notes Written on 'Chamber's Life of Joseph Smith,' by William Smith," about 1875, typescript, 17, in Marquardt and Walters, *Inventing Mormonism,* 13. See also Anderson, "Joseph Smith's New York Reputation Reappraised," 314.

76. Andrew Jenson and Edward Stevenson, *Infancy of the Church: A Series of Letters* (Salt Lake City: n.pub., 1889), 39.

77. Tucker, *The Origin, Rise and Progress of Mormonism,* 16-17.

78. Howe, *Mormonism Unvailed,* 231-71.

79. Groesbeck, "Smiths and Dreams and Visions," 24.

80. Joseph Smith, Jr., et al., *History of the Church of Jesus Christ of Latter-day Saints,* ed. B. H. Roberts, 7 vols., 2d ed. rev. (Salt Lake City: Deseret Book, 1948 printing), 2:343; Dan Vogel, "Joseph Smith's Family Dynamics," July 1998, Sunstone Symposium, Salt Lake City; copy in my possession.

81. Tucker, *Origin, Rise and Progress of Mormonism,* 17.

82. Ibid., 17-18.

83. Jessee, *Papers of Joseph Smith,* 1:5; Scott H. Faulring, ed., *An American*

Prophet's Records: The Diaries and Journals of Joseph Smith (Salt Lake City: Signature Books in association with Smith Research Associates, 1989), 4.

84. Turner, *History of the Pioneer Settlement,* 213-14.

85. Joseph's age at the time is deduced from the date when the Methodists purchased the property in the woods on the Vienna Road (July 1821; Deeds of Ontario Co., Bk. G345), and the fact that Turner left Palmyra in 1822. See Wesley P. Walters, "A Reply to Dr. Bushman," *Dialogue: A Journal of Mormon Thought* 4 (Spring 1969): 99.

86. Jessee, *Papers of Joseph Smith,* 1:5.

87. Quinn, *Magic World View,* 38-39, 41, 47, 59-62, 65-72, 123, 192-224, provides extensive documentation. Although many of the reports of Joseph's money-digging activities speak in generalities, they paint a picture of episodes dating from 1819 to 1826 during which at least eighteen separate money-digging attempts can be identified. After the founding of the Mormon church, Joseph Smith began to understate his past activities in magic. In the July 1838 issue of the *Elders' Journal,* he answered frequently asked questions. One was whether he was a money-digger. He responded, "Yes, but it was never a very profitable job to him, as he only got fourteen dollars a month for it." Qtd. in ibid., 50. Five extensively documented papers written from an orthodox and traditional perspective discussing magic in early Mormonism were published in *BYU Studies* 24 (Fall 1984): Dean C. Jessee, "New Documents and Mormon Beginnings," 397-428; Ronald W. Walker, "The Persisting Idea of American Treasure Hunting," 429-60; Ronald W. Walker, "Joseph Smith: 'The Palmyra Seer,'" 461-72; Marvin S. Hill, "Money-Digging Folklore and the Beginnings of Mormonism: An Interpretive Suggestion," 473-89; Richard L. Anderson, "The Mature Joseph Smith and Treasure Searching," 489-558. Wilford Woodruff, fourth president of the church, commented that Joseph Smith found a "seer stone ... by revelation some 30 feet under the earth" which he "carried ... through life." Journal, 18 May 1888, as quoted in Quinn, *Early Magic World View,* 148; see also Reed C. Durham, "Is There No Help for the Widow's Son?" presidential address, Mormon History Association, 20 Apr. 1974, and Jack Adamson, "The Treasure of the Widow's Son," both papers published by Martin Publishing Co., Nauvoo, Illinois, in 1980. Paul Hedengren, *In Defense of Faith: Assessing Arguments Against Latter-day Saint Belief* (Provo, UT: Bradford and Wilson, 1985), 178; Linda Sillitoe and Allen Roberts, *Salamander: The Story of the Mormon Forgery Murders* (Salt Lake City: Signature Books, 1988); Steven Naifeh and Gregory White Smith, *The Mormon Murders* (New York: Werdenfeld & Nicolson, 1988). Dan Vogel, "The Location of Joseph Smith's Early Treasure Quests," *Dialogue: A Journal of Mormon Thought* 27 (Fall 1994): 197-231, reports exploring eighteen different sites of his treasure seeking and the evidence of money-digging that still remains. Rodger I. Anderson, *Joseph Smith's New York Reputation Reexamined,* documents twenty-seven accounts of magical money-digging by the Smiths, half of which involved young Joseph.

88. Vogel, Lucy Smith History, 255-59, 278-79, 283-84, 287; Groesbeck, "Smiths and Dreams and Visions," 22-29.

89. Quinn, *Magic World View,* 33-52, summarizes Joseph's magical activities during the 1820s.

90. Howe, *Mormonism Unvailed,* 267; F. Lapham, "Interview with the Father of Joseph Smith, the Mormon Prophet, Forty Years Ago. His Account of the Finding of the Sacred Plates," *Historical Magazine ... of America,* 7, 2nd series (Morri-

sania, NY: Henry B. Dawson, 1870), reprinted in Francis W. Kirkham, *A New Witness for Christ in America* (Independence, MO: Zion's Printing and Publishing Co., 1970), 2:387, 383-91; Brett L. Holbrook, "The Sword of Laban as a Symbol of Divine Authority and Kingship" (Provo, UT: FARMS, 1993), 2:1, 39-72, esp. 59-72. These testimonies include one from Harmony, Pennsylvania, one with Joseph's father in Manchester, one from a sister, from the three witnesses to the Book of Mormon, and others. Others believed he still had the sword later in his life. The belief that the story of Laban and his sword was created to deal with the surgery is also the belief of RLDS surgeon William D. Morain, as discussed throughout his *Sword of Laban.*

91. Arnold M. Cooper, "Narcissism," in Andrew P. Morrison, ed., *Essential Papers on Narcissism* (New York: New York University Press, 1986), 139-40; see also 132-33.

92. "301.81 Narcissistic Personality Disorder," DSM4, 658-59.

93. Traditional scholars also assume that Laban is a relative. See Hugh Nibley, *Lehi in the Desert: The World of the Jaredites,* in *The Collected Works of Hugh Nibley,* ed. John W. Welch (Salt Lake City: Deseret Book Co., 1988), 5, 35ff.; and John L. Sorenson, "The Composition of Lehi's Family," in John M. Lundquist and Stephen D. Ricks, eds., *By Study and Also by Faith* (Salt Lake City: Deseret Book Co., 1990), 2:174-96. Sorenson speculates that the implausibly large population of Lehite descendants might be explained by conjecturing that Lehi's group contained many unmentioned servants and their families, although he finds such a hypothesis unlikely. He also proposes, but finds unlikely, the idea that Lehi had plural wives, since the only named or mentioned wife, Sariah, seems unlikely to be the mother of the four older sons, two younger sons born in the wilderness, and at least two otherwise unmentioned daughters, given their speculated age spread and conditions of longevity and reproductive years at the time. Ibid., 179-85. From a psychological view, I wonder if these Mormon scholars aren't sensing and trying to account for the real (Smith) family behind the fantasy.

94. Polygamy and deceit about polygamy are two prominent examples. At the same time he was breaking the laws of the states in which the Mormons resided, he was insisting that monogamy was the rule and practice of the church. See Richard S. Van Wagoner, *Mormon Polygamy: A History* (Salt Lake City: Signature Books, 1986), iii-69; Linda King Newell and Valeen Tippetts Avery, *Mormon Enigma: Emma Hale Smith, Prophet's Wife, "Elect Lady," Polygamy's Foe, 1804-1879* (Garden City, NY: Doubleday, 1984), 95-156.

95. Perhaps the most striking example is his later attack on his wife when he accused her of being "a child of hell and literally the most wicked woman on this earth." He also accused her of trying to poison him. Newell and Avery, *Mormon Enigma,* 164; see also 157-64.

96. History provides evidence that Smith's desire for power and control became extreme toward the end of his life. He formed, or at least sanctioned the activities of, a secret "Danite" band which used intimidation and threats to enforce compliance, then organized the secret Council of Fifty to set up the political kingdom of God, and had himself secretly crowned king by this group. Klaus J. Hansen, *Quest for Empire: The Political Kingdom of God and the Council of Fifty in Mormon History* (East Lansing: Michigan State University Press, 1970), 72-179.

97. Lorenzo Saunders, Unpublished manuscript taken at Reading, Michigan,

20 Sept. 1884, Library-Archives, Reorganized Church of Jesus Christ of Latter Day Saints, Independence, Missouri.

98. Riley, *Founder of Mormonism,* 26, 114-17. See also Prince, "Psychological Tests," 375; Brodie, *No Man Knows My History,* 58.

99. See Bushman, *Joseph Smith and the Beginnings of Mormonism,* 50, 204n.

100. Brodie, *No Man Knows My History,* 58-60.

101. Inconsistently, this plan did not work out. Ishmael's sons stayed with Laman and Lemuel, thus becoming enemies (BM 271; Alma 17:19). Ishmael's descendants, whom I suggest represent Isaac Hale's extended family, thus become a major element in Joseph's fantasy conquest of them that occupies so large a section of the Book of Mormon.

102. Sorenson, "Composition," 194-95; B. H. Roberts, *Studies of the Book of Mormon* (Urbana: University of Illinois Press, 1985), 259.

103. Howe, *Mormonism Unvailed,* 46; Roberts, *Studies of the Book of Mormon,* 259-62.

104. Vogel, "The Location of Joseph Smith's Early Treasure Quests."

105. Brigham Young, address to a special conference, Farmington, Utah, 17 June 1877, *Journal of Discourses,* 26 vols. (London and Liverpool: LDS Booksellers Depot, 1855-86), 19:38-39.

CHAPTER 3

Joseph Grows Up: Nephi and Jesus

From a psychoanalytic perspective, Joseph Smith's "first story" in 1-2 Nephi establishes the themes that dominate his psychological task of dealing with real-life misfortunes through fantasies of reversal and exaggerated compensation. From them, as a psychiatrist, I can anticipate hearing repeated versions of four brothers, one a leader (or four brothers and a leader), wine and swords that will introduce us to various disguised versions of his surgery, and an arduous and disruptive relocation. I can also begin looking for these same psychological coping mechanisms throughout his life as he deals with his socially inferior and disadvantaged family. In these Book of Mormon stories, the heroes are Joseph Smith's alter egos; other people from his real life are diminished or presented as evil. I hypothesize that Smith's motive is to gain power over people and reverse his childhood helplessness, particularly during his surgery. Later narratives in the Book of Mormon will provide reasons for embellishing, reinforcing, diminishing, modifying, or retracting these initial views.

I believe that the application of psychoanalytical theory to Smith's autobiography and to the Book of Mormon narratives in chapter 2 provides persuasive reasons for seeing the Book of Mormon as a disguised version of Smith's life. This conclusion is what we should expect, according to the general experience of applied psychoanalysis. But the narrative's secondary themes also merit attention. For example, the story of Lehi's family wandering in the wilderness echoes the exodus from Egypt of the children of Israel and their wandering, under Moses' guidance, in the Sinai desert for forty years.[1] Biblical motifs and events recur throughout the Book of Mormon. But I argue that Smith also braids into his book concepts from his readings and from local and national current events. This ability to integrate past, present, personal, local, national, and global events will be a major aspect of his religious genius.

I have tried to show how, in the first story in the Book of Mormon, Smith relates an abbreviated story of his life until his mid-teens, with emphasis on his childhood—his surgery when he was between five and seven, and the humiliating family migration from Vermont to New York when he was about ten. He mentions only briefly later events such as his marriage and the construction of the family homes. Throughout the Book of Mormon he tells and retells various events from his life, but the clearest, most concise, and chronologically exact review of his adolescence and early adulthood to age twenty-four (when he began dictating the present version of the Book of Mormon to Oliver Cowdery) is 3 Nephi. Believers consider this book the most important and sacred of the Book of Mormon narratives, for it recounts the spectacular visit of the resurrected Jesus to the American continent.

This chapter first describes Smith's life to age twenty-four. Then it summarizes the story of Nephi, a descendent and namesake of the first Nephi, with emphasis on the psychological parallels between the two accounts that will help build a cohesive assessment of Joseph Smith.

Splitting as Joseph Smith's Primary Psychological Defense in the Book of Mormon

The world of the Book of Mormon is dyadic: good/bad; white/black. Most psychologists agree that such polarization characterizes the child's earliest forms of thinking:

> This division of internalized object relations [i.e., people and things] into "good" and "bad" happens at first simply because of the lack of integrative capacity of the early ego ... [and later] is used defensively by the emerging ego in order to prevent the generalization of anxiety ... by [the] ... maintaining apart of mental images of these important people which contain conflicted feelings and ideas.
>
> This defensive division of the ego, in which what was at first a simple defect in integration is then used actively for other purposes [and] is in essence the mechanism of splitting. This mechanism is normally used only in an early stage of ego development during the first year of life and rapidly is replaced by higher defensive operations of the ego which center around repression and related mechanisms such as reaction formation, isolation, and undoing. ... In contrast, in pathological conditions ... this mechanism ... persists. ...
>
> Under these pathological circumstances, contradictory ego states are alternately activated; and so long as these contradictory ego states can be kept separate from each other, anxiety is prevented. Such a state of affairs is, of course, very detrimental ... and underlies the syndrome of identity diffusion.[2]

Judging people and events in these simple polarized opposites is a stage we all pass through; in attenuated form, it exists even in normal healthy adults. Usually it is relegated to the artistic part of life or emerges in creative regression. It is found in comic strips, some plays, paintings, opera, and especially movies. It is found in adult narcissistic personalities and also in fundamentalistic religions which divide the world into "us"/"them," good/bad, saved/unsaved. The Book of Mormon presents this polarized world with its division of people into "righteous" and "evil."

Nephites are white and Lamanites black (red); the Nephites tend to slip rapidly from unusually good to unusually bad. It is instructive, I believe, that Joseph Smith about fifteen years later manifested more complex thinking and articulated a view of heaven with multiple gradations (D&C 76).

For example, Nephi the son of Lehi described his vision of Joseph Smith's world. In it, Roman Catholicism, as seen through the eyes of nineteenth-century Protestantism, was a completely evil organization:

> I saw among the nations of the Gentiles, the foundation of a great church. ... which is most abominable above all other churches, which slayeth the Saints of God. ... and I saw the devil, that he was the founder of it. And I also saw gold, and silver, and silks, and scarlets, and fine twined linen, and all manner of precious clothing; and I saw many harlots. ... and also for the praise of the world do they destroy the Saints of God, and also bring them down into captivity. (BM 28-29; 1 Ne. 13:4-9)

This "abominable" church corrupted the Bible, according to the Book of Mormon, censoring and altering the scriptures until "an exceeding great many [people] do stumble, yea insomuch that Satan hath great power over them" (BM 30; 1 Ne. 13:20-29). The Book of Mormon text makes it clear that there are only two churches:

> And [the angel] saith unto me, Look. ... Behold, there is save it be, two churches: the one is the church of the Devil; wherefore, whoso belongeth not to the church of the Lamb of God, belongeth to that great church, which is the mother of abominations; and she is the whore of all the earth. ...
>
> And ... I beheld the church of the lamb of God, and its numbers were few, because of the wickedness and abominations of the whore. (BM 33; 1 Ne. 14:9-12)

Smith canonized this polarity into a religious philosophy. Lehi, in a sermon to his son Jacob, described how all would come before God to be judged, receiving the punishment affixed to their sinfulness:

> which punishment that is affixed is in opposition to that of the happiness which is affixed, to answer the ends of the atonement; for it must needs be, that there is an opposition in all things. ... [wherefore] ... even the forbidden fruit in opposition to the tree of life; the one being sweet and the other bitter; wherefore, the Lord God gave unto man, that he should act for himself. Wherefore, man could not act for himself, save it should be that he were enticed by the one or the other. (BM 63-64; 2 Ne. 2:10-16)

From a psychoanalytic perspective, seeing an "opposition in all things" requires wrenching the world into polarized images. Only occasionally do healthy people feel such tension.

I believe that splitting—or actively keeping apart identifications, internal mental images, conflicted feelings, and memories that are part of the child's personality—underlies all other psychological defenses for Joseph

Smith. When splitting becomes a permanent, major defense past early childhood, it is

> a fundamental cause of ego weakness. ... The direct clinical manifestation of splitting may be the alternative expression of complementary sides of a conflict in certain character disorders, combined with a bland denial and lack of concern over the contradiction in his behavior and internal experience. ... [But] probably the best known manifestation of splitting is the division of external objects [such as individuals or churches] into "all good" ones and "all bad" ones, with the concomitant possibility of complete, abrupt shifts of an object from one extreme compartment to the other; that is, sudden and complete reversals of all feelings and conceptualizations about a particular person.[3]

Delusion and Deception in Joseph Smith's Adolescence

As we have seen, Joseph Smith grew up in a family that experienced significant relationship problems and financial difficulties. He accepted his father's dreams as religious visions and participated with his father, brothers Alvin and sometimes Hyrum, and neighbors in money-digging and other magic practices. He himself used both a divining rod and seer stone. To deal with the inevitable failure, the participant must fuse self-deception with deception of others. In other words, convincing others reinforces one's own belief and substitutes for objective evidence. Group belief is necessary.[4] According to contemporary accounts, Joseph Jr. began using a divining rod for money-digging at about age thirteen or fourteen; before age seventeen, he became a seer searching for treasure.[5] (See chapter 2.) I take the position that the line between "magic" and "miracle" was a blurred one for the adolescent Joseph. His account of a visit from the angel and his discovery of the buried gold records have elements of both: it is a semi-magical and also semi-Christian miracle. This event is disguised in a Book of Mormon narrative.

ABSENCE OF THE FIRST VISION IN THE BOOK OF MORMON

Significantly, the Book of Mormon does not contain a version of Smith's first vision of God and Jesus, except, perhaps, in an embryonic and undifferentiated form (BM 519; Mormon 1:15) that I will discuss in chapter 7 as an example of follower enhancement. The reason, I argue, is that the story, as we have it, at least, did not exist until after the publication of the Book of Mormon. In the now-canonized version of that first vision, written in 1838 when he was thirty-three, Smith describes his turmoil during a local revival because of competition among the various religions. When he prayed to know which church to join, God and Jesus appeared to him, condemned all Christianity, told him to join "none of them," and implied he would be the means of restoring the original Church of Christ as it had existed in the days of the apostles. Although Smith dates this revival in the spring of 1820 when he was fourteen, no known revival occurred in Palmyra between 1818 and 1823, especially not one that caused the kind of furor Smith describes. The revival which matches his description occurred in 1824-25 (he turned nineteen in December 1824) and is confirmed in the Protestant church records, town newspapers, and personal memoirs. Thus Joseph moved the revival back in time four years.[6] Until Smith wrote about this experience in his late twenties, the story apparently did not exist. The most vigorous search by the most devout Mormon historians produces the same conclusion. No one—not family, friends, or enemies—knew this story. In personal writings and conversations, Smith began to develop his first vision story which makes its first written appearance in 1832, again in 1835, and finally in 1838. All three surviving versions give him a different age at the time of the vision, assign different purposes in praying, and at least partially disagree on the preliminary supernatural experiences leading up to the vision, the number of heavenly visitors, and their identity.[7]

ROLE OF THE ANGEL/GUARDIAN SPIRIT

The first official first vision account was a rambling and lengthy version written by Oliver Cowdery in association with Joseph Smith and published in the first church newspaper, the *Messenger and Advocate* in 1834.[8] Smith prayed in 1823 "for ... the all important information, if a Supreme being did exist, [and] to have an assurance that he was accepted of him." In response, the angelic guardian of the buried gold book visited him. Earlier unofficial versions (both friendly and unfriendly) place this story in the context of money-digging and magic. Lucy Smith also introduces the story of the angel in the context of magic, a context that was silently edited from all published versions until 1996:

> I shall change my theme for the present but let not my reader suppose that because I shall pursue another topic for a season that we stopt our labor and went at trying to win the faculty of Abrac drawing Magic circles or sooth saying to the neglect of all kinds of business we never during lives suffered one important interest to swallow up every other obligation but whilst we worked with our hands we endeavored to remember the service of & the welfare of our souls.[9]

Lucy thus defends her family against accusations of laziness but shows no discomfort in revealing the family's ongoing involvement with magic practices.

Mormon historian D. Michael Quinn and others have reconstructed the earliest contours of the story about the angel and the buried gold records within a magical context.[10] Seeking forgiveness for his sins, Smith prayed at about 11:00 p.m. on Sunday, 21 September 1823, the night of the autumn equinox and a full moon. Although he does not quote his prayer or suggest accompanying rituals, I argue that the act of praying on that date was itself ritualistic. In addition to the significance of the full moon and the equinox, Sunday was the only night of the week ruled by Jupiter, Smith's ruling planet. In response a dead man, guardian of a treasure book which he had buried, appeared to Smith and repeated his instructions three times, a number with magic significance, without the least variation. The first published newspaper references and early Mormon leaders equated these events to a thrice-repeated dream.[11] A close Mormon friend who became Smith's financial backer said Smith had, earlier that evening, been seer to a group of money-diggers.[12]

According to his canonized account, Smith reported in 1838 that, when he went to the hill on Monday, "owing to the distinctness of vision which I had concerning it, I knew the place the instant I arrived there." However, contemporary witnesses, both Mormon and non-Mormon, remembered that Smith said he used his seer stone to find the gold plates.[13]

Smith's earliest version of this encounter with the angel was recorded in 1832 (but not published until the late 1960s):

> It was on the 22nd day of September AD 1822 [1823]. Thus [the angel] appeared to me three times in one night and once on the next day. Then I immediately went to the place and found where the plates was deposited as the angel of the Lord had commanded me and straightway made three attempts to get them. Then being exceedingly frightened I suppose it had been a dreem of Vision, but when I consid[e]red I knew that it was not. Therefore I cried unto the Lord in the angony of my soul, "Why can I not obtain them?"
>
> Behold the angel appeared unto me again and said unto me, "You have not kept the commandments of the Lord which I gave unto you. Therefore you cannot now obtain them for the time is not yet fulfilled. Therefore thou wast left unto temptation that thou mightest be made acquainted with the power of the Lord [and] thou shalt be forgiven. And in his own due time thou shalt obtain them."
>
> For now I had been tempted of the advisary and saught the Plates to obtain riches and kept not the commandment that I should have an eye single to the glory of God. Therefore I was chastened.[14]

In the 1835 and 1838 accounts, Quinn summarizes that Smith removed four elements from this 1832 version suggesting a magic context. (1) Smith made three attempts to pull the book out of the box but could not. (2) He was "exceedingly frightened," not just "afraid" (1838 version).[15] (3) The angel rebuked him for disobedience without specifying how he was disobedient. (4) He acknowledged that he could see the plates as a source of income. In comparison, the canonized 1838 version dropped these details and any sense of his dialogue with the angel:

> On the west side of this hill [Cumorah] not far from the top, under a stone of considerable size, lay the plates deposited in a stone box[.] This

stone was thick and rounding in the middle on the upper side, and thinner toward the edges, so that the middle part of it was visible above the ground. ... Having removed the earth and obtained a lever which I got fixed under the edge of the stone ... I looked in, and there indeed did I behold the plates, the Urim and Thummin, and the Breastplate as stated by the messenger[.] The box in which they lay was formed by laying stones together in some kind of cement. ... I made an attempt to take them out, but was forbidden by the messenger, and was again informed that the time [for] bringing them forth had not yet arrived, neither would it, until four years from that time, but he told me that I should come to that place precisely in one year from that time, and that he would there meet with me, and that I should continue to do so until the time should come for obtaining the plates.[16]

Two non-Mormon neighbors, one friendly and one unfriendly, left accounts many years later that explain why Smith described himself in the early draft of his experience as "exceedingly frightened" of the angel. Both men say that, along with the plates in the box, Smith saw something "like a toad," which then transformed itself into the angel. According to one of the accounts, this being struck Smith on the side of the head. Such stories were a common part of the magic tradition.[17]

Both Lucy Mack Smith and Joseph Knight, a devoted friend in his late fifties and later a Mormon himself, also give versions of the angel story. Both leave in details which Smith later removed. They also suggest why he was unable to get the plates. He had been commanded not to let the plates out of his hands; when he set them down to look for "something else" in the box, thus violating the precise instructions, the plates vanished. Lucy described the problem:

He vis[i]ted the place where the plates were laid and thinking he could keep every commandment given him supposed that it would be possible for him to take them from their place and carry them home. But said the divine messenger you must take them into your hands and go straight to the house without delay. ... Accordingly ... he went to the place appointed. ... He put forth his hand and took them up but when he lifted them from their place the thought flashed across his mind that there might be something more in the box that would be a benefit to him in a pecuniary point of view. ... He laid the record down in order to cover up the box least some one should come along. ... When he turned again to take up the record it was gone. ... He was much alarmed at this. He asked the Lord why. ... The angel appeared to him and told him that he had not done as he was commanded in that he laid down the record in order to secure some imaginary treasure that remained. ... After some further conversation Joseph was permitted to raise the stone again and there he beheld the plates the same as before. He reached forth his hand to take them but was thrown to the ground. ... He arose and went to the house.[18]

Joseph Knight adds a critical detail:

He oncovered it [the box in the ground] and found the Book and took it out and laid [it] Down By his side and thot he would Cover the place over again

> thinkin[g] there might be something else here. But he was told to take the Book and go right away. And after he had Covered the place he turned round to take the Book and it was not there and he was astonished that the Book was gone. He thot he would look in the place again and see if it had not got Back again. He had heard people tell of such things. And he opened the Box and Behold the Book was there. He took hold of it to take it out again and Behold he Could not stur the Book any more then he Could the mountin. He exclaimed "why Cant I stur this Book?" And he was answerd, "you have not Done rite; you should have took the Book and a gone right away. You cant have it now." Joseph says, "when can I have it?" The answer was the 22nd Date of September next if you Bring the right person with you. Joseph says, "who is the right person?" The answer was "your oldest Brother."[19]

This ritual struggle is a familiar theme in other stories from Smith's period about obtaining buried treasures by magical means. Other unfriendly accounts agree with Knight. Smith was to return in one year with his "serious and industrious" brother Alvin.[20]

A couple of observations are important at this point. First, it is my professional opinion that the story of a guardian angel protecting a gold record began as a fantasy in Smith's mind but, reinforced by the belief of his family and followers, it increasingly became a psychological reality to him. Second, in the 1838 canonized account the angel is different from the 1832 crafty guardian spirit who made such strange exactions. Even the first official printed version of this story, written by Oliver Cowdery and published in 1834, describes a brilliant angel circled in nonconsuming fire who quotes Old Testament scripture and tells Smith about the record of ancient America.[21] Earlier versions of the angel/guardian, many from unfriendly and retrospective sources, are less biblical. The angel/guardian is described variously as a "little old man with a long beard," a "large, tall man dressed in an ancient suit of clothes covered with blood," a "Spaniard ... with his throat cut," a plainly dressed Quaker, "the spirit of one of the Saints that was on this continent ... previous to Columbus, and finally an angel."[22]

The traditional orthodox position is that the speakers were probably motivated by malice or were passing on much-changed hearsay. This explanation may be true or partially true; however, Smith himself, as we have seen, also gave various versions of the story and gave the angel/guardian spirit two different identities. In the manuscript of his official history (1838) and printed version (1842, published under his review) and again in 1851 (after his death), the name of the angel was Nephi—the first major prophet in the Book of Mormon. That is what his mother said in 1844 as well; so did Mary Musser Whitmer, mother of five of the Book of Mormon's eleven official witnesses. Meanwhile, in 1832, and also in 1838 (in the *Elder's Journal*), Smith called the angel Moroni, the last prophet in the book. The official version now names only Moroni; it is Moroni, not Nephi, who trumpets from atop Mormon temples around the world, and the book he holds is presumed to be the Book of Mormon.[23] Not only did Smith relate various versions of the angel story, but they progressively reduce the magic context for the angel's first interactions with him.

THE DEATH OF ALVIN SMITH

The guardian spirit assigned an important role to Alvin Smith as a necessary companion before Joseph could receive the book. Only two months afterwards, however, Alvin became ill. The family's usual physician was away and the physician from the next town gave Alvin calomel (mercurous chloride), a toxin frequently used as a purgative. Alvin died after four agonizing days. An autopsy discovered the calomel untouched in the upper bowel, surrounded by gangrene. The doctors performing the autopsy were distressed at the medical misjudgment of a "careless quack."[24] This episode was the second negative experience with physicians. A doctor had been unable to help Sophronia during the typhoid epidemic and then may have caused Joseph's leg infection; in three successive operations, he and others inflicted excruciating pain on Joseph. Now another doctor had killed Alvin, and still others had mutilated his body. During the funeral service, Presbyterian minister Benjamin Stockton implied that Alvin would go to hell because he had not joined the church. This sermon distressed all of the family and irrevocably alienated Joseph Sr. from the Presbyterians.[25]

Even given the tendency to glorify the dead, Alvin seems to have been remarkably responsible and decent. Singlehanded, he made the second payment on their land and home. Now a third payment was coming due, and the guardian angel had designated him as Joseph's companion to receive the records, yet he had died—suddenly and unnecessarily. It was a heavy blow for the family.[26]

Psychologically speaking, it is probable that Alvin's death at the hands of a physician stirred feelings and memories of Joseph's earlier surgery. These two episodes are, in my opinion, combined, expressed, and narrated in a variety of ways in the Book of Mormon. Alvin's death altered Joseph's position within the family. I see his parents passing over Hyrum to give him a central place. Unlike Alvin, he had survived the attack by physicians and he was now emerging as a seer. Both factors together suggested that he had unusual powers or that God was taking a personal interest in him. Lucy's history shows that it was Joseph Jr., not Joseph Sr., who took the dominant place in family evenings at the fireside:

> From this time forth Joseph continued to receive instructions from time to time and every evening we gathered our children together[.] I think that we presented the most peculiar aspect of any family that ever lived upon the Earth all seated in a circle[,] father[,] Mother[,] sons and Daughters listening in breathless anxiety to the religious teachings of a boy 16 y[e]ars of age who

> had never read the Bible through by course in his life for Joseph was less inclined to the study of books than any child we had but much more given to reflection and deep study[.]
>
> In the course of our evening conversations Joseph would give us some of the most amusing recitals which could be immagined[.] he would describe the ancient inhabitants of this continent[,] their dress[,] their maner of traveling[,] the animals which they rode[,] The cities that were built by them[,] the structure of their warfare[,] their religious worship as particularly as though he had spent his life with them[.][27]

Thus the Smith family was nurturing young Joseph's claims to be a person with supernatural powers, and Joseph had opportunity to develop the stories later to be found in the Book of Mormon.

THE PALMYRA REVIVALS OF 1824-25

After Alvin's death in November 1823, the religious revivals began that Smith would later date to 1820. Lucy's manuscript biography confirms that the revivals came after, not before, Alvin's death and provides some information concerning the Smith family's participation:

> when Joseph spoke of the [buried gold] record it would immediately bring Alvin to our minds ... [and] we all wept ... and we could not be comforted[.]
>
> About this time their was a great revival in religion and the whole neighborhood was very much aroused to the subject and we among the rest flocked to the meeting house to see if their was a word of comfort for us that might relieve our overcharged feelings but as there was at this time a man there laboring in that place to effect a union of all the churches that all denominations might be agreed to worship god with one mind and one heart.[28]

Again and again in the Book of Mormon, disguised versions of the revival follow immediately after a good man meets an untimely end at the hands of evildoers. It becomes an important motif to add to those already established in the Book of Mormon stories.

The revival commenced near Palmyra in the early spring of 1824, four or five months after Alvin's death, and continued with moderate enthusiasm until September under the direction of Presbyterian minister Benjamin Stockton, who had so offended Joseph Sr. at Alvin's funeral. Methodist revivalist George Lane had the reputation for being a man of good "gifts," much "grace," and "usefulness."[29] He arrived on 25 September 1824, and the intensity of the revival picked up dramatically. Lane left the area on 22 December (by which time 150 had converted), but the revival continued into the first three months of 1825, and by March nearly 400 had been converted. It was truly a local phenomenon, for over 400 people converted to the Baptists, Methodists, or Presbyterians by September 1825 from a town of 3,500.[30] Apparently the contrast in Lane's and Stockton's preaching styles made them an effective team. Book of Mormon revivals will feature

Table 1
Joseph Smith's Early Years: A Chronology

Economic	*Social/Religious*	*Year*	*Family Complications*
Working farm	Lucy receives $1,000 gift	1796	January, marriage of Lucy/Joseph
Working farm		1797	(Possible premature birth/death)
Working farm		1798	February, Alvin born
Working farm		1799	
Working farm		1800	February, Hyrum born
Working farm		1801	
Working farm	Lucy depressed, ?1802 or 1803	1802	
Move to Randolph	Move to Randolph, bankruptcy	1803	May, Sophronia born
Ginsing bankruptcy	Move to/sell farm, then Tunbridge	1804	
	Move to Sharon	1805	December, Joseph born
		1806	
?Father begins magic digging		1807	
Father's drinking begins		1808	March, Samuel Harrison born
	Move to Tunbridge	1809	
	Move to Royalton	1810	March, Ephraim is born, dies
Typhoid epidemic	Joseph's memory date for leg surgery	1811	March, William born
Typhoid epidemic	Move to Lebanon; all children ill	1812	July, Catherine born
Typhoid epidemic	?January, probable date for surgery	1813	Joseph recovers in Salem, Mass.
Episodes of hunger, bankrupt		1814	
Episodes of hunger	Tambora volcano begins long winter	1815	
Episodes of hunger, bankrupt	Fall, emigration to Palmyra	1816	March, Don Carlos born
Above hunger	Common laborers in Palmyra village	1817	
Becoming established	Built first log cabin in Palmyra	1818	
Joseph uses magic rod		1819	
Joseph's date for revival	No revivals in or around Palmyra	1820	
Joseph uses seer stone	Building second log cabin in Manchester	1821	July, Lucy born
	Joseph is Methodist exorter	1822	
October, began farmhouse	September, angel appears	1823	November, Alvin dies
March, revival begins	Grieving family seeks solace in revival	1824	
Revival converts 400-450	Fall, Joseph goes to Josiah Stowell's	1825	Joseph meets Emma Hale
March, Joseph charged with "glass-looking"	Family loses farm	1826	
	September, receives gold plates	1827	January, Joseph marries Emma

two styles of preachers—one harsh and threatening, the other preaching the love and grace of Jesus.

According to William Smith, Joseph Sr. boycotted the revivals, while Lucy, Sophronia, Hyrum, and Samuel joined the Presbyterians under Stockton. William adds that Joseph was "one of several hopeful converts" to the Methodists, but Joseph's version is only that he had been "partial" to the Methodists. Significantly, William remembered that Lane "preached a sermon on 'what church shall I join?' And the burden of his discourse was to ask God, using as a text, 'If any man lack wisdom let him ask of God who giveth to all men liberally, [James 1:5].'"[31] Lane's direction appears as an important though unattributed motivation in Joseph's first vision story, and I assume from this and other evidence within the Book of Mormon (discussed below) that Smith took a keen interest in these preaching services.

Public Humiliation and the Abandonment of Magic

Thus the five yearly visits of the angel between 1823 and 1827 overlapped significantly with the period of most intense religious revivals in and around Palmyra. Smith was seventeen at the beginning of this period, twenty-two at its close. Yet the townspeople do not remember his stories about the angel/messenger or the record in the context of Christianity or the revivals. To them, he was a youthful seer seeking treasure by magical means. Over twenty-seven testimonies survive about the Smith family's involvement in magic money-digging; half describe Joseph's involvement.[32] It seems clear that Joseph had one foot in Christian revivalism and the other in magic. However, according to Michael Quinn, after 1826 Smith minimized his involvement in magic in favor of Christianity.[33]

Quinn argues,[34] and I agree, that one crucial event was Smith's marriage, significant in itself but also because it solved the problem of taking Alvin to the yearly encounter with the guardian spirit. According to Joseph Knight, the angel told Smith at the 1826 meeting to bring someone else instead of Alvin. "Joseph says, 'who is the right Person?' The answer was you will know. Then he looked in his glass [seer stone] and found it was Emma Hale, Daughter of old Mr. Hail of Pensylvany, a girl that he had seen Before, for he had Bin Down there Before with me."[35]

THE SOUTH BAINBRIDGE TRIAL, 1826

Another event in 1826, however, was far more important than his marriage in shifting his attention away from magic. In fact, in psychological terms, I see his marriage as hardly more than a side issue in this larger context. In March 1826 Peter Bridgeman brought charges against Smith for magic and money-digging. Smith's version of the trial in South Bainbridge, New York, written by Oliver Cowdery, was that "some very officious person complained of him as a disorderly person, and brought him before the authorities of the country; but there being no cause of action he was honorably acquitted."[36] This version is considerably more positive than the actual happening.

About 120 miles from Palmyra lived a wealthy, strong-minded, industrious Dutch farmer named Josiah/Isaiah Stowell/Stoal. He was fifty-six years old, a Presbyterian deacon with grown children, who lived near South Bainbridge (now Afton), Chenango County, New York, about twenty miles from the Pennsylvania border. He believed in magic treasure seeking and believed there was a silver mine near Harmony (later Lanesboro, now Oakland), Pennsylvania, just over the state line. This supposed silver mine had been operated by the Spaniards, then lost to history along with a cache of coins and bullion. Stowell had hired diggers in the summer of 1825 but had failed to find the mine. Through his son, Simpson Stowell, who lived in the Palmyra-Manchester area, he heard of Joseph Smith and traveled to Manchester to meet him. Using his magic stone in a white stove-pipe hat, Smith described specific details about Stowell's farm, convincing Stowell of his supernatural talents. Stowell hired Smith to help find the Spanish cave and paid him $14 a month plus room and board. For the first few weeks Joseph Jr. and Joseph Sr. boarded at the nearby home of Isaac Hale. Here Joseph Jr. met Emma. A group of nine money-diggers, including the two Smiths, Stowell, Isaac Hale, and one of his sons signed an agreement on 1 November 1825 specifying how the mine's treasure would be divided when it was found.[37] Isaac Hale quickly became disillusioned and contemptuous of the treasure-seeking effort.

Meanwhile, in Manchester, panic ensued when the new owners of the Smith property arrived in Lucy's frame house with a signed deed. The new land agent had heard rumors from a neighbor who wanted the farm that the Smiths had burned sugar maple trees, torn down the fences, and were otherwise damaging the property. Hyrum sent an urgent message after his father, Joseph Sr. dashed home, and the entire family mounted a strenuous effort to reverse the sale. The land agent retrieved the deed; because the Smiths could not make the payment, they compromised on selling the land to Lemuel Durfee, a Quaker, who charitably allowed the Smiths to remain as tenants in their unfinished farmhouse for a year. One of the Smith boys would work for Durfee as rent.[38]

Joseph Jr., arguably the hope of the family, did not return home to cope with this financial crisis. I suggest that, perhaps on an unconscious level, Joseph Sr. and Lucy both saw Joseph's financial contribution as either finding the treasure through his supernatural talents or by manipulating Josiah Stowell. After his father's departure, Joseph moved to the Stowell home where Stowell's children became concerned that their father was squandering his fortune. Finally Stowell's nephew, Peter Bridgeman,[39] acted for the children and had Smith arrested as a "disorderly person and an imposter," jailed overnight, and brought up the next morning before Judge Albert Neeley for a pre-trial examination.

Two accounts of his trial have survived: one by W. D. Purple, a respected local physician and clerk, and the account from the court docket. Neither is friendly to Joseph Smith, and both differ in style and content, with Purple emphasizing the dramatic and narrative elements, while the court reporter focused on evidence that would justify (or not) a full trial.[40] Purple described the events leading to the trial:

> Mr. Stowell was a man of much force of character, of indomitable will, and well fitted as a pioneer in the unbroken wilderness that this country possessed at the close of the last century. ... He was a very industrious, exemplary man, and by severe labor and frugality had acquired surroundings that excited the envy of many of his less fortunate neighbors. He had at this time grown up sons and daughters to share his property and the honors of his name.
>
> About this time he took upon himself a monomaniacal impression to seek for hidden treasures which he believed were buried in the earth. He hired help and repaired to Northern Pennsylvania, in the vicinity of Lanesboro [previously named Harmony], to prosecute his search for untold wealth which he believed to be buried there ... and camped out on the black hills of that region for weeks at a time, [as] was freely admitted by himself and family. ...
>
> There had lived a few years previous to this date, in the vicinity of Great Bend, a poor man named Joseph Smith, who, with his family, had removed to the western part of the State, and lived in squalid poverty near Palmyra, in Ontario County. Mr. Stowell, while at Lanesboro, heard of the fame of one of his sons, named Joseph, who by the aid of a magic stone had become a famous seer of lost or hidden treasures. ... In due time he arrived at the humble log-cabin, midway between Canandaigua and Palmyra, and found the sought for treasure in the person of Joseph Smith, Jr. a lad of some eighteen years of age. He, with the magic stone, was at once transferred from his humble abode to a more pretentious mansion of Deacon Stowell. Here, in the estimation of the Deacon, he confirmed his conceded powers as a seer, by means of the stone which he placed in his hat, and by excluding the light from all other terrestrial things, could see whatever he wished, even in the depths of the earth. This omniscient attribute he firmly claimed. Deacon Stowell and others as firmly believed it. ...
>
> In February, 1826, the sons of Mr. Stowell, who lived with their father, were greatly incensed against Smith, as they plainly saw their father squandering his property in the fruitless search for hidden treasures, and saw that the youthful seer had unlimited control over the illusions of their sire. They made up their mind that "patience had ceased to be a virtue," and ... caused the arrest of Smith as a vagrant, without visible means of livelihood. The trial came on in the above mentioned month, before Albert Neeley, Esquire, the father of Bishop Neeley of the State of Maine. I was an intimate friend of the Justice, and was invited to take notes of the trial which I did.[41]

Smith, called as the first witness, confirmed but tried to downplay his money-digging activities. The docket reads:

> Prisoner examined. Says that he came from town of Palmyra, and had been at the house of Josiah Stowell in Bainbridge most of time since; had small part of time been employed in looking for mines, but the major part had been employed by said Stowell on his farm, and going to school; that he had a certain stone, which he had occasionally looked at to determine where hidden treasures in the bowels of the earth were; that he professed to tell in this manner where gold-mines were a distance under ground, and had looked for Mr. Stowell several times, and informed him where he could find those treasures, and Mr. Stowell had been engaged in digging for them; that at Palmyra he pretended to tell, by looking at this stone, where coined money was buried in Pennsylvania, and while at Palmyra he had frequently ascertained in that way where lost property was, of various kinds; that he had occasionally been in the habit of looking through this stone to find lost property for three years, but of late had pretty much given it up on account its injuring his health, especially his eyes—made them sore; that he did not solicit business of this kind, and had always rather declined having anything to do with this business.[42]

Purple's account relates how Smith says he discovered his seer stone:

> He said when he was a lad, he heard of a neighboring girl some three miles from him, who could look into a glass and see anything however hidden from others; that he was seized with a strong desire to see her and her glass; that after much effort he induced his parents to let him visit her. He did so, and was permitted to look in the glass, which was placed in a hat to exclude the light. He was greatly surprised to see but one thing, which was a small stone, a great way off. It soon became luminous, and dazzled his eyes, and after a short time it became as intense as the mid-day sun. He said that the stone was under the roots of a tree or shrub as large as his arm, situated about a mile up a stream that puts in on the South side of Lake Erie, not far from the New York and Pennsylvania line. He often had an opportunity to look in the glass, and with the same result. The luminous stone alone attracted his attention. This singular circumstance occupied his mind for some years, when he left his father's house, and with his youthful zeal traveled west in search of this luminous stone.
>
> He took a few shillings in money and some provisions with him. He stopped on the road with a farmer, and worked three days, and replenished his means of support. After traveling some one hundred and fifty miles he found himself at the mouth of the creek. He did not have the glass with him, but he knew its exact location. He borrowed an old ax and a hoe, and repaired to the tree. With some labor and exertion he found the stone, carried it to the creek, washed and wiped it dry, sat down on the bank, placed it in his hat, and discovered that time, place and distance were annihilated; that all the intervening obstacles were removed, and that he possessed one of the attributes of Deity, an All-Seeing-Eye. He arose with a thankful heart, carried his tools to their owner, turned his feet towards the rising sun, and sought with weary limbs his long deserted home.
>
> On the request of the Court, he exhibited the stone. It was about the size of a small hen's egg, in the shape of a high-instepped shoe.[43] It was

> composed of layers of different colors passing diagonally through it. It was very hard and smooth, perhaps by being carried in the pocket.

Stowell himself testified, offering unwavering support for Smith. According to the docket, he admitted that they had never discovered treasure but attributed the cause to the treasure's mobility (again a quality of treasure in the Book of Mormon):

> Josiah Stowell sworn. Says that prisoner had been at his house something like five months. Had been employed by him to work on farm part of time; that he pretended to have skill of telling where hidden treasures in the earth were, by means of looking through a certain stone; that prisoner had looked for him sometimes—once to tell him about money ... once for gold ... and once for a salt-spring—and that he positively knew that the prisoner could tell, and professed the art of seeing those valuable treasures through the medium of said stone: that he found the digging part ... as prisoner represented it; that prisoner had looked through said stone for Deacon Attelon, for a mine—did not exactly find it, but got a piece of ore, which resembled gold, he thinks; that prisoner had told by means of this stone where a Mr. Bacon had buried money; that he and prisoner had been in search of it; the prisoner said that it was in a certain root of a stump five feet from surface of the earth, and with it would be found a tail-feather; that said Stowell and prisoner there upon commenced digging, found a tail-feather, but money was gone; that he supposed that money moved down; that prisoner did offer his services; that he never deceived him; that prisoner looked through stone, and described Josiah's Stowell's house and out-houses while at Palmyra, at Simpson Stowell's, correctly; that he had told about a painted tree with a man's hand painted upon it, by means of said stone; that he had been in company with prisoner digging for gold, and had the most implicit faith in prisoner's skill.

Purple's account confirms Stowell's steadfast defense of Smith:

> He [Stowell] confirmed all that is said above in relation to himself, and delineated many other circumstances not necessary to record. He swore that the prisoner possessed all the power he claimed, and declared he could see things fifty feet below the surface of the earth, as plain as the witness could see what was on the Justice's table, and described very many circumstances to confirm his words. Justice Neeley soberly looked at the witness and in a solemn, dignified voice, said, "Deacon Stowell, do I understand you as swearing before God, under the solemn oath you have taken, that you believe the prisoner can see by the aid of the stone fifty feet below the surface of the earth, as plainly as you can see what is on my table?" "Do I believe it?" says Deacon Stowell, "do I believe it? No, it is not a matter of belief. I positively know it to be true."

Jonathan Thompson, who dug with Smith and Stowell, testified that charmed and guarded treasures were difficult and frightening to obtain. Again such stories find suggestive echoes in the earliest versions of Smith's series of "encounters" with the angel/guardian figure which would have been occurring during this same period of time. According to the docket:

> Jonathan Thompson says that prisoner was requested to look [on] Yeomans [property] for chest of money; did look, and pretended to know where it was, and that prisoner, Thompson, and Yeomans went in search of it; that Smith arrived at spot first (was in night); that Smith looked in hat while there, and when very dark, and told how the chest was situated. After digging several feet, struck upon something sounding like a board or plank. Prisoner could not look again, pretending that he was alarmed the last time that he looked, on account of the circumstances relating to the trunk being buried came all fresh to his mind; that the last time that he looked, he discovered distinctly the two Indians who buried the trunk that a quarrel ensued between them, and that one of said Indians was killed by the other, and thrown into the hole beside the trunk, to guard it, as he supposed. Thompson says that he believes in the prisoner's professed skill; that the board which he struck his spade upon was probably the chest, but, on account of an enchantment, the trunk kept settling away from under them while digging; that, notwithstanding they continued constantly removing the dirt, yet the trunk kept about the same distance from them.

Purple's summary of Thompson's testimony is very similar:

> Smith had told the Deacon that very many years before a band of robbers had buried on his flat a box of treasure, and as it was very valuable they had by a sacrifice placed a charm over it to protect it, so that it could not be obtained except by faith, accompanied by certain talismanic influences. So, after arming themselves with fasting and prayer, they sallied forth to the spot designated by Smith. Digging was commenced with fear and trembling, in the presence of this imaginary charm. In a few feet from the surface the box of treasure was struck by the shovel, on which they redoubled their energies, but it gradually receded from their grasp. One of the men placed his hand upon the box, but it gradually sunk from his reach. After some five feet in depth had been attained without success, a council of war against this spirit of darkness was called, and they resolved that the lack of faith, or some untoward mental emotion, was the cause of their failure.

As we have seen, Smith, in the earliest versions of the story about the gold records of the Book of Mormon, disobeyed the guardian's/angel's command and promptly lost possession of the book. Purple's summary of Thompson's testimony continues with a somewhat different version of Smith's strategy for satisfying the guardian spirit and obtaining the treasure:

> In this emergency the fruitful mind of Smith was called on to devise a way to obtain the prize. Mr. Stowell went to his flock and selected a fine vigorous lamb, and resolved to sacrifice it to the demon spirit who guarded the coveted treasure. Shortly after the venerable Deacon might be seen on his knees at prayer near the pit, while Smith, with a lantern in one hand to dispel the midnight darkness might be seen making a circuit around the spot, sprinkling the flowing blood from the lamb upon the ground, as a propitiation to

the spirit that thwarted them. They then descended the excavation, but the treasure still receded from their grasp, and it was never obtained.

The docket book report by Judge Albert Neeley concludes, "And thereupon the Court finds the defendent guilty," which, in context, probably meant guilty enough to go to a full trial, with the conclusion fairly obvious. In 1971 two pieces of paper—original holographs from this legal examination—were found in the basement of the county jail in Norwich, New York.[44] These were bills for the cost of the trial from Judge Albert Neeley and his constable, Philip DeZeng. These charges confirm the trial, but also include charges for notifying two more justices of the peace so that a full trial—a "Court of Special Sessions"—could be held. In apparent contradiction, Purple recorded his memory that: "As the testimony of Deacon Stowell could not be impeached, the prisoner was discharged, and in a few weeks left town." Further, the bills of all four justices of the peace in Bainbridge have been found, and there are no charges for a "Court of Special Sessions." Apparently, a full trial was never held.

These historical contradictions were largely resolved with the discovery of two more pieces of evidence. In the Library of Congress, a Protestant newspaper, the *Evangelical Magazine and Gospel Advocate,* published at Utica, New York, on 9 April 1831, contained a letter written by Dr. Abram W. Benton entitled "Mormonites."[45] Benton's letter referred to this trial, quoted some of the testimony of Deacon Stowell, then commented that the people had become tired of this imposition. They "had him [Joseph Smith] arrested as a disorderly person, tried and condemned before a court of Justice. But, considering his youth, (he then being a minor,) and thinking he might reform his conduct, he was designedly allowed to escape. This was four or five years ago."

Final clarification of the conclusion of this examination came in a letter found in the Illinois State Historical Library in Springfield, Illinois.[46] This letter had been written by Judge Joel King Noble in 1842. Judge Noble had presided at an 1830 trial of Joseph Smith in Colesville that was dismissed on a technicality, but Noble also knew about this earlier 1826 trial. He referred to some magical practices of Joseph Smith, including the sacrifice of a black dog while magically searching for a chest of money. Referring to the 1826 trial, Noble said that "Jo[seph Smith] was condemned," then added the comment that the "whisper came to Jo., 'Off, Off!'" and so Joseph "took Leg Bail." These were early slang expressions meaning "to escape from custody." Noble then commented that "Jo. was not seen in our town for 2 Years or more (except in dark corners)." The most likely explanation behind these comments "is that the three justices discussed the case, and considering that since this was Joseph Smith's first offence, privately made a deal with him" to leave town and avoid punishment.[47] Purple, not aware of these "behind the scenes" arrangements, believed that Smith had been discharged. In this charitable act, the three judges also avoided embarrassing their friend and prominent citizen, Josiah Stowell. Joseph apparently hid out "in dark corners" in Bainbridge if Purple was correct that he didn't leave for a "few weeks."

Smith was humiliated by the trial. According to Purple, Joseph Sr., who had apparently returned to Bainbridge some time after Durfee bought the farm on 20 December 1835, had testified that both he and his son

> were mortified that this wonderful power which God had so miraculously given him should be used only in search of filthy lucre, or its equivalent in earthly treasures and with a longfaced, "sanctimonious seemin," he said his constant prayer to his Heavenly Father was to manifest His will concerning this marvelous power. He trusted that the Son of Righteousness would some day illumine the heart of the boy, and enable him to see His will concerning Him.

Purple, respected and decent, reflects the community opinions of Smith and his father at the trial:

> These words have ever had a strong impression on my mind. They seemed to contain a prophetic vision of the future history of that mighty delusion of the present century, Mormonism. The "old man eloquent" with his lank and haggard visage—his form very poorly clad—indicating a wandering vagabond rather than an oracle of future events, has, in view of those events, excited my wonder. ... What a picture for the pencil of a Hogarth! How difficult to believe it could have been enacted in the nineteenth century of the Christian era! ... But as it was declared under oath, in a Court of Justice ... it is worthy of recital as evincing the spirit of delusion.

Other than humiliation, what did Joseph Smith learn from this trial? By now, I believe, he was seeing that magic was a dead end. He had already observed how Christian revivalists could enthuse and maneuver believers. His trial had proved that it was fairly easy to prosecute for fraud within a framework of magic belief. But who would dare bring Christian miracles to trial? He also learned that, while the majority of the world would think of him with contempt, he could draw from a small percentage a loyal belief that exceeded common sense or reason and crossed over the line into delusion. It is my opinion that, with this episode, Smith turns a corner; his direction increasingly leads away from magic and toward Christianity. However, a few observations may be useful:

This pretrial examination stands as a memorial against the integrity of Joseph Smith. The hearing establishes that either Smith had non-Christian—magical—supernatural powers of discernment and vision (which never produced treasures), or he was deceptive.[48] We do not know, from court records, the precise final outcome of the pretrial examination; but Dale L. Morgan, a nonbelieving Mormon historian who discovered one of the five evidences for the hearing, commented: "From the point of view of

Mormon history, it is immaterial what the finding of the court was on the technical charge of being 'a disorderly person and an imposter'; what is important is the evidence adduced, and its bearing on the life of Joseph Smith before he announced his claim to be a prophet of God."[49]

When this pretrial examination was rediscovered, many Mormons declared it to be a fabrication by evil men against a true prophet of God, and the document itself remains largely unknown to the rank and file members of the church. As evidence mounted, it and especially its implications were simply ignored. Those who acknowledge it minimized its importance. Mormon attorney Gordon A. Madsen declared the trial a mere "blip" in the life of Joseph Smith, while Mormon historian Richard L. Anderson, with rather more sophistication, suggested that Smith's spirituality was immature and that he progressed to a more mature form of supernatural "Christian" claims.[50]

But the issue for a psychiatrist is not the personality per se or spiritual development, but misrepresentation, even deceit; and the historical record documents the same general pattern for the rest of Smith's life.[51] The pretrial examination suggests that delusion had become a way of life for young Joseph. I have now presented evidence from many testimonies—and there will be more—that he originally created multiple versions of his story, progressing to a final, canonized version. The "unfriendly" testimonies form a consistent corrective to this progressive, ultimately deceptive story. For example, was the angel Moroni or Nephi? Was he a magical guardian of a treasure or a biblical angel of the gospel? Was the Palmyra revival in 1820 or 1824-25? At this point, Smith had not developed his "first vision" story of God and Jesus. I see it going through a contradictory development. Was Joseph's deception conscious or unconscious? Did he deceive himself along with others? The Book of Mormon, to the extent that it can accurately be read back into Smith's biography, makes such a suggestion plausible. Irritated by the first Nephi, his antagonistic brother, Laman, proposed to his other antagonistic brother, Lemuel, "Let us slay our father, and also our brother Nephi who has taken it upon himself to be our ruler and our teacher. ... We know he lies ... and he worketh many things by his cunning arts ... to make himself a king and a ruler over us, that he may do with us according to his will and pleasure" (BM 41; 1 Ne. 16:37-38). Is it possible that even the Smith children tired of Joseph's machinations?

Joseph Smith never referred to this humiliating pretrial examination in any of his writings, but a characteristic of the narcissistic personality is that it does not handle shame or humiliation well. Using allegory, simile, and metaphor, Smith reviews this pretrial examination twice in the Book of Mormon (discussed below). In both versions, his psychological upheavals are represented by geophysical upheavals, suggesting the extent to which he was psychologically shaken. In the second version, again using allegory, metaphor, and simile, and reading from the Book of Mormon back into Joseph's life, Josiah Stowell reappears as the sole supporter of a holy prophet beleaguered by enemies.

After the trial, Smith apparently worked in nearby Colesville and quietly boarded at Stowell's home. He also apparently used this time to court Emma Hale. Joseph had announced that the angel had instructed him to bring Alvin to the next meeting, but Alvin had died two months later. Emma Hale now became important in Joseph's readjustment of the story, and his courtship of her had a meaning beyond romance. Joseph's friend, Joseph Knight, who was in his mid-fifties, explained that, at the yearly meeting with the angel in 1826, he was told to bring someone else in place of his dead brother: "Joseph says, 'who is the right Person?' The answer was you will know. Then he looked in his glass [stone] and found it was Emma Hale, Daughter of old Mr. Hail of Pensylvany, a girl that he had seen Before, for he had Bin Down there Before with me."[52]

Joseph had told his parents that he continued to be lonely for his dead brother, wished to marry, and preferred Emma to any woman he had met.[53] He and Emma were married on 18 January 1827, in plenty of time for meeting the angel in September of that year. They were married, probably, by the one justice of the peace in Bainbridge who was not one of the three notified for the "Court of Special Sessions." The couple eloped because of the objections of Emma's family. Joseph was twenty-one, Emma twenty-two. From a psychological perspective, Joseph's decision to marry is extremely important, as was his relationship to Emma.

Joseph immediately took Emma to the Smith home to Manchester. Emma Hale, whose family was respected and financially comfortable, now found herself a member of a family who was little respected by at least a portion of the community, who engaged in nighttime rituals and money-digging, and whose financial circumstances were so reduced that they were tenants in their own house.

About six months later in July or August 1827, Emma wrote her father that she wanted to collect her belongings, including clothes, furniture, and cows. Her father agreed, and she and Smith accomplished this errand with a Manchester neighbor, Peter Ingersoll, whom Smith hired to drive them to Harmony in his wagon in August. On the night of 21 September, she and Joseph borrowed Joseph Knight's horse and carriage and drove to Cumorah to get the gold plates. Her exact role at that point is not clear. According to Emma's cousins, Joseph and Hiel Lewis, both local leaders in the Methodist Episcopal church who were writing fifty years later in Illinois, Emma turned her back while Joseph retrieved the gold plates from their vault in the ground, then hid them in a trunk of a dead tree. According to

Martin Harris, interviewed by a reporter in 1859, Emma knelt and prayed. And according to Lucy Mack Smith, she simply stayed in the wagon at the foot of the hill.[54] Emma never tried to see the plates because she was not authorized to do so by God, even though the temptation must have been overwhelming, given her father's scorn and her husband's negative reputation. She certainly had opportunity, since she believed that the plates were at times in a box underneath her bed or sitting on the furniture wrapped in cloth as she cleaned.[55] From a psychoanalytic perspective, it is possible to see Emma's great self-restraint as her assumption of what will become a full-time job—looking away from possible evidence of deception by her husband. Her behavior is the physical manifestation of the psychological defense of denial. If deceived in anything, she might be deceived in everything. It is probable that she has been caught in the web of Joseph's charisma and that her own self-esteem is becoming dependent on his claims and the reflection from his self-importance.

Six years later Ingersoll, no longer accommodating, made a sworn affidavit about driving Joseph and Emma to Harmony. From a psychoanalytic perspective, his observations are among the most important psychological evidences about Smith's motives for claiming supernatural powers. He describes Smith's conflicts as Isaac Hale pressed him to settle into conventional living, while Joseph's parents pressed him toward the supernatural.

> His father-in-law (Mr. Hale) addressed Joseph, in a flood of tears: "You have stolen my daughter and married her. I had much rather have followed her to her grave. You spend your time in digging for money—pretend to see in a stone, and thus try to deceive people." Joseph wept, and acknowledged he could not see in a stone now, nor never could; and that his former pretensions in that respect, were all false. He then promised to give up his old habits of digging for money and looking into stones. Mr. Hale told Joseph, if he would move to Pennsylvania and work for a living, he would assist him in getting into business. Joseph acceded to this proposition. I then returned with Joseph and his wife to Manchester. ... Joseph told me on his return, that he intended to keep the promise which he had made to his father-in-law; but, said he, it will be hard for me, for they will all oppose, as they want me to look in the stone for them to dig money: and in fact it was as he predicted. They urged him, day after day, to resume his old practice of looking in the stone. He seemed much perplexed as to the course he should pursue.[56]

As a psychiatrist, I hear the ring of truth in Ingersoll's description. Joseph's view of himself has been largely determined by what his family wanted to believe about him. When he is removed from their influence and confronted by his decent father-in-law, the shell of his false self temporarily cracked; but as he returned to his family, the grandiose personality with its supernatural claims reasserted itself. This tension helps explain the perpetual dyadic conflicts in the Book of Mormon that end in moral failure and destruction. In contrast to Isaac Hale stands the encouragement of his own parents and Deacon Josiah Stowell's unwavering certainty that Smith could see fifty feet into the earth. Both extremes deal with known mental forces and behavior, which develop from the elements of a person's psychological make-up. Given Joseph Smith's background of deprivation and trauma, I interpret his inner self to be struggling with inferiority, fear, and insecurity; he masks these feelings with competence, power, and "specialness." But only an audience who believes the mask provides evidence that he is succeeding. In psychological terms, Smith makes a contract: "I will become the person you want me to convince you that I am." The narcissist is permanently caught between mask and mirror: he exists as a reflection from his audience. Who he is—who he becomes to himself as well as to others—results from this combination. In therapeutic terms, if it had been possible to take Smith away—and keep him away—from people who wanted him to have supernatural powers, then he might have developed into a normal adult. But unless that happened, he would continue to victimize his believers even as their desire that he possess supernatural powers trapped him in turn. He is both victim and victimizer.

DICTATING THE FIRST 116 PAGES

In any case, Joseph Smith came to a crossroads in August 1827. In Harmony, he could see a vision of his life if he abandoned his supernatural claims and vowed to choose normalcy. Would his life be like his father's? But by late September back in Palmyra, he had made a different decision. He took Emma with him to the hill; he returned to tell his family and supporters that he had obtained the treasured book. And from that point on, he was committed to producing a translation of it. Apparently he first began dictating using the "breast plate with the seer stones." According to Lucy, who felt the seer stones through a "silk handkerchief," they consisted of "2 smooth 3 cornered diamonds set in glass and the glass was set in silver bows ... [like] old fashioned spectacles." The 1853 published version of her history contains a description, not in her 1844 manuscript, that the breastplate was "concave on one side and convex on the other, and extended from the neck downwards as far as the center of the stomach of a man of extraordinary size." It had four straps—two to go over the shoulders and two around the hips—the width of two of her fingers with "holes in the end" for easy fastening. Then she added, "The whole plate was worth at least five hundred dollars,"[57] a comment suggesting that the plates and artifacts were still associated with a money-digging context in her mind. Martin Harris and David Whitmer, who later claimed to have seen the gold plates under miraculous conditions, described the same "spectacles" in somewhat contradictory terms. Harris remembered them as "white, like polished marble, with a few grey streaks two inches in diameter, perfectly round, and about five-eighths of an inch thick at the centre," while Whitmer recalled them as "transparent stones set in a bow-shaped frame and very much resembled a pair of spectacles."[58] Interviewed in 1891, Joseph's younger brother, William, said the "two stones were placed literally between the two rims of a [double silver] bow." William claimed, with Joseph's approval, to have looked through the two stones, but "could see nothing, as he did not have the gift of Seer."[59]

Smith had agreed to share any discovered treasures not only with Stowell's money-diggers in Pennsylvania but also with his colleagues in the Palmyra/Manchester area.[60] When they heard about gold plates, they believed he was breaking his contract. Smith reports being attacked three times in the woods as he carried the plates home; he reports dislocating his thumb in fighting off one man. Treasure-seekers broke into the Smith home and repeatedly searched their property.

Two months later, in December 1827, he and Emma moved to Harmony, Pennsylvania, where the skeptical Isaac Hale let them live in a two-room shed where Emma's brother tanned deer skins.[61] While it was being readied for their habitation, they temporarily lived in a garret of the Hale house. Here the first known dictation of the Book of Mormon occurred with Emma and her brother Reuben serving as scribes.[62] Apparently Smith had covered the departure of Lehi's family from Jerusalem, Nephi's murder of Laban and possession of the brass plates, and Ishmael's death in the wilderness by February 1828 when Martin Harris arrived from Palmyra.[63]

From a psychoanalytic perspective, Harris was the first of three men who turned the Book of Mormon into reality by the simple and effective means of becoming Smith's financial backer. Psychologically speaking, he was an enabler. A forty-five-year-old moderately wealthy farmer, married with probably three children at or near adulthood, he was also a money-digger, an abusive husband,[64] and a religious addict who had already joined five different religious sects, would later be excommunicated from Mormonism, return to Mormonism, become a missionary for a Mormon splinter group, return to Mormonism, leave again, then return, and die in Utah, poor and debilitated.[65] Harris apparently never lost his belief in Smith's miraculous power to translate the Book of Mormon but found the later revelations spurious. Harris's motives were probably mixed, for others recall his plans for the book to make him rich.[66] Thirty years later Harris recalled the incident that convinced him of Smith's supernatural powers:

> I was at the house of his father in Manchester, two miles south of Palmyra village, and was picking my teeth with a pin while sitting on the bars. The pin caught in my teeth, and dropped from my fingers into shavings and straw. I jumped from the bars and looked for it. Joseph ... did the same. We could not find it. I then took Joseph on surprise, and said to him—I said,

> "take your stone." I had never seen it and did not know that he had it with him. He had it in his pocket. He took it and placed it in his hat—the old white [stove-pipe] hat—and placed his face in the hat. I watched him closely see that he did not look on one side; he reached out his hand beyond me on the right, and moved a little stick, and there I saw the pin, which he picked up and gave to me. I knew he did not look out of the hat until after he had picked up the pin.[67]

According to Peter Ingersoll, Smith spotted Harris in Palmyra and announced to him, "I have a commandment from God to ask the first man I meet in the street to give me fifty dollars to assist me in doing the work of the Lord by translating the Golden Bible." Harris gave him the money.[68] Joseph used it to move to Pennsylvania. Harris's wife was strongly opposed to Harris's interest. They separated before the Book of Mormon was published, and she wrote an affidavit, accusing him of beating her repeatedly, mad fits, and possible infidelity.[69] Lucy Harris's accusations were supported by neighbor G. W. Stoddard. Reading from the Book of Mormon back into Joseph's life and in a story I will later review, a reflection of Martin Harris will appear in the book as a woman-beating man of "much ... angry ... passion" (Alma 50:31-32).

When Harris reached Harmony in February 1828, he took some "caractors" Smith copied off the gold plates to New York City to confirm their authenticity. He showed them to Charles Anthon, a scholar of antiquities at Columbia University, and returned to Pennsylvania convinced of the divinity of the work. Anthon later wrote that the characters were "perfectly false" and "all a trick, perhaps a hoax."[70] Smith took Harris's version of the interview and worked it into the Book of Mormon as a prophecy (BM 110-11; 2 Ne. 27:14-21). In the glow of growing importance, Harris returned to Palmyra, but soon returned to Pennsylvania, accompanied by his wife. A feisty woman, convinced that Smith was trying to get her husband's money, Mrs. Harris searched the house trying to find the gold plates. She eventually returned to New York, while Harris acted as scribe for the next two months. During that time Smith finished dictating 116 foolscap pages, about one-fourth of the Book of Mormon, allegedly using the breastplate with the spectacles behind a curtain.[71]

It was apparently important to Harris to convince his wife that he was not being deluded. He repeatedly urged Smith to let him show his wife the completed pages of the manuscript. Three times Smith inquired of God, using his seer stone. After two refusals came consent, and Harris rushed to Palmyra with the dictation on 14 June 1828.

THE BIRTH OF A DEFORMED SON

The next day, 15 June 1828, Emma gave birth to a stillborn son whom they named Alvin after Smith's older (now dead) brother.[72] Midwife Rhoda

Skinner, Emma's sister-in-law, stated that the child was malformed in terms that Newell and Avery describe as "birth defects." Sophia Lewis, probably a cousin of Emma, likewise described the baby as "very much deformed."[73] Years later John C. Bennett, Smith's friend-turned-enemy, used the archaic, technically correct medical term—"monster"—to describe the infant.[74] Today mental health workers are alert to the emotional devastation of the parents of a dead baby, even if it never lived.[75] Healthy parents who know they have done "nothing wrong" may still struggle with irrational guilt. Undeniably, an extra psychological burden was added through the alarming deformations. The child's father was a man "chosen by God." How was such a thing possible? Was it a judgement from God? Had they as parents done something amiss? Smith's usual style later in life would be to blame others. Did he blame his wife, construing the child's deformities as punishment from God for siding with her family on occasion? Although there is no documentary evidence of such disagreements, beyond Isaac Hale's dismay, already described, Emma was surrounded by relatives who disapproved of her marriage and of Joseph. It seems unlikely that she would have remained immune to their criticisms of her support of her husband. With his past history of involvement in magic, it seems unlikely that it was never an issue between them and that she never challenged his attitude. The available records (granted, none from Emma) show Joseph as a concerned and tender husband, in great anxiety over Emma's difficult childbirth; he nursed her himself, and it was she who insisted that he go to Palmyra to investigate Martin Harris's silence.

Lucy Mack Smith confirms Joseph's concern for his wife's condition. The narcissistic personality is capable of saying the right thing at the right time and "being" genuinely kind and caring. In various degrees and times, such a personality may actually be concerned for others; but over time observers can see that most statements are ultimately self-serving. The narcissist strives to be convincing, and so the behavior, not just the words, become increasingly important. Joseph could wrestle a smaller man, break his leg, nurse him compassionately, then do it again. (See chapter 2.) His posture while under oath in a courtroom must also be considered. While I would not argue that he did not have romantic feelings for Emma, the reasons he gave his mother for the marriage were to relieve his own feelings of loneliness and to meet the angel's requirement for a companion. In short, Emma was doubly a substitute for his dead brother, Alvin, a point reinforced by naming his first child for his dead brother. These are not attitudes one wants in a friend or loving spouse. As a psychiatrist, I have professional skepticism about the genuineness of Joseph's concern for Emma. Was his guilt an expression of his misjudgment or because he was now caught in a corner of his own making?

Five years later three antagonistic contemporaries, one in Palmyra quoting Martin Harris, Sophia Lewis of Harmony, and Joshua M'Kune (also McKune), the Methodist Episcopal minister, also from Harmony, testified under oath that Smith had announced that his male child "would be able when two years old to translate the Gold Bible," that this "first-born child was to translate the characters, and hieroglyphics, upon the Plates into our language at the age of three years," and that the "Book of Plates could not be opened under penalty of death by any other person but his (Smith's) first-born, which was to be male." In addition, Smith told his father-in-law that a small child would be the first to see the plates.[76] These boastful predictions meant that Smith had set himself up for special devastation. Using metaphor, allegory, and simile, and reading from the Book of Mormon back into Joseph's life, he will handle this humiliation by techniques we have already seen: he will reverse it into a wonderful miracle.

Smith turned to religion—either for consolation or possibly to placate a vengeful God. He "presented himself in a very serious and humble manner" to the circuit-riding minister of Emma's faith and to the Methodist Episcopal class in Harmony. The minister, who arrived on a Wednesday in June, put his name on the class roll. Emma's first cousin, Joseph Lewis, an official in the church, heard about the new member on Saturday. On Sunday before meeting began, he and Rev. McKune pulled Smith aside and candidly told him that it would be a "disgrace to the church to have a practicing necromancer, a dealer in enchantments and bleeding ghosts, in it." Furthermore, his "habits, and moral character were at variance with the [church] discipline" and there would have to be "recantation, confession, and at least promised reformation." Smith could either remove his name from the rolls or submit to an investigation. Smith resigned although, through a clerical error, his name was not removed for six months.[77]

I consider the Bainbridge trial of 1826 to be a first blow, the deformed and stillborn child a second. Hard on its heels came a third. Anxious because he had not heard from Harris for over two weeks, Emma encouraged Joseph to leave her in her mother's care and investigate. Smith traveled most of the way by stagecoach, then walked the final twenty miles in the night. Harris confessed that his wife had let him lock the manuscript in her dresser after reading it; then in her absence, he had forced the lock and showed the manuscript to unauthorized people. Harris and other Palmyrans believed that his wife had burned the pages of dictation. These pages have never reappeared.[78] We have only Joseph's word on the content of the lost 116 pages which, reportedly, dealt with government, war, and society. Nevertheless, again, based on Joseph's word (see note 62), this history also contained more personal material. It is my opinion that Joseph's final version is more refined and contains much more Christianity, while the earlier version had more magic in it. The rising level of Christianity was enhanced by the arrival (discussed below) of his major scribe, Oliver Cowdery.

Smith implies that these lost pages contained magical elements when he tells us that the redictation of this section was more "spiritual" in nature (BM 16, 21; 1 Ne. 6; 9:4). But perhaps the best clue is how much the guardian of the treasure was still from the world of magic. Emma's cousins, Joseph and Hiel Lewis, make it clear that, during the period of this first dictation, Joseph did not talk about a visitation or about an angelic messenger. Rather, he described a "dream" in which he saw the ghost of a man with "a long beard ... down ... to the pit of his stomach ... with his throat cut from ear to ear, and the blood streaming down." They believed that the "vision" and "angels" were later additions—"afterthoughts, *revised to order.*"[79] In retrospect, I suggest that Smith had a rather well-formed idea about a pre-Columbian magical American story but only a poorly developed concept for an ancient American Christian history. Even at this late date, he needed something more for a cohesive narrative.

The loss of the 116 pages left Smith in a difficult situation. Lucy remembered Martin's cry, "Oh, I have lost my soul!" and Joseph's response, "Oh, my God! All is lost! ... Must I return to my wife with such a tale as this I dare not do it least I should kill her at once."[80] The narcissistic personality in its varied forms and mixtures with other personality issues can be capable of different degrees of concern and worry. Smith may indeed be troubled by his wife's condition, but I believe that he is also worried that his false self is at risk. Maintaining my premise that he was drawing the Book of Mormon narrative from his own experiences, I hypothesize that he thought of and discarded the most obvious alternative—redictating the story as he remembered it. There was no way he could get all the details correct; furthermore, almost certainly the manuscript still existed and would be produced for public comparison if he tried again.

On 3 July 1828 he received a revelation chastising him for delivering the sacred dictation "into the hands of a wicked man and this is the reason that thou has lost thy privileges for a season." But ironically this reminder of lost power in fact reveals a new one. This revelation is, as far as I know, the first revelation *written* down by the *prophet.* Thus it holds a unique position in Smith's development. Until this point, he has claimed only to be the translator of an ancient record. Now, in this moment of urgent crisis, he takes the step of enhancing his identify from translator to prophet—a man who speaks the words of God for today's problems. From this point on, he gives revelations that deal with new pressing issues, not just translations. Psychologically, he must rely on only his own powers. At this moment all other powers and promises have failed him, including Harris, his wife, and his promised son. The paradox of such a personality is that it truly trusts no one, yet must constantly have a sympathetic audience. For the moment, Smith had no one.

He then returned to the convalescing Emma. I see this particular time period as having intense psychological significance. If I am correct that he was motivated by a desire to control others, then this quest was temporarily blocked because of fear and criticism. He was 120 miles from his family, the chief source of expectations that he possessed and would exercise supernatural powers. If he tried, the missing manuscript might be produced at any moment to make him look like a fool. He was twenty miles from South Bainbridge where, a year and a half earlier, he had spent a night in jail, had been tried for fraudulent activities, and been found guilty. Everyone in the area knew about this episode and was still watching. And he was only 150 yards away from his in-laws and their extended family. Although some may have been supportive, he does not mention it; instead, they seem to have taken their tone from Isaac Hale who found his claims outrageous, barely tolerated him for Emma's sake, and obviously wanted him to begin living a stable and hard-working life.

SEVEN MONTHS OF NORMALCY

For the next seven months, from the chastening revelation on 3 July 1828 to February 1829, Smith yielded, retreated from his supernatural claims, and came as close to a conventional life as he ever would. He later explained this gap as punishment for losing the 116 pages: the angel had taken away the gold plates and translating spectacles; however, in late 1828 he told Lucy a different story—that these items had been returned to him 22 September 1828, on the night of the equinox.[81] He later recalled, "I did not go immediately to translating, but went to laboring with my hands upon a small farm which I had purchased of my wife's father, in order to provide for my family."[82]

During these months, Smith's parents came to visit, staying with Isaac and Elizabeth Hale for perhaps two months. Lucy remembered Joseph as so "hurried with his secular affairs, that he could not proceed with his spiritual concerns as fast as was necessary ... [and] his wife had so much of her time taken up with the care of her house, that she could write for him but a small portion of the time."[83] The traditional perspective is to see this period as a dark one, a time of spiritual loss and suffering. But from a psychological point of view, I see it as one of the healthiest periods of Smith's adult life. Smith's deception was contained by fright, sorrow, and humiliation. Fright, sorrow, and humiliation can be important positive outside forces in the treatment of narcissistic personalities. Such experiences may provide some added motivation for the patient to struggle toward change by giving up grand claims that have gotten him in trouble and to move toward ordinary commonness.

But two factors encouraged his return to the supernatural. The first was poverty. In early winter he and Emma were so poor that they paid a begging visit to Joseph's older friend, Joseph Knight, asking for help. He gave Smith food, a pair of shoes, and $3.00.[84] Only if we understand the desperateness of their economic plight can we begin to appreciate the extremity of Smith's solutions. Perhaps he looked into the future during that winter and saw himself becoming his father. Perhaps he saw a future of poverty and contempt from his neighbors. But these factors are minor compared to the enormous underlying problem of identity. Take away the façade that was now crystallizing, and what remained was a small, incomplete, and helpless shadow of a man. But for narcissists, seeing themselves as ordinary and common is to feel weak and perpetually threatened that emotional deprivation, even physical hunger, might occur at any time. Perhaps even more powerful is feeling that they simply do not know who they are. Smith's need to be important and in control was strong; he returned to the compensating personality.

I see his parents' visit as the second factor. They obviously encouraged his supernatural claims, perhaps reporting their own belief that, since the original manuscript had not resurfaced in Palmyra, it must have been destroyed. Smith could begin again.

In February 1829 Smith received a revelation for his father. From a psychological view, this revelation (Book of Commandments [BC] III; D&C 4) reveals his past Bible readings, his attendance at religious services or revivals, and his ability to weave fragments into a new creation. In two sentences—two verses—he smoothly combines segments from Isaiah, Mark, Luke, John, Peter, James, and Paul.[85] I argue that his ability to create this revelatory literature demonstrates that he is ready to weave stories together, also suggesting that his creation of personality is adequate to create the Book of Mormon.

From a psychoanalytic perspective, this moment of return to claims of supernatural power was a decisive turning point for Joseph Smith, one that closed the door on the possibility of developing a healthy self. This moment is, in therapeutic terms, the saddest for Smith—not three years later when he is tarred, beaten, and nearly castrated in Ohio; or ten years later when he is incarcerated for months in Missouri; or fifteen years later when he is jailed and shot by a mob in Illinois. At this point, on a farm in Pennsylvania, his power over others is minimal; he has not had sexual relations with dozens of women and girls; three brothers and hundreds of followers have not yet died for him, given him their properties, their lives, their wives, their time, and their finest loyalty.

Every dynamic psychiatrist or psychoanalyst I know believes that we have a say over our own destiny, but here are some of the forces Joseph Smith had to contend with: being raised in a family of poverty and inferiority by parents generally incapable of assuring their economic well-being; a mother who experienced at least two depressive episodes, one before and one after marriage, and who was, arguably, emotionally unavailable to her children when she was under intense economic stress; a father who compensated for reality by a belief in magic as a means of controlling natural forces and getting rich; the father's drinking—severe enough to have frightened five-year-old Joseph; poverty that may have included episodes of actual hunger; increasing numbers of mouths to feed; many moves and instability of environment in childhood; repeated episodes of medical incompetence that resulted in a permanent limp, while another resulted in the death of a beloved brother; being raised to believe that, instead of being like their neighbors, one's family and oneself had supernatural powers; and that the morality taught by his father was pride in how successful one was in one's "supernatural" pursuits.

From a psychoanalytic perspective, a genuine acknowledgement that one comes from a dysfunctional, inferior family is a beginning step toward health. With such an admission, one can begin working toward authentic accomplishment. But to replace an honest awareness of dysfunction with the delusion that a man's dreams are divine visions and that he can do magical ("spiritual?") acts diverts energies from potential progress and mires him more deeply in fantasy.

Dictating the Book of Mormon

The revelation to his father was the first of a number of similar revelations to men who were beginning to gather around Smith, each one, I suggest, hungry for something extraordinary to give his life purpose and distinction. This revelation predicted that "a marvelous work is about to come forth among the children of men," a statement of capitulation on Smith's part to the pressures to reconstruct the Book of Mormon. Smith began dictating again, this time to Emma and her brother Reuben, Smith's own brother, Samuel Harrison, and Martin Harris.[86]

However, because the angel refused to return the breastplate and seer stones set in spectacles, Smith produced the entire Book of Mormon, as it now exists, using his old instrument of magic: a single seer stone in a hat.[87] Martin Harris called this method more "convenient," and it had its advantages. Smith did not need the gold plates in front of him; they could be safely hidden, in any locale he chose. Now other people could watch the translation process; and at least eight people described Smith's "new" method of dictation.[88] David Whitmer commented:

> Joseph would put the seer stone into a hat, and put his face in the hat, drawing it closely around his face to exclude the light; and in the darkness the spiritual light would shine. A piece of something resembling parchment would appear, and on that appeared the writing. One character at a time

> would appear, and under it was the interpretation in English. Brother Joseph would read off the English to ... his ... scribe, and when it was written down and repeated to Brother Joseph to see if it was correct, then it would disappear, and another character with the interpretation would appear.[89]

Joseph Knight, then in his late fifties, whose black carriage had been borrowed without his knowledge to retrieve the gold plates in September 1827, also described the process:

> Now the way he translated was he put the urim and thummim [seer stone] into his hat and Darkened his Eyes then he would take a sentance and it would apper in Brite Roman Letters. Then he would tell the writer and he would write it. Then that would go away the next sentance would Come and so on. But if it was not Spelt rite it would not go away till it was rite. so we see it was marvelous. Thus was the hol translated.[90]

Emma Smith described the process on more than one occasion to her son: "Now the first that my husband translated, was translated by use of Urim and Thummim [breastplate and seer stones], and that was the part that Martin Harris lost, after that [my husband] used a small stone, not exactly black, but was rather a dark color." She later added: "In writing for your father I frequently wrote day after day, sitting by the table close to him, he sitting with his face buried in his hat, with the stone in it, and dictating hour after hour with nothing between us."[91]

Comparatively few pages of text had been dictated when around 5:00 on Sunday evening, 5 April 1829, Oliver Cowdery came to the door.[92] Cowdery, accompanied by Smith's twenty-one-year-old brother Samuel, had walked the 120 miles from Manchester where he had been teaching school and boarding with Joseph Sr. and Lucy. Joseph Sr. had, over the course of the winter, told him about his son's special calling from God; and fired by religious zeal and personal experiences in prayer that confirmed to him the truth of what Joseph Sr. had told him, Cowdery was presenting himself to assist Joseph Jr. If Harris was the enabler, Cowdery was the facilitator.

OLIVER COWDERY'S BACKGROUND

It is my opinion that Cowdery brought with him the over-arching conceptual plans and some of the important details that made it possible for Smith to complete the Book of Mormon. Cowdery's qualifications for teaching were minimal; in fact, Hyrum Smith as school trustee had actually hired Lyman Cowdery, who accepted the job, then urged them to accept his brother Oliver as his replacement. Oliver had worked as a blacksmith, farmhand, and store clerk; according to John Gilbert, the Book of Mormon's typesetter, he was not capable of correcting the grammar in the dictation.[93] In the next nine to thirteen weeks, twenty-three-year-old Joseph Smith dictated to twenty-two-year-old Oliver Cowdery a book of 275,000 words; the printer, John H. Gilbert, who set its 588 pages, also corrected the grammar.[94] It reached an estimated less than .1 percent of the population, but the effect was so profound that it changed American history.

Critical in understanding this process is understanding Oliver Cowdery. Like Joseph Smith, he approached the world with a dual perspective, one of which was magic. Cowdery had been born in Middleton, Vermont, only fifty miles from Smith. They may not have known they were related; Cowdery was a third cousin to Lucy Mack Smith and was also related by marriage.[95] His father, William Cowdery, had been enmeshed in a scandal involving magic about 1800 near their home and had used divining rods in seeking treasure.[96] Within two days of their meeting, Cowdery was writing full time as Smith's scribe; and within the month Smith gave Cowdery a series of revelations. In the first, God told Cowdery that he had the divine gift of revelation and in the second that he had the gift "of working with the rod: behold it has told you things: behold there is no power save God, that can cause this rod of nature, to work in your hands, for it is the work of God; and therefore whatsoever you shall ask me to tell you by that means, that will I grant unto you, that you shall know."[97] In psychological terms, the narcissist had found an absolutely necessary figure: an awestruck, encouraging, and supportive individual who responded fully to his charisma. For her part, I see Emma as caught in Joseph's narcissism, as well. If this is true (and the documentation is absent to decide the case conclusively one way or the other), then she gained her importance from association or reflection of the narcissist. Thus, when someone attempted to comfort her on the day of Joseph's murder by assuring her that this sorrow would be the crown of her life, she responded, *"My husband was my crown."*[98] Though uttered in grief, it does not suggest successful individual maturation.

Cowdery's second perspective was the Hebrew origins of the Native Americans. This interest, like the interest in magic, he also shared with Smith. In 1803 the Cowdery family, including seven-year-old Oliver, moved to Poultney, Vermont, in Rutland County, which shares a border with Windsor County, where Smith was born and lived for ten years. In Poultney, Oliver's stepmother joined the Congregational church in 1810 followed by his stepsisters in 1818. In 1821 Ethan Smith (no relation to the Joseph Smith family) became their pastor.[99] Although there is no documentation that Ethan Smith and Oliver Cowdery had any kind of relationship, I argue that it requires more effort to believe they did not than that they did. As a consequence, I see Ethan Smith as the unwitting third man to help Joseph Smith produce the Book of Mormon by acting as an absent but necessary theologian.

In 1823 Ethan Smith published *A View of the Hebrews; or The Tribes of Israel in America,*[100] which brought together writings by authors as far back as the sixteenth century promoting a popular belief of the day—that the Native Americans were the descendants of the lost ten tribes of Israel. Because of widespread interest, a second enlarged edition was printed in 1825. Ethan Smith visited Palmyra, perhaps in 1827, for the *Wayne Sentinel* printed notices that he should call at the post office for letters.[101] The year after Ethan Smith's first edition appeared, Josiah Priest, whose works were a compilation of curious, dramatic, and historical items, printed fifty-six pages from Ethan Smith's book word for word in his own *Wonders of Nature and Providence Displayed* (Rochester, NY: n.p., 1824), only twenty miles from Palmyra, with a second edition following the next year.[102] The Manchester library, five miles from the Smith home, owned a copy; and according to Robert Paul, it was repeatedly checked out in 1826-27.[103] Hence it is highly likely—B. H. Roberts called it a "close certainty"—that Joseph Smith knew Ethan Smith's book, especially given thc family's interest in pre-Columbian America.[104] From a naturalistic perspective, I argue that Ethan Smith's book provided the concept and outline for much of the Book of Mormon. Although Ethan Smith was a distinguished theologian and successful author of the most influential book of the period promoting a Hebrew-Christian ancestry for the Native American, as well as being pastor to Cowdery's family, neither Cowdery nor Joseph Smith ever mention him. As a psychiatrist, I find this silence telling.

In the early 1920s, B. H. Roberts, the leading intellectual Mormon general authority and historian, wrote a 284-page manuscript comparing these two books and finding multiple similarities. Some of Ethan Smith's slight misquotations from the Bible appear in the Book of Mormon with similar near-quotations from Josiah Priest's book.[105] Joseph Smith undoubtedly knew the common view about Indian origins; with specific details from Ethan Smith's views provided by Oliver Cowdery, Smith was in a position to unify Christian magic and Christian miracle, pre-Columbian fantasy and Bible myth.

As I read the Book of Mormon, I see Joseph Smith and Oliver Cowdery constructing narratives of Joseph's personal life within Ethan Smith's conceptual framework, if not following the outline of his book. I also hypothesize that, dictating to Oliver Cowdery, who was ignorant of the similarities between Joseph's life and the narratives he was writing down, Joseph could be less restrained in fantasy than he had been with his wife or Martin Harris.

According to most devout and nonbelieving students of the Book of Mormon alike, Smith began the dictation where he had left off (Mosiah). I feel that he was waiting for time to pass and his confidence to increase that the 116 pages would not resurface. After dictating from Mosiah through (probably) the short book individually named "Book of Mormon" almost at its end by the end of May, he returned to the beginning, retelling the story of the departure from Jerusalem, Laban, the sword, the plates, and the arrival in the promised land. For reasons I discuss in chapter 6, he dictated the book of Ether next, then finished off with the book of Moroni, a clear announcement that he was ready to start a church.[106]

Preparing for the possibility that the lost 116 pages might reappear, he created an explanation: God had foreseen this loss of the 116 pages over 2,000 years earlier and knew that evil men would alter the record to diminish Smith's credibility as a translator. So God inspired Nephi and several generations of his descendants to write a similar, but not identical, history on "small plates" which were added to the record without being edited and condensed. Smith translated this second "more spiritual and personal" version.

From a psychoanalytic perspective, this story provided a reason for belief to those who desperately wanted proof that God, in an eternal world of omnipotent perfection, had touched one spot—one person—on earth. But among men and women who approached life in a more common sense way, the complexities of this scenario create difficulties. Some of them might also have sensed, without knowing the term, that Smith was using the defense mechanism of projection in accusing his enemies of forgery. Such projection appears in the interactions between Nephi and Laban, who first threatens Nephi and his brothers with his sword but then turns up, literally, at Nephi's feet, still armed but helpless to use his sword. Joseph Smith/Nephi had projected his anger and deception onto the surgeon Nathan Smith/Laban, and turned him into a drunk thieving murderer.

Revenge and Compensation for Humiliation: The Second Nephi

> Vulnerability in self-esteem makes individuals with Narcissistic Personality Disorder very sensitive to "injury" from criticism or defeat. Although they may not show it outwardly, criticism may haunt these individuals and may leave them feeling humiliated, degraded, hollow, and empty. They may react with disdain, rage, or defiant counterattack. Such experiences often lead to social withdrawal or an appearance of humility that may mask and protect the grandiosity. Interpersonal relations are typically impaired due to problems derived from entitlement, the need for admiration, and the relative disregard for the sensitivities of others. Though overweening ambition and confidence may lead to high achievement, performance may be disrupted due to intolerance of criticism or defeat. Sometimes vocational functioning can be very low, reflecting an unwillingness to take a risk in competitive or other situations in which defeat is possible.[107]

> Although the specific form of the environmental trauma may vary, we suggest that there is a common denominator in that these environmental traumata induce the formation of a precocious and premature sense of self—which retains its fragility and must be supported by omnipotent and

> grandiose fantasies. ... [and this creates] a state of illusionary self-sufficiency. ... By means of the illusion of self-sufficiency the individual is removed from the fear of closeness to objects [people], for he denies any instinctual demand made upon the object.[108]

> [The child] escapes the painful feeling of nothingness by molding himself in fancy into something outstanding—the more he is alienated, not only from others but also from himself, the more easily such notions acquire a psychic reality. His notions of himself become a substitute for his undermined self-esteem; they become his "real me". ... In rather simplified terms, a person clings to illusions about himself because, and as far as, he has lost himself.[109]

Nephi, the son of Nephi, the son of Helaman, in 3 Nephi may be another major alter ego for Smith. (To distinguish clearly between them, I call them Nephi Sr. [son of Helaman] and Nephi Jr. [son of Nephi].) This narrative again demonstrates how key events from Joseph Smith's early adulthood appear in the Book of Mormon text. It is striking that, of all Smith's possible alter egos in the Book of Mormon, the two most important are named Nephi, a psychological clue that they are mirrors of each other and serve the same psychological function.

Nephi Jr., namesake of the first Nephi, lived some 500 years later, just before the coming of Jesus Christ to the Americas. The narrative of the first Nephi, as I have argued, told in disguised form the story of Joseph Smith's childhood and early adolescence. In the 3 Nephi account, Smith may refer briefly to his surgery, the years of intermittent hunger, the religious revival, Alvin's death, the Bainbridge trial, the death of his firstborn son, loss of the manuscript, and seven months of normal living before he again began dictating the Book of Mormon. The account in 3 Nephi thus focused on the second and third decade of Smith's life but used many of the same psychological patterns of relation demonstrated by the first retelling and that will be demonstrated throughout the book. Strikingly, the chronology for a disguised reliving of Smith's story matches the chronology of Smith's life virtually year for year.

The summary of the Book of Mormon narrative in chapter 2 brought us to the point where Lehi and the heroic Nephi had died, the latter about age seventy around 540 B.C.E. The period from around 500 B.C.E. to 200 B.C.E.—30 percent of Nephite history—is covered in only five to seven pages, a little over 1 percent of the whole Book of Mormon. Each king or keeper of the record commented on his own degree of righteousness and personal religious experience, then passed the record on. Around 200 B.C.E. this rapid pace slowed and the story unfolded in greater detail for the next century. Extended wars began between the Nephites and the Lamanites. The Nephites moved to new territory and established various "Christian" communities (see chapter 4), complete with baptism, a king's statesmanlike sermon, a prophet's martyrdom, marvelous conversions, and dedicated missionary work by five young men. Around 92 B.C.E. a peaceful revolution transformed the Nephite government from a monarchy to a monarchy/democracy, followed by thirty-two years of virulent warfare between the Nephites and Lamanites. Temporarily, reversing the usual pattern, the Lamanites, largely converted by a miracle, became righteous. War between the two major races was then replaced by internal conflict between the legitimate government and a secret evil brotherhood (the Gadianton band) that corrupted individuals and infiltrated the administrative and judicial branches of the government, as if Masonry and the Mafia had joined forces. This band of secret robbers and murderers expanded with the tolerance and collusion of the Nephite people as they slowly slid into iniquity. The government was in danger of collapsing.

Around 6 B.C.E. a Lamanite prophet, Samuel, foretold Jesus Christ's birth. He predicted two confirming signs: the star of Bethlehem and a dramatic night without darkness. He warned the people to repent or suffer terrible destruction at the time of Jesus' crucifixion. During this time the keepers of the sacred plates of brass as well as their own were a righteous father-son dyad, Nephi Sr. and Nephi Jr.

Nephi Jr. received the plates of brass from his father, who then "departed" from the land, disappearing forever.[110] Unbelievers insisted that the time for Samuel's prophecies had passed, and designated a day for killing the believers. Nephi Jr., sorrowful and distraught, engaged in lengthy prayer far into the night and was comforted when the Lord spoke: "This night shall the sign be given and on the morrow come I into the world" (BM 453; 3 Ne. 1:13). The signs appeared, the wicked repented, and there was a "great remission of sins." However, the next thirty-three years, while Christ was fulfilling his mission in Palestine, were given over to resistance against the thriving Gadianton band, which began with flattery and deceit and ended with robbery, murder, and rebellion against the government.

The Nephites in the Book of Mormon are characterized by the constancy of their inconstancy. By 3 C.E.—three years after the "great remission of sins"—they were beginning "to wax strong in wickedness and abominations." This trend continued for the next ten years, despite preaching and prophesying by the shrinking number of the righteous. Meanwhile the Gadianton robbers steadily enlarged their power base (BM 452-456; 3 Ne. 1, 2).

Converted Lamanites joined with Nephites in defense against these robbers; and, once again, reading from the Book of Mormon back into Smith's life provides a sort of "evidence" of periods of hunger for the family. The Gadianton band threatened the destruction of the country in 13 C.E.; the Nephites gained the upper hand one year later, only to suffer another attack in 15 C.E. In 16 C.E. Giddianhi, the robber chief, sent a written ultimatum to Lachoneus, the Nephite chief executive: capitulation or extermination. The Latin name is startling in a book of supposedly Hebrew and Egyptian origins; when a patient says something contradictory to facts and his level of knowledge, the therapist becomes alerted to possible strong psychological factors at play. This raising of consciousness is now justified by the following event; for, more significantly, the letter is a simplistic, almost boyish one, of bluster and threats. It alerts us to pay close attention. The robber praised Lachoneus for his firmness in maintaining "defense of your liberty, and your property, and your country. ... And it seemeth a pity unto me, most noble Lachoneus that ye should be so foolish and vain to suppose that ye can stand against so many brave men, which are at my command. ... and do await. ... for the word, Go down. ... and destroy." Giddianhi gave Lachoneus a month to make up his mind. If he capitulated, he may join the band of robbers on an equal footing. If not, "on the morrow month, I will command that my armies shall come down ... and shall let fall the sword upon you" (BM 457-58; 3 Ne. 3).

From a psychoanalytic perspective, the message is familiar: "You are very brave, but I am giving you two terrible choices." I think the source of the story lies in this event from Lucy's history:

> Said I, "Doctor ... can you not try once more by cutting round the bone. ... and thus you may save the leg. You will [not] take off the leg until you try once more. ..." The Doctor said, my poor boy, we have come again. "Yes," said Joseph, "I see you have; but you have not come to take off my leg, have you sir?" "No," said the surgeon, "it is your mothers request, that we should make one more effort."[111]

In this retelling of Joseph Smith's autobiography, Lachoneus is Lucy, negotiating with the robbers with swords (the surgeons), who are giving her the two choices of amputation or operation. It is Lucy, not Joseph Sr., who negotiates; Joseph Sr. is weeping at Joseph Jr.'s bedside, in what is certainly a demonstration of unhelpful emotional lability in a time of crisis. Joseph Jr. demonstrates his bravery by refusing to be bound with cords or drugged with alcohol. He chooses to face the surgery with his father, not his mother. His bravery did not keep him from pain.

In the Book of Mormon, the Nephites made a drastic choice. They gathered by the tens of thousands to a fortified place and prepared to withstand a seven-year siege, bringing with them their horses, chariots, cattle, flocks, and grain. Because they had stripped the land of food, the robbers also had only two choices: attack or starve (BM 459-460; 3 Ne. 3-4:7). The seven years in 3 Nephi corresponds to eight years in the wilderness in the 1-2 Nephi version.

In this, our second reading, the bloody private event is transformed by the Book of Mormon into a national war which occurred in "the sixth month" of 19 C.E. and corresponds to the year 1811 C.E. in Smith's memory:[112] "great and terrible was the slaughter thereof, insomuch that there never was known so great a slaughter among the people of Lehi since he left Jerusalem." The Gadianton band attacked with lamb skins around their loins, heads shorn and bodies dyed in blood and "great and terrible was the appearance of the armies" (BM 460-61; 3 Ne. 4:7). This description corresponds both to Joseph's living memory of the surgery and also to Lucy's description: "Oh! My God what a spectacle for a mother's eye. The wound torn open to view and my boy and the bed on which he covered with the blood which was still gushing from the wound. He was pale as a corpse and ... his face every feature of which depicted agony that cannot be described."[113]

In short, surgery has been transformed imaginatively into a major battle. The Nephites fought off this attack, pursuing the robbers to the borders of the wilderness. Giddianhi, "weary because of his much fighting," was "overtaken and slain" (BM 461; 3 Ne. 4:14). Like Laban, Giddianhi is a robber who is cut down by the sword. Joseph has, in fantasy, taken his vengeance on the pain-inflicting surgeon.

The Nephites then returned to their fortification. The next two and a half years of the siege were eventless and correspond historically, in my opinion, to the first years of recovery after Joseph's surgery. Then the Lamanites besieged the Nephite fortress under the command of another leader, Zemnarihah (21 C.E.) This event corresponds, I believe, to the beginning of the three years of crop failure and economic desperation for the Smiths (1813-16). In a fantasy reversal, the Nephites (the Smith family) have ample stores while the robbers (the surgeons) subsist on a dwindling supply of wilderness game, "insomuch that the robbers were about to perish with hunger" (BM 462-63; 3 Ne. 4:15-21). In this case, the hunger suggested by Lucy's history of three years of crop failures has been projected onto the enemy.[114] In an example of expansiveness, both the family and the surgeons have become the equivalent of national groups. In the decisive battle, the Nephites decimate the robbers, require them to repent, and hang Zemnarihah. Again, a representative of the surgeon has been killed.

Lucy summarizes the family's gratitude when it is clear that they have all survived typhoid and that Joseph will recover from the surgery: "We realized the blessing for I believe we felt more to acknowledge the hand of God in preserving our lives through such a desperate siege."[115] This family thanksgiving is exaggerated in the Book of Mormon: the people "did break forth, all as one, in singing and praising their God, for the great thing which he had done for them, in preserving them from falling into the hands of their enemies; yea, they did cry Hosanna to the Most High God" (BM 463; Ne. 4:29-33).

From a psychoanalytic perspective, the drive and fantasies for omnipotence that began before the surgery and were enhanced by the surgery and following events are now temporarily contained and reversed. Frightened by the surgery and periods of hunger, Smith's fantasies of omnipotence are briefly squelched and reversed into humility. In the Book of Mormon, God is praised for saving them:

> They knew it was because of their repentance and their humility that they had been delivered from everlasting destruction. And now behold there was not a living soul among all the people of the Nephites which did doubt in the least thing in the words of all the holy prophets which had spoken. ... [they forsook] all their sins ... abominations ... and whoredoms, and did serve God. (BM 463; 3 Ne. 5:1)

This beatific state occurred in 21 or 22 C.E. (1813-14). But Joseph Smith did not have enough ego strength to renounce narcissism. The desperate need for compensating fantasies of power slowly returned as he felt increasingly safe during his recovery. Three years passed without incident—the length of time that the Nephites' faith and repentance endured. At that point (26 C.E.//1818), seven years after the great battle, the people "did return to their own lands" from their fortress encampment, taking with them their animals, treasures, remaining food, and other goods. This episode corresponds with the Smith family's move to Palmyra in 1817 and settling in their own cabin in 1818, seven years after the surgery (BM 465; 3 Ne. 6:1-3).

The next three years comprise a period of relative tranquility in both the life of the family and in the Book of Mormon narrative:

> There was great order in the land; and they had formed their laws according to equity and justice. And now there was nothing in all the land to hinder the people from prospering continually. ... There were many cities built anew, and ... many highways cast up, and many roads made, which led from city to city, and from land to land, and from place to place. And thus passed twenty and eighth year [1820], and the people had continued peace. (BM 465; 3 Ne. 6:1-10)

The period of relative tranquility for the Smith family paralleled the historical "era of good feeling" during the first of U.S. president James Monroe's two terms (1816-24). In 1818 the Cumberland Road (the "National Road") reached Ohio and opened up Kentucky, Tennessee, and lands westward.[116] Thus the larger social context also found its way in disguised form into the Book of Mormon. Supporting evidence is Orsamus Turner's memory that Joseph came into the printer's shop weekly to get his father's paper, participated in the debating club, and read extensively.[117]

In 29 C.E. (1821) the Nephites' prosperity is disrupted by "disputings ... pride and boastings, because of ... riches." "Lawyers," "merchants," and "officers" began forming social "ranks, according to their riches, and their chances for learning; yea, some were ignorant because of their poverty, and others did receive great learning because of their riches" (BM 466; 3 Ne. 6:11-14). This hierarchical view of social privilege, from a psychological perspective, is consistent with how an ill-educated and poor fifteen-year-old could view his own lack of privilege (encouraged perhaps by his socially aware mother). Smith had written that because of "indigent circumstances. ... we were deprived of the bennifit of an education."[118]

In 30 C.E. Book of Mormon society degenerated into "awful wickedness." The 30-33 C.E. era in Nephite history corresponds roughly to 1823-26 for the Smiths. In September 1826 New York was rocked by the disappearance and presumed murder of William Morgan, a brick-and-stone mason of Batavia, New York, and also a member of the Masonic order. He was in jail in Canandaigua, New York, nine miles from the Smith farmhouse for a debt of $2.69, but the real reason for his imprisonment was his determination to publish a book revealing the secrets of Masonry. Someone paid his debt, and Morgan was released from jail; but as he stepped into the street, he was seized, gagged, and thrust into a carriage. A wild drive followed, with relays of horses to the Canadian border where all traces of Morgan disappeared.[119] This event fed into a widespread belief that Masons were secretly controlling the government, courts, and elections; the resulting national paranoia lasted for over a decade.[120] Five Masons were tried for Morgan's murder. Three were acquitted, and two received sentences of less than a year. I argue that this story appears in the Book of Mormon as the Gadianton band's corruption of the Nephite judges, who were bought off "to deliver those which were guilty of murder from the grasp of justice" (BM 467; 3 Ne. 6:28-30). The band also murdered "the Chief Judge of the land" in the thirtieth year, a period of violence during which the Nephite government actually collapsed. The church "began to be broken up," and the people "were divided one against another ... into tribes, every man according to his family, and his kindred and friends; and thus they did destroy the government of the land" (BM 467-68; 3 Ne. 6:15-7:2).

Monroe's second term (1820-24), rather than continuing the "era of good feeling," was characterized by sectional hostility, individual political rivalries, bitter conflict over slavery (Maine, no; Missouri, yes), and the one-party election of 1824 with four candidates. Andrew Jackson won a plurality of votes, but the electoral college was split with 99 votes for Jackson, 84 for John Quincy Adams, 41 for W. H. Crawford, and 37 for Henry Clay. No one had a constitutional majority, although the will of the people was reasonably clear. By law the election was decided in the U.S. House of Representatives, where, according to common belief, Henry Clay, in a secret agreement, gave his votes to John Quincy Adams in exchange for an appointment as Secretary of State. Cries of corruption erupted. One newspaper editorialized: "Expired at Washington on the ninth of February, of poison administered by the assassin hands of John Quincy Adams, the usurper, and Henry Clay[:] the virtue, liberty and independence of the United States."[121]

In Palmyra the years 1823-24 (31-32 C.E.) also commenced, as we have seen, a period of competitive religious revivalism. Smith later stigmatized the "great love" professed by converts of various sects as "more pretended than real; for a feeling of great confusion and bad feeling ensued—priest contending against priest, and convert against convert; so that all their good feelings for one another, if they ever had any, were entirely lost in a strife of words."[122] Similarly, in the Book of Mormon, "six years had not passed away, since the more part of the people had turned from their righteousness, like the dog to his vomit, or the sow to her wallowing in the mire" (BM 468; 3 Ne. 7:8).

In 31 C.E. (1823) the tribal division resulted in "strict laws" so that "in some degree they had peace in the land." The faithless Nephites actively persecuted the prophets; they stoned Nephi's brother near the end of that year. Significantly, Smith here compensated strikingly for Alvin's death, which coincided with the first visits of the angel/guardian spirit. Similarly, Joseph Smith's alter ego Nephi Jr. heard the voice of the Lord, saw angels, and began to "minister with power and great authority, ... and even his brother did he raise from the dead" (BM 469; 3 Ne. 7:19). Psychologically, Smith was ranking himself with Elijah and Elisha, who had raised one dead person apiece, and Jesus who had restored Lazarus and the daughter of Jairus to life (1 Kgs. 17:17-24; 2 Kgs. 4:14-37; Matt. 9:18-26; John 11:32-45). But who had also repaired a broken body, perhaps with a crushed skull? Those who had stoned Nephi's brother witnessed this miracle but "were angry with him [Nephi], because of his power: and he did also many more miracles, in the sight of the people, in the name of Jesus" (BM 469; 3 Ne. 7:20). Smith conquered the tragedy of Alvin's death by a reversed fantasy that also, incidentally, showed his power and authority over an older brother.

Nephi's preaching began a revival of religious activity among the people: "the thirty and first year [1823] did pass away, and there were but few which were converted unto the Lord," a historically accurate statement. The next year, 1824, was similar. However, by the "thirty and third year [1825]," there were "many in the commencement of this year, that were baptized unto repentance; and thus the more part of the year did pass away" (BM 467-70; 3 Ne. 7:20-26). The parallels between Nephi's revival and the Palmyra revival are striking, not only the description of the slow beginning and the sudden jump in conversions when George Lane arrived to work with Benjamin Stockton, but also in its chronology. The revival commenced in the spring of 1824, a few months after Alvin's death in November 1823 and continued moderately for almost a year. About 150 were baptized in late 1824, and another 250 were added in the first three months of 1825. Or, as Nephi recorded, "there were many in the commencement of this year [33 C.E.//1825] ... that were baptized ... and the year did pass away." By September 1825, when the Palmyra churches looked back over the previous twelve months, over 400 had been baptized; of these 208 were Methodists, 94 Baptists, and 99 Presbyterians.[123] Apparently the effects of Rev. George Lane continued after his departure. The revival was over in both the Book of Mormon and Palmyra one and a half to two years after the brother's death. As a psychiatrist, I would expect the revival to be transformed in fantasy to become a sign of Smith's own emerging religious power and authority. In real life he almost returned to the Methodist church; in the Book of Mormon fantasy, he has replaced Stockton and Lane as the religious leader.

The next event was Christ's crucifixion, which occurred in the Book of Mormon "in the thirty and fourth year, in the first month, in the fourth day of the month" (BM 470; 3 Ne. 8:5). Nephi's brother had been stoned in the latter part of the thirty-first year—more than twenty-four months earlier but probably less than thirty. Significantly, the space between Alvin's death and early 1826 was twenty-seven months. The New Testament records that the "earth did quake and rocks rent"; there were three hours of darkness, and the temple veil was rent (Mark 15:33-38; Luke 23:55-56; Matt. 27:51). The Book of Mormon exaggerates these events into a geophysical holocaust, as, throughout the book, it exaggerates biblical miracles. This three-hour cataclysm began with a terrible storm; tidal waves, fire, and earthquakes destroyed sixteen cities and changed the "whole face" of the northern land, breaking up highways and roads. Thousands died, presumably including children, infants, and pregnant mothers.

Next came a darkness so thick that the survivors could feel it, and no fire or candle could be lit for the next three days. The survivors wept and mourned: "O that we had repented ... and not stoned the prophets. ... Then would our mothers, and our fair daughters, and our children have been spared." This selective miracle spared the "more righteous" but slew those guilty of "iniquity and abominations." Then the survivors heard a voice, twice without comprehending it, but the third time understanding as it said:

> Wo, wo, wo unto this people; wo unto the inhabitants of the whole earth, except they shall repent. ... Behold, that great city Zarahemla have I burned with fire. ... and the great city Moroni have I caused to be sunk in the depths of the sea. ... and. ... the great city Moronihah have I covered with earth. ... And ... the city of Gilgal ... sunk ... and city of Onihah ... and ... Mocumi ... Gadiandi ... Gadiomnah ... Jacob ... and ... Gimgimno ... to be sunk. ... and made hills and valleys in the places thereof. ... and [the cities of] Laman ... and Josh ... Gad ... and Kishkumen have I caused to be burned with fire. (BM 470-472; 3 Ne. 8:19-9:19)

Who has destroyed lands, cities, men and women who were perhaps "wicked," but also innocent children and infants? "Behold I am Jesus

Christ, the Son of God. ... I am the light and the life of the world" (BM 473; 3 Ne. 9:11-22). The resurrected Christ then descended and preached his gospel of love and compassion, including the Sermon on the Mount. As a psychiatrist, I see a contradiction between behavior and words that the author does not appreciate. Such failure to recognize paradox is typical of the narcissistic personality.

Today Mormon geologists look for evidence of this geophysical holocaust in the oceans off Chile and Peru,[124] while Mormon archaeologists search for evidence of a Middle Eastern culture or language throughout the Americas. With no historical or scientific findings anywhere for this story, I believe we are justified in looking to the personal story of Joseph Smith.

A more fruitful source for this geophysical holocaust is Smith's inner life. The catastrophe in the Book of Mormon comes as a judgment from God—mirroring, I argue, the time when Smith stood before a literal judgment bar in South Bainbridge and was declared guilty. Psychologically, this fantasy of external destruction reveals how shattered he was by his trial for magic and money-digging, and his difficulty in handling the resulting shame and humiliation is proportional to the magnitude of the devastation.[125] He combines his internal devastation with a fantasy act of revenge on those who killed his brother and humiliated him. Every psychiatrist has heard patients present dreams and fantasies of volcanos and earthquakes, suggesting intensity of emotional upheaval. The narcissistic personality cannot handle shame or humiliation; it feels even ordinary slights, rebuffs, or insults with frightening emotional intensity. The narcissist's defenses include surrounding himself or herself with compliant people who buffer the narcissist from the outside world. But if these buffers are inadequate or unavailable, as was the case for Smith during his trial, then the narcissist's personality is terribly shaken. This story makes a contribution to the diagnostic profile of Joseph Smith.[126]

Up to this point, Smith has followed both the chronological order and timing of his autobiography in creating the Book of Mormon narrative. He continues the order, but not the close time parallels. As already discussed, the five events following Smith's humiliating trial are the death of Smith's deformed and stillborn son, his rejection by Emma's church, his loss of the manuscript, a period of conventional living, then a return to dictation. All five events in this same chronological order can be found in the Book of Mormon story in the book of 3 Nephi, but these incidents are more highly disguised than the autobiographical parallels with the story of the first Nephi and Lehi. These events happened within two years of the time when Smith dictated them to Cowdery, sufficient reason, in my opinion, to take special pains with disguising them.

From a psychoanalytic perspective, we would expect the "very much deformed" stillborn son to be transformed by compensatory exaggerated fantasy into a child of unearthly beauty. Therefore, I see the Book of Mormon story of Christ blessing the children as the transformation of this painful and frightening loss:

> [Jesus] commanded that their little children should be brought. So they brought their little children and sat them down upon the ground round about him, and Jesus stood in their midst ... and ... groaned ... and prayed ... and he took their little children one by one, and blessed them, and prayed unto the Father for them ... and spoke unto the multitude. ... Behold your little ones. And as they looked to behold, they cast their eyes toward heaven, and they saw the Heavens open, and they saw angels descending out of Heaven as it were, in the midst of fire; and they came down and encircled those little ones about; and they were encircled about with fire; and the angels did minister unto them, and the multitude did see and hear, and bear record. (BM 490; 3 Ne. 17:21-24)

Rather than one horribly deformed child, we here have a multitude of children encircled by the glory of God and ministered to by angels. No scene could have more completely erased the sorrowful memory of the dead child and the humiliating memory of how Smith had boasted of this child's ability to his skeptical in-laws.

Chronologically, the disguised version of Smith's application to Emma's church should follow this scene of the children and precede the lost manuscript. In fact, we find Jesus counseling the people against the kind of behavior that humiliated the grieving Joseph.

> And now behold, this is the commandment which I give unto you, that ye shall not suffer any one, knowingly, to partake of my flesh, and blood unworthily ... For whoso eateth and drinketh my flesh and blood unworthily eateth and drinketh damnation to his soul. ... Nevertheless ye shall not cast him out from among you, but ye shall minister unto him and shall pray for him unto the Father, in my name and if it so be that he repenteth, and is baptized in my name, then shall ye receive him, and shall minister unto him of my flesh and blood. ... Nevertheless, ye shall not cast him out of your ... places of worship ... for ye know not but what they will return and repent. (BM 492; 3 Ne. 18:28-32)

This statement of tolerance and compassion thus becomes a condemnation, put in God's mouth, against the Methodist Episcopal church of Harmony. In fact, Smith never forgave the Methodist Episcopals and later the Methodists, whom he said God had singled out as especially unworthy.[127] The quotation from Jesus about the sacrament paraphrases 1 Corinthians 11:24-30, and the rest of the passage can be read as Smith's complaint that, even if his in-laws felt he was unworthy of the sacrament, they should have let him attend church.

The stillbirth occurred only eighteen days before Smith discovered the loss of the manuscript, and the application to the Methodist Episcopal church came in between. One would expect the disguised representations

Table 2
Parallels between 3-4 Nephi and the Teenage Joseph Smith

3 Nephi	*Joseph Smith, Jr.*
(C.E. 1) Nephi Sr. disappears, leaving Nephi Jr. with the plates.	Joseph Smith Sr. presents a disappointing figure and is being replaced by Joseph Smith Jr.
(C.E. 1-2) Signs of Christ's birth; people in "great remission of sins"; evil Gadianton band in the mountains.	
(C.E. 3-15) Robbers grow in number and attack; people ignore miracles and become wicked; preliminary defensive wars of Nephites.	
(C.E. 16) Gadianton band sends letter to Lachoneus demanding that the Nephites capitulate or be destroyed; describes Lachoneus as brave but foolish.	(Early C.E. 1811) Joseph's memory date for his surgery: "five years old or thereabouts." Surgeons tell Lucy she must choose between leg amputation or surgery. Joseph demonstrates bravery in surgery.
(C.E. 19, early) Nephites all move to one fortified area, taking all possessions and food.	
(C.E. 19, June) Robbers attack in lambskins, heads shorn, bodies in blood. Nephites win, retaliate by killing the lead robber. Nephites praise God, repent.	(C.E. 1811) Joseph's surgery with blood all over bed linen. Actual date probably early 1813. Smith family praises God for help through such a "desperate siege."
(C.E. 21-22) Robbers are starving; the Nephites have left no food outside their fortification. Nephites win, hang leader of robbers, kill others.	(C.E. 1813-15) Hunger time of Smiths while Joseph recovers. Hunger psychologically projected onto the enemy.
(C.E. 23-25) Continuing conquest of robbers and peace.	(C.E. 1815-16) Continued failure in crops and day-to-day living with probable hunger.
(C.E. 26) Nephites return home with flocks, cattle, and possessions. Warfare is over.	(C.E. 1816-18) Smith family immigrates to Palmyra, New York, improves, and moves to their own farm.
(C.E. 26-28) Prosperity: new roads, new cities, expansion and cooperation.	(C.E. 1816-20) James Monroe "era of good feelings," Cumberland road, U.S. expansion.
(C.E. 29) Beginning of pride, social class ranks, difficulty in getting "learning," iniquity, secret murders.	(C.E. 1821) Smith family endures amiable contempt; Joseph is without "bennifit of education."
(C.E. 30-34) Composite: collapse of government because of conflict and sectional divisions; "awful wickedness, "secret combinations," wickedness of most people.	(C.E. 1822-26) Composite: U.S. sectional hostilities; end of "era of good feelings." Corrupt election (1824); people believe in Masonic conspiracies; Masonic uproar; beginning of religious revivals and competition.

Table 2 (continued)
Parallels between 3-4 Nephi and the Teenage Joseph Smith

3 Nephi	*Joseph Smith, Jr.*
(C.E. 31). Nephi sees angels daily, ministers with "great authority," performs miracles though few believe, and (end of year) stone his brother to death. Nephi raises brother from the dead. People angry, but a few are converted.	(C.E. 1823) Story of angel and gold plates. Few believe story. Prerevival period. (End of year) Alvin Smith killed by medical incompetence, November 1823.
(C.E. 32) Nephi cries repentance and remission of sins, followed by baptism.	(C.E. 1824) Revival begins in March, accelerates in last quarter of the year.
(C.E. 33). Many converted in the first part of year.	(C.E. 1825). Revival continues; last two-thirds of converts are baptised in first part of year.
(C.E. 34, 4 Jan.) Death of Jesus and geophysical holocaust, people destroyed, about twenty-seven months after death/resurrection of Nephi's brother.	(C.E. 1826, Mar.). Joseph charged with "glass-looking," endures humiliation, one night in jail, about twenty-seven months after death of his brother Alvin.
(C.E. 34) Destruction of children and Jesus visits, blesses surviving children miraculously.	(C.E. 1828, 15 June) Stillborn birth of Joseph's malformed son.
(C.E. 34) Jesus encourages all, including sinners, to attend church but avoid communion.	(C.E. 1828, late June) Joseph rejected by Methodist Episcopal class in Harmony, Pennsylvania.
(C.E. 34) Jesus chastises Nephi for not writing Samuel's words.	(C.E. 1828, June/July) Joseph in despair for not making a copy of the manuscript of the Book of Mormon translation, for not writing it down twice.
(C.E. 34) Children speak miraculous things without Jesus present.	(C.E. 1828, June/July) Son was to "translate gold plates."
(C.E. 34-194) Period of peace (C.E. 194-201). Social class replaces Christian communism (C.E. 201-31). Division into Lamanites and Nephites marks beginning of extreme evil. 197 years of declining righteousness.	(C.E. 1828, 3 July-Feb. 1829) Joseph forced by outside factors into a nonsupernatural, normal life of farming. After seven months (perhaps one day for each of the 197 Nephite years), he returns to supernatural claims.

of these events in the Book of Mormon to follow each other in quick succession. Smith's self-chastisement for not making a copy of the manuscript appears as Jesus chastising Smith's alter ego Nephi Jr. for not recording events at all:

> I commanded my servant Samuel, the Lamanite, that he should testify unto this people ... that there were many saints which should arise from the dead. ... Were it not so? And his disciples answered him and said, Yea, Lord, Samuel did prophesy according to thy words, and they were all fulfilled. And Jesus saith unto them, How be it that ye have not written this thing? ... And ... Nephi remembered that this thing had not been written. And it came to pass that Jesus commanded that it should be written; therefore it was written according as he commanded. (BM 503; 3 Ne. 23:6-14)

Psychiatrists agree that major psychological conflicts and emotional trauma cannot be totally suppressed in our communications, even with conscious intent. This event involving the record makes an important pattern between events in Smith's life and events in the Book of Mormon: Smith projects his self-chastisement onto God.

Interestingly, at this point in the Book of Mormon narrative there is another episode of Jesus and the children. This repetition of compensatory fantasy underscores how traumatized Smith was by the malformed stillbirth, especially since the fantasy is even more miraculous:

> [Jesus] did teach and minister unto the children of the multitude ... and he did loose their tongues, and they did speak unto their fathers great and marvellous things ... and ... after he had ascended into Heaven the second time ... behold, it came to pass on the morrow, that the multitude gathered themselves together, and they both saw and heard these children; yea, even babes did open their mouths, and utter marvellous things; and the things which they did utter were forbidden, that there should not any man write them. (BM 506-507; 3 Ne. 26:16)

Smith's child, who, he boasted, would translate the golden plates, is here transformed into a multitude of children speaking the secrets of God.

After Christ departed from the Nephites, they experienced approximately two generations (160 years, 34-194 C.E.) of peace, a period that corresponded to Smith's relatively normal life between 3 July 1828 and February 1829. Nephi's son, Amos, "kept [the record] eighty and four years and there was still peace in the land, save it were for a small part of the people, which had revolted from the church, and took upon them the name of Lamanites" (BM 516; 4 Ne. 19-21). During this time the people repaired the destruction and "spread upon all the face of the land." The church prospered, and

> there was no contention in the land, because of the love of God which did dwell in the hearts of the people. And there were no envyings, nor strifes, nor tumults, nor whoredoms, nor lyings, nor murders, nor any manner of

> lasciviousness: and surely there could not be a happier people among all the people of God: There were no robbers, nor no murderers, neither were there Lamanites, nor no manner of Ites; but they were in one, the children of Christ, and heirs to the kingdom of God: And how blessed were they. (BM 515-16; 4 Ne. 12-18)

From a psychoanalytic perspective, this passage strongly suggests that Smith, temporarily controlled by outside pressures, found peace from his internal conflicts for a time. This ideal peace deteriorated in 201 C.E. when social classes replaced Christian communalism; thirty years later (231 C.E.), a "great division" into Lamanites, Nephites, and other subdivisions recurred. The peace from Jesus' visit in 33 C.E. to this division lasted 197 years. The seven months of Smith's retreat into conventional living lasted, in round months of thirty days each, 210 days. The two figures are so close that, as a psychiatrist, I suspect a simple mental substitution of days for years. In seventy more years, all righteousness had evaporated from among the people. Tellingly, in Smith's real life, after giving his father a revelation some time in February, he began dictating the Book of Mormon to Oliver Cowdery in early April—a little more than sixty days. As Smith intensified his supernatural claims, the Book of Mormon peoples intensified their evil. These parallels are very suggestive.

In his final addition to the Book of Mormon, Ether, I argue that Smith will disclose important information about his dictation of the Book of Mormon. (See chapter 6.) This self-disclosure is one of three reasons for the addition of this otherwise puzzling book.

Notes

1. Wesley P. Walters, "The Use of the Old Testament in the Book of Mormon," M.A. thesis, Covenant Theological Seminary, St. Louis, MO, 1981, 25-29. Walters ascribes this pattern to Smith's use of Old Testament motifs. The orthodox Mormon position is that Nephi saw his exodus to a promised land as symbolically parallel to the original exodus from Egypt. John L. Sorenson, "Composition of Lehi's Family," in *By Study and Also by Faith,* eds., John M. Lundquist and Stephen D. Ricks (Salt Lake City: Deseret Book, 1990), 182; and George S. Tate, "The Typology of the Exodus Pattern in the Book of Mormon," in *Literature of Belief,* ed. Neal E. Lambert (Provo, UT: BYU Religious Studies Center, 1981), 245-62.

2. Otto Kernberg, *Borderline Conditions and Pathological Narcissism* (New York: Jason Aronson, 1975), 25-26.

3. Ibid., 29.

4. Sigmund Freud, "Group Psychology and the Analysis of the Ego," (1922) *Complete Psychological Works of Sigmund Freud* (hereafter *Standard Edition)* (London: Hogarth Press, 1955), 18:69-143. Nietzsche's well-known dictum applies: "With individuals, insanity is the exception; with groups it is the rule." Irving L. Janis, *Groupthink: Psychological Studies of Policy Decisions and Fiascoes* (Boston: Houghton Mifflin, 1983), 9, 13.

5. D. Michael Quinn, *Early Mormonism and the Magic World View* (Salt Lake City: Signature Books, 1987), 36, 206-208.

6. Wesley P. Walters, "New Light on Mormon Origins from the Palmyra Revival," 59-81, and response by Richard L. Bushman, 82-100, in *Dialogue: A Journal of Mormon Thought* 4 (Spring 1969). Orthodox Mormon attempts to keep the 1820 date may be found in Milton V. Backman, *Joseph Smith's First Vision* (Salt Lake City: Bookcraft, 1890), and Richard L. Anderson, "Circumstantial Confirmation of the First Vision through Reminiscences," *BYU Studies* 9 (Spring 1969): 373-404. Mormon historian Marvin S. Hill accepts the 1824 date in "The First Vision Controversy: A Critique and Reconciliation," *Dialogue: A Journal of Mormon Thought* 15 (Summer 1982): 31-46. In 1842 Smith summarized his 1838 version in a letter to a Chicago newspaper editor, John Wentworth. Qtd in Backman, *First Vision,* 168-69.

7. Dean C. Jessee, "The Early Accounts of Joseph Smith's First Vision," *BYU Studies* 9 (1969): 275-94; Dean C. Jessee, ed., *The Papers of Joseph Smith* (Salt Lake City: Deseret Book, 1989), 1:6-7, 127, 272-73.

8. Cowdery, with Smith, in *Latter Day Saints' Messenger and Advocate,* Kirtland, Ohio, 1834-35, 1:13, 40, 79-80. Cowdery explains his collaboration with Smith: "That our narrative may be correct, and particularly the introduction, it is proper to inform our patrons, that our brother J. Smith, Jr. has offered to assist us. Indeed there are many items connected with the fore part of this subject that render his labor indispensable." Letter III, 1 (Dec. 1834): 42-43, starts the description of the first vision (in which the divine visitor is an angel); it continues in Letter IV, 1 (Feb. 1835): 78, and Letter VII, 1 (July 1835): 155-59.

9. "Lucy Smith History, 1845," in *Early Mormon Documents,* Vol. 1, ed. Dan Vogel (Salt Lake City: Signature Books, 1996), 285, hereafter cited as Vogel, Lucy Smith History.

10. Quinn, *Magic World View,* ix-xxii; 1-149. See discussion in chapter 2.

11. Ibid., 114, quotes an 1829 newspaper account that Smith had been "visited in a dream by the spirit of the Almighty [and was] thrice thus visited." One month later a Rochester newspaper quoted Martin Harris: Smith "said that he had been visited by the spirit of the Almighty ... and after a third visit from the same spirit in a dream he proceeded to the spot [Cumorah]."

12. Ibid., 120.

13. Ibid., 112-23; see especially seven references to Smith needing his seer stone to find the plates, 122-23.

14. Dean C. Jessee, *The Personal Writings of Joseph Smith* (Salt Lake City: Deseret Book, 1984), 7; see also Jessee, *Papers of Joseph Smith,* 1:8-9; Scott H. Faulring, ed., *An American Prophet's Record: The Diaries and Journals of Joseph Smith* (Salt Lake City: Signature Books in association with Smith Research Associates, 1989), 6-7.

15. Quinn, *Magic World View,* 123.

16. Jessee, *Papers of Joseph Smith,* 1:281-82. Compare the even more refined 1838 version in the *Pearl of Great Price,* JS-H 2:51-53.

17. These men are Willard Chase, affidavit, 11 Dec. 1833, in E. D. Howe, *Mormonism Unvailed* (Painesville, OH: Author, 1834), and Benjamin Saunders, interviewed in 1884, Miscellany, 1795-1948, Box 2, fd. 44, 2, 19, RLDS Library-Archives; both quoted in Quinn, *Magic World View,* 124-28. Quinn then reviews ancient and European historical sources providing context from the world of magic for such a happening (128-33).

18. Vogel, Lucy Smith History, 297-98. Compare the report sixty years later by Joseph's brother, William: "He took [the plates] from the stone box in which they were found, and placed them on the ground behind him, when the thought came into his mind that there might be a treasure hidden with them. While stooping forward to see, he was overpowered, so that could not look farther. Turning to get the plates, he found they had gone; and on looking around found that they were in the box again; but he could not get them." "Statement," *Saints' Herald* 2 (4 Oct. 1884): 643.

19. Dean C. Jessee, "Joseph Knight's Recollection of Early Mormon History," *BYU Studies* 17 (Autumn 1976): 29-39. See also Quinn, *Magic World View*, 139, who provides three additional references to this story.

20. Quinn, *Magic World View*, 133-37.

21. *Latter Day Saints Messenger and Advocate* 1 (Oct. 1834): 13, 78-80, 156-59.

22. John Phillip Walker, ed., *Dale Morgan on Early Mormonism: Correspondence and a New History* (Salt Lake City: Signature Books, 1986), 266, 380n16-21, who summarizes quotations from 1828, 1830-31, 1851, 1870, 1879, and 1880.

23. Quinn, *Magic World View*, 157. See also chapter 1, n27.

24. Vogel, Lucy Smith History, 304 ("careless quack" crossed out, and not printed).

25. According to Joseph's younger brother William in 1894, "Rev. Stockton was the president of the meeting and suggested that it was their meeting and under their care and they had a church there and they [the Smiths] ought to join the Presbyterians, but as father did not like Rev. Stockton very well, our folks hesitated." The reason for the dislike was Stockton's funeral sermon for Alvin when he implied that Alvin "had gone to hell, for Alvin was not a church member, but he was a good boy and my father did not like it." William adds that Joseph Sr. attended one of Stockton's revival meetings, then stopped. H. Michael Marquardt and Wesley P. Walters, *Inventing Mormonism: Tradition and the Historical Record* (San Francisco: Smith Research Associates, 1994), 19-20; 36-37n16; William Smith, interviewed by E. C. Briggs as reported by J. W. Petersen to *Zion's Ensign* (Independence, MO), and reprinted in *Deseret News*, 20 Jan. 1894, qtd. in Walters, "New Light on Mormon Origins from the Palmyra Revival," 75n10.

26. Rumors in town may have suggested that Alvin's body was disinterred—perhaps to get part of the corpse to satisfy the angelic messenger during Joseph's yearly visit. Joseph Smith, Sr., published a notice in six consecutive issues of the Palmyra *Wayne Sentinel* beginning 25 September 1824:

> TO THE PUBLIC: Whereas reports have been industriously put in circulation, that my son, Alvin, had been removed from the place of his interment and dissected; which reports every person possessed of human sensibility must know, are peculiarly calculated to harrow up the mind of a parent and deeply wound the feelings of relations—therefore, for the purpose of ascertaining the truth of such reports, I, with some of my neighbors this morning, repaired to the grave, and removing the earth, found the body which had not been disturbed. This method is taken for the purpose of satisfying the minds of those who may have heard the report, and of informing those who have put it into circulation, that it is earnestly requested that they would desist therefrom; and that it is believed by some that they have been stimulated to injure the reputation of certain persons than a philanthropy for the peace and welfare of myself and friends. /s/ Joseph Smith.

27. Vogel, Lucy Smith History, 295-96.

28. Ibid., 306.

29. Larry C. Porter, "Reverend George Lane: Good 'Gifts,' Much 'Grace,' and Marked 'Usefulness,'" *BYU Studies* 9 (Spring 1969): 321-40.

30. Walters, "New Light on Mormon Origins," 64-66: "[By March 1925] in Palmyra and Macedon ... more than 400 have already testified ... [and] the work is still progressing." *Wayne Sentinel* (Palmyra), 2 Mar. 1825, 3-4.

31. William Smith, qtd. in Marquardt and Walters, *Inventing Mormonism,* 19, 36n16. William's statement contradicts Joseph's 1838 canonized account of the first vision in which God commands him in 1820 not to "join with any of them." Jessee, *Papers of Joseph Smith,* 1:272-73.

32. Rodger I. Anderson, *Joseph Smith's New York Reputation Reexamined* (Salt Lake City: Signature Books, 1990), 117-72. Anderson's list includes episodes of animal sacrifice: a dog named Tray when Joseph was nineteen or twenty; a lamb (reviewed later in this chapter); and a black sheep.

33. Quinn, *Magic World View,* 47-51.

34. Ibid., 135-41.

35. Jessee, "Joseph Knight's Recollection," 31-32; also Quinn, *Magic World View,* 139, with three additional references to this story.

36. Oliver Cowdery, with Joseph Smith, *Messenger and Advocate* 2 (Oct. 1835): 200-201. This account briefly discusses a legend about a Spanish treasure cave near Harmony and presents Smith as a reluctant participant.

37. The "Articles of Agreement" was kept by "a citizen of Thompson township," who passed it on to a journalist in 1880. It was published in the anti-Mormon *Daily Tribune* (Salt Lake City), 23 Apr. 1880, and reprinted in Francis W. Kirkham, *New Witness for Christ in America* (Independence, MO: Zion's Printing and Publishing Co., 1951), 1:492-94 (my source here). The signers were Isaac Hale, David Hale, P. Newton, Charles A. Newton, Joseph Smith, Sr., Joseph Smith, Jr., Isaiah [Josiah] Stowell, Calvin Stowell, and William I. Wiley.

38. Marquardt and Walters, *Inventing Mormonism,* 69, 82, 120-22, 141. This agreement apparently extended for another two years, for Durfee recorded on 16 April 1827 that "S. Harrison Smith son of Joseph Smith began to work for me by the month ... for 7 months for the use of the place where Said Joseph Smith lives. Lemuel Durfee, Account Book, 1813-29, 15, Ontario County Historical Society, Canandaigua, New York, quoted by Marquart and Walters, *Inventing Mormonism,* 142n31; see also Vogel, Lucy Smith History, 322n129.

39. Peter Bridgeman was a crusading twenty-two-year-old Methodist exhorter, later a minister who helped found the West Bainbridge Methodist church. Marquardt and Walters, *Inventing Mormonism,* 83n34.

40. The records of the trial of Joseph Smith, Jr., are so potentially injurious to his reputation as a prophet of God that their rediscovery met with firm opposition from the Mormon establishment. This led to further investigation and discoveries, so that the provenance of the records can now be established with a high degree of assurance. Wesley P. Walters, "Joseph Smith's Bainbridge, N.Y., Court Trials," *Westminster Theological Journal* 36 (Winter 1974): 123-37, including nn. 1-23, and his "From Occult to Cult with Joseph Smith, Jr.," *Journal of Pastoral Practice* 1 (Summer 1977), published together by Utah Lighthouse Ministry (Salt Lake City, n.d.). See also Marquardt and Walters, *Inventing Mormonism,* 63-87, unnumbered pages between 199-201, 223-30.

41. W. D. Purple, "Joseph Smith, the Originator of Mormonism: Historical Reminiscences of the Town of Afton," *Chenango Union* 20 (3 May 1877): 3, Norwich, New York, reprinted in Kirkham, *A New Witness for Christ,* 2:362-68; Marquardt and Walter, *Inventing Mormonism,* 63-87, 222-30.

42. "Mormonism," *New Schaff-Herzog Encyclopedia of Religious Knowledge* (New York, 1883), 2:1576, qtd. in Fawn M. Brodie, *No Man Knows My History,* 2d ed. rev. and enl. (New York: Alfred A. Knopf, 1971), 427-29.

43. Smith used this stone while he produced the Book of Mormon. It is today in the First Presidency's vault, Church of Jesus Christ of Latter-day Saints, Salt Lake City. Quinn, *Magic World View,* 195-96.

44. Walters, "Joseph Smith's Bainbridge ... Trials," 121-31.

45. Walker, *Dale Morgan on Early Mormonism,* letter dated 19 Aug. 1947, 129-30; and Jerald and Sandra Tanner, *Joseph Smith and Money Digging* (Salt Lake City: Modern Microfilm, 1970), photographic copy, 120.

46. Walters, "From Occult to Cult, 121-37.

47. Marquardt and Walters, *Inventing Mormonism,* 73.

48. Dan Vogel, "'The Prophet Puzzle' Revisited," *Dialogue: A Journal of Mormon Thought* 31 (Fall 1998): 125-40.

49. Walker, *Dale Morgan on Early Mormonism,* 373n44.

50. Gordon A. Madsen, "Joseph Smith's 1826 Trial: The Legal Setting," *BYU Studies* 30 (Spring 1990), 91; Richard L. Anderson, "The Mature Joseph Smith and Treasure Seeking," *BYU Studies* 24 (Fall 1984): 489-560.

51. Susan Staker, "The Lord Said, 'Thy Wife Is a Very Fair Woman to Look Upon': The Book of Abraham, Secrets, and Lying for the Lord," 17 Aug. 1996, Sunstone Symposium, Salt Lake City, photocopy of paper in my possession; Linda King Newell and Valeen Tippetts Avery, *Mormon Enigma: Emma Hale Smith, Prophet's Wife, "Elect Lady," Polygamy's Foe, 1804-1879,* 95-168; George D. Smith, ed., *An Intimate Chronicle: The Journals of William Clayton* (Salt Lake City: Signature Books in association with Smith Research Associates, 1995), 93-136.

52. Jessee, "Joseph Knight's Recollection," 31-32; Quinn, *Magic World View,* 139, provides three additional references to this story.

53. Vogel, Lucy Smith History, 312.

54. "Mormon History," *Amboy Journal* 24 (30 Apr. 1879): 1; Joel Tiffany, "Mormonism," *Tiffany's Monthly* (New York) 5 (Aug. 1859): 163-64, qtd. in Kirkham, *New Witness,* 2:377; Vogel, Lucy Smith History, 326-30. See also summaries in Quinn, *Magic World View,* 112-48, and Marquardt and Walters, *Inventing Mormonism,* 96-115.

55. Richard L. Bushman, "The Recovery of the Book of Mormon," in *Book of Mormon Authorship Revisited: The Evidence for Ancient Origins* (Provo, UT: FARMS, 1997), 24.

56. Howe, *Mormonism Unvailed,* 231-37.

57. Vogel, Lucy Smith History, 328-29, 339-40.

58. Martin Harris, "Mormonism," *Tiffany's Monthly* 5 (May 1859): 116, reprt. in Kirkham, *New Witness,* 2:372-82, esp. 378. See also *Richmond Democrat,* 26 Jan. 1886, from *Plattsburg Democrat,* reprt. in *Saints Herald* 4 (Feb. 1888): 67, and qtd. in James E. Lancaster, "The Translation of the Book of Mormon," in *The Word of God: Essays on Mormon Scripture,* ed. Dan Vogel (Salt Lake City: Signature Books, 1990), 100.

59. Lancaster, "The Translation of the Book of Mormon," 105.

60. Harris, "Mormonism," 376-80. These were apparently oral agreements.

61. Walker, *Dale Morgan on Early Mormonism,* 277-78.

62. Ibid. A more detailed chronology of the translation period may be found in Stephen D. Ricks, "Joseph Smith's Means and Methods of Translating the Book of Mormon," and in John W. Welch and Tim Rathbone, "The Translation of the Book of Mormon: Basic Historical Information," published under one cover, #WRR-86 (Provo, UT: FARMS, 1986).

63. The contents of the lost 116 pages can be inferred from a sermon given by Mormon apostle Erastus Snow in May 1882. He remembered, "The Prophet Joseph informed us that the record of Lehi was contained on the 116 pages that were first translated and subsequently stolen, and of which an abridgment is given us in the first Book of Nephi, which is the record of Nephi individually, he himself being of the lineage of Manasseh; but that Ishmael was of the lineage of Ephraim, and that his sons married into Lehi's family, and Lehi's sons married Ishmael's daughters." *Journal of Discourses* (Liverpool and London: LDS Booksellers Depot, 1855-86), 23:184.

64. Howe, *Mormonism Unvailed,* 254-55; 260-61; Alma 50:30-31.

65. Ronald Walker, "Martin Harris: Mormonism's Early Convert," *Dialogue: A Journal of Mormon Thought* 19 (Winter 1986): 29-43; see also Jerald and Sandra Tanner, *The Case Against Mormonism* (Salt Lake City: Lighthouse Ministry, 1968), 2:2-33. Howe, *Mormonism Unvailed,* 261, prints the testimony of neighbor G. W. Stoddard who lists orthodox Quaker, Universalist, Restorationer, Baptist, and Presbyterian as Harris's previous religious affiliations. Stoddard also confirms Harris's wife-beating.

66. Howe, *Mormonism Unvailed,* quotes Harris's wife (256) and neighbor Abigail Harris (254), no known relation to Martin, on this point.

67. Harris, "Mormonism," 376-77.

68. Howe, *Mormonism Unvailed,* 236. Neighbor Willard Chase (246), who is probably quoting Ingersoll, repeats this sentence. Lucy Mack Smith recorded a more benign but not incompatible version in which Harris spontaneously gave Smith $50 in the presence of others "to do the Lords work with." Vogel, Lucy Smith History, 349.

69. Howe, *Mormonism Unvailed,* 254-57.

70. Bushman, *Joseph Smith and the Beginnings of Mormonism,* 80-92; Anthon letters in Kirkham, *New Witness,* 1:415-22. Harris also saw a prominent and "knowledgeable" physician, Samuel L. Mitchell. Mitchell, who died in 1831, may have encouraged Harris, for Mitchell was corresponding with Dr. Francis Corroy at the Mayan ceremonial ruin of Palenque. Corroy, a French physician and amateur archaeologist, believed alternately that they were either 4,600 or 1,300 years old and that the ruins had been built by the Egyptians, among others. Robert L. Brunhouse, *In Search of the Maya* (New York: Ballantine Books, 1973), 65-68.

71. Lancaster, "The Translation of the Book of Mormon," 97-112, 111-12n25. As an old man, Harris said Joseph also used a seer stone to translate, perhaps referring to the second translation period. Ricks, "Joseph Smith's Means and Methods," 4, 7n25, 7n13, Welch and Rathbone, "The Translation of the Book of Mormon," 9-10.

72. Vogel, Lucy Smith History, 357-58. Newell and Avery, *Mormon Enigma,* 314n12; Richard L. Anderson reported to Welch and Rathbone that "the Smith

family Bible clearly reads 'Alvin.'" Welch and Rathbone, "The Translation of the Book of Mormon," 12n36.

73. Howe, *Mormonism Unvailed,* 269; see also Newell and Avery, *Mormon Enigma,* 16-29.

74. I. Woodbridge Riley, *The Founder of Mormonism* (New York: Dodd, Mead, and Co., 1902), 350n16. Bennett had not seen the child, of course, but was probably relying on Joseph's description.

75. Psychological responses to stillbirth include "emptiness," "low self-esteem," "unbearable helplessness," "underlying shame," and feelings of inferiority, inadequacy, failure, and worthlessness. Irving G. Leon, "The Psychoanalytic Conceptualization of Perinatal Loss: A Multidimensional Model," *American Journal of Psychiatry* 149 (Nov. 1992): 1464-71, esp. 1465, 1470. Emma was surrounded by family members, but these relatives did not respect her husband and probably condemned her choice to elope in the face of her father's clear disapproval. "When a mother gives birth to a stillborn infant, *the reaction of others,* especially doctors, nurses, and family members, may influence the processes of grief." Elizabeth Kirkley-Best and Kenneth R. Kellner, "The Forgotten Grief: A Review of the Psychology of Stillbirth," *American Journal of Orthopsychiatry* 52 (July 1982): 425; emphasis theirs.

76. Howe, *Mormonism Unvailed,* 246-47, 264, 267, 269.

77. "Mormon History," *Amboy [Illinois] Journal,* 30 Mar. 1879, 30 Apr. 1879, 21 May 1879, and 11 June 1879. Emma's cousins, Joseph and Hiel Lewis, lived in Amboy but had been officers in the church in Harmony fifty years earlier. Reverend Wesley P. Walters published their comments in the *Utah Christian Tract Society Newsletter* (La Mesa, CA), July-Aug. 1971, 1. Newell and Avery, *Mormon Enigma,* 25, and Bushman, *Joseph Smith and the Beginnings of Mormonism,* 94-95, report the incident but do not explore its significance in showing Hale family and community feeling about Smith's reputation.

78. Vogel, Lucy Smith History, 356-68, 67-68n176; Pomeroy Tucker, *Origin, Rise and Progress of Mormonism* (New York: D. Appleton, 1867), 45-46.

79. Joseph and Hiel Lewis, "Mormon History," *Amboy Journal,* 30 Apr. 1879: 1, recalled their memories of what Smith had told them of the coming forth of the Book of Mormon, fifty years after Smith's 1826-27 residence near the family home:

> He [Joseph] said that by a dream he was informed that at such a place in a certain hill, in an iron box, were some gold plates with curious engravings, which he must get and translate, and write a book; that the plates were to be kept concealed from every human being for a certain time, some two or three years; that he went to the place and dug till he came to the stone that covered the box, when he was knocked down; that he again attempted to remove the stone, and was again knocked down; this attempt was made the third time, and the third time he was knocked down. Then he exclaimed, "Why can't I get it?" or words to that effect; and then he saw a man standing over the spot, which to him appeared like a Spaniard, having a long beard coming down over his breast to about here (Smith putting his hand to the pit of his stomach) with his (the ghost's) throat cut from ear to ear, and the blood streaming down, who told him that he could not get it alone; that another person whom he, Smith, would know at first sight, must come with him, and

> then he could get it. And when Smith saw Miss Emma Hale, he knew that she was the person ...
>
> In all this narrative, there was not one word about "visions of God," or of angels, or heavenly revelations. All his information was by that dream, and that bleeding ghost. The heavenly visions and messages of angels, etc., contained in Mormon books, were after-thoughts, *revised to order*. (Emphasis theirs.)

When challenged by Edwin Cadwell of the RLDS church, the Lewis brothers acknowledged that they may have misremembered that the box was "iron" but stated that others still living could attest to the rest of the story. Hiel Lewis, "Review of Mormonism," *Amboy Journal,* 4 June 1879, 1.

80. Vogel, Lucy Smith History, 364-65.

81. Ibid., 369-70.

82. Joseph Smith, Jr., et al., *History of the Church of Jesus Christ of Latter-day Saints,* 7 vols., ed. Brigham H. Roberts (Salt Lake City: Deseret Book Co., 1951), 1:28.

83. Vogel, Lucy Smith History, 380.

84. Jessee, "Joseph Knight's Recollection," 29-39.

85. "Now, behold, a marvelous work is about to come forth among the children of men, [//Isaiah 29:14], therefore, O ye that embark in the service of God, see that ye serve him with all your heart[,] might, mind and strength, that ye may stand blameless at the last day: [//Mark 12:30, Luke 10:24, 1 Cor. 1:8] Therefore if ye have desires to serve God, ye are called to the work, for behold, the field is white already to harvest, and lo, he that thrusteth in his sickle with his might, the same layeth up in store that he perisheth not, but bringeth salvation to his soul, [//John 4:35, 36] and faith, hope, charity, and love, with an eye single to the glory of God, qualifies him for the work [//1 Cor. 13:13]. Remember temperance, patience, humility, diligence, &c., ask and ye shall receive, knock and it shall be opened unto you: Amen" [//2 Peter 1:5-7; Matt. 7:7, 8, Luke 18:1, James 1:5]. See Bushman, *Joseph Smith and the Beginnings of Mormonism,* 95, 221n54.

86. Jessee, *Papers of Joseph Smith,* 1:9; Quinn, *Early Mormonism and the Magic World View,* 144-46; Walker, *Dale Morgan on Early Mormonism,* 278, 386; *Saint's Herald* 26 (1 Oct. 1879): 290. Joseph lists Martin Harris and his brother as scribes; Emma adds herself and Reuben. Later scribes included John and David Whitmer, and finally Oliver Cowdery, who would become Joseph's main scribe.

87. There is apparently universal agreement on this point from many eyewitnesses to Smith's dictation technique after the 116 pages were lost. However, Oliver Cowdery, who afterward became Smith's main scribe, testified in an 1830 trial that "said Smith found with the plates, from which he translated his book, two transparent stones, resembling glass, set in silver bows. That by looking through these, he was able to read in English, the reformed Egyptian characters, which were engraved on the plates." He reaffirms that his experience was with Joseph when Joseph was using the "Urim and Thummin, or, as the Nephites would have said, 'Interpreters.'" These statements, at variance with those of so many other witnesses, may raise the question of Cowdery's honesty. Possibly protecting Cowdery, devout Mormonism allows for the possibility that Smith continued to use both the seer stone in a hat and the spectacles attached to the breastplate, although a number of people, including Emma, said that it did not

happen. Ricks, "Joseph Smith's Means," 5; Welch and Rathbone, "The Translation of the Book of Mormon," 10-20; Bushman, *Joseph Smith and the Beginnings of Mormonism,* 221n51; Vogel, Lucy Smith History, 369-71; Tanner and Tanner, *Joseph Smith and Money Digging,* 7-9. Some apparent contradictions in the testimony of observers, but not all, occur because they used the Bible phrase "urim and thummin" to describe both the two seer stones attached to the breastplate and the single seer stone which he viewed in his white stove-pipe hat.

The mechanical description of translation, in which the translated words in English were viewed by Joseph when he looked into the stone, and not as a product of his own mental effort was accepted throughout the nineteenth century, but it makes God speak in New England idiom with flawed grammar. B. H. Roberts, *Defense of the Faith of the Saints, Vol. 1* (Salt Lake City: Deseret News Press, 1907), 305-307, insisted in 1907: "The theory of [the mechanical translation will] invite ridicule, and make of those who advocate it candidates for contempt. ... [It is] contrary to common sense and reason. ... The old theory must be abandoned." He advances instead the scenario that "the Prophet saw the Nephite characters in the Urim and Thummin; through strenuous mental effort, the exercise of faith and the operation of the inspiration of God upon his mind, he obtained the thought represented by the Nephite characters, understood them in the Nephite characters, understood them in the Nephite language, and then expressed the understanding, the thought, in such language as he was master of; which language, as his mind by mental processes arranged it, was reflected and held to his vision in Urim and Thummin until written by his amanuensis." See also 275-311.

However, Royal Skousen, who has done the most detailed work on the surviving manuscript pages, argues for a return to the mechanistic method: "Joseph Smith was not the author of the Book of Mormon, not even its English language translation. ... [He] could actually see ... the translated English text—word for word and letter for letter." Royal Skousen, "Translating the Book of Mormon: Evidence from the Original Manuscript," in Reynolds, *Book of Mormon Authorship Revisited,* 61-94.

88. Lancaster, "The Translation of the Book of Mormon," 97-112. Lancaster quotes from the following eyewitnesses: Oliver Cowdery, Martin Harris, Elizabeth Ann Whitmer Cowdery Johnson, Michael Morse (husband of Emma's sister, Trial Hale), and William Smith. Lancaster also gives sources for the other quotations in this section, except that of Joseph Knight. The Martin Harris quotation is quoted on 102-103.

89. David Whitmer, *An Address to All Believers in Christ* (Richmond, MO: Author, 1887), 12.

90. Jessee, "Joseph Knight's Recollection," 35.

91. Emma Smith Bidamon, letter, Nauvoo, Illinois, 27 Mar. 1876, quoted in Lancaster, 99-100; see also Quinn, *Magic World View,* 143-49.

92. Jessee, *Papers of Joseph Smith,* 1:29.

93. B. H. Roberts, *A Comprehensive History of the Church of Jesus Christ of Latter-day Saints,* 7 vols. (Provo, UT: BYU Press, 1965), 1:119-20.

94. Welch and Rathbone, "The Translation of the Book of Mormon," 38; "Memorandum made by John H. Gilbert, esq.," 8 Sept. 1892, in Wilford C. Wood, *Joseph Smith Begins His Work* (Salt Lake City: Deseret News Press, 1963), preface, n.p.

95. Stanley P. Gunn, *Oliver Cowdery: Second Elder and Scribe* (Salt Lake City:

Bookcraft, 1962); Richard L. Anderson, "The Second Witness of Priesthood Restoration," *Improvement Era* 82 (Sept. 1968): 15-24; Bushman, *Joseph Smith and the Beginnings of Mormonism,* 94-98; David Persuitte, *Joseph Smith and the Origins of the Book of Mormon* (Jefferson, NC: McFarland & Co., 1985), 56, 235-38.

96. Quinn, *Magic World View,* 84-86; Tanner and Tanner, *Joseph Smith and Money Digging,* 16-18; Persuitte, *Joseph Smith and the Origins,* 57; Bushman, *Joseph Smith and the Beginnings of Mormonism,* 96-104.

97. As part of his general pattern of erasing magical references from Mormonism, Smith edited this revelation for the 1835 version of the Doctrine and Covenants to read: "for you have another gift, which is the gift of Aaron; behold it has told you many things" (D&C 8:7-8). This was one of a thousand changes—102 in one revelation alone—that Joseph made in his revelations between 1833 and 1835. Most of the changes are stylistic; but some, such as this one, are substantive. See Richard P. Howard, "Latter Day Scriptures and the Doctrine of Propositional Revelation," in Vogel, *Word of God,* 1-18.

98. Newell and Avery, *Mormon Enigma,* 196.

99. Ethan Smith (1762-1849) wrote and edited a number of books, including *A View of the Hebrews* when he was sixty-one. Members of the Poultney Historical Society had known about the Ethan Smith/Oliver Cowdery connection, but no one had commented publicly on it until David Persuitte described it to Presbyterian minister Wesley P. Walters, who included it in his master's thesis in 1981. Persuitte, personal communication, 1990; see also Persuitte, *Joseph Smith,* 7, 270: "When I examined and took photos of [the church records] in the summer of 1977, the original church records were in the possession of the Poultney Historical Society. The records were apparently stolen from the museum when it was closed during the following winter, but the Society still has photocopies of the original, as well as the transcription of the births, baptisms, etc. that the WPA made from the records during the thirties."

100. Ethan Smith, *A View of the Hebrews or the Tribes of Israel in America,* 2d ed. (Poultney, VT: Smith and Shute, 1825; first edition, 1823).

101. Brigham H. Roberts, *Studies of the Book of Mormon,* edited by Brigham D. Madsen, with a biographical essay by Sterling M. McMurrin (Urbana: University of Illinois Press, 1985), 27; Richard S. Van Wagoner, *Sidney Rigdon: A Portrait of Religious Excess* (Salt Lake City: Signature Books, 1994), 464-65, see also 461-66.

102. Josiah Priest, *Wonders of Nature and Providence Displayed,* 2d ed. (Albany, NY: Author and E. and E. Hosford, 1825), 290-324.

103. Roberts, *Studies of the Book of Mormon,* 28-29; Robert Paul, "Joseph Smith and the Manchester (New York) Library," *BYU Studies* 22 (Summer 1982): 333-56. The book's accession number is 208.

104. Roberts, *Studies of the Book of Mormon,* 235.

105. Persuitte, *Joseph Smith,* lists more than fifty-five prominent and detailed parallels in his index, 292, 138-50. For example, the ancestors of the Indians were white and of Israelitish origin; they had an Urim with precious stones and had a book; they divided into two groups, one civilized, one barbaric, engaged in wars that demolished the civilized sector, and experienced earthquakes at Christ's crucifixion; they used Egyptian writing and had legends of Moses "as a type of Christ." Compare Roberts's twenty-six major parallels in his *Studies of the Book of Mormon,* 241-42. Ethan Smith misquotes Isaiah 11: "And it shall come to pass in that day that the Lord shall set his hand again ... to gather the remnant of his peo-

ple ... from the isles [*islands* in Isaiah] of the sea. ... and four quarters [*corners* in Isaiah] of the earth." In the Book of Mormon, the prophet Zenos says that the Lord will "remember the isles of the sea ... and ... gather in ... the House of Israel ... from the four quarters of the earth" (BM 51-52; 1 Ne. 19:15-16; Persuitte, *Joseph Smith,* 141-42). As another example, Lehi admonishes his sons: "Awake! and arise from the dust, and hear the words of a trembling parent, whose limbs ye must soon lay down in the cold and silent grave, from whence no traveler can return" (BM 61; 2 Ne. 1:14). This statement paraphrases Hamlet's soliloquy, Act III.1, "death, the undiscovered country from whose bourn no traveller returns," but it is much closer to Priest's allusion: "my time was short, and I had some preparation to make before I went to 'that bourne from whence no traveller returns.'" Ibid., 147.

106. Dean C. Jessee, "The Original Book of Mormon Manuscript," *BYU Studies* 10 (Spring 1970): 259-78, was able to show from the scribal hands on the surviving pages of the original manuscript that Smith had not simply started over with Lehi's family in Jerusalem when he began dictating again in February 1829. Additional evidence is the number of interpolations and "corrections" Smith progressively made in quoting biblical scriptures in the Book of Mormon. Walters, "The Use of the Old Testament in the Book of Mormon," 32-94. The most comprehensive review of this issue is Brent Lee Metcalfe, "The Priority of Mosiah: A Prelude to Book of Mormon Exegesis," in *New Approaches to the Book of Mormon: Explorations in Critical Methodology,* ed. Metcalfe (Salt Lake City: Signature Books, 1993), 395-444.

107. "Associated Features and Disorders of the Narcissistic Personality," American Psychiatric Association, *Diagnostic and Statistical Manual of Mental Disorders,* 4th ed. (Washington, DC: American Psychiatric Association, 1994), 660-61.

108. Arnold H. Modell, "A Narcissistic Defense Against Affects and the Illusion of Self-Sufficiency," in *Essential Papers on Narcissism,* ed. Andrew P. Morrison (New York: New York Universities Press, 1986), 296, see also 293-307.

109. Karen Horney, *New Ways in Psychoanalysis* (New York: Norton, 1939), 92-93, 100.

110. Psychologically speaking, the erasure of this father, who has given his own name to his son, seems significant. I hypothesize that Joseph Smith may be taking this method of writing out his own increasing disappointment at his father's inadequacies, his drinking (which I assume continued), and his apparent inability to make an adequate living for the family. During this second decade of Joseph Smith's life, as he acquires the father's magical gifts with the divining rod and the seer stone and goes beyond them, I think it is obvious that the son replaces the father as the family's key figure.

111. Vogel, Lucy Smith History, 265-66.

112. This date, which begins a fifteen-year chronology correlating the Book of Mormon with Smith's life, is based on Joseph's memories and fantasies. As he remembers, this sequence began when he was "five years old or thereabouts" with the surgery—hence, 1811. As discussed in chapter 2, a more probable date is the winter of 1812-13.

113. Vogel, Lucy Smith History, 268.

114. Ibid., 269-70.

115. Ibid., 268-69.

116. I am grateful to Brigham D. Madsen for bringing this parallel to my attention.

117. Orsamus Turner, *History of the Pioneer Settlement of Phelps and Gorham's Purchase* (Rochester, NY: William Alling, 1851), 213-215, 400; see also Tucker, *Origin, Rise, and Progress of Mormonism,* 17.

118. Jessee, *Papers of Joseph Smith,* 5.

119. Glyndon G. VanDusen, *The Jacksonian Era: 1828-1848* (New York: Harper Torchbooks, 1963), 55.

120. Charles McCarthy, "The Antimasonic Party," *Annual Report of the American Historical Association for the Year 1902* (Washington, D.C.: Government Printing Office, 1903), 1:367-574, esp. 371-87, 531-43; see also VanDusen, *The Jacksonian Era.*

121. Qtd. in B. Davis, *Old Hickory: A Life of Andrew Jackson* (New York: Dial Press, 1977), 211.

122. Jessee, *Papers of Joseph Smith,* 270.

123. Marquardt and Walters, *Inventing Mormonism,* 16-20.

124. James L. Baer, "The Third Nephi Disaster: A Geological View," *Dialogue: A Journal of Mormon Thought* 19 (Spring 1986): 129-32.

125. Marvin Hill, *Quest for Refuge: The Mormon Flight from American Pluralism* (Salt Lake City: Signature Books, 1989), 193n62, stated: "It is significant that Joseph Smith never mentioned this trial in any of his writings." Smith was silent on this episode in his autobiographical writings, I argue, because his shame was so deep; yet in a setting where he was free to exercise his fantasies, this episode becomes the most dramatic in the Book of Mormon.

126. I argue that Smith was inspired by Josiah Priest's *Wonders of Nature and Providence Displayed* (Albany, NY: Author and E. and E. Hosford, 1825), 527. Priest quotes Adam Clarke, LL.D, as saying that the plagues of Egypt including "darkness which may be felt. ... [and] thick clammy vapours [that] would prevent lamps, etc. from burning; or even if they could be ignited, the light, through the palpable obscurity could diffuse itself to no distance from the burning body ... [and] lasted for three days" (527). Priest also describes "a most violent whirlwind. ... typhones. ... with such fury and violence as to threaten the destruction of the whole fleet" at Charleston, South Carolina (558), and was combined with a terrible storm in Ireland (174): "a violent wind ... a dreadful clap of thunder ... a thick darkness. ... that continued for half a quarter of an hour. ... Continued lightning broke out without ceasing, so that heaven and earth seemed to be united in flame" (174). Priest vividly portrays the terrors of volcanic upheavals, earthquakes and burning islands: Mount Etna (1669, 1755) some of Vesuvius' twenty eruptions (79, 1631, 1698, 1754, 1770), Santorini (1707), the earthquake sinking of Port Royal, Jamaica (1692), similar devastations in Lima (1747), and many other events. These extensive descriptions (257-84) provide an adequate source for the Book of Mormon cataclysms.

127. In an interview with Alexander Neibaur on 24 May 1844, Joseph reported that he asked "must I join the Methodist Church." God answered, "No—they are not my People. They have gone astray and there is none that doeth good no not one." Qtd. in *Improvement Era,* Apr. 1970, 12.

Joseph Smith

Emma Smith

Martin Harris

Oliver Cowdery

Hill Cumorah

Title page, Book of Mormon, first edition

THE

BOOK OF MORMON:

AN ACCOUNT WRITTEN BY THE HAND OF MORMON, UPON PLATES TAKEN FROM THE PLATES OF NEPHI.

Wherefore it is an abridgment of the Record of the People of Nephi; and also of the Lamanites; written to the Lamanites, which are a remnant of the House of Israel; and also to Jew and Gentile; written by way of commandment, and also by the spirit of Prophesy and of Revelation. Written, and sealed up, and hid up unto the LORD, that they might not be destroyed; to come forth by the gift and power of GOD, unto the interpretation thereof; sealed by the hand of Moroni, and hid up unto the LORD, to come forth in due time by the way of Gentile; the interpretation thereof by the gift of GOD; an abridgment taken from the Book of Ether.

Also, which is a Record of the People of Jared, which were scattered at the time the LORD confounded the language of the people when they were building a tower to get to Heaven: which is to shew unto the remnant of the House of Israel how great things the LORD hath done for their fathers; and that they may know the covenants of the LORD, that they are not cast off forever; and also to the convincing of the Jew and Gentile that JESUS is the CHRIST, the ETERNAL GOD, manifesting Himself unto all nations. And now if there be fault, it be the mistake of men; wherefore condemn not the things of GOD, that ye may be found spotless at the judgment seat of CHRIST.

BY JOSEPH SMITH, JUNIOR,

AUTHOR AND PROPRIETOR.

PALMYRA:

PRINTED BY E. B. GRANDIN, FOR THE AUTHOR.

1830.

CHAPTER 4

A Book of Intricate Complexity: Mosiah and Alma

I believe that the first major attempt to understand Joseph Smith was that of his antagonist, Eber D. Howe, in *Mormonism Unvailed.*[1] Howe proposed that the Book of Mormon had been adapted from a romance written by a poverty-stricken Presbyterian minister, Solomon Spaulding, fifteen years earlier. This proposal, supported in his book by many testimonies from individuals, lasted until the original Spaulding manuscript was rediscovered in 1884, when no meaningful connection between it and the Book of Mormon could be found. This theory, however, had successfully blocked more sophisticated inquiry into the source(s) of the Book of Mormon for fifty years. From that point, further examination explored other hypotheses besides that accepted by devout Mormons. Evidence began to accumulate suggesting that the book reflected the early nineteenth-century American frontier.[2] Further, travel, geographic, and population claims in the book seemed implausible.[3] While no Mormon acknowledgment has been forthcoming, M. T. Lamb's 1887 book was probably the impetus for the "new geographic theory" of the Book of Mormon which put Cumorah in Central America and limited the whole Book of Mormon history to a geographic diameter of 400 miles.

The first attempt to understand Joseph Smith psychologically occurred in 1902 and relied on what was by then the canonized version of his "first vision" of God and Jesus. In his doctoral dissertation, I. Woodbridge Riley proposed that Smith suffered from a migraine-type of epilepsy, a possibility that no longer fits medical knowledge.[4] Riley believed that the Book of Mormon was a product of the American environment, discarded the Spaulding theory, and mentioned a few items that suggested the autobiographical possibilities of Smith in the Book of Mormon. He was the first to notice the parallels between the dreams of Joseph Smith, Sr., and Lehi in the Book of Mormon.[5] Walter F. Prince in 1917 found evidence that was satisfying to him that Smith was the sole author of the Book of Mormon. Prince's views were challenged by Theodore Schroeder, who, however, began his argument by insisting on the outdated hypothesis that Solomon Spaulding wrote the Book of Mormon. Some of his conclusions will be reviewed in chapter 5.[6]

During the first part of the twentieth century, various diagnoses were given to Joseph Smith. Harry M. Beardsley offered "demential Praecox," a "voluntarily induced schizophrenia," and "dissociation," while Bernard DeVoto hypothesized that Smith was a "paranoid" who heard "auditory hallucinations." Most recently, William D. Morain, a plastic surgeon with ties to the RLDS church, has proposed that Smith "dissociated," and dictated the Book of Mormon in a "trance."[7]

The problem with these proposals is that they see Smith dictating the Book of Mormon without full mental functioning. He is "not all there," but rather is limited by or under the influence of a severe mental illness that decreases function. In contrast, if not in response to the earlier chapters, I hope readers will appreciate what every devout student of the Book of Mormon knows—its complexity. This complexity initially hid the population and travel improbabilities in the text. Dates, places, and stories interlock in confusing, but internally consistent patterns, with almost no errors. (I will mention one, perhaps two, clear errors in chapter 6.) Such a feat required clear, sharp calculations during the dictation. In my professional opinion, such an achievement was not possible for someone of even temporarily limited mental functioning. Yet even with such integration of cognitive function, the book required some framework. I am proposing that the theology, stories, and geography came from Joseph's life, expanded into "greater than life" episodes, and being modified as required to allow him to conquer in fantastic fantasy.

The previous two chapters have reviewed the personal story of Smith to the point where he began dictating the Book of Mormon as it currently exists, each one focusing on a story of one of the two important Nephis in the book. The activities of these Smith alter egos show a clear, compact, and close chronological fit between events in the Book of Mormon and events in Smith's own life. Even though 3 Nephi was written before the current version of 1-2 Nephi, it is my belief that Smith had, in the lost 116 pages, basically covered the same material that he revisited in 1-2 Nephi. Thus the story of the first Nephi emphasized the first decade of Smith's life, the story of the second Nephi the second and third decades. Events in their life stories, I have argued, present a pattern of distinctive themes and figures from key events in Smith's life.

As the Book of Mormon proceeds, elements of Smith's autobiography repeatedly recur, though seldom in such crystalline form and precise chronological order. This chapter will confirm the motifs previously identified and add two or three more: a revival that follows a good man's death (see also chapter 2), the appearance of an angel, and the mention of a gold record that needed translation. This chapter will not only attempt to confirm how Smith used reversal and compensation as fantasy techniques for dealing with his misfortunes, but also document his use of a second psychological technique—exaggerating biblical stories to tell and "correct" his life.[8]

As a psychiatrist, I argue that the formula to understanding the Book of Mormon is that, beneath its exaggeration and reversal of misfortune, lies the original episode from Joseph Smith's life—or, in parallel fashion, adds to his life story exaggeration and reversal to find the Book of Mormon version. Familiar motifs will continue to be groups of four or five men, often brothers; the mention of wine with swords; travel following an armed conflict with robbers; and revivals following the death of a good man, often occurring at the same time that an angel appears. Other characters from his life reappear in disguise as Smith becomes one alter-ego hero after another within the plots of the Book of Mormon.

In the previous two chapters, Smith's life has been the central theme, the Book of Mormon stories their mirror. In this chapter and the next, I reverse the order, summarizing Book of Mormon stories and briefly presenting their correlation with Smith's life. Although it would certainly be rewarding to analyze in detail literally hundreds of Book of Mormon episodes, space precludes such an approach. I wish to present the most important parallels and let the reader fill in the details through additional study. From a psychoanalytic perspective, the book's heros and despots stir the deepest and most primitive childhood fantasies of magic and power. The theology has real content and conflict, for it distills four centuries of problems in Protestant thought.[9] The next section is an example.

Polygamy and Doubt

> [The] emotional life [of narcissists] is shallow. They experience little empathy for the feelings of others, they obtain very little enjoyment from life other than from the tributes they receive from others or from their own grandiose fantasies, and they feel restless and bored when external glitter wears off and no new sources feed their self-regard. ... In general, their relationships with other people are clearly exploitative and sometimes parasitic. It is as if they feel they have the right to control and possess others and to exploit them without guilt feelings—and behind a surface which very often is charming and engaging, one senses coldness and ruthlessness.[10]

The first Nephi's death is recorded in the short book kept by Jacob, his younger brother, who replaced him as religious and political leader. Jacob then chastised the entire assembled Nephite nation for materialism and for the sin of polygamy, which Jacob calls the "abominable" sin of "whoredoms." Jacob condemns David's and Solomon's polygamy, for the Lord has

> seen the sorrow, and heard the mourning of the daughters of my people. ... Ye have broken the hearts of your tender wives ... and the sobbing of their

> hearts ascendeth up to God against you. ... Behold, the Lamanites ... are more righteous than you; for they have not forgotten the commandments of the Lord. ... that they should have save it were one wife; and concubines they should have none. ... Their husbands love their wives, and their wives love their husbands, and their husbands and their wives love their children.

The sole exception is: "For if I will, saith the Lord of Hosts, raise up seed unto me, I will command my people; otherwise they shall hearken unto these things" (BM 124-28; Jacob 1:15-3:7).

Smith would have known that polygamy was a Protestant problem. Polygamy was apparently practiced during Jesus' ministry without a word of condemnation (see Matt. 25:1-12). Some Christians during apostolic times would have been converted Jewish men with multiple wives, for Paul had advised Timothy that bishops and deacons should be the husbands of only one wife (1 Tim. 3:2). Polygamy continued among the European Jews until around 1000 C.E. In 1531 Luther advocated its practice to Henry VIII and, in 1539, gave permission to Prince Philip of Hesse to take a second wife. The Anabaptists in Germany in the sixteenth century practiced polygamy, and others in Protestantism continued to press for its return.[11] Smith, under "command" from God, married more than thirty women before his death in 1844, including already married women and pubescent girls. The historical record confirms my suspicion as a psychiatrist that such behavior would be devastating for Emma, even though he concealed as many of these relationships as possible. Joseph Smith had dictated this first (and later lost) section of the Book of Mormon during early 1828, when Emma entered the last half of her pregnancy with the stillborn child, Alvin. She may have been sexually unavailable or sexually unattractive to him. If this first 116 pages was similar to his redictation—or if, when he redictated this section, he was reflecting on his past experiences—then this section may contain evidence of marital disharmony. One outside accusation appears to provide support for this conjecture. In August 1830 Joseph and Emma abruptly left Harmony. Fifty years later Hiel Lewis commented, as quoted in the *Amboy Journal,* that one "Levi Lewis states that he has heard Joseph Smith and Martin Harris both say that adultery was no crime. Harris said that 'he did not blame Smith for attempting to seduce E. W., (Eliza Winters).'"[12] Hiel Lewis had been an official in Emma's religious congregation in Harmony, Pennsylvania, fifty years earlier. While devout Mormons correctly point out that the report is second hand and that it emerges after a lapse of fifty years, from a professional perspective, I find it worth considering as the beginning of Joseph Smith's sexual expansion. Consider the progress:

In 1831 Smith privately stated that plural marriage was a "correct principle," but the time had "not yet come to teach and practice it." If he received this knowledge by revelation, it remains unrecorded or at least unpublished. In that year he also told early convert, Mary Elizabeth Rollins, then twelve years old, that God had commanded him to take her as a plural wife—which he did eleven years later. He also stated that the Lamanites (American Indians) would become "white and delightsome" through their plural marriages to white men. In 1833 he was, in the words of Oliver Cowdery, caught by his wife in a "dirty, filthy affair" with sixteen-year-old Fanny Alger. Years later, in Utah, Mormon pioneer and leader Heber C. Kimball referred to Alger as Smith's first plural wife, while Alger's cousin remembered that his father had performed a marriage uniting Joseph and Fanny. In November 1835 Joseph declared all religious and civil marriages null and void, for they had not been performed by the Mormon priesthood, a declaration that opened the door to taking already "married" women as his plural wives.[13]

The difference between the sexual expansiveness of Joseph Smith and others is that he put his multiple marriages within a theological framework and made the practice a command from God. Although the exact date when he began practicing polygamy is unknown, he was certainly involved with plural wives and teaching the principle secretly to devoted followers by the early 1840s. The major revelation on it, now canonized as Doctrine and Covenants 132, is dated July 1843. Thirty-three wives (twelve of whom, already married, continued to live with their husbands to conceal their marriages to Smith) can now be confirmed from the records, and another seven are possible. He married girls as young as fourteen and sixteen years old.[14]

Smith used coercion and emotional pressure to persuade at least some of these women to marry him. He told two women—Mary Elizabeth Rollins, then a married twenty-three-year-old, and Eliza R. Snow, age thirty-eight—that he was forced by God to take his wives in this illegal practice. An angel had come to him and commanded him, he stated. He had balked. The angel came again, and again he resisted. As Mary Elizabeth recalled, Smith "talked to him [the angel] soberly about it, and told him it was an abomination and quoted scripture to him." On the third time, the angel appeared, sword in hand, and commanded him to begin the practice or he "would slay him." Therapeutically speaking, this "vision" is a manifestation of the ghost of scalpel-wielding surgeon Nathan Smith, suggesting a focus on childhood issues. According to Eliza, Joseph told her that the angel had said his "priesthood would be taken from him and he would be destroyed." Both women married him.[15] Reading from the Book of Mormon back into Joseph's life suggests that Emma knew of some sexual dalliance by Joseph and that her reaction may have been a possible source for the prophet Jacob's accusation that adulterous Nephite men had "broken the hearts of your tender wives" but that God had heard their "sobbing" and "mourning" (Jacob 2:35, 31).

To someone who doubts or does not believe in the supernatural (or in Smith's version of the supernatural), questions about his ability to truly care for his wife, as well as for people in general, are now increasingly obvious. From my professional perspective, I see the marital dynamic as unhealthy—a continuation of the earlier encouragement to believe in his supernatural money-digging powers. In addition to this distressing naturalistic view of his coercion of Eliza R. Snow and Mary Elizabeth Rollins Lightner, as well as the psychological pain he inflicted on Emma (if not at this point in time, then certainly later), a psychiatrist sees this sad fact: each of these women was responding to Smith's projected image and married him because of his claims. Not once did he know what it was to be loved for himself. Nor could he love any of these women for herself.

The book of Jacob continues with an extensive, complex allegory of the tame and wild olive tree, reflecting God's plans for the house of Israel. It is a exaggeration of Paul's allegory (Rom. 11), and elaborates several references by Ethan Smith who applied the same metaphor to the American Indians. There are several interpretations of this extensive allegory by traditional Mormons.[16]

The book ends with a debate between Jacob and Sherem, the first of three anti-Christs in the Book of Mormon. Sherem denies that anyone "knows" that Christ will come, demands a sign, is struck down, and confesses his sin before dying. Though probably based on a real individual in Smith's life, he also epitomizes the rational atheism of Thomas Paine's influential *Age of Reason.* Paine, a major influence behind the Declaration of Independence, had then turned his attention to religion. He wrote: "Of all the tyrannies that effect mankind, tyranny in religion is the worst; every other species of tyranny is limited to the world we live in; but this attempts to stride beyond the grave, and seeks to pursue us into eternity."[17] Paine wrote in "simple and clear language for the common man. He took Deism [a belief in a creator who did not interact in the affairs of men] ... and made it a living creed for the average man. By doing so ... he threatened the hold of the clergy upon the people."[18]

The Final Part of the "Small Plates"

Next come the very short books of Enos, Jarom, and Omni (BM 143-53). An anomaly in the Book of Mormon, they cover 314 years—31 percent of the Nephite history—in only 1.5 percent of the entire book. Each of the recordkeepers comments briefly on his personal behavior or religious experience and passes the record on. Omni spins through the records of four keepers in only twelve verses.

Psychologically, it makes sense to explain this section as Smith's attempt to quickly reach the point at which this new record joins the already finished section. Because he was writing these "small plates" to cover the lost 116 pages after dictating the rest of the Book of Mormon, I suggest that both time and the size of the book were pressing on him and that his tendency to elaborate—as with the allegory of the tame and wild olive tree—had gotten out of hand. He bridged these three centuries to bring him to the joining point.

The Revival Begun

TIME: 124 B.C.E.//1824-25 C.E.
PERSONAE: KING BENJAMIN//REV. BENJAMIN STOCKTON

The interlocking and overlapping stories in the book of Mosiah and the early sections of Alma demonstrate how Smith continued to rewrite his life within the Book of Mormon text. The main story line follows the Nephite civilization through the reigns of Mosiah I, Benjamin, and Mosiah II, and the judgeship of Alma II (Alma the younger). However, three stories are embedded within and intersect with it—Zeniff's colony, the missionary sons of Mosiah, and the mission of Alma and Amulek. The narratives of the two Nephis are organized chain fashion, each story succeeding the previous story in neat chronological order. In contrast, the Mosiah/Alma texts are nested or stacked, often happening at the same time, interrupting and repeating each other. From a psychoanalytic perspective, I argue that each of the stacked stories occurring simultaneously in the Book of Mormon reveals part of the original incident in Smith's life and that reading the paired stories will provide the complete incident.

These interlocking stories are not only framed by but are linked together by the familiar motif of the journey. Other familiar motifs include Alvin's death, Smith's encounter with the angel and gold plates, the religious revival, Smith's imprisonment and trial, his troubled relations with the Hale family, the death of the firstborn child, and the transforming trauma of Smith's childhood—the bloody surgery.

The main story line follows the central body of Nephites. Mosiah I, the Nephite king, obeys God's commandment to flee with his people from the land of Nephi to provide a buffer of wilderness between themselves and the Lamanites. They find the land of Zarahemla, which is populated by the Mulekites, who fled from Jerusalem at about the same time as Lehi; but lacking records, they are becoming uncivilized. (The Mulekites have found the record of a third people, the Jaredites, who reached the promised land from the tower of Babel. I will review the story of the Jaredites and the book of Ether in chapter 6.) Mosiah translates the Jaredite record (the book of Ether) and unites his people with the Mulekites. His son, Benjamin, is a righteous ruler. Benjamin's son, Mosiah II, is also a righteous king. Mosiah II has four sons: Ammon, Aaron, Omner, and Himni.

During Benjamin's reign, the Lamanites discover them, resulting in "a serious war and much bloodshed between the Nephites and Lamanites" (BM 150; Omni 24). Mormon, summarizing these events 500 years later, adds an intriguing detail: "King Benjamin gathered together his armies, and he did stand against them; and he did fight with the strength of his own arm, with the sword of Laban" (BM 152; Words of Mormon 13). This sequence is important. The first story is framed by two journeys: that of the Nephites into the land of Zarahemla and that of the Mulekites from Jerusalem. The journeys suggest, psychologically, the point at which the Smiths moved to New York, while the sword of Laban, the "serious war," and "much bloodshed" suggest both Smith's surgery ("much bloodshed") and Alvin's death (because of the chronology). We may speculatively date these events to Joseph Smith's winter of 1823-24.

This speculation seems confirmed because the next event is the beginning of a religious revival—the "proper" event to follow Alvin's death. Benjamin, in relinquishing the kingdom to his son, Mosiah II, gave him the plates of brass, the plates engraved by Nephi, the magic compass used in the wilderness, and Laban's sword (BM 155; Mosiah 1:15-16). He called his people together in a great encampment in tents and addressed them from a tower near the temple. The crowd was too great to hear his voice, so he had his message written and delivered by runners. The people, convicted of sin, fell to the ground, implored the mercy of God, converted universally, took on the name of Christ, made a life-long covenant of obedience to God, were reborn as children of Christ (124 years before Christ), and had their names listed by King Benjamin (BM 155-68; Mosiah 1:18-6:7).

From a psychoanalytic perspective, this episode exaggerates frontier America camp meetings, with those present falling to the earth due to the intense emotion. As historian Michael T. Walton summarizes:

> The camp meeting began in the "second great awakening" at the turn of the 19th century as an ecumenical revival meeting. By the 1820's, however, it had become the exclusive property of the Methodists. In over 600 such gatherings a year, Methodist preachers hoped to bring religion to unchurched America. The camp meeting was one of the most significant social institutions on the frontier. People came for miles to help clear the land, erect the raised speakers stand and set up their family tents around the compound. For days various preachers would deliver sermons on man's sinfulness and the need for atonement. Many would be stricken with their sense of sin and collapse in what was known as the falling exercise. At the end of the encampment, those who had been converted were enrolled in the Methodist records so that they could be visited by circuit preachers. Those who were not able to feel a manifestation of the divine were exhorted to "go to the grove to seek God."[19]

Benjamin's lengthy sermon, moreover, fits the condemnatory tone we would expect from the first Benjamin (Stockton), the minister who stated publicly that Alvin was in hell because he had lived unchurched. Benjamin's exhortations to altruism are phrased as commandments of God, fueled by guilt. Psychologically, Reverend Benjamin speaks through the persona of King Benjamin, oppressive, intense, relentless in his pressure:

> And even I [King Benjamin], myself, have labored with mine own hands that I might serve you, and that ye should not be laden with taxes. ... I tell you these things that ye may know that I can answer a clear conscience before God this day. ... that ye may learn that when ye are in the service of your fellow beings ye are only in the service of your God. ... and if I who has spent his days in your service, and yet has been in the service of God, do merit any thanks from you, O how you ought to thank your heavenly King! ... If ye should serve him with all your whole souls yet ye would be unprofitable servants. ...
>
> And now in the first place, he hath created you, and granted unto you your lives for which ye are indebted unto him. And secondly, he doth require that ye should do as he hath commanded you; for which if ye do, he doth immediately bless you; and therefore he hath paid you. And ye are still indebted unto him, and are, and will be, forever and ever; therefore, of what have ye to boast ... (BM 156-59; Mosiah 2:14-16, 22-24)
>
> And ye will not have a mind to injure one another, but to live peaceably, and to render to every man according to that which is his due. And ye will not suffer your children that they go hungry, or naked; neither will ye suffer that they transgress the laws of God and fight and quarrel one with another, and serve the devil who is the master of sin ... and ... ye will not suffer that the beggar putteth up his petition to you in vain, and turn him out to perish. Perhaps thou shalt say: the man has brought upon himself his misery; therefore I will stay my hand, and will not give unto him of my food, nor impart unto him my substance that he may not suffer, for his punishments are just. But I say unto you, O man, whosoever doeth this the same has great cause to repent; and except he repenteth of that which he hath done he perisheth forever, and hath no interest in the kingdom of God. For behold, are we not all beggars? ... And ... all you who deny the beggar, because ye have not; I would that ye say in your hearts that: I give not because I have not but if I had I would give. And now, if ye say this in your hearts ye remain guiltless, otherwise ye are condemned; and your condemnation is just for ye covet that which ye have not received. ...
>
> And see that all these things are done in wisdom and order; for it is not requisite that a man should run faster than he has strength. And again, it is expedient that he should be diligent that thereby he might win the prize; therefore, all things must be done in order.
>
> And ... remember ... that whosoever among you borroweth of his neighbor should return the thing that he borroweth ... or else thou shalt commit sin; and perhaps thou shalt cause thy neighbor to commit sin also. (BM 160-62; Mosiah 4:13-14, 16-19, 28)

This call to altruism and common sense is magnificent, but underlying it is fear of God's punishment:

> And finally, I cannot tell you all the things whereby ye may commit sin; for there are divers ways and means, even so many that I cannot number them. But this much I can tell you, that if ye do not watch yourselves, and

> your thoughts, and your words, and your deeds, and observe the commandments of God, and continue in the faith of what ye have heard concerning the coming of our Lord, even unto the end of your lives, ye must perish. And now, O man, remember, and perish not.[20] (BM 165; Mosiah 4:29-30)

If we can assume—and I do—that Smith recalled themes from Stockton's sermons to put in the mouth of his Nephite king, the people who attended the Palmyra revival in 1824-25 resisted this guilt-laden approach. The Stockton/Benjamin view emphasizes the sufferings of Jesus and threatens punishment if the people do not repent. From a psychoanalytic perspective, it is a despair-producing sermon, for salvation requires perfection in behavior and even thought. In September 1825 Reverend George Lane arrived, and the tempo of conversions increased, with almost all of the 400 baptisms occurring in the next six months.[21] As far as I know, there is no record of Lane's preaching style and content;[22] but I believe that the Book of Mormon preserves his hope in Christ's saving grace.

The Revival Concluded

TIME: 200-123 B.C.E.//1816-25 C.E.
PERSONAE: ABINADI//ALVIN; REV. GEORGE LANE
AMMON//JOSEPH SMITH
ALMA//JOSEPH SMITH; REV. GEORGE LANE
KING NOAH//A REPRESENTATIVE OF CORRUPT POWER;
PHYSICIANS, JUDGES, LAND OWNERS
ALMA THE YOUNGER//JOSEPH SMITH; THE APOSTLE PAUL

The second story, stacked over these events in the reign of Benjamin's successor-son, Mosiah II, and hence part of the revival narrative, is that of Zeniff, his son Noah, and his grandson Limhi. In about 200 B.C.E., Zeniff received permission from Mosiah I, Benjamin's father, to lead a party of Nephites from the land of Zarahemla back to the land of Nephi, now populated by Lamanites (BM 151; Omni 27-30). Nothing more was heard from them until Mosiah II sent a search party of sixteen led by Ammon, "a strong and mighty man" (BM 168; Mosiah 7:1-6). The narrative of Ammon's journey and the history of this Nephite colony—an embedded story beginning in the "past" of the main narrative—dominates the book of Mosiah, but concludes by moving forward quickly to nearly the same period as King Benjamin's sermon.

As a psychiatrist, I hear in Ammon's story the experience of the Smith family: "they knew not the course they should travel in the wilderness, to go up to the land of ... Nephi; therefore they wandered many days in the wilderness, even forty days did they wander" (BM 168; Mosiah 7: 5). Ammon's group found the Nephite colony led by King Limhi, Zeniff's grandson, who is "exceeding glad." This meeting, I feel, recalls the Smith family's joyful reunion with Joseph Sr. in Palmyra. Limhi invites Ammon's group to "eat, and drink and rest themselves from the labors of their journey; for they had suffered many things: they had suffered hunger, thirst, and fatigue" (BM 169-70; Mosiah 7:9-20)—Smith's own memory of how, as a lame boy laboring through the snow, he had "suffered the most excruciating weariness and pain." Furthermore, Limhi's group was in "bondage to the Lamanites, and are taxed with a tax grievous to be borne" (BM 169; Mosiah 7:15), suggesting the Smiths' straitened finances—Lucy was almost literally penniless by the time they arrived.

A third story is stacked onto these two, as Limhi recounts his people's history for the last three generations. This story within a story again presents events from Smith's life in disguised and fragmentary form. For example, Zeniff's followers battle repeatedly with the Lamanites, thus presenting the familiar sequence of a journey, conflict, and blood. The narrative exaggerates the fatalities (3,043 Lamanites and 279 of Zeniff's followers), thus underscoring the psychological significance of these motifs.[23] In a second battle nine years later, the dead are too numerous to count. From a psychoanalytic perspective, these deaths signal not only an extravagant version of Alvin's death but also, I think, echoes of Smith's surgery.

Succeeding Zeniff was his son Noah, a successful warrior but a wicked king who reveled with "wives and concubines" and constructed "many elegant and spacious buildings. ... a spacious palace. ... and throne in the midst thereof. ... ornamented with gold and silver" (BM 177-80; Mosiah 11). He taxed his people heavily and surrounded himself with priests who also spent "their time with harlots." Abinadi, who seems to have been modeled after the prophet Nathan who chastised the adulterous King David, launched an aggressive mission of calling the people to repentance. Noah eventually captured, imprisoned, and tried him. Confronting Noah and his priests, Abinadi was so filled with the power of God that "his face shone with exceeding luster, even as Moses did while in the Mount of Sinai, while speaking with the Lord" (BM 181-83; Mosiah 13). He preached and prophesied concerning Christ and the resurrection, mixing scriptures fluently from the Old and New Testaments in a style reminiscent of revivals during the Second Great Awakening. He preaches, not the wrath of God, but the grace of Christ, thus leading me to speculate that the Reverend George Lane had taken a similar approach during the Palmyra revival:

> Behold, they [humankind] would have been endlessly lost, were it not that God redeemed his people from their lost and fallen state. But remember, that he that persists in his own carnal nature, and goes on in the ways of sin and rebellion against God, he remaineth in his fallen state, and the devil hath all power over him. ... And now if Christ had not come into the world, speaking of things to come, as though they had already come,[24] there could have been no redemption. ... But there is a resurrection, therefore the grave hath no vic-

> tory, and the sting of death is swallowed up in Christ: He is the light and the life of the world; yea, a light that is endless, that can never be darkened; yea, and also a life which is endless, that there can be no more death. ... This mortal shall put on immortality, and this corruption shall put on incorruption ... to be judged of him according to their works ... If they be good, to the resurrection of endless life and happiness, and if they be evil, to the resurrection of endless damnation ... having never called upon the Lord while the arms of mercy was extended towards them; for ... they would not. ... And now had ye not to ... remember only in and through Christ ye can be saved ... (BM 189; Mosiah 16)

Furious at Abinadi's condemnation of their wickedness, Noah and his priests sentence him to death. I argue that, even though Abinadi was burned alive, not killed by the sword, his death is a replay of Alvin's motif: a good man killed by one of high position.[25] Alma, one of Noah's priests, was inspired by Abinadi, tried to save him, recorded the prophet's words, repented of his own sins, went into hiding to save his life from Noah's wrath, and quietly began preaching to and baptizing converts. I hypothesize that this scenario was Smith's transformation of George Lane into Abinadi and himself into Alma. Alma hid in

> a place which was called Mormon,[26] having received its name from the king, being in the borders of the land. ... by wild beasts. ... Now, there was in Mormon a fountain of pure water, and Alma resorted thither, there being near the water a thicket of small trees, where he did hide himself in the day-time from the searches of the king. ... As many as believed him went thither to hear his words. ... and he did teach them and did preach repentance, and redemption, and faith on the Lord. (BM 191; Mosiah 18:4-7)

This small community was idyllic, a loving flock in the wilderness, bound together in faith and charity. Those baptized agreed to enter

> into the fold of God, to bear one another's burdens. ... to mourn with those that mourn and comfort those that stand in need of comfort, and to stand as witnesses of God at all times, and all places, and in all things. ... [They] were filled with the Grace of God. And they were called the Church of God, or the church of Christ, from that time forward. ... And he commanded them that there should be no contention one with another, but that they should look forward with one eye, having one faith and one baptism, having their hearts knit together in unity and in love one toward another ... and thus they became the children of God.
>
> And now it came to pass that all this was done in Mormon, yea, by the waters of Mormon, in the forest that was near the waters of Mormon; yea, the place of Mormon, the waters of Mormon, the forest of Mormon, now beautiful are they to the eyes of them who there came to the knowledge of their Redeemer; yea, and how blessed are they. ... And these things were done in the borders of the land, that they might not come to the knowledge of the king. (BM 192-93; Mosiah 18:9-30)

When the king sent his army after them, forewarned of God, "they took their tents and their families and departed into the wilderness. And they were in number about four hundred and fifty souls" (BM 190-94; Mosiah 17, 18).

This scene by the waters of Mormon is a moment of supreme beauty in the Book of Mormon, a paradisiacal Eden in ancient America. The people are saved by their faith in Jesus and then, automatically, have hearts filled with charity. It is no accident that their numbers were almost exactly those of the Palmyra harvest ("over 400"), baptized in the area's rivers, streams, and lakes. This scene of Alma (Reverend Lane) ministering tenderly to his little flock is a pleasant complement to King Benjamin (Benjamin Stockton) with his practical, heavy-handed, and guilt-producing commandments. Although I have no historic evidence to support my views, I suspect that Lane comforted Smith as he mourned his brother's death, temporarily becoming a superficial role model.

From a psychoanalytic perspective, the stacked stories of Benjamin in Zarahemla and Zeniff's people in the land of Nephi tell two versions of Smith's story. Together, they tell the complete history of the Palmyra revival. Significantly, the Book of Mormon merges these two stories and continues Smith's story through the experience yet another alter ego: Alma's son, who is also named Alma (yet another "Jr." or, in Book of Mormon terms, Alma the younger).

Alma's flock of 450, after fleeing from Noah's army, found a fertile location in the wilderness and farmed for about twenty years. They were discovered by Noah's priests who had followed the escaping Noah, lost themselves in the wilderness, then teamed up with a party of Lamanites. The renegade priests and Lamanites oppressed Alma's people until the Lord caused a "deep sleep" to overcome their guards and Alma could lead his people to safety (Mosiah 24:19). This time Alma and his people reached Zarahemla where King Mosiah II greeted them with joy and authorized Alma to organize the church (BM 202-208; Mosiah 23, 24).

The two episodes of revival, occurring in different places but within the same time frame, are completed by this point. The problems in interpreting these stories may be helpful in understanding the rest of this book. In reading this and later sections of the book, devout Mormons have emphasized the "flimsy" or fragmentary nature of the parallels. In this case, we have only the Book of Mormon sermons and no extant documents of the manner and style of either George Lane or Benjamin Stockton for comparison. Not only do I agree that this omission makes a conclusive evaluation impossible, but there are also some particular problems with my interpretation. I chose the parallels between Benjamin Stockton//King Benjamin, and Abinadi//George Lane as the most probable. But another hypothesis is possible. Perhaps Joseph Smith, for purposes of disguise, reversed these parallels, and it is King Benjamin who is the fantasy representative of George Lane. This conjecture is supported by three pieces of evidence. (1) Camp meetings by the 1820s were largely the domain of the Methodists, and George Lane was a Methodist. (2) King Benjamin's sermon emphasized altruistic, charitable behavior, yet the Presbyterians were criticized for being niggardly. (3) I think that Smith does a similar intentional reversal to disguise Book of Mormon geography, making it more difficult to parallel it with his biographical geography. (See chapter 5.)

It is hard to determine what is going on in a person's mind even with a live, cooperative, and honest patient. Smith, dead for 150 years and from a different culture, is not, to my way of thinking, cooperative. Still, I don't think my manner of interpretation can be lightly dismissed. Although academic history, by definition, excludes the supernatural as the explanation for events, let us permit Smith's description of the ancient and divine origins of the Book of Mormon to enter into the discussion, weighing it against what I am trying to do and remembering that a theory has only to be better than the alternate(s) it seeks to replace, not completely satisfactory in all respects.

Smith sketched three migrations from the Middle East to the New World. The major body was of Jews from Jerusalem. American archaeology fails to support this proposal. He proposed that, 125 years before the birth of Christ, these Jewish people were preaching "Christ and him crucified," performing baptisms, and enjoying the Holy Spirit. This proposal receives no support from theologians or historians of Judaism nor from the rest of Christianity. In this story of revival, Smith describes the Nephite form of Christianity as having the specific characteristics of an early nineteenth-century American frontier camp meeting, with phrases and terminology borrowed straight from the Second Great Awakening. Again, the history of religion does not support the proposition that either the camp meeting as a form or the specific evangelical language of frontier Methodists and Presbyterians can be dated back to that early period of Mesoamerican history.

To these negative responses, there are at least two positive findings: Smith claimed he could miraculously translate ancient languages, but that has been put to the test and found wanting.[27] The second explanation is the position I take that Smith is a man who engaged in deceit and coercion from early adulthood throughout his life. My position is that belief in the Book of Mormon is an act of faith, not the result of scientific or academic inquiry.

I acknowledge that psychodynamic concepts are a "soft science" and that applied psychoanalysis is even softer. But it is rooted in the natural world and the body of knowledge that has accumulated about how both mentally healthy people and mentally ill patients react and think, and how the works of artists and writers reflect their personalities in one way or another. In the rest of this book I will continue to look for a consistent chronological picture of Joseph Smith's life, making tentative interpretations on unavoidably fragmentary information.

The stories of these two families come together in the next generation. Alma II and the four sons of Mosiah were rebellious and apostate youths until an angel confronted them and punished Alma II with the torments of hell for three days. Alma II (yet another Jr.) is another of Smith's alter egos; and in writing this narrative, Smith paints what may be a striking portrait, in psychological terms, of himself before his conversion: "He became a very wicked and an idolatrous man. And he was a man of many words, and did speak much flattery to the people; therefore he led many of the people to do after the manner of his iniquities. And he became a great hinderment to the prosperity of the church of God; stealing away the hearts of the people; causing much dissension" (BM 212; Mosiah 27:8-10).

I do not think Smith was confessing his personal sins as much as he was depicting himself from an orthodox Protestant perspective. I have proposed that Smith sometimes quoted his antagonists in their negative opinion of him. For example, his siblings, if they are reflected in Laman and Lemuel, commented that he lied and used cunning as a means to gain power over them. He will do this again. He does not seem bothered by their views. Before and after the revival, Smith continued magic activities, dug for money, and used his seer stone. Protestants of his day saw such behavior as less than fully righteous at best and traffic with the devil at worst. Psychologically, Smith can be said to document the completion of his "grandiose [false] self" as he/Alma sees an angel. In fact Alma's conversion recalls the earliest versions of Smith's own conversion story, which, as we have seen, did not feature God and Jesus but rather an angel and forgiveness of his sins. In this Book of Mormon version, he exaggerates and dramatizes the angelic visitation to the wayward Alma Jr.: "Behold the angel of the Lord ... descended as it were in a cloud; and he spoke with a voice of thunder, which caused the earth to shake upon which they stood. ... and ... he cried. ... Alma, arise and stand forth, for why persecutest thou the church of God? ... for ... the Lord has heard the prayers of thy father." After three days of torment, Alma calls upon Christ, is forgiven, revives, and bears ecstatic witness: "My soul hath been redeemed from the gall of bitterness and bonds of iniquity. I was in the darkest abyss; but now I behold the marvelous light of God. My soul was wrecked with eternal torment; but I am snatched, and my soul is pained no more" (BM 212, 214; Mosiah 27:11-14, 29). This phrase and others come directly from the unmodified revivalist rhetoric of the Second Great Awakening in the 1820s.[28] The four sons of Mosiah are also converted and become missionaries to the Lamanites of legendary endurance and effectiveness. They renounce political aspirations, as well, an event that triggers a change in the form of government from monarchy to a more democratic system of elected judges. Alma II becomes a missionary, but rather to renegade Nephites. I see in their number, five, a Smith family parallel, for four converted to Presbyterianism, and Smith was swayed toward Methodism. (Eventually two of Mosiah's four sons also become alter egos for variations of Smith's autobiographical narratives. See below.)

After the "revival" episodes in the Book of Mormon, we would predict, according to Smith's psychic map, gold treasure or a gold book. In fact, in the next chapter (BM 216; Mosiah 28), Smith discusses how Mosiah II translated the Jaredites' gold records using the breastplate and two seer stones. I discuss the Jaredite story in chapter 6, but the sequence confirms that Smith uses it, a story within a story, as an expanded fantasy of his own life as he has the other narratives up to this point.

The Order of Nehor

> Narcissistic rage occurs in many forms; they all share, however, a specific psychological flavor which gives them a distinct position within the wide realm of human aggressions. The need for revenge, for righting a wrong, for undoing a hurt by whatever means, and a deeply anchored, unrelenting compulsion in the pursuit to all these aims which gives no rest to those who have suffered a narcissistic injury—[such as ridicule, contempt, and conspicuous defeat]—these are features which are characteristic for the phenomenon of narcissistic rage in all its forms and which set it apart from other kinds of aggression.[29]

TIME:	92-81 B.C.E.//1823-27 C.E.
PLACE:	ZARAHEMLA//PALMYRA; THEN AMMONIHAH// SOUTH BAINBRIDGE
PERSONAE:	ALMA THE YOUNGER//JOSEPH SMITH, JR.
	NEHOR//ALVIN'S PHYSICIAN
	THE ORDER OF NEHOR//ANY IN POSITIONS OF POWER AND PRESTIGE WITH SOME CONTROL OVER THE SMITH FAMILY
	GIDEON//ALVIN, PERHAPS WITH ELEMENTS OF JOSEPH AS A CHILD
	AMLICI//DUPLICATE OF NEHOR, AND POSSIBLY JOHN QUINCY ADAMS
	AMULEK//JOSIAH STOWELL
	FOREMOST LAWYER ZEEZROM//JUDGE ALBERT NEELEY

In the book of Alma, the Book of Mormon's longest, the four sons of Mosiah began missionary work among the Lamanites, leaving Mosiah II without an heir. Before his death in 92 B.C.E., he supervised the transformation of the government from a hereditary monarchy to a "rule of judges," in which the chief judge, once elected, could retain that position for life. Alma II was the first man elected to that office, adding its functions to the position he already held as high priest of the church.[30] Mosiah transmitted to him the symbols of power: the brass plates, the gold plates, etc., but not the sword of Laban. It disappears from the Book of Mormon narrative; but because Smith had not been able to find a more mature way to deal with humiliation and disappointment than his compensatory fantasies, no psychiatrist would be surprised to see it reappear with even more awesome powers.[31] It does—as Ammon's almost-magical weapon.

The book of Alma chronicles various missionary endeavors of faith and hope played out against the background of a civilization descending steadily into war. From a psychoanalytic perspective, these wars embody Smith's narcissistic rage, caused by his public humiliation over the stillborn death of his first son.

The first part of the book of Alma deals, however, with personal narratives. Alma first achieves an important political triumph over Nehor, the second of the Book of Mormon's three anti-Christs. A physically strong and evil man, Nehor had assured the people that they need not fear God, for all will be "saved at the last day. ... and, in the end, all men should have eternal life."[32] When an aged warrior, Gideon, argued with him, Nehor killed Gideon with his sword, and Alma condemned Nehor to death for the murder but not his theology, because the law allowed freedom of belief.

Viewed from a psychoanalytic perspective, Smith has dictated another compensatory fantasy of retribution for the death of a good man. I see in this tale, not only Alvin's death, but also, because of the blood and violence, Smith's surgery. If so, then Smith, through his alter ego, Alma, administers justice. I also read the triumph over Nehor as being so psychologically satisfying that Smith expanded the story to the larger society. His rewritings of the local excitement caused by the revival and the national political turmoil during the period of Alvin's death show his "power" in providing solutions, a pattern that will intensify in this section of the Book of Mormon.

Next Amlici, a follower of Nehor, tried to persuade the people to repudiate the judge system and name him king. But "the voice of the people came against Amlici" (BM 225; Alma 2:7). He organized his followers, they consecrated him king, and he launched a rebellion. In one day the Nephites killed 12,532 Amlicites while losing 6,562 of their own. In a climactic sword fight, Amlici and Alma met

> face to face; and they did contend mightily one with another. And it came to pass that Alma, being a man of God, being exercised with much faith, cried saying: O Lord, have mercy and spare my life, that I may be an instrument in thy hands to save and preserve this people. Now when Alma said these words he contended again with Amlici; and he was strengthened, insomuch that he slew Amlici with the sword. (BM 227; Alma 2:28-30)

Once again Smith, in Alma's persona, has taken revenge on Nathan Smith and Alvin's physician, also saving the government from the injustice that had denied Andrew Jackson the presidency in 1824 through trickery with the electoral college. (See chapters 3 and 5.) The next two autobiographical events are the Smith family's mourning for Alvin's death and the revival. The book of Alma records both simultaneously:

> The people were afflicted, yea greatly afflicted for the loss of their brethren ... and every soul had cause to mourn; and they believed it was the judgments of God sent upon them, because of their wickedness and their abominations; therefore they were awakened to a remembrance of their duty, and they began to establish the church more fully; yea, and many were baptized in the waters of Sidon and were joined to the church of God. (BM 230; Alma 4:1-4)

In this compensatory fantasy, Alma himself baptized 3,500. In fact, the motif of revival preaching takes over at this point in the Book of Mormon (see, for example, BM 232-38; Alma 5) with Alma giving up his position as chief judge to become a sometimes rejected but always powerful preacher. In Alma's transition from temporal to spiritual power, I see the transition period in Smith's life after Alvin's death. Also the angel reappeared as if on cue, recapitulating the sequence of angel, sword, and revival.

In this Book of Mormon episode, Alma had gone to preach in Ammonihah, a town "on the west of the river Sidon by the borders of the wilderness" (BM 236-42; Alma 7; [83 B.C.E.//1826 C.E.]). These phrases communicate to me that Smith is recalling the move from Palmyra to the border of Pennsylvania by the Susquehanna River. These "lands, and their cities, and their villages, yea, even all their small villages [were named] after him who first possessed them; and thus it was with the city of Ammonihah" (BM 242-43; Alma 8:3-7). Tellingly with the exception of Bainbridge and South Bainbridge, the surrounding towns and hamlets are named for individuals: Colesville, Harpersville, Taylortown, Bennettsville, Masonville, Bettsburgh, Quinntown (now Quinnville), Doraville, etc.

This geographical point is worth developing. I suggest a simple naturalistic solution to the Book of Mormon geography problems discussed in my introduction: I hypothesize that Smith conceptualized Book of Mormon geography by turning his own locale upside down and superimposing it on an exaggerated and unsophisticated view of the Americas. For example, he put oxen, cows, asses, sheep, domesticated goats and swine, horses (with chariots), and elephants in pre-Columbian America. Zarahemla/Palmyra, the Nephite capitol in the center of their civilization, was multiplied ten-fold to the size of Washington, D.C., in 1830 which had 27,000 whites, 6,100 slaves, and 6,100 free blacks totalling 39,000. These Nephite lands reversed in polarity and became southern until the end-battles in the book, and the northern Lamanite country usually represented Joseph's travels south to the area of southeastern New York and Pennsylvania. The only river in the Book of Mormon, Sidon, was an exaggeration of the Susquehanna to the size of the Mississippi. But the river Sidon also ran by Zarahemla/Palmyra which the Susquehanna does not do. Here Joseph seemed to have followed the plan for the "Chenango Canal" which in 1827-29 was the cause of one of the two loudest debates between the opposing parties in New York State. The plan was to connect Maryland and Pennsylvania with the Great Lakes interior by extending the Susquehanna River north through the proposed "Chenango Canal" up to the Erie Canal, which, in Smith's day ran west, alongside of Zarahemla/Palmyra.[33] This inverted-geography thesis gives Smith an outline easy to bring to mind and visualize as he dictated for those thirteen weeks, thus keeping his story straight. The geography had to be disguised enough to avoid obvious correlation with his known life. From a naturalistic approach, the geography, like the stories, could only come from his personal life, which, to this point, had a diameter of 345 miles as the crow flies, extending from Lebanon, New Hampshire, on the east to the edge of Lake Erie (where he found his seer stone) on the west.

To return to the parallels between Smith's life and the experiences of Alma and Amulek: The citizens of Ammonihah reviled Alma and spat upon him. In sorrow he left, but the same angel who converted him fourteen years earlier commended his sincerity and sent him back, promising him a companion. Amulek, the promised companion, had also seen the angel; together they preach, having some success in making converts.

From a psychoanalytic perspective, I suggest that Amulek represents Smith's main supporter in his magic endeavors in South Bainbridge, Josiah Stowell. Just as Stowell defended Smith from those who ridiculed his supernatural claims (Stowell's relatives and the Hales), so does Amulek defend Alma. Alma and Amulek are tried before Ammonihah's "foremost" lawyer, Zeezrom, and both are imprisoned—a clear second version, in my opinion, of Smith's 1826 trial. God demolishes the prison, and they escape (see Alma 8-15). Continuing the compensating fantasy, Zeezrom, unlike his real-life counterpart, Judge Albert Neeley, repents, converts, and becomes a missionary. The impoverished Smith lived in Stowell's affluent home, despite Stowell's family's opposition; but as another element of reversal and compensatory fantasy, Alma rewarded Amulek for his loyalty. Amulek had "forsaken all his gold, and silver, and precious things ... for the word of God, he being rejected by those who were once his friends and also by his father and his kindred[,] ... Alma ... took Amulek and came over to the land of Zarahemla ... to his own house, and did administer unto him his tribulations, and strengthened him in the Lord" (BM 266; Alma 15:16-18).

In Smith's first fantasy version of the Bainbridge trial (the cataclysm accompanying Christ's death), its devastating impact can be measured by the magnitude of destruction and by the specificity of the date on which it occurred. In this second version, the impact of the trial can be measured by the extensive sermonizing, digressions, martyrdom of Alma's converts, the conversion of Zeezrom, and the destruction of the prison—covering twenty-five pages and seven chapters (BM 249, 264; Alma 10:6, 14:23).

However, the fantasy went a step farther in seeking retribution for his humiliation. A few months later, the Lamanites destroyed Ammonihah. Smith also assigned a precise date to this final moment of vindication—in the

> eleventh year of the reign of the judges ... on the fifth day of the second month ... the people of Ammonihah were destroyed; yea, every living soul ... and also their great city, which they said God could not destroy because of its greatness. But behold, in one day it was left desolate; and their carcasses were mangled by dogs and wild beasts of the wilderness. ... And so great was the scent thereof, that the people did not go in to possess the land of Ammonihah for many years. And it was called the desolation of Nehors; for they were of the profession of Nehor. (BM 267; Alma 16)

Smith's compensatory vengeance on those who had humiliated him is graphic, extreme, and specifically dated. The emphasis on a literal connection to Nehor, also slain in psychological retribution, recalls Smith's earlier acts of revenge on the physicians—here broadened to anyone in positions of power and prestige—who had inflicted pain on the child Smith, caused the death of his brother, taken away their farmhouse, and disdained his family.

Embedded within the Ammonihah narrative is an addendum that psychologically suggests Smith's experiences with money-digging near South Bainbridge. Although he had been humiliated, he also detached his future wife from her disbelieving relatives and attached her to himself. In the Book of Mormon, the Lamanites who destroyed Ammonihah took hostages from "around" the area. Alma petitioned the Lord for their safety and release, and God instructed Alma where the Nephite army could intercept the Lamanites and free the hostages (BM 267; Alma 16).

This embedded story also explains why Smith dated the occurrence; because Isaac Hale refused permission for Emma to wed Joseph, they eloped in January 1827, emancipating her from her father and making her the companion demanded by the angel so Smith could get the gold plates seven months later.

Meanwhile, in another stacked story, Mosiah's sons (whom I suggest correspond to the four Smiths who converted to Presbyterianism during the revival) rejected the monarchy in favor of serving God as missionaries for fourteen years among the Lamanites. The experiences of two, Ammon (not to be confused with the Ammon who rescued Limhi's people) and Aaron, again enact portions of Smith's history and are chronologically stacked over Alma's storyline.

Their story—particularly Ammon's—is the core of this chapter for two reasons. It culminates in Smith's failed boast about his firstborn son in front of his enemies, an experience that I argue is even more painful than the South Bainbridge trial. Like the trial, he never wrote about his child's deformities, I hypothesize, because the subject was too painful—but because it was so painful, he could not keep the event fully hidden. Second, Ammon represents the unconscious prototype of Smith's later life in its most exposed form in the Book of Mormon. From a psychoanalytic perspective, Ammon is an example of phallic narcissism, and his sword is an awesome phallic symbol.

Invincibility Confronts Overwhelming Devastation

All infants are narcissists, and these traits are well developed by age two: the search for power, self-centeredness, greed, and the assumption of control over others, usually the mother. In normal development, a caring mother will mold herself to the newborn's needs. All mothers know how exhausting this is. Then, over time, in sensitive response to the readiness of the child, the mother will slow down, modify, and even stop some of her "on-constant-call" behavior. In "good enough" mothering, these steps will be small, incremental, and paced to the child's physical and neurological development. These will be "mini-jolts" which might get "mini-rages" as the child loses control of his world, but they are small enough to be handled progressively by the child. Further, the child begins to take genuine pride in his own accomplishments. But if the emotional or physical deprivation and frustrations are too great for him at that particular stage, the initial crying and screaming give way to an internal world of compensating omnipotent fantasy. The narcissistic personality remains fixated on the quest for power, frequently characterized by expanded fantasies of omnipotence and conquest and, when possible, by exploitation in the real world. The infantile desire to overcome opposition effortlessly, as if by magic, is frequently carried forward to the later stages of childhood. In the Oedipal stage, a narcissistic boy adds, to the normal intense feelings about his phallus, an extra element of magic; he becomes preoccupied with sexual success, power, brilliance, and specialness.

The male narcissistic personality has been unofficially divided into four subtypes. The least functional two are the craving and the paranoid, while the more effective two are the manipulative and phallic types. As I read Joseph Smith's personality, he combines characteristics of the manipulative and phallic types:

> The manipulator perceives that another person's goal conflicts with his own [and] he intends to influence the other person and employs deception in the influencing process, and he has the satisfying feeling of having put something over on the other person when the manipulation works. ... These components of manipulation are readily available to consciousness; the manipulator knows what he is doing. ...
>
> The phallic narcissistic personality ... are the "men's men." ... They

> parade their masculinity, often along athletic or aggressive lines. In common with some manipulative personalities, they tend to be both exhibitionist and reckless. While the exhibitionism of the manipulative personality tends more to call attention to his "good behavior" and reputation, the phallic narcissist tends more to show himself off and to exhibit his body, clothes, and manliness. The manipulative person is more reckless in his schemes, deceptions and manipulations; the phallic narcissist tends more towards feats of reckless daring. ... Many phallic narcissistic men seem to have a dual attitude to women. On the one hand, they talk about them in the contemptuous terms of locker-room language. On the other hand, they are the defenders of motherhood and the sanctity of women.[34]

> Phallic narcissism stems from the period of development in which the penis in males prototypically becomes invested with narcissistic [self-centered] libido [attachment] and thus becomes highly valued and prized. This is the so-called phallic stage of development, usually occurring around the third to fifth year—also known as the oedipal phase. Along with this investment in the penis or its symbolic equivalents comes the threat of its loss in the form of castration anxiety. ... Qualities associated with this narcissistic configuration are pride in phallic prowess and performance, the search for admiration especially of skill or mastery, a sense of daring, counterphobic behaviors, unwillingness to accept defeat, omnipotence in the face of seemingly impossible obstacles, exhibitionism, assertiveness, and self-aggrandizement. The underlying themes are the wish for admiration of the phallic accomplishment and the need to defend against anxiety from castration fears and vulnerability. Individuals with these character traits tend to be self-centered, independent, difficult to intimidate, often fearless, ready to spring into action—strong personalities that step readily and willingly into positions of leadership. ... Reich described them as "self-confident, often arrogant, elastic, vigorous and often impressive. ... The outspoken types tend to achieve leading positions in life and resent subordination." To this Kernberg adds, "Because narcissistic personalities are often driven by intense needs for power and prestige to assume positions of authority and leadership, individuals with such characteristics are found rather frequently in top leadership positions." The narcissistic need in such a personality compels him to take risks and undertake arduous tasks for the sake of winning a narcissistic prize and gaining a position of power and grandiose satisfaction. Moreover, the capacity to maintain self-esteem and integral psychic functioning depends on gaining the required narcissistic gratifications.[35]

As I analyze Joseph Smith, I suggest that his Oedipal phase would be characterized by intense anxiety to him because of the repeated operations on his leg, requiring extreme compensation through fantasy conquests and omnipotence. A weak father also contributes to phallic narcissism, for the boy child finds compensating super strength in his fantasies. If I am correct in seeing Joseph Sr. as weak, then Joseph Jr. was doubly at risk for never finding adequate means of dealing maturely with his underlying narcissism.

Some may be surprised at the lack of direct sexual morality and conflict in the Book of Mormon. What made Smith different from the ordinary "womanizing" man are the unusual characteristics he brought to the relationships. In both the Book of Mormon and in his official documented history, women are underrepresented, almost ignored. His sexuality differed from others in that he put it within a theologic framework and made it a commandment of God. Further, he lied about his sexuality to his wife (for a while), his friends, church, state, and nation. It is the grandiosity and daring deceit that are the unusual characteristics worthy of note of his sexual expansion. From a naturalistic view, the next story in the Book of Mormon may represent as close as we can get to the underlying fantasy behind his sexual behavior.

TIME: 92-77 B.C.E.//1826-28 C.E.
PLACE: THE LAND OF NEPHI, NOW POSSESSED BY LAMANITES// ISAAC HALE'S HOMESTEAD AND NEIGHBORHOOD
PERSONAE: AMMON//JOSEPH SMITH
KING LAMONI//ISAAC HALE
ABISH//EMMA HALE SMITH
THE SHEEP THIEVES//THE HALE BROTHERS
KING LAMONI'S FATHER//PERHAPS JUDGE NEELEY, THE LOCAL MINISTER, OR MEMBERS OF THE STOWELL FAMILY
AMALEKITES AND AMULONITES//HALE, LEWIS, AND/ OR STOWELL FAMILIES
ZORAMITE SYNAGOGUE//METHODIST EPISCOPAL CHURCH
THE ANTI-NEPHI-LEHIES//THE STILLBORN, DEFORMED FIRST SON

Ammon and his brothers separated at the Lamanite border, and Ammon went to "the land of Ishmael, the land being called after the sons of Ishmael, who also became Lamanites" (BM 271; Alma 17:19).[36] The Lamanites captured Ammon and took him bound before King Lamoni, a descendant of Ishmael. This genealogical connection is a clue, I suggest, that Ammon's story will rework Smith's experience in Pennsylvania with Isaac Hale, who strongly disapproved of him as a son-in-law, would have preferred to see his daughter dead rather than married to him, and exerted maximum pressure to remake Smith into a stable, hard-working farmer. According to one of Emma's brothers-in-law, her brothers deliberately provoked Smith "at every opportunity"; once, on a fishing trip, they intentionally "vexed" Smith until he tore off his coat and challenged them to a fight.[37]

Lamoni (Isaac Hale) began the acquaintance by inquiring if Ammon wanted to live among the Lamanites: "And Ammon said unto him: Yea, I desire to dwell among this people for a time; yea, and perhaps until the day I die. ... Lamoni was much pleased with Ammon and caused that his bands should be loosed; and he would that Ammon should take one of his daughters to wife. But Ammon said unto him: Nay, but I will be thy servant" (BM 270-761; Alma 17:18-25).

The elements of compensation are obvious. Almost as soon as Lamoni laid eyes on Ammon, he saw him as not only an acceptable resident but a desirable son-in-law. Yet Ammon declined the proffered marriage. Why? Obviously for the satisfaction of refusing the king and of taking an exaggeratedly humble position as a servant that recalls all of the fairy tales of the disguised prince. From this very lowly position, his true worth would be even more dazzling. Here he reverses the humiliating need to elope.

Ammon's glamorous career began almost immediately as he accompanied the king's shepherds "to the place of water, which was called the water of Sebus" where "a certain number of Lamanites who had been with their flocks to water, stood and scattered the flocks of Ammon, and the servants of the king, ... insomuch that they fled many ways" (BM 271; Alma 17:26-27).

If Smith had been metaphorically "scattered" by the teasing or rudeness of his brothers-in-law, possibly because they were attempting to make him look worse in Isaac Hale's eyes than he already did, he psychologically took revenge on them in this story. The other servants begin to weep, frightened that Lamoni will kill them for losing the sheep. Confidently Ammon thought: "I will shew forth my power ... which is in me, in restoring these flocks unto the king, that I may win the hearts of these my fellow servants ... to believe in my words" (BM 272; Alma 17:29).

Ammon took on the whole pack of "vexers" singlehandedly, first killing some with a slingshot, like David against Goliath. When they attacked with clubs, he drew his sword, that already charged motif: "But behold, every man that lifted his club to smite Ammon, he smote off their arms with his sword; for he did withstand their blows by smiting off their arms with the edge of his sword, insomuch that they began to be astonished ... and flee ... yea, and they were not a few in number" (BM 272-73; Alma 17: 34-38).

Ammon's companions took these severed limbs to King Lamoni, who was "astonished exceedingly" and decided that Ammon must be "the Great Spirit; and he hath come down at this time to preserve your lives, that I might not slay you as I did your brethren." When the king next saw Ammon, he was frightened and suppliant, asking Ammon if he was the Great Spirit (BM 272-74; Alma 17:34-18:11). As a psychiatrist, I suspect that Smith is reveling in this compensatory story. Not only did the father-in-law figure petition Ammon/Joseph to marry his daughter, but he was ready to see him as a god and promises Ammon/Joseph anything he wanted.

At this point, a striking event occurs. Ammon, promised anything he might wish or desire, decides to use "guile" or trickery. In short, Ammon will exploit the king: "Now Ammon being wise yet harmless he saith unto

Lamoni, Wilt thou hearken unto my words, if I tell thee by what power I do these things? and this is the thing I desire of thee. And the king answered him, and said, Yea, I will believe all thy words; and thus he was caught with guile" (BM 275; Alma 18:22-23). And while Lamoni is duped, the reader is being encouraged to admire Ammon's cleverness.

Ammon's next step in exercising power over the king is to require him to "hearken" and "believe" his preaching. Lamoni agrees to do so and, after listening to Ammon, is struck by what nineteenth-century revivalists called "the falling exercise," or an ecstatic swoon that, from a psychiatric perspective, was a trance-like state resulting in a period of psychologically caused bodily paralysis and partial or complete unconsciousness. It was then seen as a sign of conversion.[38] After forty-eight hours, the queen begins to wonder if he is dead; some have said that he is decomposing, but, she says, "as for myself, he doth not stink." She believes Ammon when he confidently tells her that the king "sleepeth in God and on the morrow he shall rise again." He praises her: "There has not been such great faith among all the people of the Nephites" (BM 277; Alma 19:8-10). The next morning Lamoni awakes and declares that he has seen his "Redeemer; and he shall come forth, and be born of a woman, and he shall redeem all mankind who believe on his name" (BM 277; Alma 19:12-13). Upon hearing this testimony, Lamoni again comes under the falling power, this time joined by the queen and Ammon.

This extravagant demonstration frightens all of the servants "save it were one of the Lamanitish women, whose name was Abish, she having been converted to the Lord for many years, on account of a remarkable vision of her father [but] never had made it known [and] she ran from house to house, making it known to the people." At her call many gather, including relatives of the sheep thieves Ammon has killed. One of them tries to kill the unconscious Ammon, but God strikes him dead. Then Abish takes the queen by the hand, who immediately rises and declares, "O blessed Jesus, who has saved me from an awful hell. ... And when she had said this, she clasped her hands, being filled with joy, speaking many words which were not understood ..." The rest of this episode, including speaking in tongues, proceeds with revivalist exaggeration. Everyone who has witnessed this scene is converted by the heroic Ammon and joins the church he establishes (BM 277-79; Alma 19:14-36).

From a psychoanalytic perspective, I suggest that Emma, who has been almost completely absent from the Book of Mormon version of Smith's life, is Abish. She is the one person in the king's court (besides the unconscious king and queen) who believes Ammon/Joseph. In a fairy tale, she would be the king's daughter and Ammon's future wife; but in this story, her function is to express absolute and unwavering confidence in Ammon—not to "reward" his efforts or to raise his status.

In the next incident, Ammon goes from triumph to triumph, reversing, I suggest, the stinging encounters with his in-laws, reviewed in chapter 3. Reading from the Book of Mormon back into Joseph Smith's life, I hypothesize that perhaps even some of the dialogue may have come from these conflicts: "Why did ye not come to the feast on that great day when I made a feast?", etc. God tells Ammon that Lamoni's father will try to kill him and that Ammon's brothers are in jail in Middoni. Lamoni assures Ammon that the king of Middoni is his personal friend, and the two set out to rescue Ammon's brothers.

On the way Ammon and Lamoni encounter the king's father, who promptly orders his son to kill this Nephite who is "one of the children of a liar," planning "by their cunning and their lyings, [to] deceive us, that they may again rob us of our property" (BM 280-81; Alma 20: 8-13). This is the second time in the Book of Mormon that the protagonist is called a liar by his antagonists (BM 41; 1 Ne. 16:38; see chapter 2). Again reading from the Book of Mormon back into Smith's life suggests historical statements of the Hale and Lewis families. If so, Joseph seems little troubled by the attack. From a naturalistic view, he does not counter this attack by speaking the truth but by constructing a conquering fantasy of omnipotence. When Lamoni refuses his father's command, the father attempts to kill Ammon; but Ammon easily deflects his blows, wounds the father's arm, and then at sword point demands the release of his brothers, a guarantee to allow Lamoni to hold his kingdom without fealty, and the promise of freedom of belief for Lamoni. The father, overjoyed at not being killed, had originally offered Ammon half his kingdom and gratefully accepts these lesser requests (BM 280-82; Alma 20:16, 20-27).

Smith's fantasy thus psychologically reverses the scornful attitudes of Emma's father, the rejection of her cousins from the Methodist Episcopal church, the obvious belief of Judge Neeley (the king of the whole land) that Smith was a fraud, and Josiah Stowell's relatives who took Smith to court as an "impostor." The three jailed sons of Mosiah represent Smith, psychologically, when he was imprisoned for the night in South Bainbridge. Although the Smith family was able to remain as tenants in their frame house, after the year expired, they all, including Oliver Cowdery who refused to leave the family, had to return to the small crowded cabin. Perhaps it was a symbolic jail cell. Certainly, their straitened economic circumstances were oppressive. In fantasy Smith saw himself as the only one who could free them. (A year after dictating this story, Smith's father went to jail for non-payment of debt and his brother Hyrum escaped jail only by permanently fleeing from the Palmyra/Manchester area.)[39]

On a fantasy level, Smith wipes out his humiliation from his in-laws. Yet, psychologically, Smith is still trying to process his experience as a child, conquering the surgeon by holding the sword in his own hand and defeating those in power. Within this context, the Book of Mormon can be read as an answer to Smith's childhood question: "How can I avoid ever being helpless and in pain again with the limited tools my family has given me?" Beneath this representation of surgery is the magic power of the sword and Smith's fantasy of himself as invincible.

Ammon's story reveals coercion and manipulation, characteristics of the narcissistic personality. Ammon catches the terrified king "with guile," by asking him if he would "believe" and "hearken to" whatever he said—the equivalent of frightening someone into signing a contract before reading it. Ammon describes himself as "wise yet harmless." From a psychological perspective, the fact that Smith, speaking through an alter ego, finds deceit and manipulation "harmless" is one of the most troubling admissions of the Book of Mormon. Similarly, Ammon offers Lamoni's father a choice between death and accepting his terms, and apparently accepts at face value that Lamoni's father is truly grateful. Ammon does not appreciate—or care—that individuals coerced by intimidation and threats do not respond with genuine gratitude. As a psychiatrist, I would fear that, if these techniques are working for Smith in early adulthood, he will continue to use them.[40]

Ammon's story demonstrates the multilayered meanings that therapists must pay attention to simultaneously. In the story of Nephi and Laban, the surgeon becomes a wealthy robber, made absolutely helpless through drunkenness, and is decapitated. Although the sword of Laban is not identified by name in the rest of the Book of Mormon, it is possible that it could be Ammon's sword, handed down to him by his father (BM 216; Mosiah 28:20). In either case, Ammon's weapon is symbolically, if not literally, Laban's sword.

Keeping this possible genealogy in mind, it requires no effort to read Ammon's encounter with the sheep thieves—robbers like Laban and like the Gadianton band. All of them are figures of the surgeon Nathan Smith. A symbol of absolute power is Smith's ability to amputate—arms by Ammon, head by Nephi. By using the symbolic instrument used against him in the surgery, Smith causes their deaths and symbolic castrations instead of his own.

Each fantasy briefly soothes Smith's fears—which is the purpose of fantasy—but they return and must be conquered again. Ammon's fearless courage stems from his secret—that he cannot be killed. He is literally invincible. Mosiah II, worried if he should let his sons be missionaries to the savage Lamanites, was reassured when God promised him: "Let them go up, for ... I will deliver thy sons out of the hands of the Lamanites" (BM 215-16; Mosiah 28:7). While Ammon is fighting the sheep-scatterers, the narrative notes that they "knew not that the Lord had promised Mosiah that he would deliver his sons out of their hands" (BM 272; Alma 17:35). The narrator insists again on this point when one of his victim's brothers tries to kill the unconscious Ammon in the throne room but is struck dead himself. Again the narrative confirms: "Now we see that Ammon could not be slain, for the Lord had said ... I will spare him" (BM 27:8; Alma 19:23). In the Book of Mormon, Smith does not need to fear surgery or physicians or anyone else again. In psychological terms, however, the fact that Ammon knows he is invincible while the other characters within the narrative do not means that he manipulates their ignorance to his advantage, another example of his "guile."

From this episode, the Book of Mormon next relates another stacked story: the experiences of Ammon's imprisoned brother Aaron and Aaron's companion, Muloki. As we might predict, their story presents yet another version of the Smiths' life story at Harmony. This story of compensatory fantasy deals with what I consider the most intense humiliation Smith experienced, a story so humiliating that he dare not tell it, yet so devastating that he cannot avoid it. This is his boast that his firstborn will be a miracle child who can open and translate the gold book, when the reality is that the child is a malformed stillbirth.[41]

Smith's alter ego Aaron proselytes among hardened strangers who have "built synagogues after the order of the Nehors," a signal that he is dealing with the powerful and prestigious—like the Hale and Lewis families:

> Now the Lamanites ... had built a great city, which was called Jerusalem. ... [and] were sufficiently hardened, but the Amalekites, and Amulonites, were still harder. ... Aaron came to the city of Jerusalem, and firstly began to preach to the Amalekites. And he began to preach to them in their synagogues ... built ... after the order of the Nehors; for many of the Amalekites and Amulonites were after the order of the Nehors. Therefore, as Aaron entered into one of their synagogues to preach unto the people, and as he was speaking unto them, behold, there arose an Amalekite, and began to contend with him, saying: What is that thou has testified? Hast thou seen an angel? Why do not angels appear unto us? Behold, are not this people as good as thy people? (BM 283; Alma 21:2-5)

Except for the king and queen, only Abish (Emma) believed Ammon in the court of King Lamoni. Aaron has the same experience: "The Amalekites were not converted, save only one; neither was any of the Amulonites, but they did harden their hearts, and also the hearts of the Lamanites in that part of the land whithersoever they dwelt" (BM 290; Alma 23:13-14).

This more generalized story still, in my professional opinion, represents either Josiah Stowell, Smith's first convert, and Stowell's disbelieving family, or Emma and her extended family. The Amalekite challenge about the angel would accurately represent the views of the Stowells, Hales, and/or Lewises. As discussed in chapter 3, fifty years after these events,

Joseph and Hiel Lewis, brothers who were officials in Emma's church, described the first "angel" described by Smith; this being lacked any Christian characteristics and had "his throat cut ear to ear, and blood streaming down." They rejected Smith's application to the church, in part, because of his "necromancy." Reading from the Book of Mormon back into his life, are these sentences from an Amalekite a fantasy enlargement of Joseph's interchange with the Lewises?

Aaron left Jerusalem, encountered Muloki, and continued preaching with him in Middoni. "Few believed on the words they taught." Instead, repeating the theme of imprisonment and judgement, Aaron and his companions are "taken and cast into prison." Ammon and Lamoni, as we have already seen, deliver them, bringing these two overlapping versions of Smith's life together (BM 283-84; Alma 21:11-14). Revival follows imprisonment: Aaron completes the conversion of Lamoni's father, who experiences the same "falling" ecstasy. Aaron restores him in the presence of his queen and servants. The king issues a proclamation recommending these missionaries to his people, and thousands of Lamanites are converted.

In Smith's compensatory fiction, rather than being humiliated before all the people in the area of Harmony and South Bainbridge, he converts them to his view. But Aaron's success is even more grandiose than Ammon's. In fact, from this point forward, the events become more extreme in portraying resolutions to the conflicts in Smith's life. The extreme compensation in this case begins when the converted abandon the name of Lamanite and call themselves, first, "Anti-Nephi-Lehies" (BM 290; Alma 23:16-17), then "Ammonites," or the people of Ammon, thus implying that Ammon/Joseph Smith is the father of a new nation. In addition to a new name, these converts take a vow of absolute pacifism, which remains unshaken even though thousands are eventually massacred by their unconverted savage Lamanite brothers. In yet another compensatory fantasy, the Lamanite slayers are so struck by the Ammonites' steadfastness that more are converted than were killed. Among those who remain unconverted are Aaron's foes, the Amalekites and Amulonites: "And thus we can plainly discern, that after a people has been once enlightened by the spirit of God, and hath had great knowledge of things pertaining to righteousness, and then have fallen away into sin and transgression, they become more hardened, and thus their estate becometh worse than as though they had never known these things" (BM 293; Alma 24:30). From a psychoanalytic perspective, this passage means that Smith damns Emma's family and others in the New York and Pennsylvania area because they refuse to believe him. The intensity of his anger is shown by the vengeance he takes upon them: "almost all the seed of Amulon and his brethren" are killed by the Nephites (BM 294; Alma 25:3-4) and by internal fighting among the Lamanites (BM 294-95; Alma 25:3-13).

These narrative events demonstrate the remarkable strength of Smith's psychological defenses. Episodes of inferiority, shame, humiliation, and failure have, through fantasy reversal, become glorious conquests, destruction of his enemies, and personal invulnerability. From a narrative perspective, the missionary success of Ammon and Aaron has come at a fearful cost in deaths. Yet in an episode of hypomania (an elevation of mood and excitement that, in more extreme forms, becomes mania), Ammon ignores the deaths, tragedies, wounds, rapes, dismemberings, burning of towns, dislocations, grievings, and general devastation that would occur from savages driven by hatred, and begins an ill-timed extended exultation (four pages in the text) which causes even his brother Aaron discomfort: "Ammon, I fear that thy joy doth carry thee away unto boasting" (BM 296; Alma 26:10). Ammon is only spurred on to greater heights:

> My joy is full, yea, my heart is brim with joy, and I will rejoice in my God; yea, I know that I am nothing; as to my strength, I am weak; therefore I will not boast of myself, but I will boast of my God; for in his strength I can do all things; yea, behold the many miracles we have wrought in this land. ... Behold, how many thousands of our brethren hath he loosed from the pains of hell; and they are brought to sing redeeming love. ... and they are encircled about with the matchless bounty of his love. ... therefore let us glory, yea, we will glory in the Lord; yea we will rejoice for our joy is full; yea, we will praise our God forever. ... Yea, who can say too much of his great power, and of his mercy, and of his long suffering towards the children of men? Behold I say unto you, I cannot say the smallest part which I feel. ... And we have entered into their houses and taught them ... and we have entered into their temples and synagogues ... and we have been cast out, and mocked, and spit upon, and smote upon our cheeks; and we have been stoned. ... Now behold ... and see the fruits of our labors; and are they few? I say unto you, Nay, there are many. ... How many of these have laid down their lives; and we know that they have gone to their God. ... Now have we not reason to rejoice? Yea, I say unto you, there never was men that had so great reason to rejoice as we, since the world began; yea, and my joy is carried away, even unto boasting in my God ... and he is a merciful Being; even unto salvation. ... Now if this is boasting, even so will I boast; for this is my life and my light, my joy and my salvation, and my redemption from everlasting wo ... and my great thanksgiving; yea, and I will give thanks unto my God forever. (BM 296-98; Alma 26)

Certainly a belief in ultimate happiness for the righteous dead helps to compensate for death and suffering. But still in such traumatic circumstances, one expects grief and mourning for the dead and exhaustion in the temporary relief from bloody, hand-to-hand battles. What despairing, traumatic experience can this exaggerated, bizarre euphoria be guarding against? I argue that it is the malformed stillbirth whose glorious future Smith had boasted of to Emma's family. The turmoil and suffering it inflicted on Smith becomes increasingly evident in the narrative as bloody carnage followed by hypomanic euphoria. It is the same psychological process I identified in the incidents involving children in 3 Nephi.

The narrative follows this pattern exactly: carnage during a Lamanite attack, then mourning, then Ammon's overwrought euphoria:

> And now this was a time that there was a great mourning and lamentation heard throughout all the land, among all the people of Nephi; yea the cry of widows mourning for their husbands, and also of fathers mourning for their sons, and the daughter for the brother; yea the brother for the father: and thus the cry of mourning was heard among everyone of them; mourning for their kindred which had been slain. And now surely this was a sorrowful day; yea a time of solemnity. (BM 302; Alma 28:1-6)

As a psychotherapist, I note that the anguish of a mother for her son is absent in this litany of loss. Was it too obvious, or temporarily too painful, to contemplate? Yet at this point of the narrative, Alma also returns, concluding with his famous descant, "O that I were an angel ..." It is the theme of the descant, not its poetry, that is important. I read this passage as Smith's confession that his grandiose view is genuinely shaken: "O that I were an angel, and could have the wish of mine heart, that I might go forth and speak with the trump of God, with a voice to shake the earth, and cry repentance unto every people. ... But behold, I am a man, and do sin in my wish; for I ought to be content with the things which the Lord hath allotted unto me" (BM 303; Alma 29:1-9). In psychological terms, he is struggling to acknowledge his vulnerability and to accept the mortal reality "allotted" to him.

These scenes written out of and around, as I am conjecturing, the death of his firstborn son provide crucial context for the narrative's forecast of a more general period of war and struggle to follow: "And this is the account of the wars and contentions among the Nephites, and also the wars between the Nephites and Lamanites" (BM 302: Alma 28:9). Smith's turmoil over the humiliating death of his son occupies the next twelve chapters; when he finally finds his fantasy compensation, he also announces the intensification of the wars. These wars are decreed by the death of his son, and what I see as his retaliatory rage at this humiliation will increasingly dominate the pages of the text and continue to the end of the Book of Mormon.

As I read the record Smith left, he attempts to divert himself from his anguish to engage in a long philosophical debate in Alma 30. Yet even in this diversion, he cannot completely get away from his conflict and returns more explicitly to his humiliation over his dead son. From my professional perspective, this psychological reason explains why Korihor, the third, last, and greatest anti-Christ in the Book of Mormon, appears, seemingly out of nowhere at a moment of peace (BM 305-10; Alma 30). The contest with

Korihor represents Smith's continued struggle with fate or the existence of God.

The narrative contextualizes Korihor with an affirmation of personal liberty: "Now there was no law against a man's belief; for it was strictly contrary to the commands of God, that there should be a law which should bring men on unequal grounds. ... and this Anti-Christ, whose name was Korihor, and the law could have no hold on him" (BM 305; Alma 30:7-1). Putting Korihor's arguments in Zarahemla into modern English makes them more easily comparable with the religious arguments of Joseph Smith's day:

> You people are unnecessarily tied down by your religious beliefs. Why are you waiting for Christ? No one can foretell the future. The prophecies you believe in are foolish traditions only. What assurance do you have of their truth? You can't know that Christ will come. The idea of a remission of sins is the effect of a mental illness brought on by the traditions of your fathers. These traditions are not true. Further the idea of an atonement is unreasonable, for each man is responsible for himself and the results of his life are his own doing. If a man becomes prosperous, it is because of his self-discipline, intellect, and strength. Whatever a man does is no crime.

The people of Zarahemla who believe Korihor ignore morality and indulge in wickedness including, specifically, whoredoms. Their reasoning is: If death is the end, then no bar to self-indulgence exists.

Korihor next enters the land of Jershon, inhabited by the Ammonites. "More wise" than the Nephites, "they took him, and bound him, and carried him before Ammon, which was a High Priest over that people" (BM 306; Alma 30:13-20). Ammon, the swordsman/missionary, has him "carried out of the land." In Gideon the inhabitants again take him "bound and carried" before Giddonah, the high priest/chief judge. Giddonah asks Korihor why he has perverted the ways of the Lord, interfered with the peoples' happiness, and spoken against the prophets. Korihor explains (again paraphrased in modern English):

> I don't teach tradition as fact and don't like seeing people tied down unnecessarily by illusion. You do these ancient ordinances and rituals to gain control over the people, keep them in ignorance, and keep them suppressed. This is not emotional freedom but bondage. You don't know that those ancient prophecies are true, and it is unreasonable to blame these people for the sin committed by a parent in the Garden of Eden. No child should be blamed for what a parent does. You say Christ shall come to make this right. But you don't know Christ will come. You say he will be slain for the sins of the world, and thereby you lead this people after foolish traditions for your own ends. You keep them in bondage so you can glut yourselves with their work, and they dare not be assertive or enjoy their rights or enjoy their own possessions lest they offend you, your traditions, whims, dreams, visions, and pretended mysteries, and your unknown God—a being they have never seen or known, which never was nor ever will be.

Giddonah's officers bind Korihor and return him to the land of Zarahemla, where the original statement about religious freedom was made. In Zarahemla Korihor confronts both the chief judge and Alma as high priest. Again Korihor accuses the priests and teachers of misleading the people into foolish traditions so they can "glut" themselves on the labors of the people. Alma counters with his arguments for the existence of God—the testimony of the brethren, the holy prophets, the scriptures, and all of nature. Korihor insists on a stubborn agnosticism: "I do not deny the existence of God, but I do not believe that there is a God; and I say also, that ye do not know that there is a God; and except ye show me a sign, I will not believe."

From a psychodynamic perspective, Korihor's two-sided position on God may reflect Joseph's. Does God exist, and, if so, why did he do this to us? Is this stillborn child a sign from God of something? Of his existence? Of punishment for misbehavior? Or does it mean God doesn't exist? Or, if he exists, doesn't care? Even rational parents of a stillborn child today who know they did nothing wrong may struggle with the feelings that they are being punished for *something* and find themselves, with feelings of irrational guilt, searching for what it might be.

Certainly this post-Enlightenment argument recurred many times in upstate New York between 1800 and 1830. Those familiar with Thomas Paine's *Age of Reason* would have recognized Korihor's voice, his demand for some kind of proof, and his suspicion of the oppression of superstition.[42] But Korihor's arguments are almost unanswerably strong; Smith, to bring the story back under his control, has God strike Korihor dumb. Korihor then writes a retraction of sorts, explaining that an angel once appeared to him, convincing him that there was no God and appealing to his "carnal mind ... and for this cause, I withstood the truth." Even so Alma refuses to remove the curse and Korihor "was cast out, and went about from house to house, a begging for his food ... and as he went forth amongst them, behold, he was run upon, and trodden down, even until he was dead"[43] (BM 306-310; Alma 30:21-60).

Psychologically speaking, the contradictions in this story are instructive, pinpointing disasters that still lie in Smith's future. In addition to the fact that God's intervention is fantastic—like a debater who strikes his opponent whose arguments he is unable to answer with logic and reason—a more important insight is Smith's attitude toward civil liberties. Despite Mosiah's laws guaranteeing freedom of speech, Korihor is arrested, deported, and brought repeatedly before authorities. He has lost his freedom because of what he has *said*. I suggest that Smith similarly will give lip service to freedom of speech but truly does not understand it and eventually ignores constitutional protections of religion and speech. His destruction of the *Nauvoo Expositor* in 1844 is only the most conspicuous, and most deadly, example.[44] I also think it is instructive that Korihor said he deceived himself because an angel lied to him. Is Smith considering making a similar confession? Is Joseph reflecting on what he is doing with his angel story? Does Korihor represent not only the Age of Enlightenment doubter but also a guilty Smith who has been punished by God?

Theologically, it is also interesting that the theme of the philosophical question—does God exist?—is answered with punishing violence. Does Smith here suggest that he believes in fate (astrology and magic) rather than God, because the randomness of fate giving him a dead deformed son is still preferable to the punishment of a vengeful God?

The incident that follows Korihor's death is psychological confirmation to me that Smith is still working through the trauma of his stillborn son, specifically the rebuff from Joseph and Hiel Lewis when he tried to join Emma's church. In the Book of Mormon, after Korihor's death, word reaches Alma that the Zoramites, a Nephite faction, are becoming wicked. Alma launches a missionary crusade with three of Mosiah's four missionary sons, Amulek, the formerly evil judge Zeezrom, and two of his own three sons, here mentioned for the first time. These Zoramites have built a high altar, the Holy Stand or "Rameumptom," in the center of their synagogue. One person at a time ascends the narrow, elevated platform and recites a ritual prayer:

> Holy God, we believe that thou hast separated us from our brethren ... and thou hast elected us, that we shall be saved, whilst all around us are elected to be cast by thy wrath down to hell; ... and we also thank thee that thou hast elected us, that we may not be led away after the foolish traditions of our brethren, which doth bind them down to a belief in Christ, which doth lead their hearts to wander far from thee, our God. And again: We thank thee, O God, that we are a chosen and holy people. Amen. (BM 309-11; Alma 31:1-18)

Alma is "astonished beyond all measure" at this unseemly pride and grieves for this "wicked and perverse people; yea, he saw that their hearts were set upon gold and upon silver, and upon all manner of fine goods ... [and] their costly apparel, and their ringlets, and their bracelets, and their ornaments of gold." Their conversion efforts find

> success among the poor class of people for behold, they were cast out of the synagogues because of the coarseness of their apparel; therefore they were not permitted to enter into their synagogues to worship God, being esteemed as filthiness; therefore they were poor; yea, they were esteemed by their brethren as dross; therefore they were poor as to things of the world; and also they were poor in heart.

Alma assures them that they can worship outside of church and points out a positive side to their poverty: "It is well that ye are cast out of your synagogues, that ye may be humble, and that ye may learn wisdom; for it is because [of this] that ye are brought to a lowliness of heart. ... And now because ye are compelled to be humble, blessed are ye; for a man sometimes, if he is compelled to be humble, seeketh repentance; and ... shall find mercy" (BM 311-14; Alma 31:19-38; 32:1-14). The parallels between Smith's rejection and the poorer Zoramites are, psychologically speaking, very thinly disguised. Smith's parody of Protestant rituals in general and of the Hales' congregation is savage and unforgiving. Once again Smith has transformed and reversed the scene of his pain and humiliation.

Alma delivers a famous lecture on faith to these poorer converts, a sermon that, in my judgement, attempts for the third time to deal with the infant's death. He has described the child once as the radiant miracle of angels ministering to the children during Jesus' visit and again as the mass slaughter of the innocent Ammonites. Now he finds yet another metaphor: the child as a growing seed.

> Now, if ye give place, that a seed may be planted in your heart, behold, if it be a true seed, or a good seed, if ye do not cast it out by your unbelief ... behold, it will begin to swell within your breasts,[45] and when you feel these swelling motions, ye will begin to say within yourselves, it must needs be that this is a good seed ... for it beginneth to enlarge my soul; yea, it beginneth to enlighten my understanding; yea, and it beginneth to be delicious to me. ... Nevertheless it hath not grown up to a perfect knowledge. But behold, as the seed swelleth, and sprouteth, and beginneth to grow, and then ye must needs say, that the seed is good. ... Yea; for every seed bringeth forth unto its own likeness; therefore, if a seed groweth, it is good, but if it groweth not, behold, it is not good; therefore it is cast away. ...
>
> But if ye neglect the tree, and take no thought for its nourishment, behold it will not get any root; and when the heat of the sun cometh and scorcheth it, because it has no root it withers away, and ye pluck it up and cast it out ... because your ground is barren; and ye will not nourish the tree, therefore ye cannot have the fruit thereof.
>
> And because of your diligence and your faith and your patience with the word, in nourishing it; that it may take root in you, behold, by and by, ye shall pluck the fruit thereof, which is most precious, which is sweet above all that is sweet, and which is white above all that is white; yea, and pure above all that is pure. (BM 314-16; Alma 32:21-43)

Reading from the Book of Mormon back into his life, we note that the failure of the tree occurs because of inadequate nourishment. Joseph may be feeling guilty over not providing adequately for his wife, but there is insufficient information to reach a firm conclusion. Smith was farming land rented from his father-in-law, and they were living in a building owned by either Isaac Hale or his son.

Alma adds a quotation from the unknown Old Testament prophet Zenos:

> Thou has heard my prayer ... concerning ... my enemies, and thou didst turn them to me. ... Yea, thou art merciful unto thy children, when they cry unto

> thee to be heard of thee, and not of men. ... O God, thou hast been merciful unto me, and heard my cries in the midst of thy congregation. ... Also ... when I have been cast out, and have been despised by mine enemies ... thou didst visit them in thine anger, with speedy destruction; and thou didst hear me because of mine afflictions and my sincerity.

Once again in Smith's story God sides with him against Joseph and Hiel Lewis, who refused him entrance to the church. Strikingly, God is merciful because, in a passage quoted from another unknown Bible prophet, Zenock, he has a son. It is striking indeed that *son* appears nine times in twelve verses:

> It is because of thy Son that thou hast been thus merciful to me. ... Thou has turned thy judgments away from me, because of thy Son. ... He saith, Thou hast turned away thy judgments because of thy Son. ... How can ye disbelieve on the Son of God? ... Thou art angry, O Lord, with this people, because they will not understand of thy mercies which thou hast bestowed upon them, because of thy Son. And now my brethren, ye see that a second prophet of old has testified of the Son of God. ... These are not the only ones who have spoken concerning the Son of God. ... He was spoken of by Moses. ... Begin to believe in the Son of God, that he will come to redeem his people. ... And then may God grant unto you that your burdens may be light, through the joy of his Son. (BM 317-18; Alma 33:4-23)

As I read this defensive accusation, I hear Smith's bitterness over the gross humiliation in front of his wife's family, combined with the loss of masculine pride in failing to have his miraculous son, as determining his final direction, using any means for conquest available. But Smith has still not finished telling us about the loss of his son. He has described his conquest over those who rejected him in his pain. He has reversed his internal emotions from depression to euphoria. But he still has no son.[46]

Therefore, in the final section of this series of stacked stories, Alma, Smith's alter ego, tells his life story to his three sons (one does not suffice). To his righteous son Helaman (BM 323-30; Alma 36-37), Alma speaks of his conversion, a version of Smith's move from Methodism to his own new religion, in exaggerated revival terms. To this same son, he entrusts the records he has received. Psychologically, Smith has succeeded in having a son work with the records. In a grandiose statement, he attributes the salvation of thousands to his work; continuing to read from the Book of Mormon back into his life tells us that he is aware that a successful dictation of the Book of Mormon will bring followers:

> Were it not for these things that these records do contain, which are on these plates, Ammon and his brethren could not have convinced so many thousands of the Lamanites, of the incorrect traditions of their fathers. ... And who knoweth but what they will be the means of bringing many thousands of [Lamanites], yea, and also many thousands of our stiffnecked brethren, the Nephites, which are now hardening their hearts in sin and iniquities.

Smith seems to interweave his own miraculous story with Protestant evangelizing, preparing to present himself as a prophet. To his second son Shiblon (BM 330-32; Alma 38), Alma briefly recounts his miraculous conversion by the angel, then advises: "See that ye are not lifted up unto pride; yea, see that ye do not boast in your own wisdom, nor of your much strength; use boldness, but not overbearance; and also see that ye bridle all your passions, that ye may be filled with love; see that ye refrain from idleness." Smith may thus reveal some of his own struggles with narcissistic arrogance.

But the third son, Corianton (BM 332-40; Alma 39-42), has been immoral and faithless: "Thou didst do that which was grievous unto me; for thou didst forsake the ministry and go over into the land of Sidon, among the borders of the Lamanites, after the harlot Isabel; yea, she did steal away the hearts of many; but this was no excuse for thee, my son." Isabel is one of three female Book of Mormon characters. (The biblical personages Eve and Mary are named in the text.) The other two are Lucy Mack Smith, represented by Lehi's wife Sariah, and Emma, who appears briefly as the believing Abish. Who is Isabel? Alma denounces harlotry as the third most serious sin: "Know ye not, my son, that these things are an abomination in the sight of the Lord; yea, most abominable above all sins, save it be the shedding of innocent blood, or denying the Holy Ghost ... which is unpardonable." Furthermore, Corianton's sexual laxness brought "great iniquity" on the Zoramites, "for when they saw your conduct they would not believe in my words."

Within a psychoanalytic framework, Smith may be writing out either a mental struggle or disguising an actual lapse in sexual fidelity. No conclusive answer is possible; but the incident in which Hiel Lewis, quoting Levi Lewis's accusation fifty years later that Smith had attempted to seduce Eliza Winters, is suggestive. I may now conjecture that the problem occurred before this approximate dictation time of May 1829. If Smith did, in fact, attempt to seduce Winters and if the sequence of attempt and dictating this passage of the Book of Mormon is correct, Smith seems to be admitting that, because of his behavior, Emma's cousins would not believe his story, an outcome that seems probable. As always, reading from the Book of Mormon back into Smith's life is only suggestive, but this story finds some support, again inconclusive, with the "sobbing" of "tender wives" described by Nephi's brother, Jacob, in his sermon against polygamy (BM 126-7; Jac. 2:28-3:7; see above).

After expressing concern about his son's sexual misconduct, Alma discusses the resurrection, the judgments of God, and the eternal states of the righteous and damned. According to Alma, the final judgment will consider both deeds and desires. Then, interestingly, he argues that, while repentance, atonement, law, and punishment are all necessary, so is sin:

> The plan of redemption could not be brought about, only on conditions of repentance of men in the [earthly] probationary state ... for except it were for these conditions, mercy could not take effect except it should destroy the work of justice ... [and] God would cease to be God. ... The plan of mercy could not be brought about except an atonement should be made; therefore God himself atoneth for the sins of the world, to bring about the plan of mercy, to appease the demands of justice, that God might be perfect ... just ... and merciful. ... Now, how could a man repent except he should sin?

From a psychological perspective, this elaborate explanation of the necessity of sin to operationalize mercy, judgment, repentance, and justice suggests that Smith was troubled with guilt and having a difficult time finding psychological equilibrium.[47]

After these patriarchal lectures, a major shift occurs in the Book of Mormon. Until now personal stories have dominated, nearly all of them featuring Smith's alter egos and acting out fantasies to compensate for his own life; they all have a basis in reality. Now the Nephite-Lamanite wars dominate the action; their basis in Smith's autobiography is more tenuous, suggesting to me that he is revealing deeper issues, not just repeating his life's story. In psychological terms, he has achieved fantasy compensation for the deformed stillbirth, but he has not come to terms with his public humiliation. These wars, covering the next thirty-two years, express a shocking level of retaliatory bitterness.

Notes

1. Eber D. Howe, *Mormonism Unvailed; or, a Faithful Account of That Singular Imposition and Delusion* (Painesville, OH: Author, 1834); see also Thomas G. Alexander, "The Place of Joseph Smith in the Development of American Religion: A Historiographical Inquiry," *Journal of Mormon History* 5 (1978): 3-17.

2. M. T. Lamb, *The Golden Bible ... or The Book of Mormon. Is It from God?* (New York: Ward and Drummond, 1887), 196-252.

3. Ibid., 96-101.

4. I. Woodbridge Riley, *The Founder of Mormonism: A Psychological Study of Joseph Smith, Jr.* (New York: Dodd, Mead, 1902), 68-70. For a description of the creation of a major Mormon vision of the three degrees of heaven, see Philo Dibble's eyewitness account in Richard S. Van Wagoner, *Sidney Rigdon: A Portrait of Religious Excess* (Salt Lake City: Signature Books, 1994), 112-13. Little in this description fits the accepted medical profile. E. H. Reynolds and M. R. Trimble, eds., *Epilepsy and Psychiatry* (London and New York: Churchill Livingstone, 1981), esp. M. R. Trimble, "The Limbic System," 216-226, and B. Toone, "Psychoses of Epilepsy," 113-37; they classify epilepsy with psychosis into

1. Psychoses directly related to the occurrence of seizure activity; including
   a. Abnormal mental states that are a direct and immediate consequence of underlying seizure activity and which may have some of the features of a psychotic state: continuous auras, petit mal status, temporal lobe status
   b. Postictal psychoses
2. Interictal psychoses:

a. Schizophrenia-like and paranoid psychoses
b. Affective psychoses.

See also Jerome Kroll and Bernard Bachrach, "Visions and Psychopathology in the Middle Ages," *Journal of Nervous and Mental Disease* 170:41-49.

For an excellent study of the complexity of pathological environment, genetic contribution, and toxic enhancement in an artistic genius, see Russell D. Monroe, "The Episodic Psychoses of Vincent Van Gogh," *Journal of Nervous and Mental Disease* 166 (1978): 480-88. No specific conclusions can be drawn concerning Van Gogh's behavior and artistry. Monroe comments, "Every conceivable diagnosis has been applied to Vincent's illness, including schizophrenia, paranoia, manic-depressive psychosis, epilepsy, complex psychic seizures, delirium tremens, and many more esoteric labels. Today, Vincent's illness might be diagnosed as a reactive schizophrenia, acute schizophrenia, schizoid-affective disorder, psychosis with epilepsy, limbic system disorder, or, as preferred by the author, the descriptive but etiologically noncommittal term, episodic psychotic reaction. ... It should be pointed out that few patients with episodic disorders demonstrate creativity and few geniuses manifest behavior suggesting episodic behavioral disorders. Also, a neurophysiological explanation, no matter how elegant (and limbic seizures are more simplistic than elegant), can never fully explain creativity. Such an explanation demands an introspective, social, and historical perspective." See also W. W. Meissner, *Vincent's Religion: The Search for Meaning* (New York: Peter Lang, 1997).

5. Riley, *Psychological Study of Joseph Smith,* 105-74, 376-96.

6. Walter F. Prince, "Psychological Tests for the Authorship of the Book of Mormon" *American Journal of Psychology* 28 (July 1917): 373-89; Theodore Schroeder, "Authorship of the Book of Mormon," *American Journal of Psychology* 30 (1919): 66-72; and Prince's convincing response in his "A Footnote: 'Authorship of the Book of Mormon,'" same vol., 427-28.

7. Francis W. Kirkham, *A New Witness For Christ in America: Attempts to Prove the Book of Mormon Man-Made* (Independence, MO: Zion's Printing and Publishing, 1951), quoting Harry M. Beardsley, *Joseph Smith and His Mormon Empire,* 1931, in 2:79-84, and Bernard DeVoto, "The Centennial of Mormonism," *American Mercury,* Jan. 1930, qtd. in ibid., 1:351-53; William D. Morain, *The Sword of Laban: Joseph Smith, Jr. and the Dissociated Mind* (Washington, D.C.: American Psychiatric Press, 1998), 87-128.

8. "The daughter of Jared, like Salome, danced before a king and a decapitation followed. Abinadi, like Daniel, deciphered handwriting on a wall, and Alma was converted after the exact fashion of St. Paul. The daughters of the Lamanites were abducted like the dancing daughters of Shiloh; and Ammon, the American counterpart of David, for want of a Goliath slew six sheep-rustlers with his sling." Fawn M. Brodie, *No Man Knows My History,* 2d ed., rev. and enl. (New York: Alfred A. Knopf, 1971), 62-63. See also Wesley P. Walters, "The Use of the Old Testament in the Book of Mormon," M.A. thesis, Covenant Theological Seminary, St. Louis, MO, 1981, 25-30, and H. Michael Marquardt, "The Use of the Bible in the Book of Mormon," *Journal of Pastoral Practice* 2 (1978): 118-32. Marquardt lists 200 New Testament verses used in the Book of Mormon before 33 C.E.

9. According to Smith's contemporary, Alexander Campbell, founder of the Church of Christ, "The Mormonites," *Millennial Harbinger* 2 (Feb. 1831): 93: "This

prophet Smith, through his stone spectacles, wrote on the plates of Nephi, in his book of Mormon, every error and almost every truth discussed in New York for the last ten years. He decides all the great controversies—infant baptism, ordination, the trinity, regeneration, repentance, justification, the fall of man, the atonement, transubstantiation, fasting, penance, church government, religious experience, the call to the ministry, the general resurrection, eternal punishment, who may baptize, and even the question of free masonry, republican government, and the rights of man."

10. Otto Kernberg, *Borderline Conditions and Pathological Narcissism* (New York: Jason Aronson, 1975), 17.

11. George D. Smith, "Nauvoo Roots of Mormon Polygamy, 1841-46: A Preliminary Demographic Report," *Dialogue: Journal of Mormon Thought* 27 (Spring 1994): 1-72. See also Richard S. Van Wagoner, *Mormon Polygamy: A History* (Salt Lake City: Signature Books, 1986), 4-12.

12. "That Mormon History," *Amboy [Illinois] Journal,* 6 Aug. 1879, 1. Levi Lewis may be a relative of Hiel and Joseph Lewis, cousins of Emma Smith; but I have been unable to find any information identifying him. The parentheses around "Eliza Winters" are in the original.

13. Van Wagoner, *Mormon Polygamy,* 4-5, 8; Van Wagoner, "Joseph and Marriage," *Sunstone* 10 (1985): 32-33; Linda King Newell and Valeen Tippetts Avery, *Mormon Enigma: Emma Hale Smith* (Garden City, NY: Doubleday, 1984), 64-67; Todd Compton, "Fawn Brodie on Joseph Smith's Plural Wives and Polygamy: A Critical View," in *Reconsidering* No Man Knows My History: *Fawn M. Brodie and Joseph Smith in Retrospect,* ed. Newell G. Bringhurst (Logan: Utah State University Press, 1996), 161-62; Compton, "Fanny Alger Smith Custer: Mormonism's First Plural Wife?" *Journal of Mormon History* 22 (Spring 1996): 174-207; Compton, *In Sacred Loneliness: The Plural Wives of Joseph Smith* (Salt Lake City: Signature Books, 1997), 25-42.

14. Compton, "Fawn Brodie on ... Polygamy," 175-84.

15. Mary Elizabeth Rollins Lightner, partly quoted in Newell and Avery, *Mormon Enigma,* 100-101, from "Remarks," Address at Brigham Young University, 14 Apr. 1905; Eliza R. Snow, qtd. in Klaus J. Hansen, *Quest for Empire: The Political Kingdom of God and the Council of Fifty in Mormon History* (East Lansing: Michigan State University Press, 1970), 53. While conflicts between divine and national law are not unknown, the New Testament also specifically counsels Christians to be "subject to principalities and powers, to obey magistrates ..." (Titus 3:1).

16. Ethan Smith, *A View of the Hebrews* (Poultney, VT: Smith & Shute, 1825), 62-63. Jacob attributes the allegory to Zenos, a prophet not mentioned in the Old Testament. Zenos may, in fact, be Ethan Smith. See also Paul Y. Hoskisson, "Explicating the Mystery of the Rejected Foundation Stone: The Allegory of the Olive Tree," *BYU Studies* 30 (Summer 1990): 77-87; Stephen D. Ricks and John W. Welch, eds., *The Allegory of the Olive Tree: The Olive, the Bible, and Jacob 5* (Salt Lake City: Deseret Book/FARMS, 1994).

17. Thomas Paine, "Letter to Erskine," qtd. in "Introduction" to *The Age of Reason* (Paris: Barras, 1794; reprint, Secaucus, NJ: Citadel Press, 1974), 35.

18. Philip S. Foner, "Biographical Introduction," in Paine, *Age of Reason,* 35.

19. Michael T. Walton, "Joseph Smith and Science: The Methodist Connection. A Case Study in Mormonism as a Response to 19th Century American Revi-

valism," Sunstone presentation, Aug. 1984, photocopy in my possession; see also Brigham H. Roberts, *Studies of the Book of Mormon* (Urbana: University of Illinois Press, 1985), 284-318.

20. According to Dan Vogel, *Religious Seekers and the Advent of Mormonism* (Salt Lake City: Signature Books, 1988), 32, 44n34, Benjamin's sermon contains nothing specifically Presbyterian, and his sermon might be hypocritical, for the Presbyterians were seen as neglecting the poor and downtrodden.

21. Michael H. Marquardt and Wesley P. Walters, *Inventing Mormonism: Tradition and the Historical Record* (Salt Lake City: Smith Research Associates, 1994), 27.

22. Larry C. Porter, "Reverend George Lane—Good 'Gifts,' Much 'Grace,' and Marked 'Usefullness,'" *BYU Studies* 9 (Spring 1969): 321-40, documents his life but not details of personality or preaching.

23. Although the Book of Mormon does not give direct population figures, John C. Kunich, "Multiply Exceedingly: Book of Mormon Population Sizes," in *New Approaches to the Book of Mormon: Explorations in Critical Methodology*, ed. Brent Lee Metcalfe (Salt Lake City: Signature Books, 1993), 231-68, has calculated normal growth curves and concluded that some "of the details of events in the Book of Mormon are not literally historical" (265).

24. This sentence by Abinadi conflates two time periods, and seems to be an error with rapid correction by Joseph Smith. It initially refers to Christ who had already come—i.e., as viewed from Smith's day, and then corrects it to Abinadi's day.

25. Later Noah had to deal simultaneously with a Lamanite attack and a revolt by his own people. He ordered his followers to abandon their families and flee with him into the wilderness. Later ashamed of their cowardice, these followers rebelled and put him to death "by fire," thus fulfilling Abinadi's dying curse. I consider this symmetry to be another compensatory fantasy by which Smith dealt psychologically with Alvin's death.

26. This is the origin of the name within the Book of Mormon.

27. In 1835 an Egyptian papyrus came into the possession of Joseph Smith who declared its writings to be from the hand of the ancient patriarch, Abraham. His translation from this papyrus was canonized by the LDS church as the Book of Abraham, now contained in a small volume of Mormon scripture entitled the Pearl of Great Price. In 1967 the original papyrus was rediscovered. According to Mormon historian Klaus J. Hansen, "A scholarly translation published in 1968 revealed the papyri as rather common funerary documents bearing absolutely no relationship to the Book of Abraham. Significantly, this translation caused nary a ripple among the faithful, who are secure in the knowledge that scholarly apologists are at work reconciling the seeming discrepancy." Hansen, *Mormonism and the American Experience* (Chicago: University of Chicago Press, 1981), 31-32. See also "The Joseph Smith Egyptian Papyri: Translations and Interpretations," *Dialogue: A Journal of Mormon Thought* 3 (Summer 1968): 67-105, with a translation by John A. Wilson, 67-85, and five articles of commentary.

28. Lamb, a Baptist minister, in *The Golden Bible*, 222-28, identified phrases from Methodist camp meetings that had been transferred into the Book of Mormon, including "'Encircled about eternally in the arms of his love ...' [BM 61; 2 Ne. 1:15] 'The hands of hell which encircled them about were loosed and their souls did sing redeeming love ...' [BM 233; Alma 5:9] 'My brethren, if ye have ex-

perienced a change of heart, and if ye have felt to sing the song of redeeming love ...' [BM 234; Alma 5:26] 'For the arms of mercy are extended toward them ...' [BM 235; Alma 5:33]." Also: "But behold, your days of probation is past; ye have procrastinated the day of your salvation until it is everlastingly too late, [and your destruction is made sure] [BM 445; Hel. 13:38]." A good single example is the whole of Alma [Jr.]'s sermon of salvationist exhortation (BM 232-38; Alma 5). Each of these phrases finds explicit parallel(s) in Methodist literature of the time.

29. Heinz Kohut, "Thoughts on Narcissism and Narcissistic Rage," *The Psychoanalytic Study of the Child* (New York: Quadrant Books, 1973), 380; see also 360-400.

30. This is perhaps the first indicator of Smith's vision of the kingdom of God in which he attempted to dissolve the separation of church and state, an effort which led to difficulties in Ohio, Missouri, and Illinois. The persecution of the Mormons as they moved westward became intense in Ohio and extreme in Missouri and, shortly before and after Smith's murder, in Illinois. However, wherever they went, Mormons lied about illegal polygamy, formed secret societies of intimidation and threats, attempted to control politics by bloc voting, and struggled to create a theocratic government, with the ultimate desire to form an independent Mormon empire or at least a separate state within the nation. The local populace responded to these injuries to democracy with violence. See Hansen, *Quest for Empire,* 72-179.

31. Some traditional Mormons agree that Ammon's sword is probably the sword of Laban but not identified as such. Brett L. Holbrook, "The Sword of Laban as a Symbol of Divine Authority and Kingship," *Journal of Book of Mormon Studies* 2 (Spring 1993): 39-69, esp. 54.

32. This "universalist" teaching dates from the early nineteenth century. See Dan Vogel, "Anti-Universalist Rhetoric in the Book of Mormon," in Metcalfe, *New Approaches to the Book of Mormon,* 21-52.

33. Charles McCarthy, "The Anti-Masonic Party," in *Annual Report of the American Historical Association* (Washington, D.C.: Government Printing Office, 1903), 365-574, esp. 390.

34. Ben Bursten, "Some Narcissistic Personality Types," in *Essential Papers on Narcissism,* ed. A. P. Morrison (New York: New York Universities Press, 1986), 385-86.

35. W. W. Meissner, *Ignatius of Loyola: The Psychology of a Saint* (New Haven, CT: Yale University Press, 1992), 429n6, also 26.

36. The Book of Mormon never explains in detail the marriages of Lehi's and Ishmael's children. One insight into the contents of the lost 116 pages can be inferred from a sermon given by Mormon pioneer Erastus Snow in May 1882. He remembered, "The Prophet Joseph informed us that the record of Lehi was contained on the 116 pages that were first translated and subsequently stolen, and of which an abridgment is given us in the first Book of Nephi, which is the record of Nephi individually, he himself being of the lineage of Manasseh; but that Ishmael was of the lineage of Ephraim, and that his sons married into Lehi's family, and Lehi's sons married Ishmael's daughters." *Journal of Discourses,* 26 vols. (London and Liverpool: LDS Booksellers Depot, 1855-86), 23:184.

37. Donna Hill, *Joseph Smith: The First Mormon* (Garden City, NY: Doubleday, 1977), 68. She does not cite a source for her conclusion that the brothers-in-law frequently and deliberately provoked Smith for this fishing incident.

38. B. H. Roberts, *Studies of the Book of Mormon*, ed. Brigham D. Madsen (Urbana: University of Illinois Press, 1985), 290-316, discusses the replication of nineteenth-century Methodist revivalist phenomena in the Book of Mormon.

39. Marquardt and Walters, *Inventing Mormonism*, 117-28.

40. Ammon would not need guile to encourage Lamoni to listen to him, nor would Ammon need to deny that he intended harm unless he planned to lie. Furthermore, *hearken*, or some form of it, is used over eighty times in the Book of Mormon; in every instance except possibly 2 Nephi 23:5, it means not only to listen but also to obey.

41. The psychodynamic interpretation of Smith's antagonism with his wife's family and church, including his reaction to the loss of his firstborn son, is, according to my hypothesis, processed in over forty pages of the Book of Mormon (282-320; Alma 21-42) and requires significant conjecture. My basis for seeing him as humiliated is the grandiose statements he reportedly made to his wife's family about his future son's miraculous translating power. (See chapter 3). These testimonies are suspect in the eyes of devout Mormons because Smith himself made no known statements about being humiliated. My assumption of his response is based on what would be expected from someone with a narcissistic profile, his application to join his wife's religious class, and his silence about his 1826 trial, which was a far more public humiliation.

42. Thomas Paine, *The Age of Reason,* introduction by Philip S. Foner (1794; Secaucus, NY: Citadel Press, 1974), wrote:

> And now, ye priests of every description, who have preached and written against the former part of "The Age of Reason," what have ye to say? Will ye, with all this mass of evidence against you, and staring you in the face, still have the assurance to march into your pulpits and continue to impose these books on your congregations as the works of *inspired penmen*, and the Word of God, when it is as evident as demonstration can make truth appear that the persons who ye say are the authors are *not* the authors, and that ye know not who the authors are?
>
> What shadow of pretense have ye now to produce for continuing the blasphemous fraud? What have ye still of offer against the pure and moral religion of Deism, in support of your system of falsehood, idolatry and pretended revelation? Had the cruel and murderous orders with which the Bible is filled, and the numberless torturing executions of men, women and children, in consequence of those orders, been ascribed to some friend whose memory you revered, you would have glowed with satisfaction at detecting the falsehood of the charge, and gloried in defending his injured fame. Is it because ye are sunk in the cruelty of superstition, or feel no interest in the honor of your Creator, that ye listen to the horrid tales of the Bible, or hear them with callous indifference? The evidence I have produced, and shall produce in the course of this work, to prove that the Bible is without authority, will, while it wounds the stubbornness of a priest, relieve and tranquillize the minds of millions; it will free them from all those hard thoughts of the Almighty which priestcraft and the Bible had infused into their minds, and which stood in everlasting opposition to all their ideas of His moral justice and benevolence. (123-124)
>
> ... The Bible and the Testament are impositions upon the world, .. . the fall of man, the account of Jesus Christ being the Son of God, and of his dy-

> ing to appease the wrath of God, and of salvation by that strange means are all fabulous inventions, dishonorable to the wisdom and power of the Almighty. ... (168)
>
> But though, speaking for myself, I thus admit the possibility of revelation, I totally disbelieve that the Almighty ever did communicate anything to man, by any mode of speech, in any language, or by any kind of vision, or appearance, or by any means which our senses are capable of receiving, otherwise than by the universal display of Himself in the works of the creation. ...
>
> The most detestable wickedness, the most horrid cruelties, and the greatest miseries that have afflicted the human race have had their origin in this thing called revelation, or revealed religion. It has been the most dishonorable belief against the character of the Divinity, the most destructive to morality and the peace and happiness of man that ever was propagated since man began to exist. (182)

43. Roberts, *Studies of the Book of Mormon*, 271, concludes his discussion concerning the three anti-Christs (Sherem, Nehor, Korihor): there is a "strong implication that [all three] have their origin in one mind," with "rawness" and "amateurishness" "increasingly evident. ... [carrying] 'proof' that it is the work of a pious youth dealing with the commonplace stock arguments clumsily put together for the belief in the existence of God. ... The evidence, I sorrowfully submit, points to Joseph Smith as their creator. It is difficult to believe that they are the product of history ..."

44. Marvin Hill, *Quest for Refuge: The Mormon Flight from American Pluralism* (Salt Lake City: Signature Books, 1989), 142-51, but see his technique of escaping from previous arrests by his illicit use of *habeas corpus*, 99-151.

45. This word, which appears on the printer's manuscript copy, is probably a Freudian slip. The word, from the context, would more likely be *breast* or *heart*, which he has already used once. As a psychiatrist, I see Smith as recalling literally though perhaps unconsciously Emma's breasts, swollen first with the pregnancy and, after delivery, with milk for the dead infant. However, since Alma is talking to more than one person, his reference to the breasts (plural) of his hearers (plural) is literally correct; and no definite conclusion can be made.

46. A valid question is to what degree Smith's emotional reaction to this child's death was grief. Grief, a healthy and normal reaction to pain, is what we would ordinarily expect. Like the question of humiliation, we have no direct statements of Smith's feelings. But the naturalistic evidence is discouraging. The hypomania of Ammon/Joseph Smith is an abnormal response, perhaps countering depression, which is also abnormal. During the visit of Jesus, Smith turned the reaction triggered by children into a magnificently expanded Bible story of wonder, again sidestepping the pain of the loss. In this instance, he turns it into a sermon and makes use of it in the Book of Mormon. Finally, the content of the stories with the representatives of the Hale and Lewis families is vengeful. The platform for this material in the Book of Mormon is to convince people of his miraculous powers. We are left to wonder how much Smith genuinely cared about others or was capable of love.

The alternate view is to believe that the unknown Bible prophets Zenos and Zenock really did exist and that these selected sermons from them about enemy congregations and the importance of having a son are coincidental; that their writings were known to the Nephites who really did exist; and that Smith is not deceitful about his ability to translate this story. See Linda King Newell and Valeen Tippetts Avery, *Mormon Enigma: Emma Hale Smith, Prophet's Wife, "Elect Lady," Polygamy's Foe, 1804-1879* (Garden City, NY: Doubleday, 1984), 95-168, and George D. Smith, ed., *An Intimate Chronicle: The Journals of William Clayton* (Salt Lake City: Signature Books in association with Smith Research Associates, 1995), 193-36.

47. Theologically, this argument would have been common during Smith's day. While Smith, in my opinion, uses it to reveal/hide his struggle over guilt and sin, he drew its specifics from Josiah Priest's *Wonders of Nature and Providence Displayed* (Rochester, NY: Author, 1824; Albany. NY: E. and E. Hosford, 1825, 1826), 127-37. The 1825 edition argues: Adam and Eve were prohibited from eating the fruit to test their "homage and obedience," and show gratitude for God's benevolence. Because of disobedience, they earned only degradation and woe. The Deist sees no reason for the death of Christ, for surely God could have rescued man without such a process. The Christian asks, "Do you admit the attributes of God to be essential to his nature?" and, when the Deist agrees, the Christian and the Deist further agree justice is an attribute of God. Christian: "Can then ... a being necessarily just, suspend his justice? If he can, he must, during that suspension, be destitute of justice; and this will prove that justice is not essential to his nature. ... But if God cannot suspend his justice, you must admit the necessity of that atonement. ... [For i]f mercy can overcome justice, what is become of that Omnipotence by which justice is supported?" (133-35)

CHAPTER 5

Regression and Recapitulation: The End of Alma, the Book of Helaman

Despite Joseph Smith's traumatic childhood surgery, I would not formally diagnose him as suffering from post-traumatic stress disorder. Even though his silence on typical symptoms cannot be taken as proof that he did *not* experience such symptoms, the historical record does not show the typical pattern: a victim distressed by intrusive and unwanted images of the traumatic experience; awaking from repeated nightmares, body and bed drenched in perspiration; involuntary triggering of fearful reactions (veterans, for instance, may find themselves shaking and crying when a helicopter flies overhead), disruptions to thinking or concentration on a task; and conscious organization of their lives so that they can avoid anything that might remind them of the trauma. When the former soldier dissociates into "flashbacks," others are in physical danger from him, for he is back in the jungle and ready to attack.

It seems likely that Smith experienced such symptoms when he was a child following the surgery; but by the time he dictated the Book of Mormon, seventeen years later, I think he was actually expanding and embellishing the details for the purpose of gaining power and prestige. They had changed from "ego-alien" (repugnant and distressing to him) to "ego-syntonic" (acceptable to his goals and feelings). The violence of the surgery had become part of his personality. He had partially "mastered" it by making it his own. This diagnosis still allows for the possibility that he dictated the Book of Mormon hoping for some therapeutic benefit. From my perspective, this young man may have benefited greatly from psychotherapy dealing with his surgery and family deprivation; without access to such aid, at least one of the Book of Mormon's several purposes may charitably be seen as his effort to find relief.

If my analysis of this situation is correct, some part of Smith sought greater mastery over his childhood trauma and, sensing his emotional and economic difference from his neighbors, longed for ordinary commonness. It is possible to see in his dictating style some elements of intensive psychotherapy, including unrestrained free association and minimal noncondemning responses from his scribes. In addition, he reduced outside stimuli by looking at his stone in a hat. A patient on the couch can talk about the ceiling tiles for only so long. Then the relative vacuum in his or her conscious mind begins to draw on past emotions and experiences in his or her unconscious, and the monologue increases in intensity, coloring, and distortion. This voice from the unconscious sometimes frightens patients; they find themselves trembling and crying "for no reason at all." They may say, "I can't believe I'm saying this. Where is this stuff coming from?" They may say, as they begin to experience childhood feelings but without enough clarity to know what is happening, "You seem like a nice person and haven't said anything mean, but I'm frightened of you. It doesn't make sense." Even in the public and highly ritualized setting of a Mormon testimony meeting, we have all seen that talking about an intense experience may force an emotional reliving of that experience. In treatment, the encouragement to talk with minimal assignment of content pressures an emotional return to times of troubles. Patients may experience this awareness with surprise and disbelief. Smith was reliving his humiliation and possible grief when his child was born dead and, I hope, his concern for Emma's physical pain and worry about whether she would survive the birth. This event had occurred less than a year earlier; he countered the emotional pain with hypomania, obvious by its inappropriate timing in the story. As a psychiatrist, I suspect that this incident stirred feelings and memories of past tragedies, including Alvin's death, Sophronia's near-death experience during the typhoid epidemic, and the death of baby Ephraim when Joseph was four. His hypomania was probably dealing with all of these layered experiences.

The essential difference between Smith's dictation of the Book of Mormon and a therapeutic setting is the listener's attitude. As bonding between the therapist and client develops, the therapist begins to understand and then to clarify the association between Smith's personal history and his fantasies. He or she would begin to confront Joseph about the origin of his stories, help him deal directly with his painful memories, and raise questions about his intent in using these fantasies with other people. This last issue would become the main therapeutic task of the interchange, for Smith's efforts to enlist converts to join his self-deceit (and/or his own certain knowledge about the origin of his fantasies) constitutes a coercive claim that he could own their lives. Either Smith would have to begin withdrawing from this search for power, or the therapist would have to withdraw, for he or she would be either wasting time or reinforcing Smith's behavior by remaining. He or she would thus be "owned" by Smith, and the therapy would become only a training ground for enhanced techniques in manipulating others. Smith may have chosen those who dictated for him because they were not inclined to confront him. In turn, they cooperated for their own reasons of attached or reflected glory or gain. (See further discussion of this point in chapter 7.) Their acceptance validated his claims and began the process of turning a fantasy into a psychological reality.

In the final diagnostic chapter, I will analyze Smith's personality according to the five components identified in the introduction; the most important is narcissism. Narcissists, despite sometimes impressive public personae, never achieve full integration of feeling or function. Observers are most likely to be struck by the grandiose self, but its foundation is inferiority, shame, and inadequacy. These individuals have strong psychological defenses; their apparent invulnerability draws followers to them. But they lack the perspective that maturity and humility bring; humiliation triggers an internal fury that only slowly abates. They commonly surround themselves with compliant admirers who accept their propaganda of supernormal abilities. Narcissists demonstrating grandiosity buffer themselves from the outside world with these people, focusing on their admiration so they can ignore criticism.

But in Harmony, in the spring of 1829, Smith had few admirers: Emma, Josiah Stowell, and Joseph Knight. Although Stowell and Knight lived only a few miles away, he probably did not see them daily. His own family was 120 miles away, absorbed in problems of their own. If Joseph Lewis and Hiel Lewis were telling the truth, Smith made grandiose claims about magic, bleeding ghosts, gold records, and a son who could open the gold book. Emma's cousins were incensed at these non-Christian claims of near-omnipotence. Why did he think he was better than they? Why did angels never visit them? When his magical son was born deformed and dead, I assume that his public humiliation could not have been worse. Even Emma had failed him by not producing the son he expected. Although her family was no doubt motivated in its hostility toward Smith by a wish to protect her, her acceptance of Smith's claims of supernatural abilities angered them, I hypothesize; and the Lewis cousins' rejection of his membership amounts to a public judgement. According to my hypothesis, despite his attempts at normalcy, he seethed in silence for seven months, then returned to his grand claims.

In summary, I have argued that the book of Alma presents the following autobiographical events: Alvin's death in November 1823 (Nehor's murder of Gideon), the Palmyra revival of March 1824 to March 1825 (Alma II's conversion), Smith's imprisonment and trial at South Bainbridge in March 1826 (Alma and Amulek in Ammonihah), Smith's rejection by Emma's family in 1827 (Ammon's contest against the sheep thieves, his conversion of Lamoni's household, and Abish's support), the stillborn in June 1828 (the massacre of the innocent pacificist Anti-Nephi-Lehies, Ammon's hypomanic response, the survivors' grief, Alma's sermon of the swelling seed and God's redeeming son), Smith's expulsion from Emma's church by her cousins, also in June 1828 (the hypocritical Zoramites), and

Smith's unspoken humiliation (Alma's instructions to his three sons). These events bring Smith's life to the year 1828.

As already mentioned, narcissistic individuals show child-like thinking. Their grandiose fantasies compensate for the inadequacies in their lives. They cannot handle complex feelings. They polarize their world into good/bad, white/black, us/them categories. This pattern characterizes the entire Book of Mormon, but, as I read the section focused mainly on Book of Mormon wars, beginning in the last part of Alma and continuing through the genocidal last battle, I see Smith expressing his expanding fury; at least psychologically, he will destroy his world in vengeance.

War: The Polarization of Personality into Extremes

> Individuals with Narcissistic Personality Disorder believe that they are superior, special, or unique and expect others to recognize them as such. ... They may feel that they can only be understood by, and should only associate with, other people who are special or of high status and may attribute "unique," "perfect," or "gifted" qualities to those with whom they associate. Individuals with this disorder believe that their needs are special and beyond the ken of ordinary people. Their own self-esteem is enhanced (i.e., "mirrored") by the idealized value that they assign to those with whom they associate. They are likely to insist on having only the "top" person (doctor, lawyer, hairdresser, instructor) or being affiliated with the "best" institutions, but may devalue the credentials of those who disappoint them. ... Individuals with this disorder generally require excessive admiration.[1]

> On the surface [narcissistic personalities] appear to present a remarkable absence of object relationships; on a deeper level, their interactions reflect very intense, primitive, internalized object relationships of a frightening kind and an incapacity to depend on internalized good objects. ... [They use the mental mechanisms of omnipotence and devaluation and] may shift between the need to establish a demanding, clinging relationship to an idealized "magic" object at some times, and fantasies and behavior betraying a deep feeling of magical omnipotence of their own at other times ... [Splitting is the] division of internalized object relations into "good" and "bad" [and] happens at first simply because of the [immaturity of the] early ego, [but later] is used defensively.[2]

MORONI, ZARAHEMNAH, AND AMALAKIAH: GOOD AND BAD ALTER EGOS

In the war stories of Alma and Helaman, Joseph Smith continues, through the technique of splitting, to identify with political leaders in the United States. Psychologically speaking, these fantasies are frightening.

TIME:	74-69 B.C.E.//1823-28 C.E.
PLACE:	THE LAND OF NEPHI (LAMANITES)//ISAAC HALE HOMESTEAD AND ENVIRONS; THE UNITED STATES
PERSONAE:	ZARAHEMNAH//POSSIBLY NATHAN SMITH, ALVIN'S PHYSICIAN, AND/OR JOHN QUINCY ADAMS

MORONI//JOSEPH SMITH, JR.; ANDREW JACKSON
AMALICKIAH//JOSEPH SMITH, JR.; JOHN QUINCY ADAMS
THE TITLE OF LIBERTY//THE HICKORY POLE
MORIANTON//MARTIN HARRIS

The war sections of Alma and Helaman reveal, I submit, polarized extremes as Smith emotionally regresses under the pressure of his humiliation and rage. Here he demonstrated the thinking of a young child or of an unintegrated, immature personality who has difficulty dealing with ambiguity and complexity.

The conflicts between the heroic Nephite Moroni, an alter ego of Joseph Smith (not to be confused with Moroni, the son of Mormon, who is the final writer in the Book of Mormon), and his military opponents, Zarahemnah and Amalickiah, demonstrate how abstract and mythic the struggles are becoming. The sole episode of triangular—Oedipal—conflict in the overwhelming dyadic Book of Mormon occurs in this section. Moroni is introduced with no background. He simply appears out of nowhere just at the moment of need: "Now the leader of the Nephites ... was Moroni; and Moroni took all the command, and the government of their wars—and he was only twenty and five years old" (BM 341; Alma 43:16-17). Smith was twenty-three and a half. This magnificent national leader is, in psychological terms, an idealized version of Smith's self:

> And Moroni was a strong and mighty man; he was a man of perfect understanding; yea, a man that did not delight in bloodshed; a man whose soul did joy in the liberty and the freedom of his country ... a man who did labor exceedingly for the welfare and safety of his people ... and this was the faith of Moroni; and his heart did glory in it; not in the shedding of blood, but in doing good, in preserving his people; yea, in keeping the commandments of God; yea, and resisting iniquity. (BM 358-59; Alma 48:11-48)

This alter ego is balanced by two dark doubles who represent the polar opposite. The first is Zarahemnah, leader of the Lamanites and dissident Nephites. War maneuvers, secrecy, strategies, and miracles blend as Moroni consults Alma for military counsel. The armor-clad Nephites rout the naked Lamanites; Moroni offers to let them surrender, reiterating that the Nephites are fighting, not for conquest, but for their "religion ... wives and ... children ... liberty ... and sacred word of God."

Zarahemnah attributes Moroni's success in battle to "cunning" and superior equipment, then attacks Moroni during the parley. A Nephite soldier scalps Zarahemnah with a single sword stroke, and the battle recommences. This time the Lamanites, Zarahemnah included, are forced to surrender and take an oath of peace. Although the Lamanites are assumed to be crafty savages, and although the oath is coerced from them, the Book of Mormon assumes that it will be scrupulously kept. The number of the dead is so "exceeding great" that they cannot be counted; their bodies are thrown in the river Sidon "and are buried in the depths of the sea" (BM 347; Alma 44). Alma then relinquishes the sacred records to his son, Helaman, leaves Zarahemla, and disappears forever. It is the nineteenth year of the reign of the judges (73 B.C.E.). Helaman, a righteous and effective warrior in the Lamanite conflicts, deals with the Nephites' "many little dissen[s]ions and disturbances" by preaching, establishing churches, and appointing priests and teachers (BM 349; Alma 45:20-24).

At the start of the book of Alma, he began with a personal confrontation between the anti-Christ Nehor and an aged warrior Gideon, and then expanded that one-to-one conflict into a social narrative between followers of Nehor (the Amlicites) and Alma. He now does the same thing, and the battle between Moroni and Zarahemnah now takes on a government enlargement.

Smith's second dark double is Amalickiah, the Book of Mormon's supreme villain. A "large and strong man," he covets the kingship, attracts a following among dissatisfied minor judges, and begins to undermine "the church of God and [to] destroy the foundation of liberty." Moroni, furious at Amalakiah,

> rent his coat; and he took a piece thereof, and wrote upon it, in memory of our God, our religion, and freedom, and our peace, our wives, and our children; and he fastened it upon the end of a pole thereof. And he fastened on his headplate ... breastplate, and his shields ... and ... his armor about his loins; and he took the pole, which had on the end thereof his rent coat, (and he called it the title of liberty,) ... And ... he went forth among the people, waving the rent of his garment in the air, that all might see the writing which he had wrote upon the rent ...

The people "came running together, with their armors girded about their loins, rending their garments in token, or as a covenant," constituting an army made up from "all parts of the land." Amalickiah, seeing his followers' fear "that he should not gain the point," fled into Lamanite country, hotly pursued by Moroni's army. Moroni, now twenty-six and battle-hardened, received full powers under what we would call martial law declared in a national emergency. Amalickiah roused the Lamanites' savage anger toward the Nephites. By ruse and deception, he rapidly rose to second in military command, poisoned his superior, and became chief. Amalickiah marched back to the Lamanite capital where his servants "stabbed the king to the heart" and then accused his terror-stricken servants, who had taken to their heels, of the murder (BM 355-56; Alma 47:1-25). The army, outraged to see the king "lying in his gore," pursued the fleeing servants, killing those they could capture. Some escaped into Nephite territory and reported events to Moroni. Meanwhile, Amalickiah's report satisfied the queen, whom he wooed and married, "and thus ... he obtained the kingdom; yea, he was acknowledged king throughout all the land" (BM 356-57; Alma 47:26-35).

At first glance, this story looks like the timeless triangle of *Oedipus Rex* and Shakespeare's *Hamlet:* the protagonist kills the father figure and marries the mother. Yet Amalakiah does not fit the pattern in the usual way. He seeks raw political power through cunning, cruelty, deception, and murder. Sexual desire is irrelevant; the queen is simply one means to an end, not the goal. Rather than fitting the classical Freudian model of the Oedipal triangle, I argue that it matches the more subtle and complex reworkings of Oedipal development by Freud's successors.[3] According to this revised hypothesis, the child between birth and three identifies almost totally, first, with the mother, then with both the mother and father. The child's ability to handle this simplest and most basic triangle is largely determined by his or her previous development, security, and parents' response. Trauma during the Oedipal period—Joseph Smith's surgery, for instance—regresses the child to these earlier developmental stages, sometimes permanently, characterized by extreme fantasies of omnipotence, magical thinking, and the polarization of personality and thinking into opposites. Smith's father was so weak that Lucy had already made the youthful seer "her man" long before his supernatural claims. And, I think, Smith's father, with his economic failings, delusional belief in magic, and problems with drinking, through the years presents a picture of fragility. We know that Joseph Jr. had become central to the family by his mid-teens with his role as magician and seer stone peeping, but I suspect that his mother viewed him as special from the time of his "miraculous" survival from leg surgery—and perhaps even before, for he was given the father's name. Such preeminence teaches the child that he has special rights, a view that certainly would affect his later behavior, including his sexual attitudes.

THE HARRIS MARRIAGE

In June 1828 Martin Harris coaxed the 116 manuscript pages out of Smith to show to his immediate family, and they disappeared permanently while in his charge. In 1833, after the disintegration of the Harris marriage, Mrs. Harris described Martin Harris in unflattering terms:

> Martin Harris was once industrious[,] attentive to his domestic concerns, and thought to be worth about ten thousand dollars. He is naturally quick in temper ... he has whipped, kicked, and turned me out of the house. ... Because I would not give credit [to Joseph Smith's claims] he became more austere toward me. In one of his fits of rage he struck me with the butt end of a whip ... beat me on the head four or five times ... turned me out of doors twice, and beat me in a shameful manner. ... My flesh was black and blue in many places.[4]

A neighbor, G. W. Stoddard, agreed that Harris "was known to frequently abuse his wife, by whipping her, kicking her out of bed and turning her out of doors. etc."[5]

Tellingly, at this point in the not-yet-resolved conflict between Moroni and Amalakiah, the Book of Mormon narrative contains an embedded subplot involving Morianton, a "man of much ... angry ... passion." When Moroni settles a land dispute against Morianton, he takes his followers and flees "into the land northward." However, "being a man of much passion," Morianton "fell upon" a maidservant "and beat her much" (BM 365; Alma 50:30-31). She fled to Moroni and revealed Morianton's flight; to prevent Morianton's escape, Moroni sent an army under Teancum who slew the "wicked and stubborn" dissident and brought back his group as prisoners. Moroni then negotiated a final peace.

I hypothesize that this story suggests both the conflict between Martin and Lucy Harris and also between the Harris family and Smith family. Harris/Morianton is presented as a woman beater, "wicked and stubborn" and subject to "mad fits." Teancum had to follow Morianton north; Smith had to go north from Harmony to confront Harris. As a final detail, the story suggests a property dispute between the Harris and Smith families. In fact, Lucy Harris protested the diversion of Martin's property to underwrite the Book of Mormon; Martin, by supporting the Book of Mormon, was asserting that Smith as prophet was the property's true owner (BM 365-66; Alma 50:25-36, esp. 30).[6]

NATIONAL PARALLELS: THE JACKSON ELECTION OF 1828

In addition to parallels with Harris, I hypothesize that the Moroni/Amalakiah conflict is a disguised reworking of national politics. As a corroborating detail, as soon as "the people of Nephi had peace restored" from the Morianton rebellion, then "Nephihah, the second chief judge, died," necessitating an election (BM 366; Alma 50:37 [67 B.C.E.//fall 1828]).

The Oedipal conflict in Amalakiah's story is weak by comparison with the search for power, a pattern in keeping with the fact that women are generally irrelevant in the Book of Mormon. Therefore, I find the queen's presence to be strong circumstantial evidence that Smith was writing out sectional rivalries and national dissensions as part of his darkest conflicts, using the U.S. election in disguised form. A major issue in the presidential election of 1828 was a contest between the perceived aristocrats of the eastern seaboard and the "common man" of the interior. In 1824 Henry Clay and John Quincy Adams colluded, as we have seen, to deprive Andrew Jackson, the candidate with the plurality, by using the electoral college.[7] Jackson seemed initially accepting of this arrangement but rapidly changed his position and began acting with the next election in mind, which he won by a popular vote of 648,000 to 508,000 and an electoral vote of 178 to 83.

Jackson (1767-1845) was seen as a man of the ordinary people, while the people were looking for "a government that would be more responsive to their needs and interests." Stubborn, quarrelsome, a gambler and drinker, vigorous, sensitive and humorless, Jackson the hero was a plain, simple, virtuous man.[8] He had become major general of the Tennessee militia in 1802, and the War of 1812 provided him an opportunity to show his abilities. In March 1814 he crushed the Creek Indians who were allies of the British, then further punished them by taking away 20 million acres of their lands. Nine months later his motley army won an amazing victory at the battle of New Orleans, and he became an instant national hero. He was a warrior hero among "free-men" and had demonstrated that he could defeat "Lamanites." His nickname, earned as a young man, was "Old Hickory," an admiring tribute to his unyielding determination. Born in Tennessee rather than among the perceived elites of the eastern seaboard, he took as his motto: "Let the people rule." One biographer described the class conflict represented in the election of 1828: "Nearly all the talent, nearly all the learning, nearly all the ancient wealth, nearly all the business activity, nearly all the book-nourished intelligence, nearly all the silver-forked civilization of the country, united in opposition to [Andrew] Jackson."[9] In contrast, John Quincy Adams, Jackson's opponent in both 1824 and 1828, was called "'King John the Second.'"[10] Common men saw him as a corrupt "blue-blood ... an unprincipled hypocrite whose mania for office had brought him money from the public treasury ... from the date of his birth." Rumors circulated. He had been "corrupted by long residence in European courts, especially the Russian court, where he had prostituted a beautiful American girl to the carnal desires of Czar Alexander I ... and [he] hated popular government, and inwardly detested the heroes of the American Revolution." In the eyes of the ordinary U.S. citizen, he had cheated them out of their choice for president and imposed himself like a tyrannous monarch.[11] He was a king among king-men.

According to one biographer, "The symbol of his [Jackson's] campaign, the hickory pole, appeared in astonishing numbers, set up in every village ... throughout the country. In the train of noisy demonstrations around the poles came new trappings of political campaigning designed to excite the electorate and appeal to its basic emotions—barbecues, ox roasts, torchlight parades, bonfire, and firework displays."[12] I argue that Smith used the hickory pole as the model for the pole on which Moroni hoisted his title of liberty (BM 351-53; Alma 46:11-36), as part of the larger contest about national leadership between an elitist faction and the "voice of the people."

In the Book of Mormon, Pahoran, the chief judge, resisted pressure from certain factions "that a few particular points of the law should be altered. ... Therefore there arose a warm dispute concerning the matter, but not unto bloodshed." The political issues of 1828 were large. Should the U.S. continue to support, by providing financial advantages, to the privately owned "Bank of United States"? Could the federal government impose tariffs on manufactured goods produced in the state of South Carolina? If South Carolina resisted, should the government send an army to force compliance? There were land development issues, Indian problems, and internal improvements such as canals, roads, and railroads to attend to. Issues were drowned, however, in the contest between the two personalities of Jackson and Adams, and a campaign became a morality play of "virtue and republican simplicity over corruption and unprincipled aristocracy."[13]

In the Book of Mormon, Pahoran's opponents "were called king-men, for they were desirous ... to overthrow the free government and to establish a king over the land." The free-men wished to retain the system of judges. At the election "the voice of the people came in favor of the free-men, and Pahoran retained the judgement seat. ... Now those which were in favor of kings were those of high birth; and they sought to be kings; and they were supported by those which sought power and authority over the people" (BM 367; Alma 51:8). At this "critical time for such contentions," Amalickiah reappeared, posing an immediate military challenge. From a psychoanalytic perspective, victory and survival depend on Joseph Smith through his surrogate, Moroni. When the sulky king-men refuse to take up arms, Moroni was "exceeding wroth." Armed with authority from the chief judge, he executed 4,000 king-men, imprisoned others without trial, and conscripted the rest: "And thus Moroni put an end to those king-men ... the stubbornness, and the pride of those people which professed the blood of nobility; but they were brought down to humble themselves like unto their brethren, and to fight valiantly for their freedom from bondage." He also forced them "to hoist the title of liberty upon their towers, and in their cities" (BM 367-68; Alma 51:4-21).

This statement not only recalls the ubiquity of Jackson's hickory poles, but also the fact that Jackson's supporters in Tennessee threatened to tar and feather anyone voting for Adams. On Jackson's inauguration, 4 March 1829, the frontiersmen, backwoodsmen, war veterans, and laborers stormed the White House in triumph. They trampled broken china into the carpets with their muddy boots and broke furniture by standing on it. Women fainted. A phalanx of friends formed around Jackson to save him from being crushed, and he escaped from the White House. Thirty-two days after this national event, Oliver Cowdery arrived in Harmony, and the prodigious feat of dictating the Book of Mormon in less than thirteen weeks began.

However, Jackson's political triumph was marred by a personal tragedy which I believe appears in a much attenuated form in Amalakiah's preemption of the Lamanite queen. Women, and their real-life prototypes, are so underrepresented in the Book of Mormon that one assumes they must have had some special significance to Smith to appear at all. I think the death of Rachel Jackson, attributed to the viciousness of the campaign, motivated Smith to introduce a Lamanite queen into the story. Jackson had married Rachel Donelson Robards in August 1791. She had been told that her husband, Lewis Robards, had been granted a divorce by the Virginia legislature on grounds of her desertion and adultery in mid-1791. She had married Jackson only to discover later that the divorce had not been finalized.

As already mentioned (chapter 3), the 1824 election had been a one-party contest. Jackson had gained the most electoral votes, but Adams and Henry Clay had joined forces and became president and secretary of state in what Jackson and the nation believed was a back-room bargain. Jackson began campaigning for the next election soon afterward and continued for four years. The campaign was the most brutal, vicious, and mud-slinging in U.S. history. The questions of "Bank of the United States" and the question of forceful compliance of federal tariffs against the state of South Carolina were swept away by "chicanery, slippery tactics, and downright falsehoods upon which the politicians relied to win the contest."[14] Rachel Jackson was a sensitive person, and the campaign by the opposition represented her as an adulteress. Jackson tried to protect her from these attacks on her morality, but she was devastated and died of a stroke on 22 December 1828, as he prepared to move to the White House. At her grave after they had covered her coffin, Jackson said loudly, "In the presence of this dear saint I can and do forgive my enemies. But those vile wretches who have slandered her must look to God for mercy." A few days later he said, "May God Almighty forgive her murderers as I know she forgave them. I never can!"[15]

Smith now stands at the point where both his personal narrative and his national history encounter the dictation of the Book of Mormon. I hope to show that Alma's final chapters write out a version of 1828-29 events, focusing on the anti-Masonic hysteria which also reached its height during that election year. But once again he begins with the traumatic, defining experiences of his childhood: the bloody surgery and the years of intermittent hunger which followed.

War Continued: Invincibility

> [In the phallic narcissist] the unconscious shame from the fear of castration is continually denied by phallic assertiveness. This may even be accompanied by a sense of omnipotence and a feeling of invulnerability which allows such

individuals, feeling that some miraculous fate of good luck will carry them through, to continually take risks.[16]

TIME: 73-53 B.C.E.//1811-26 C.E.
PERSONAE: THE 2,060 AMMONITE YOUTHS (SONS OF HELAMAN)// THE CHILD JOSEPH SMITH
MORONI//THE IDEALIZED JOSEPH SMITH, JR.
AMALICKIAH; AMMORON//NATHAN SMITH; JOHN QUINCY ADAMS; DARK ALTER EGO OF JOSEPH SMITH, JR.
PAHORAN//JOSEPH SMITH, SR.

Smith next writes a Book of Mormon narrative in which 2,060 youths are miraculously protected against bodily injury from swords and knives, an extreme fantasy in which he probably protects himself from the surgeon's threat. At this point, from a psychoanalytic perspective, the autobiographical elements are both more disguised and more extreme. It is my professional opinion that, rather than dealing with his childhood trauma in a mature way, Smith is regressing farther, returning as well to a child's structuring imagination.

For example, Nephite society became more polarized. Moroni and the Nephites continued their struggle against the Lamanites, led by the initially successful evil Amalickiah. Teancum assassinated Amalickiah by night with "a javelin to his heart." Amalickiah's brother, Ammoron, regrouped the army, then, after a series of skirmishes, attacked the main army "with exceeding fury." Moroni was wounded but recovered. The war seesawed back and forth, with the narrative following campaigns on two and sometimes three fronts, wounds, the taking, guarding, and exchanges of prisoners, and political problems on the home front. Many Book of Mormon readers are puzzled and bored by these maneuvers, particularly by their length. The usual explanation is that Mormon, the last great general and the book's abridger, had a special interest in his people's military history.[17] A more plausible explanation, I feel, is that Joseph Smith had a special interest in these wars; he is battling both his mortality and his surgeon; he must face the pain, come close to death, and then conquer absolutely. His solution is not, however, the psychologically healthy one of coming to terms with the inevitability of suffering and death but the child's fantasy solution of becoming invincible.

The plight of the Nephites was exacerbated because they needed to protect the people of Ammon, who, confronted by the dangerous situation, contemplated breaking their vow of pacifism to enter the war as allies to the Nephites.

> But behold as they were about to take their weapons of war, they were overpowered by the persuasions of Helaman and his brethren, for they were

> about to break the oath which they had made; and Helaman feared lest by so doing, they should lose their souls; therefore all those which had entered into this covenant, were compelled to behold their brethren wade through their afflictions, in their dangerous circumstances, at this time. (BM 376; Alma 53:13-16)

However, their 2,000 sons, not bound by the same covenant, enlisted under Helaman

> to protect the land unto the laying down of their lives. ... And they were all young men, and they were exceeding valiant for courage, and also for strength and activity; but behold, this was not all: they were men which were true at all times in whatsoever thing they were entrusted; yea, they were men of truth and soberness, for they had been taught to keep the commandments of God, and to walk uprightly before him. (BM 376; Alma 53:17-21)

Meanwhile, complications from these battles were mounting. Moroni had taken so many captives that guarding and feeding them were becoming problems, even though he was also using them to fortify Bountiful and Mulek. Then his enemy, Ammaron, who held many wives and children prisoner in addition to soldiers, petitioned for an exchange of prisoners. Moroni also desired this but tactlessly sent a letter of sermonizing damnation to Ammaron, who angrily withdrew his petition. Moroni found a "descendent of Laman," who was named Laman, among his soldiers, and sent him to the enemy camp with the tale that he had escaped from the Nephites while they slept and that he, with some other escapees, had brought wine they had stolen from the Nephites.

The mention of wine should alert us to the possibility that Joseph will begin another fantasy variation of his childhood surgery and, in fact, I believe he does, importing a sort of regressed logic into the text. Given the extremity and gravity of the situation developing within the Book of Mormon, providing wine to the all-too-willing guards is both overelaborate yet trivial. The guards get drunk and fall asleep. At one point Moroni manages to get arms to the Nephite prisoners—not just to the soldiers, but "even to their women, and all those of their children, as many as were able to use a weapon of war." This is possible because of the drunkenness of the Lamanite guards. As a result, the Nephites turn the tables on their Lamanite guards. Thereafter, as Mormon proudly records,

> Many times did the Lamanites attempt to encircle them about by night, but in these attempts they did lose many prisoners—And many times did they attempt to administer of their wine to the Nephites, that they might destroy them with poison or with drunkenness. But behold, the Nephites were not slow to remember the Lord their God, in this their times of affliction. They could not be taken in their snares; yea, they would not partake of their wine; yea, they would not take of wine, save they had firstly given to some of the Lamanite prisoners. And they were thus cautious, that no poison should be

administered among them; for if wine would poison a Lamanite, it would also poison a Nephite. (BM 381; Alma 55: 28-32)

This simple comedy of drunken guards is emphasized and repeated to the point of becoming ludicrous, like a child who has discovered a pun. But the motifs in this story are suggestive: helpless women and children suddenly become armed and dangerous; wine becomes, not a drink, but a drug. These signals refer us again to little Joseph's surgery. In my opinion, both the story content and literary style suggest that Smith has, under the influence of reliving his childhood surgery, regressed in emotional age.

Moroni was victorious in capturing the Lamanite guards and releasing the Nephite captives, men, women, and children. This was but one episode in ongoing war, and Moroni needed to attack the fortified city of Morianton. At this point he received a letter from Helaman, a general engaged in complicated battles in a different area where the Lamanites had been victorious until Helaman arrived with the 2,000 youths—his "sons" who were the children of those who had taken an oath of pacificism—to swell the Nephite army to 10,000 troops and assist in the battles. Helaman proudly described these young men: "Now they never had fought, yet they did not fear death; and they did think more upon the liberty of their fathers, than they did upon their lives; yea, they had been taught by their mothers, that if they did not doubt, that God would deliver them. And they rehearsed unto me the words of their mothers saying: We do not doubt our mothers knew it."

This statement is, theologically, nonsensical: how can their faith in their mothers' faith save them? Yet, psychologically, it is familiar. Lucy had insisted that the doctors "must try one more time" to save Joseph's leg. Now Joseph Jr. has metamorphosed into 2,000 invulnerable youths. After the first battle, Helaman "numbered those young men which had fought with me, fearing lest there were many of them slain. But behold, to my great joy, there had not one soul of them fallen to the earth; yea, and they had fought as if with the strength of God; yea, never was men known to have to have fought with such miraculous strength (BM 381-86; Alma 55:33-35; 56:1-57). He repeats, "And I did remember the words which they said unto me that their mothers had taught them." From a psychoanalytic perspective, Smith here pays tribute to his mother for saving his leg.

In the second battle, at which sixty more youths join the sons of Helaman, over 1,000 Nephite soldiers die out of a total 16,000; still the Ammonites are invulnerable:

> Two hundred ... had fainted because of the loss of blood ... [but] not one soul of them ... did perish; yea, and neither was there one soul among them which had not received many wounds. ... and we do justly ascribe it to the miraculous power of God, because of their exceeding faith in that which they had

> been taught to believe ... that ... whosoever did not doubt ... should be preserved. (BM 388-89; Alma 57:22-26)

Early in his life Brigham H. Roberts, LDS general authority, reviewed this story of the Lamanite youths:

> Yes, they were preserved according to their faith in God. They had no fear of death, they loved their own and their father[s'] liberty more than life, and they fought with the fierceness of young lions, and more than once by the prowess given them of God, snatched victory from the very jaws of defeat. And though at times many of them were wounded, and on one occasion two hundred fainted from loss of blood, yet not one of them were killed in battle.[18]

But years later he approached this incident in a more questioning spirit as a "beautiful story of faith! Beautiful story of mother-assurance! Is it History? Or is it a wonder-tale of a pious but immature mind?"[19] In my judgement, Roberts has correctly identified the logic of childhood in this retelling of Smith's surgery. Increasingly broad, sweeping, and generalized, it speaks to Smith's wish for invulnerability in the most extravagant terms yet seen.

The next chronological element in Smith's autobiography is the years of economic stress and deprivation which followed between 1813 and 1816 until the family moved to Palmyra. Previous accounts (Lehi's family's wandering in the wilderness; the Gadianton band's unsuccessful seven-year siege of the Nephites) underplayed the narrative; but this retelling consumes three chapters (BM 389-96; Alma 58-60).

Desperate for supplies, Helaman wrote to Moroni: "Now we do not know the cause that the government does not grant us more strength. ... We do not desire to murmur ... [but] we fear that there is some faction in the government. ... We trust God will deliver us, not withstanding the weakness of our armies." When the Nephites lost the city of Nephihah to the Lamanites, Moroni angrily wrote to the chief judge, Pahoran: "We desire to know the cause of this exceeding great neglect. ... Can you think to sit upon your thrones, in a state of thoughtless stupor, while your enemies are ... murdering thousands of your brethren? ... Ye have withheld provisions ... when they were about to perish with hunger." He accused Pahoran of treason and threatens to attack the capital and dethrone Pahoran unless aid was forthcoming:

> Yea, behold I do not fear your power nor your authority, but it is my God whom I fear. ... The sword of justice doth hang over you. ... God will not suffer that we should perish with hunger; therefore he will give unto us of your food, even if it must be by the sword. Now see ye fulfill the word of God. Behold, I am Moroni, your Chief Captain. I seek not for power but to pull it down. I seek not for honor of the world, but for the glory of my God, and the freedom and welfare of my country.

Even though there is no documentary evidence that the Smith family actually went hungry, reading from the Book of Mormon back into Joseph's life, I argue that this passage provides psychological evidence that it occurred. I hear the voice of young Joseph expressing fury about physical deprivation, daily physical hunger, and the squabbling at the table which must have made antagonists of everyone in the family. The phrase "thoughtless stupor" even suggests the possibility that Joseph Sr. was drunk, contributing to the crisis.

Finally a grieving letter arrived from Pahoran, describing an insurrection that had shattered the government and forced him to flee from Zarahemla. He was the one who needs rescue: "I am not angry, but do rejoice in the greatness of your heart. I, Pahoran, do not seek for power, save only to retain my judgement-seat that I may preserve the rights and the liberty of my people" (BM 399; Alma 61:9). Thus Smith not only voiced his anger but also exonerated his parents' failures as beyond their control.

In Alma's final two chapters, Smith retells his history to the point of discovering the gold record but in a more diffuse and ambiguous form than in previous stories because of the on-going military conflict. When Pahoran tells Moroni to join him in Zarahemla (62:1-11), Smith may be alluding to the family's reunion in Palmyra. They put down the insurrection, restoring peace to Zarahemla, possibly a version of the family settling into Palmyra. Reinforcements go to the various Nephite armies (vv. 11-12) and Nephihah returns to Nephite possession with the loss of only one Nephite life (vv. 14-26). The Lamanite prisoners join the Nephites in peaceful farming, suggesting the family's move to their farm (v. 29). The heroic Teancum, trying to assassinate the Lamanite captain, as he had earlier killed Amalakiah by stealth, is himself killed (vv. 32-37), sounding the theme of Alvin's death. Moroni drives the remaining Lamanites from the land "with a great slaughter"; and in the following peace, Helaman and his brothers convert many—the revival scene (vv. 38, 44-47). Even more striking, the final chapter of Alma both opens and closes with a mention of a sacred record—the record Smith is now translating. Again I must emphasize the speculative nature of this interpretation.

The book of Alma ends with the peaceful deaths of a series of record-keepers: Alma, Helaman, Shiblon, and Helaman II.[20] After thirty years of intensive warfare came four years of peace, a final effort by the Lamanites, and the Nephite success in repelling it. The book ends in the fortieth year of the judges (52 B.C.E.). If my last interpretations are correct, these stories correlate to the life of Joseph Smith after 1825.

Internal Corrosion and Inconstancy

> [The Narcissistic personality] is preoccupied with fantasies of unlimited success, power, brilliance, beauty, or ideal love ... [He] is often envious of others

> [and] may begrudge others their successes or possessions, feeling that [he] better [deserves] those achievements, admiration, or privileges.[21]

> These people are envious of everything, even of other people's object relations.[22]

> It is postulated that under optimum circumstances the very young infant enjoys some vague sense of omnipotence, autarchy, and perfect union with mother and environment, since all needs are gratified relatively quickly upon their being experienced and with no special effort on the part of the infant. ... This experience of satisfactory unity with the caretaking environment, usually the mother, builds in the young psyche a sense of omnipotence, a fantasy of total bliss and power. ... Those infants who are able to begin gradually to delegate their own sense of omnipotence to a parent for whom they have loving feelings, and to share that omnipotence while gaining a feeling of greater effectiveness, both individually and through sharing, are likely to develop a sturdy and joyful sense of self. Those infants who respond with increasing frustration and rage to the recognition of their own helplessness in satisfying their needs, or who find that the mother on whom they are dependent is an unreliable gratifier of their needs, are likely to develop rage tinged with inadequate feelings of themselves as beings incapable of providing for their own gratification [and will make] reparative attempts [by] omnipotent fantasies.[23]

TIME: 52-51 B.C.E.//1826-28 C.E.

PERSONAE: THE GADIANTON BAND//THE MASONIC ORDER
FIVE SUSPECTS IN THE MURDER OF THE CHIEF JUDGE//
FIVE SUSPECTS IN THE MURDER OF WILLIAM MORGAN
CANDIDATES FOR CHIEF JUDGE//CANDIDATES
FOR U.S. PRESIDENT AND NEW YORK GOVERNORSHIP

In the book of Helaman, I argue that Smith writes out contemporary events—particularly the anti-Masonic turmoil of 1826-27—and that he again indulges in dreams of omnipotence by having God grant total power to Nephi Jr. (See also chapter 3.)

William Morgan, a disgruntled Mason, wrote an exposé of Masonic secret rites; but while it was being published in Batavia, New York, in September 1826, Masons burned the printing press, beat the owner, and charged Morgan with theft. At Canandaigua, nine miles from Smith's home, Morgan was acquitted, then rearrested for a debt of $2.69 and jailed. Someone paid his debt; but, remember from chapter 3, as he walked out of jail, he was seized, gagged, thrust into a yellow carriage, and driven to the Canadian border. There he disappeared, presumably murdered. His book, published in 1827, was an immediate sensation and fanned flames of national outrage against Masonry as a secret society that was controlling courts and government offices. Five men were tried for the murder in January 1827. Three were acquitted and two received light sentences, providing "proof" to many of Masonic control of the courts.

During this time the city of Rochester, twenty miles from Palmyra, was the bitterest center of the conflict. Pamphlets reviewing the trial appeared in large numbers, Rochester had the first of thirty-two anti-Masonic papers in the state, and speakers traveled "from town to town to divulge Masonic secrets." They focused on the rites of initiates that pledged protection to Masonic brothers whether they were "right or wrong," and on the threats "of death to anyone who divulged Masonic secrets." Eighteen trials of Masonic "conspirators" occurred in western New York between October 1826 and 1831.[24] The anti-Masonic hysteria swept the country until about 1838 when it was replaced by the slavery conflict. In New York state, over two-thirds of the 600 Masonic lodges were abandoned.[25] Andrew Jackson was a high-ranking Mason, while John Quincy Adams declared, "I state that I am not, never was, and never shall be a Freemason." Baptists, Presbyterians, and Methodists saw the Masons as evil competition; Masons were forbidden communion. The Dutch Reform Church in New York called Masonry "a mixture of Paganism and Mohammedanism. ... We also find that it perverts the meaning [of Christianity] and is full of names of blasphemy and [is guilty of] administering illegal, profane, and horrible oaths."[26] The three candidates for governor of New York in 1828 each took positions on Masonry. Martin Van Buren won but resigned after twelve weeks to become Jackson's secretary of state. His replacement took the public position that the Masons should dissolve their organization because it was "founded on principles which tend to subvert all government." The anti-Masonic movement had grown large enough for a convention at Le Roy, New York, in February 1829, with plans to hold a national convention in September 1830. Both state and federal congresses had investigative committees.[27]

Joseph Smith retells this political history but in a way that reveals an internal moral struggle over hidden corruption. Ironically, Smith himself later became a high-ranking Mason, played some role with the vigilante Danites, and organized a secret political Council of Fifty, which some see as the equivalent of a Gadianton band.

Our clue about the time frame is a contested election, again drawing our attention to 1827-28. When Pahoran dies, three of his sons contend for the judgement seat: Pahoran II, Paanchi, and Pacumeni. Pahoran II wins the election. Paanchi leads a revolt but is captured and executed. His followers retaliate by hiring an assassin, Kishkumen, who kills Pahoran and escapes, his band of assassins mingling successfully with ordinary citizens. Kishkumen had belonged to the secret band led by one Gadianton "who was exceeding expert in many words, and also in his craft, to carry out the secret work of murder and robbery." Pacumeni is elected chief judge to replace his murdered brother. Preoccupied with these political intrigues, the Nephites are caught off guard when the Lamanites attack, capture Zarahemla, and kill Pacumeni. The nation rallies under Moronihah, son of

Moroni, to regain their territories after much bloody conflict; and Helaman II, son of Helaman, is elected chief judge. Kishkumen again plots to murder him; but a disguised servant of Helaman, who has been attending the secret meetings, gets Kishkumen alone and "did stab Kishkumen, even to the heart, that he fell dead without a groan" (BM 407-12; Hel. 1-3).

Gadianton, alarmed by Kishkumen's absence, abandons his plan to take over the government and flees with his band into the wilderness. The group remains cohesive, however; and in years to come will corrupt the Nephite nation from within. After a period of righteousness and peace, the Nephites become proud and wicked. Helaman II dies and is replaced by Nephi Jr. in 39 B.C.E., Joseph Smith's surrogate. Dissensions intensify, some Nephites join the Lamanites, and the "work of death" begins in 35 B.C.E. with the Lamanites retaking Zarahemla. In the social struggle that follows, the racial polarization (good Nephites/bad Lamanites) is erased, then reversed, with the Nephites becoming wicked and harboring the secret Gadianton band.

> Now this great loss of the Nephites, and the great slaughter which was among them, would not have happened, had it not been for their wickedness and their abomination which was among them; yea, and it was among those which professed to belong to the church of God; and it was because of their exceeding riches ... [and] oppression to the poor ... [and] withholding their food from the hungry ... [and] clothing from the naked ... [and] smiting their humble brethren upon the cheek, making a mock of that which was sacred, denying the spirit of prophecy and revelation, murdering, plundering, lying, steeling, committing adultery, raising up great contentions, and deserting away into the land of Nephi, among the Lamanites; and because of their great wickedness, and their boastings in their own strength, they were left in their own strength; therefore they did not prosper, but were afflicted, and smitten, and driven before the Lamanites, until they had lost possession of almost all their lands. (BM 416; Hel. 4:10-13)

From a psychoanalytic perspective, Smith is retelling the national fantasies that began even before Morgan's murder in 1826. The next section, however, is personal. Nephi Jr. resigns the chief judgeship (like Alma) and, with his brother Lehi, preaches "with power and authority." In Zarahemla they convert 8,000 Lamanites. Imprisoned in the land of Nephi, they are encircled with fire while their would-be slayers are terrified by the quaking prison and a voice that warns: "Repent ye, repent ye, and seek no more to destroy my servants whom I have sent unto you to declare good tidings. ... And ... it was not a voice of thunder, neither was it a voice of great tumultuous noise, but behold, it was a still voice of perfect mildness, as if it had been a whisper, and it did pierce to the very soul" (BM 419-20; Hel. 5:14-33). The walls continue to shake. The voice speaks twice more. The brothers' faces "did shine exceedingly, even as the face of angels." The Lamanites repent, are encircled with the same fire, and "the Holy Spirit of God did come down from Heaven, and did enter into their hearts, and they were filled as if with fire; and could speak forth marvelous words. And it came to pass that there came a voice unto them, yea, a pleasant voice, as if it were a whisper, saying, Peace, peace be unto you, because of your faith in my well beloved." Angels minister to them, and they become missionaries in turn, converting the majority of the Lamanites who laid down their weapons and returned the conquered land to the Nephites (BM 420-22; Hel. 5:34-52).

This is the most extreme fantasy yet derived from Smith's brush with jail. His humiliation has become a nation-saving miracle that, according to Baptist minister M. T. Lamb, combines and outperforms the angelic escapes from prison by the apostles Peter (Acts 5, 12) and Paul (Acts 16), the fiery furnace of Shadrach, Meshach, and Abednego (Dan. 3), the darkness and awful dread of Sinai (Ex. 19), the shining face of Moses (Ex. 34), the still small voice heard by Elijah (1 Kgs. 19) and the outpouring of the spirit on the day of Pentecost (Acts 2).[28]

In a refreshing reversal, the Lamanites accept the prophets, repent, convert, and become preachers and missionaries. In contrast, the Nephites are "hardened and impenitent and grossly wicked." During this odd transitional phase, the two groups have "free intercourse, one with another, to buy and sell, and to get gain, according to their desire." This trade results in increased wealth: "They did raise grain in abundance ... and they did flourish exceedingly. And they did multiply and wax exceedingly strong in the land. And they did raise many flocks and herds. ... Behold, their women did toil and spin, and did make all manner of cloth, of fine twined linen, and cloth of every kind, to clothe their nakedness" (BM 422-23; Hel. 6:1-13). But because they were blessed with peace and prosperity, they "began to set their hearts upon their riches ... [and] to get gain, that they might be lifted up one above another; therefore they began to commit secret murders" (BM 423; Hel. 6:14-17).

We have seen this cycle before in the Book of Mormon: obedience results in God's blessings of prosperity; material well-being brings hard hearts and pride; God awakens the unrighteous with war and afflictions until the people repent. But there is no maturing as a result of these experiences, no escape from these repeated cycles. And the rapidity of the cycling becomes absurd in this phase of the narrative.

> And thus ended the eighty and first year of the reign of the Judges [11 B.C.E.]. And in the eighty and second year, they began again to forget the Lord their God. And in the eighty and third year, they began to wax strong in iniquity. And in the eighty and fourth year, they did not mend their ways. And it came to pass in the eighty and fifth year, they did wax stronger and stronger in their pride, and in their wickedness; and thus they were ripening again for destruction. ... And thus we can behold how false, and also the unsteadiness of the hearts of the children of men. (BM 439; Hel. 12:1-6)

I suspect that the description of free trade is an echo of Smith's life in 1827-28, when he traveled back and forth between Palmyra and Harmony, married, and hosted his parents at the Hales'. It follows, then, that the immature cycle of greed and pride as a source of maintaining self-esteem represents Smith's personal maturity. Eventually even his concept of heaven is structured by competition with one's peers over possessions and dominions, including who would have the most wives and father the most children.[29]

Even more dangerous than this struggle for possessions is the increasing influence of the Gadianton band. As the Lamanites are transformed into "good objects," the Nephites become "bad objects"—a striking example of Otto Kernberg's observation about the abrupt shifts and reversals that occur between "good objects and bad objects" in the narcissist.[30] This secret band has an obvious external referent in the secret Masonic society; but I would argue as well that it simultaneously points to Smith's deeper psychological terrain.

When Nephi had left the judgment seat to preach the gospel, Cezoram became chief judge. He "was murdered by an unknown hand," and replaced by his son, also soon murdered. The motive for these "secret murders" is greed: "They began to set their hearts upon their riches ... and to get gain, that they might be lifted up one above another" (BM 423; Hel. 6:17). Although most of Nephite society seems to fall under the condemnation of being materialistic, it is the Gadianton robbers who are willing to resort to murder and to protect themselves in a parody of unity with "secret signs, and their secret words. ... that whatsoever wickedness his brother should do, he should not be injured by his brother, ... thus they might murder, and plunder, and steal, and commit whoredoms, and all manner of wickedness." The source of these secret oaths is "the same being who did entice our first parents to partake of the forbidden fruit; yea, that same being who did plot with Cain, that if he would murder his brother Abel, it should not be known unto the world. ... And it was the same being ... which is the author of all sin" (BM 423-24; Hel. 6:14-30).

The Nephite/Lamanite reversal is tied to their response to this secret organization. The Lamanites, in a two-pronged action, hunt down the Gadianton band and also preach the gospel to its members with the result that the band is "utterly destroyed from among the Lamanites." In contrast, the Nephites allow the band to "obtain sole management of the government, insomuch that they did trample under their feet, and smite, and rend, and turn their backs upon the poor, and the meek, and humble followers of God. And thus we see that they were in an awful state, and ripening for everlasting destruction" (BM 425-26; Hel. 6:37-41).

At this point Nephi/Joseph returns home to Zarahemla/Palmyra from his missionary/family journeys. This area was the very center of the national Gadianton/anti-Masonic conflict. He discovers the Nephites in a state of "awful wickedness" with the Gadianton robbers in "the judgment seats ... doing no justice ... condemning the righteous because of their righteousness; letting the wicked go unpunished, because of their money ... to rule according to their wills ... [and] commit adultery, and steal, and kill" (BM 426; Hel. 7:1-6).

Heartsore, Nephi begins praying in his garden tower, which is near the main road to Zarahemla's central market. When he realizes that he has attracted a crowd of the curious, he chastises them, warning them by name of Gadianton band members who are among them. Inspired, Nephi announces that the chief judge has just been murdered by his power-hungry brother and, furthermore, predicts the brother's guilty reaction to the accusation (BM 426-31; Hel. 7, 8). Some of Nephi's listeners conclude that he is either a prophet or a God "for except he was a God, he could not know of all things. For behold, he hath told us the thoughts of our hearts" (BM 434; Hel. 9:40-41). Still, despite the precise fulfillment of his prophecies, only a few of the Nephites are converted. In a private manifestation, God consoles him:

> Blessed art thou. ... I will make thee mighty in word and in deed, in faith and in works; yea, even that all things shall be done unto thee according to thy word, for thou shalt not ask that which is contrary to my will. ... I am God ... [and] declare it unto thee in the presence of mine angels,[31] that ye shall have power over this people, and shall smite the earth with famine, and with pestilence, and destruction. ... Behold, I give unto you power that whatsoever ye shall seal on earth shall be sealed in heaven; and whatsoever ye shall loose on earth, shall be loosed in heaven. ... And thus, if ye shall say unto this temple, it shall be rent in twain, and it shall be done ... [and] unto this mountain, be thou cast down ... it shall be done. (BM 434-35; Hel. 10:1-10)

Nephi uses this power to bring a famine in an attempt to encourage repentance. It works briefly, but the Nephites remain inconstant, immature, incapable of self-discipline, with the Gadianton band always growing.

Readers have long seen in these stories an expression of public fears about Masonry and its secrets. Lamb, writing sixty years later, could remember "when almost all of the above accusations [in the Book of Mormon], and in almost the same language, were freely hurled against the Masonic Brotherhood by hot-headed and radical opponents."[32] Walter Prince made an extended comparison of the Morgan episode and the Book of Mormon in 1917:

> Now in at least twenty-one chapters in seven out of the sixteen "books" of the Book of Mormon are to be found passages ... plainly referring to Masonry under the guise of a pretended similar organization in ancient America. ... The warning of [George] Washington in his Farewell Address, against "combinations ... with real design to direct, control, counteract or awe the regular deliberation and action of the constituted authorities" was

> quoted a thousand times in Anti-Masonic speeches and writings, and accordingly we find the Book of Mormon employing the term *"combination"* fives times ... and *"secret combination"* fifteen times. ... The claim or poetic fiction of the Masons that their order is from very old times is reflected in "which had been handed down from Cain" (BM 553; Ether 8:15).
>
> ... No charge was more frequently sounded in the furor of 1826-33 than that the Masons monopolized the offices, and defeated justice in the courts in the interest of their members, and accordingly we read in the Book of Mormon of the "secret combinations" "filling the judgement-seats, having usurped the power and authority of the land ... letting the wicked go unpunished because of their money." ... Not only are the general charges against the Masons faithfully impressed upon these many passages ... but so also is the tragedy of William Morgan. Twenty-eight times, and in almost every passage, are the "secret combinations" coupled with "murder" and "murderers" while the words "kill," "slay" and "blood," with similar implications are employed. The source of the obsessing idea becomes more patent with the four-fold use of the expression "secret murder" (BM 416-18; Hel. 6:29; 8:4) since Morgan was murdered secretly. ... At any rate, it is impossible to mistake the connection between the belief of the masses that the light sentences of the several men convicted of Morgan's abduction was an insult to justice and the statement in the Book of Mormon that lawyers and others connected with the ancient covenants conspired to "deliver those who were guilty of murder from the grasp of justice." (BM 467; 3 Ne. 6:29)[33]

Further correlations include a secret trial by the Masons by the "laws of their wickedness," and the publication of the pamphlet despite opposition: "Their secret abominations have been brought out of darkness and made known unto us" (BM 328; Alma 37:26).[34] Smith juxtaposes this story of secret organizations immediately after his (Nephi's) imprisonment, thus grounding it firmly in his life history. As a psychiatrist, I am most struck by what this narrative of secret combinations and compensatory power suggests about Smith's psyche. Any patient who talks so incessantly about an evil hidden brotherhood is revealing an unending conflict. What the patient opposes is the underside of the conflict, in this case recognizing the advantages of such secret oaths and contracts in binding people together, even illicitly. Tellingly, in the Nephite narrative, the evil powers are steadily gaining, corroding from within. And the compensatory fantasy of "good" within this context of extreme evil is absolute power.

As I read this scenario, Smith feels intensely envious of others and their possessions; he declared that the desire for possessions is evil, yet repeatedly and secretly tries to obtain "gain," even by illicit means. Ultimately he attempts to deal with his envy, not by acceptance and humility, but by asserting absolute God-given omnipotence. Psychologically speaking, this story of moral conflict and the eventual ascendancy of secret evil is a troubling prediction that sadly is borne out by Smith's future. Within a few years, he declares all marriages void except those performed by the Mormon priesthood; he not only stepped outside the religious and legal bounds of monogamy, but also took other men's wives as his own.[35] Within ten years Mormonism gave rise to the Danites, a secret organization that began with self-protection and loyalty to Mormon priesthood leaders, whether "right or wrong," and ended with vigilantism. Lying, control of judges, and bloc voting contributed to violent expulsion from Ohio, Missouri, and Illinois. The Mormons demonstrated repeatedly that they could not live with anyone, including those who originally welcomed them with Christian kindness. The Mormon temple ceremony of the early 1840s eventually included secret oaths and covenants of obedience that had their counterpart in Masonic oaths, including covenants to kill or be killed if secrets were divulged, and an oath of vengeance that remained part of the ceremony for almost 100 years. Smith's secret political Council of Fifty, which crowned him president, high priest, and king, was resolved to make him president of the United States or, failing that, to establish a new Mormon empire in the West. These secret oaths reemerged as an element at Mountain Meadows in 1857 where over 100 non-Mormon men, women, and children were murdered. Then, united by oaths and fear of retaliation from within the church, the Mormons delivered up a single scapegoat and successfully blocked U.S. territorial courts from delivering justice.[36] Mormonism became America's most despised religion.

The last incident in the Book of Mormon before Christ's birth marks the completion of the righteous-Lamanite/wicked-Nephite reversal. For the first time, a Lamanite prophet appears. Through Samuel's language and images, Smith temporarily fuses his two worlds: the world of magic (the world of his father, the world of treasures and gold plates) and Protestant revivalism (the world of his mother, the world of revivals and camp meetings). Samuel, another alter ego for Smith, appears from nowhere at a critical moment, preaches from the city wall (symbolic of borders and transitions), cannot be killed by arrows, and disappears as quickly as he came. He foretells the destruction of the Nephite people in 400 years, the signs of Christ's birth in five years, and the signs of Christ's death and the accompanying destruction. He is a modified John the Baptist in the Book of Mormon.

But he serves another purpose as well, for he explains to Smith's nineteenth-century followers why the gold plates are his only money-digging success:

> Whoso shall hide up treasures in the earth, shall find them again no more, because of the great curse on the land, save he be a righteous man, and shall hide it up unto the Lord. ... And he that hideth not up his treasures unto me [God], cursed is he, and also the treasure, and none shall redeem it because of the curse of the land. ... And then shall ye lament, and say, O that I had repented, and had not killed the prophets, and stoned them, and cast them out ... and then they would not have become slippery, that we should lose them.

> ... Behold, we layeth a tool here, and on the morrow it is gone; and behold, our swords are taken from us in the day we have sought them for battle. Yea, we have hid up our treasures, and they have slipped away from us, because of the curse of the land ... Behold, we are surrounded by demons ... Behold, our iniquities are great: O Lord, canst thou not turn away thine anger from us? And this shall be your language in them days. But behold, your days of probation is past; ye have procrastinated the day of your salvation until it is everlastingly too late, and your destruction is made sure; yea, for ye have sought all the days of your lives for that which ye could not obtain; and ye have sought for happiness in doing iniquity, which thing is contrary to the nature of that righteousness which is in our great and Eternal Head. (BM 443-445; Hel. 13)[37]

I consider Smith's remarkable ability to fuse the two opposite supernatural worlds a major indicator that he is ready to found a new church.

Notes

1. American Psychiatric Association, *Diagnostic and Statistical Manual of Mental Disorders, Fourth Edition* (Washington, D.C.: American Psychiatric Association, 1994), 658-59.

2. Otto Kernberg, *Borderline Conditions and Pathological Narcissism* (New York: Jason Aronson, 1975), 17-18, 25, 33.

3. Jay R. Greenberg and Stephen A. Mitchell, *Object Relations in Psychoanalytic Theory* (Cambridge, MA: Harvard University Press, 1983); Lawrence H. Schwartz, "The Role of Psychodynamic Concepts in Psychiatry: New Developments," paper presented at the annual meeting of the Washington State Psychiatric Association, 15 Apr. 1989, Vancouver, B.C.; photocopy in my possession.

4. E. D. Howe, *Mormonism Unvailed* (Painesville, OH: Author, 1834), 254-55.

5. Ibid., 260-61.

6. In an eighty-year-old study of Book of Mormon names, Walter F. Prince, "Psychological Tests for the Authorship of the Book of Mormon," *American Journal of Psychology* 28 (3 July 1917): 373-89, used the then-new concept of Freud's "psychic censor" to trace their origin—primarily finding such parallels between the Gadianton band and anti-Masonry as Smith's use of *Morgan* as a base for the many uses of Mor*** in the Book of Mormon, and also that the "anti" of the anti-Masonic phrase as the source of similar terms used in the Book of Mormon. He also pointed to the similarities between Chesebro, the surname of the principal Mason, and Book of Mormon characters Zeezrom, Cezorum, and Seezorum. See Theodore Schroeder's negative response in the same journal, "Authorship of the Book of Mormon," 30 (Jan. 1919): 66-72, in which he takes issue with Prince on the basis of the discredited hypothesis that Solomon Spaulding, not Joseph Smith, wrote the Book of Mormon. See also Prince's brusque response in "A Footnote: 'Authorship of the Book of Mormon,'" ibid., 427-28.

7. I knew nothing about the politics or government during this period, but it seemed clear from the Book of Mormon that there were prominent issues. Nevertheless, I was still surprised to find the close parallels. See R. K. Andrist, *Andrew Jackson: Soldier and Statesman* (New York: American Heritage Publishing Co., 1963), and B. Davis, *Old Hickory: A Life of Andrew Jackson* (New York: Dial Press, 1977), esp. 201-44.

8. Glyndon G. VanDeusen, *The Jacksonian Era: 1828-1848* (New York: Harper Torchbooks, 1963), 26-27; Davis, *Old Hickory*, 46-65, 175-84, 213-31.

9. Davis, *Old Hickory*, 219.

10. Ibid., 227.

11. Van Deusen, *The Jacksonian Era*, 27.

12. Ibid.

13. Davis, *Old Hickory*, 214, 222, 262-64.

14. Van Deusen, *The Jacksonian Era*, 27.

15. Davis, *Old Hickory*, 230.

16. W. W. Meissner, "Narcissistic Personalities and Borderline Conditions: Differential Diagnosis," in *Essential Papers on Narcissism*, ed., A. P. Morrison (New York: New York University Press, 1986), 407-408.

17. R. Douglas Phillips, "Why Is So Much of the Book of Mormon Given Over to Military Accounts?" in *Warfare in the Book of Mormon*, eds. Stephen D. Ricks and William J. Hamblin (Salt Lake City: Deseret Book Co., 1990), 25-28.

18. B. H. Roberts, "Moroni IX," *Contributor* 11:335-40, reprinted in B. H. Roberts, *A Scrap Book, Vol. 1* (Provo, UT: Pulsipher Publishers, n.d.), 227. I would argue that Smith borrowed another incident from Josiah Priest's *Wonders of Nature and Providence Displayed* (Albany, NY: Author and E. E. Hosford, 1825), 530-32. When the British army practiced some maneuvers on Sunday, the Methodist minister told his flock to avoid these Sabbath-breakers. Putting patriotism above religious obedience, ten Methodist youths asked the officer for arms. Irritated at the minister, the officer threatened to place them in the front line. One replied, "We are not afraid to die. ... Place us in the front of the hottest battle, and we shall die fighting for king and country." The officer placed them at a bridge and ordered them to retreat after firing once on the Irish rebels. "No sir," responded the youth, "we will not retreat; we will stand our ground and die upon the spot." After four volleys, the rest of the soldiers joined them "and in about an hour and a half, the rebels began to fly in all directions. ... [Later] one of the ten young men ... informed them that the Lord had so wonderfully preserved them all, that not one of them had received the slightest wound."

19. B. H. Roberts, *Studies of the Book of Mormon* (Urbana: University of Illinois Press, 1985), 272-73.

20. During this period Hagoth, a "curious" man, builds boats and makes two settlement voyages, not returning from the second (BM 405-406; Alma 63:4-8). The traditional explanation is that Hagoth's people are the ancestors of the Polynesians. This episode has a contemporary counterpart. According to LaRue W. Piercy, *Hawaii: Truth Stranger Than Fiction* (Honolulu: Fisher Printing Co., 1985), 79, Hawaiian Bibles were being printed at Rochester in 1827-28, and newspapers reported the departure of Christian missionaries in November 1822 and 1827. The boats would have returned about a year later.

21. American Psychiatric Association, *Diagnostic and Statistical Manual*, 658-61.

22. Otto Kernberg, in an aside comment at a discussion group in 1973; see also Alice Miller, "Depression and Grandiosity as Related Forms of Narcissistic Disturbances," in Morrison, *Essential Papers*, 323-37.

23. Arnold M. Cooper, "Narcissism," in Morrison, *Essential Papers on Narcissism*, 132-33, 139-40.

24. Richard L. Bushman, *Joseph Smith and the Beginnings of Mormonism* (Urbana: University of Illinois Press, 1988), 129.

25. Charles McCarthy, "The Antimasonic Party," *Annual Report of the American Historical Association for the Year 1902* (Washington, D.C.: Government Printing Office, 1903), 1:539.

26. Ibid., 541.

27. Ibid., 367-574.

28. M. T. Lamb, *The Golden Bible ... or the Book of Mormon. Is it from God?* (New York: Ward and Drummond, 1887), 74.

29. Orson Pratt, "Celestial Marriage," *The Seer*, May-Dec. 1853, 65-192, photographic reprint (Salt Lake City: Eborn Books and Publishers Press, 1990); David John Buerger, "The Adam-God Doctrine," *Dialogue: A Journal of Mormon Thought* 15 (Spring 1982): 14-58; Boyd Kirkland, "The Development of the Mormon Doctrine of God," 32-52, and "Eternal Progression and the Second Death of the Theology of Brigham Young," 171-82, both in Gary J. Bergera, *Line Upon Line: Essays on Mormon Doctrine* (Salt Lake City: Signature Books, 1989); Gary J. Bergera, "The Orson Pratt—Brigham Young Controversies: Conflict within the Quorums, 1853 to 1868," *Dialogue: A Journal of Mormon Thought* 13 (Summer 1980): 7-49.

30. Kernberg, *Borderline Conditions*, 29.

31. This remarkable sentence implies that a statement by God can be made *more* trustworthy by having angels as witnesses. In other words, Smith's view of absolute truth, here stated by God, is that it exists in varying degrees.

32. Lamb, *Golden Bible*, 230-31; Alexander Campbell, *Delusions: An Analysis of the Book of Mormon* (Boston: Benjamin H. Greene, 1832), 9; Fawn M. Brodie, *No Man Knows My History*, 2d ed., rev. and enl. (New York: Alfred A. Knopf, 1971) 65-66; Thomas F. O'Dea, *The Mormons* (Chicago: University of Chicago Press, 1957), 35.

33. Prince, "Psychological Tests for the Authorship of the Book of Mormon," 375-78.

34. The principal Mason acting legally in arresting Morgan was surnamed Chesebro, arguably the source of both Cezorum (leader of robbers) and Seezorum (judge elected by robbers). Chesebro received a light sentence. Ibid., 381.

35. Richard S. Van Wagoner, *Mormon Polygamy: A History* (Salt Lake City: Signature Books, 1986), 7-8, 38, 43-46; see also his discussion "Joseph and Marriage," *Sunstone* 10 (1985): 32-33.

36. For a summary of Smith's search for political power and intimidating organizations, see Klaus J. Hansen, *Quest for Empire: The Political Kingdom of God and the Council of Fifty in Mormon History* (East Lansing: Michigan State University Press, 1970); Marvin S. Hill, *Quest for Refuge: The Mormon Flight from American Pluralism* (Salt Lake City: Signature Books, 1989); D. Michael Quinn, *The Mormon Hierarchy: Origins of Power* (Salt Lake City: Signature Books, 1994), and his *The Mormon Hierarchy: Extensions of Power* (Salt Lake City: Signature Books, 1997), throughout, but esp. 226-372, and notes for analysis of Mormonism's "culture of violence" and secret government control in the West. The classic work on the Mountain Meadows Massacre is Juanita Brooks, *Mountain Meadows Massacre* (Norman: University of Oklahoma Press, 1962). Brooks, a practicing Mormon, maintained her own oath of secrecy by deftly avoiding the exact wording and therefore the full impact of the temple oaths on the crime in this otherwise excellent work. Mormon church presidents were secretly crowned king until at least

1885. D. Michael Quinn, "The Council of Fifty and Its Members, 1844 to 1945," *BYU Studies* 20 (Winter 1980): 163-97, esp. 188, emphasizes the council's symbolic and spiritual, rather than political, meaning; but Quinn's position changed with his later writings. See his *Mormon Hierarchy: Extensions of Power.* Under governmental pressure and Supreme Court decisions threatening disenfranchisement of the church, the failure of Jesus to appear before the deaths of the first generation of Mormons, and because of the basic loyalty of the majority of the members of the church, the reversal of Mormonism from an anti-democratic antagonist to the United States that began in 1890 was largely completed by 1930. See Thomas G. Alexander, *Mormonism in Transition: A History of the Latter-day Saints, 1890-1930* (Urbana: University of Illinois Press, 1986). Today, American Mormons are a conservative people dedicated to the United States, but still can move *en bloc* in political action. Under direction of the male Mormon leadership, Mormon women flooded the meetings supporting the Equal Rights Amendment, and blocked or derailed agendas. These acts of religious fundamentalism "tipped the scales" in defeating the Equal Rights Amendment in 1982. See Quinn, *Mormon Hierarchy: Extension of Power,* 373-408.

37. For Samuel's importance in explaining the failure of money-digging, see Brent Lee Metcalfe, response to Edgar Snow, "A Narrative Critical Exegesis of the Samuel the Lamanite Narrative," Sunstone Symposium, Aug. 1994, Salt Lake City. See also: "And behold, if a man hideth up a treasure in the earth, and the Lord shall say, let it be accursed, because of the iniquity of him that hath hid it up, behold, it shall be accursed, that no man shall find thee from this time hence forth and forever" (BM 440: Hel. 12:18-20).

CHAPTER 6

Descent into Hell

> Analytic exploration very often demonstrates that their [narcissistic personalities'] haughty, grandiose, and controlling behavior is a defense against paranoid traits related to the projection of oral rage, which is central to their pathology. ... Their [internal] interactions reflect very intense primitive ... object relationships of a frightening kind.[1]

Samuel had prophesied and disappeared (5 B.C.E.); the signs of Jesus' birth in Bethlehem had brought the people to a temporary repentance; the Gadianton band had revived (1-33 C.E.); Nephi had resurrected his brother who had been stoned by a mob (31 C.E.); the landscape had been devastated and the people decimated at the crucifixion of Christ (34 C.E.); Jesus had come and gone; and the people had two centuries of peace and harmony. Then, as predicted, the inconstant Nephites slid again into evil, this time as part of a pattern that would not be permanently reversed and that would end in their extermination by the Lamanites. From my psychoanalytic perspective, this corruption represents Joseph Smith's capitulation to the temptation to control people by illicit means and, to use a psychiatric expression, to allow his "false self" to take its final form. He will now elaborate on this drift and acknowledge, through the Nephite people, the triumph of unethical forces in his personality. He will also give us clues as to the origin of these forces.

Those who have spent their lives studying the narcissistic personality believe that its psychological origin begins at birth and partly, or largely, occurs with repeated frustrations too big for the child to handle. The child responds with "oral rage"—screaming, crying, and whining; and its expression through the years may be in temper outbursts, unrestrained attacks on things and people, and explosive verbal outbursts that are without purpose or specific goals, but that unnerve witnesses. In the developing narcissistic personality, oral rage provides no rewards and gives way, early in life—in the first two years, it is believed—to compensatory mental processes that focus the child intensely on an internal world of wonderful and powerful satisfaction. The mental experiences of the child contain raging and destructive images but provide magical means by which the child conquers opposition. As the years pass, these mental experiences may take on certain specific qualities: particular fantasies may become stories of magic, killings, dangers, and conquests but always with the main theme that the child, in fantasy, defeats enemies and overcomes obstacles. As the developing narcissistic boy enters the Oedipal stage, he uses these early methods to struggle with his attraction for his mother, fear of retaliation from his father, and fears of bodily injury—various forms of symbolic castration. What sets these children apart is the massive use of primitive rageful, vengeful fantasies in trying to solve the conflict, but it is believed that the central level of emotional development remains at the pre-Oedipal period, despite superficial appearances of social abilities.

My discussion of the book of Ether is unquestionably the most speculative in this volume, for it attempts to understand the thinking, emotions, and images of a preverbal child, represented by stories that come from the interface of oral legends and the first writings of these legends. The early stories from Babylon and Mesopotamia, the Homeric stories, and Icelandic sagas all contain primitive magic and heroes of gigantic proportions. The beginning chapters of the Bible, many believe, fit into this category. In the Book of Mormon, the book of Ether, like the ending of the Nephite civilization, descends first into a world of magic, then into a hell of sheer hatred.

I have already quoted psychoanalyst Phyllis Greenacre's assessment of artists, including prophets:

> In using the term *artist* I designate the creative individual ... whose work-product shows ... unusual capacity for imaginative creation, original thought, invention or discovery [and] would ... include those prophets, religious leaders and scientists whose philosophies and discoveries have influenced the course of their times and left an imprint on history.
>
> After reading a great many accounts of artists, I was struck with the prominence of the family romance in their lives. The germ of the family romance is ubiquitous [universal] in the hankering of growing children for a return to the real or fancied conditions at or before the dawn of conscious memory when adults were Olympians.[2]

If my speculation about Ether is correct, then it will be even more miraculous than the rest of the Book of Mormon, even more revealing of early childhood fantasies. No one has said that these fantasies must be pleasant; they may be gigantic in terror as well as size.

The final three books—Mormon, Ether, and Moroni—present a puzzle. Mormon, born around 311 C.E., tells the destruction of his people. His son, Moroni, tells of Mormon's death and the final remnants of the Nephites. Smith disrupts this obvious progress from one generation to the next by inserting Ether between them. Thus Ether is anomalous in placement as well as subject. It provides a synoptic, abbreviated history of the Jaredites, who immigrated to the New World in about 2500 B.C.E.—approximately 1,900 years before Lehi left Jerusalem. The Jaredites had just barely wiped each other out in civil strife when the Nephites arrived in the new world.

Chronologically this book should commence the Book of Mormon or perhaps become an appendix to the main story. But its placement is so chronologically inconsistent that, from a psychoanalytic perspective, it signals an opportunity to view the deeper logic of Smith's unconscious. I argue that Smith placed Ether between Mormon and Moroni because it fits his personal chronology. In previous stories he has taken us right up to the point where he is dictating the book. With Ether, he comes as close as he can to telling us about the dictation period that he has just completed.

The Small Book of Mormon

The text of the book of Mormon brings the story to the eve of Nephite destruction. Mormon, the son of Mormon, is yet another surrogate for Smith. His name (another Jr.) is the first signal, but the narrative also presents a thinly veiled version of Mormon's/Smith's childhood. Mormon is ten or eleven, about young Joseph's age when he followed his father south from New England toward Palmyra, New York.

> I began to be learned somewhat after the manner of the learning of my people [when] Ammaron saith unto me, I perceive that thou art a sober child, and art quick to observe; therefore when ye are about twenty and four years old ... go to the land of Antum, unto a hill, which shall be called Shim, and there I have deposited unto the Lord, all the sacred engravings concerning this people. ... And I ... remembered the things which Ammaron had commanded me. ... And ... I, being eleven years old, was carried by my father into the land southward, even to the land of Zarahemla ... (BM 518-19; Morm. 1:1-7)

Smith would also be nearly twenty-four years old when he "discovered" the record in the hill and wrote from it the history of his "people," his own autobiography.

Mormon continues: "And I being fifteen years of age and being somewhat of a sober mind, therefore I was visited of the Lord, and tasted and knew of the goodness of Jesus" (BM 519; Morm. 1:15). This description of Mormon's experience, revealing the mental world of Joseph Smith, is the very first version, still in embryonic and undifferentiated form, of the future first vision story. At fifteen, Mormon because of his physical and spiritual prowess became general of the armies—which I read as another statement of Smith's compensatory drive toward power and accomplishment. God forbade Mormon to preach because of the iniquity of the people:

> Because of the hardness of their hearts, the land was cursed for their sake. And these Gadianton robbers, which were among the Lamanites, did infest the land, insomuch that the inhabitants thereof began to hide up their treasures in the earth; and they became slippery, because the Lord had cursed the land, that they could not hold them, nor retain them again. And it came to

> pass that there were sorceries, and witchcrafts, and magics: and the power of the evil one was wrought upon all the face of the land. (BM 519-20; Morm. 1:7-19)

This passage calls up echoes of anti-Masonry and Smith's experience with magic and money-digging. The narrative returns later to this same theme: "For behold no man could keep that which was his own, for the thieves and the robbers, and the murders, and the magic art, and the witchcraft which was in the land" (BM 521; Morm. 2:1-10). These complaints against magic are curious: Smith, a magician and the son of a magician, condemns magic and sorcery as evidence of extreme evil in a story dictated by means of his magic seer stone and with the help of Oliver Cowdery, a divining rod magician and son of another magician rodsman. Yet the text reveals no observable discomfort with this moral contradiction—typical of the psychological defense of splitting used by narcissistic personalities.

"Blood and carnage" rule, and "it was one complete revolution throughout all the face of the land." Years wear away in battle: 42,000 soldiers versus 44,000; 30,000 versus 50,000. Cities are taken, lost, and retaken. Thousands die. Mormon and his Lamanite counterpart agree on a migration in preparation for the final battles. Women and children are sacrificed to idols. The people lament, mourn and sorrow, but "not unto repentance. ... but it was rather the sorrowing of the damned. ... and the day of grace was past with them" (BM 521; Morm. 2:11-14). These sentences signal that Smith's internal warfare is not moving toward any kind of integration or reconciliation.

Because certain motifs have been so obsessively repeated and reworked, it is possible to catch glimpses—albeit increasingly uncertain ones because of their brevity—of other events in the pages of Mormon's story. For example, at one point Mormon "did utterly refuse from this time forth to be a commander and a leader of this people, because of their wickedness and abomination" (BM 523; Morm. 3:11). Is this withdrawal connected to Smith's seven-month withdrawal from supernatural claims after Martin Harris lost the 116 pages of manuscript? The glimpse is suggestive but not conclusive. The Lamanites consistently advance against the Nephites, who persist in their wickedness:

> And it is impossible to describe, or for man to write a perfect description of the horrible scene of the blood and carnage, both of the Nephites and the Lamanites; and every heart was hardened so that they delighted in the shedding of blood continually. And there never had been so great wickedness among all the children of Lehi; nor even among all the house of Israel, according to ... the Lord, as was among this people. (BM 525; Morm. 4:10-12)

To a psychiatrist, this passage communicates that Smith's internal morality and personal ethics, battered by fury ever since the death of his son, are giving way, as represented by the Nephite capitulation to evil and their inability to withstand the Lamanites: "And from this time forth did the Nephites gain no power over the Lamanites, but began to be swept off by them even as a dew before the sun" (BM 526; Morm. 4:18). Finally Mormon returns to the battles, paralleling Smith's return to his claims of supernatural power after the seven-month hiatus. "But behold, I was without hopes, for I knew the judgements of the Lord which should come upon them: for they repented not of their iniquities, but did struggle for their lives, without calling upon that Being who had created them" (BM 526; Morm. 4:23, 5:2). Reading from the Book of Mormon back into Joseph's life, does this statement of Mormon's hopelessness reflect Joseph's abandonment of all hope to seek a decent ordinary life, as Isaac Hale had encouraged him to do? His comments to Peter Ingersoll, as they returned to Palmyra/Manchester, are a confession that he felt vulnerable to pressure from his family to return to magic.

The book of Mormon draws to an end as Mormon, now seventy-four years old, waits for death. He has gathered together the stacks of gold records, abridged them, and hidden them in the hill Cumorah after experiences so terrible that he censors his report so that we, the modern readers, will not have "too great sorrow" (BM 529; Morm. 5:9). The opposing forces agree that the final battle will be at the hill Cumorah. In a place Mormon describes as beautiful, he watches as the Lamanites approach:

> And it came to pass that my people, with their wives and their children, did now behold the armies of the Lamanites marching toward them; and with that awful fear of death which fills the breasts of all the wicked, did they await to receive them. ... And it came to pass that they did fall upon my people with the sword, and with the bow, and with the arrow, and with the ax, and with all manner of weapons of war. (BM 529; Morm. 6:9)

Mormon is wounded and left for dead. His 10,000 men are massacred, as are 10,000 men under each of twenty-two others, each with uncounted wives and children. Only twenty-four Nephites remain, including Mormon and his son, Moroni. They mourn: "O ye fair ones, how could ye have departed from the ways of the Lord! [and] rejected that Jesus. ... But behold, ye are gone" (BM 529-30; Morm. 6:7, 16-18).

Then Mormon and the others are killed, leaving only Moroni. Moroni writes the final message in the warning style of a revivalist preacher to the future readers:

> Jesus Christ hath shown you unto me, and I know your doing ... and there are none, save a few only, which do not lift themselves up in the pride of their hearts, unto the wearing of very fine apparel, unto envyings, and strifes, and malice, and persecutions, and all manner of iniquities; and your churches, yea, even every one, have become polluted. ... For behold, ye do love money, and your substances, and your fine apparel, and the adorning of

your churches, more than ye love the poor and needy, the sick and afflicted. (BM 531-538; Morm. 8, 9)

These words and the story flow by in a torrential stream; the fluidity is striking. Smith is truly caught up in his images. The Book of Mormon is not a book of love, but of terror, hatred, and destruction. Until historical evidence is presented for the Nephite-Lamanite civilizations, these terrible stories can possibly best be seen as reflecting Joseph's emotions and mental images—filled with violence and hatred—dating from the developmental period when the basic units of his personality were being laid down. The fiction that Moroni is speaking to future readers allows Smith to excoriate, in envy and rage, those who have caused the personal humiliations and difficulties which have been disguised and replayed again and again within the Book of Mormon. With Mormon's death, the narrative seems complete. The Nephite people have fought against dark forces from the beginning of their civilizations, the trajectory of their conflict representing the course of Smith's internal struggles. In psychological terms, he has waged—and lost—his battle for decent civilized behavior.

With Mormon's death, the preliminary and preparatory Joseph Smith dies. He is almost ready to be a prophet to his church. But he has not yet expressed and exorcised his hatred. Ether repeats and expands this theme.

The Book of Ether

Ether begins in or near ancient Babylon in Mesopotamia, around 2500 B.C.E. In the days of Noah, God saw the scope of human wickedness and "repented ... that he had made man on the earth," because "every imagination of the thoughts of his heart was only evil continually" (Gen. 9:13-18). He destroyed all humankind except for one family by the flood, then repentantly established the rainbow as a promise that he would never again commit such widescale slaughter. Lacking trust in God's benevolence, the people of Babel built a tower of fired brick "whose top may reach unto heaven. ... And the Lord came down to see ... the tower ... and ... said ... the people is one, and they have all one language ... and now nothing will be restrained from them" (Gen. 9-11). God, fearful of competition from his socially cooperative children, confounded the language and scattered the people.

Ether begins when Jared asks his extraordinarily righteous brother, referred to only as "the brother of Jared," to save their family and friends by pleading with God not to confound their language but rather to lead them away from this evil place. The Lord answers the brother of Jared's prayer, and they set forth on a journey that will take them to the Americas "where there never had man been" (BM 541; Ether 2:5). This context explains the first of Smith's three reasons for writing Ether: it is a second explanation for the origin of the Native Americans, second in popularity only to the belief that they descended from the lost ten tribes of Israel.[3] With this story, Smith has covered both theories.

The second reason Smith dictates the book of Ether is both to tell us and to avoid telling us that he has dictated the Book of Mormon to this point. The Book of Mormon has concealed and revealed similar secrets before now, such as his conjectured humiliation about his stillborn malformed son. The secrets tell themselves by fantasies that parallel the reality, by words and phrases with double meanings, by "Freudian slips," similarities of names and beginning letters of names, and by errors. Perhaps Smith would have been less revealing if he had written down the story and revised it repeatedly, but he is dictating rapidly to others in a fashion close to the free association so revealing in psychotherapy. At this point he makes two technical errors, both worth noting, for while Smith was naive about American archaeology, he was remarkably consistent in his book.

I conjecture that he is trying to tell us/not tell us about how he made the Book of Mormon, including the angel, gold book story, the miraculous translating seer stones, and the period of dictation which included Oliver Cowdery and the contributions of Ethan Smith's *View of the Hebrews.* B. H. Roberts suspected a connection between "Ether" and "Ethan," but was even more struck by the route traveled by Ethan Smith's emigrants and by the Jaredites. In both, Roberts wrote,

> the motive for their journey [is] the same; the direction of the journey in both cases being northward; both peoples entering a valley at the commencement of their journey; both of them encountering many bodies of water in their journey; the journey in both cases being an immense one; and to a land in one case "Where never a man dwelt" ([Ethan] Smith's book); and in the other case, "into a quarter where there never had man been" (Ether 2:5). Where such striking parallels as these obtain, it is not unreasonable to hold that where one account precedes the other, and if the one constructing the later account has had the opportunity of contact with the first account, then it is not impossible that the first account could have suggested the second; and if the points of resemblance and possible suggestion are frequent and striking then it would have to be conceded that the first might even have supplied the ground plan for the second.
>
> Also let it be borne in mind, that the facts and the arguments employed here are cumulative and progressive, and that we have not yet reached the end of our story.[4]

In addition to the Ethan/Ether parallels, Joseph Smith is dealing with the whole period of development of the Book of Mormon itself. To see the bigger picture, we connect the Jaredites to the Nephite story. Smith found his book with the help of an angel and/or seer stone; the Nephites found the book of Ether by divine accident. The Nephite discovery of the book of Ether occurs in two parts, beginning about 200 B.C.E.

Mosiah I, warned by God, abandons the land of Nephi to the Lamanites and leads his people into the wilderness to the north. Unexpectedly, they came upon the city of Zarahemla, whose inhabitants, the Mulekites, left Jerusalem in a separate migration, about ten years after Lehi and Nephi. They were Jews (Lehi was a descendant of Joseph through Manesseh), but had failed to bring their holy scriptures with them. As a result, they had deteriorated into near savages, their language had been corrupted and they had become atheistic. Mosiah taught them language and Bible stories, became their king, "saved them," and merged the two peoples under the name of Nephites. The Mulekites thus disappear after a few verses, but they are the connecting link to the Jaredite civilization. The Mulekites brought "a large stone" to King Mosiah "with engravings on it; and he did interpret the engravings by the gift and power of God" (BM 150; Omni 20-21).[5]

From this stone, Mosiah learns that the Nephites and the Mulekites are the second and third migrations to the New World. They had been preceded by the Jaredites. The narrative does not describe how Mosiah I supernaturally translates the large carved stone; specifically there is no mention of the two glass "interpreters" later attached to a breastplate, or even a seer stone. But with God's help, Mosiah translated it, for the record includes a summary: "[The stone] gave an account of [a last king of a previous civilization,] one Coriantumr, and the slain of his people. And Coriantumr was discovered by the people of Zarahemla; and he dwelt with them nine moons. It also spoke a few words concerning his fathers. And his first parents came out from the tower, at the time the Lord confounded the language ..." (BM 149-50; Omni 15-22). We are not told how long the Mulekites had kept the stone or how long they had known about Coriantumr. It could have been a few years or as long as four centuries. Nevertheless, Coriantumr is established as the survivor from this earliest migration.

Here we can begin to see the parallels between the book of Ether and the Book of Mormon. An ancient record of a long-dead civilization, it is translated by mysterious means through a man from a much later period. The last survivor of this extinct civilization is responsible for passing on part of the history.

The second part of the discovery is recorded in the book of Ether and is related in the complex flashback of Zeniff, who received Mosiah I's permission to take a settlement party back to the land of Nephi, even though it was now in the possession of Lamanites. His grandson, Limhi, vassal-king to the Lamanites, secretly sent out search parties, trying to find a way back to Zarahemla. One of these parties, lost in the wilderness, came across "a land which was covered with dry bones; yea, a land which had been peopled and destroyed" (BM 200; Mosiah 21:25-28). They erroneously believed that they had discovered the ruins of Zarahemla and despondently returned to semi-bondage, bringing with them their finds: a book of twenty-four gold plates, rusty swords, and breastplates. Two generations later Ammon, heading a Zarahemla search party with the permission of Mosiah II, the son of Benjamin and the grandson of Mosiah I, finds Limhi's people. Limhi asks: "Canst thou translate [these gold records]? ... Knowest thou of anyone that can translate?" (BM 172; Mosiah 8:11-12). Ammon answered:

> I can assuredly tell thee, O king, of a man that can translate the records; for he has wherewith that he can look and translate all records that are of ancient date; and it is a gift from God. And these things are called interpreters, and no man can look in them except he be commanded ... lest ... he should perish ... and whosoever is commanded to look in them, the same is called seer. ... And Ammon said that a seer is a revelator and a prophet also; and a gift which is greater can no man have, except he should possess the power of God. ... But a seer can know of things past ... and ... to come ... and ... secret ... and hidden things. ... Thus God had provided a means that man, through faith, might work mighty miracles; therefore, he becometh a great benefit to his fellow beings. (BM 173; Mosiah 8:12-18)
>
> ... And now Limhi was again filled with joy on learning from the mouth of Ammon that King Benjamin had a gift from God, whereby he could interpret such engravings. (BM 173, 200; Mosiah 8:12-18, 21:28)

The first error is a slip in the chronology. King Benjamin had died soon after turning the kingdom over to his son, Mosiah II, who authorized Ammon's expedition (BM 168; Mosiah 6:3-7; 7:1). Moroni also refers to Benjamin as the translator of the book of Ether (BM 546; Ether 4:1), wording which appears in the printer's manuscript copy of the text. In the second edition of the Book of Mormon (1837), Smith changed the name of the translating king to Benjamin's son, Mosiah II.[6]

The second error is a mistake in geography. Mosiah has not specified the means of translation, and there is nothing in his account that would preclude the use of the (plural) items that Ammon describes. However, these "interpreters" had not been found with the engraved stone of the Mulekites but with the twenty-four gold plates (the book of Ether) found by Limhi's people. The interpreters originated in a miracle documented by the twenty-four gold plates themselves. When Jared's family reaches the ocean, God commands the brother of Jared to build eight submarine-like barges, built "tight" and without windows. To light them, the brother of Jared melts sixteen glass stones from a mountain and, at his prayer, God touches them to make them luminous. God praises the brother of Jared's faith, then says: "These two [extra] stones will I give unto thee, and ye shall seal them up also with the things ye shall write. For behold, the language which ye shall write I have confounded; wherefore I will cause in my own due time that these stones shall magnify to the eyes of men these things which ye shall write." Moroni records that he has obediently kept these interpreters sealed up with the record of the Jaredites (BM 545-6; Ether 3:23-4:5). Thus King Benjamin (or Mosiah) is supposedly capable of translating because he has the "interpreters" back in Zarahemla. But this claim of possession occurs before the storyline permits it, for God had commanded that the "interpreters" remain with the twenty-four gold plates, which had never been in Zarahemla, and were at the moment in the land of Nephi with Ammon and Limhi. Besides "interpreters," Joseph Smith had a stone in a hat, but we are not told what means Benjamin or Mosiah used in the translation.

Although there is no evidence to support my conjecture, I hypothesize that both errors occurred because Smith had just reconstructed the first part of the Book of Mormon in 1-2 Nephi, to replace the lost 116 pages. Too much time had passed, and connecting 1-2 Nephi with the last three-fourths of the book, dictating rapidly, was too complex a task for his memory.

In either case, Smith is describing himself with his "seer stones" attached to a breastplate. In Ammon's description of the seer is the language Smith would soon formalize when he became president of the church—its "prophet, seer, and revelator." This story emphasizes the importance of the "interpreters" he received from the angel; but it also creates an extraordinarily complex story. He is conflating the story within the Book of Mormon with his personal story of discovery and translation which began with two stones attached to a breastplate. Yet the angel confiscated the translators as punishment when Smith lost the 116 pages, leaving Smith to translate without the "interpreters" that had, according to the narrative, been prepared and preserved for that purpose.

Whatever else these complexities and mistakes signify, the very fact of expending such prodigious narrative energy to set up the story about discovering and translating the twenty-four gold plates underscores the parallels between Ether and the larger Book of Mormon which contains it. This explanation begins to account for Ether's distinctive complexities. The book is only thirty-five pages long (6 percent of the entire text), yet it is a condensed or miniaturized version of the whole Book of Mormon. I suggest that Smith put the book at the end of his story because that is where the Book of Mormon belongs in his personal chronology. Considering Ether as a fantasized version of the Book of Mormon itself also provides a useful context for understanding the complicated and sometimes contradictory stories suggested for its origins.

The Book of Mormon, as I hope I have demonstrated, is an expanded version of Joseph Smith's life. Ether is a more extreme fantasy version of the Book of Mormon. Everything in the story is more extreme: the wars, miracles, evil intrigue, and ultimate destruction. This two-step removal from Smith's life story also means that it is very disguised. But once we understand its relation to the larger Book of Mormon, we can use the Nephite stories to decode Ether. Smith, I would argue, is developing his own creative abilities—becoming a prophet whose creations are increasingly removed from their original source.

Here are a few of the similarities between Smith's life and his Book of Mormon alter egos, then paralleled again to the book of Ether alter egos:

1. The book of Ether is named after the final prophet who, like Mormon, observes and records the final wars of his civilization.

2. Joseph Smith was large. Nephi describes himself as "a man large in stature" (BM 13; 1 Ne. 4:20-38), and the brother of Jared is "a large and mighty man" (BM 539; Ether 1:34).

3. God tells the brother of Jared that he will be directed to a "land choice above all the lands of the earth"; God had told Nephi that "ye ... shall be led to a land choice above all other lands" (BM 540; Ether 1:42; and BM 9; 1 Ne. 2:20). The Smith family travels to New York in hopes of abundant grain harvests.

4. The brother of Jared is commanded to gather all animals and species; they camp in the wilderness for four years. Lehi's family wanders in the wilderness and provisions their ship. The Smith family experiences economic privation until they reach New York.

5. The eight Jaredite barges may suggest the eight Smith children traveling from Vermont to New York.

6. The luminous stones of the brother of Jared are reminiscent of Smith's peepstone.

7. The brother of Jared sees God's finger when he touches the stones and, because of his faith, God (who introduces himself as the pre-mortal Jesus) shows himself to this prophet. Smith will later claim to see Jesus Christ and God the Father.[7]

8. The watery trip of Lehi and Nephi had taken "many days." The Jaredite voyage took 344 days. The painful trip from Vermont to New York must have seemed very long to a lame child.

9. The Jaredite group, like Lehi's family, includes a father and four sons; this fact is mentioned twice within seven sentences. The Smith family has a similar configuration.

In addition to these parallels, there are differences, the most important being the condensation of the Jaredite story. Ether covers twenty-nine generations in thirty-five pages, using many of the same motifs as the Nephite story. The destructiveness is more terrible. The people divide into two genocidal factions, but both groups are equally filled with hate and equally unrepentant. Episodes of righteousness, whether individual or collective, are sparse. In the Nephite-Lamanite story, the Nephites intermittently repent and struggle (though unsuccessfully) against evil. Other motifs are familiar: a famine, a secret criminal society, assassinations, knifings, intrigue, and wars. Even in abbreviated form, King Noah and the Jaredite king

Riplakish share twelve similarities.[8] Both civilizations end in a gigantic battle at the hill Cumorah, called Ramah in this earlier period.

In the later Nephite battle, 240,000 soldiers die on one side, but a significant portion of the Lamanites survives. The Jaredites spend over four years in preparation for the final battle, and over 2 million soldiers die on one side alone. (In comparison, more American lives were lost in the Civil War than any other war: 25,000 soldiers were killed at Antietam in one day and 620,000 had died by the war's end. Mormon apostle Orson Pratt estimated the Jaredite civilization at 10-15 million.[9]) Nightly the soldiers retire to their camps, wailing their grief, sleeping on their swords so they will not magically disappear, and returning to battle the next day. Women and children are massacred. The people are "drunken with anger, even as a man which is drunken with wine" (BM 572; Ether 15:22). This is the final image of wine and swords in the Book of Mormon and signals yet another battle between Smith and his surgeon.

This time no one escapes. The numbers dwindle daily: fifty-two versus sixty-nine, thirty-two versus twenty-nine. Then all faint from loss of blood, revive, and fight again. Finally only two remain:

> And it came to pass that when they had all fallen by the sword; save it were Coriantumr and Shiz, behold Shiz had fainted with loss of blood. And it came to pass that when Coriantumr had leaned upon his sword, that he rested a little, he smote off the head of Shiz. And it came to pass that after he had smote off the head of Shiz, that Shiz raised upon his hands and fell; and after that he had struggled for breath, he died. (BM 573; Ether 15:29-31)

As a psychiatrist, I hypothesize that, in Smith's mind, sheer hatred was magic enough to make Shiz's corpse move after decapitation. In these terrible pages, Coriantumr is wounded in the thigh, arm, and other places. He faints three times from loss of blood. It is hard to imagine a more extreme version of the bloody surgery.

The hermit prophet Ether witnessed this debacle and recorded the story, including Coriantumr's survival. What happened to Ether is unknown, but Coriantumr lived "nine moons" with the Mulekites. During this period the carved stone was discovered, then the twenty-four gold plates, probably with the luminous interpreters, as God had commanded. I think most dynamic psychiatrists and psychoanalysts will appreciate that Shiz and Coriantumr are the final regressed versions of the two antagonists who began the Book of Mormon, Nephi and Laban, and, hence, of Joseph Smith and his surgeon.

The third way to account for the Ether narrative is as a final terrible descent into Smith's psychological conflicts. Sometimes in treating a patient who initially appears to have personality strengths and the capacity to care for others, the therapist may realize that this façade covers deep conflicts and very incomplete development. A successful outcome is unlikely, and the prospect of continuing will be exhausting. That is the feeling I had in reading Ether as a description of Smith's psychological state. Here are some disturbing aspects:

1. The book was found amid destruction, skeletons, and ruins. Limhi preserves but cannot read it. In psychological terms, these people (like the Mulekites with the carved rock) have information in their unconscious which they cannot tap. Since a large part of the Book of Mormon already reflects part of Smith's unconscious mind, these symbols suggest that we are dealing with the deepest layers in his unconscious.

2. Ether comes from the dawn of human history. The legends and myths about this period tell stories about humankind's earliest consciousness of itself. That is why the story of Adam and Eve remains such a fixed part of our culture, symbolically repeating our early childhood experiences. Here is nudity without embarrassment, a world where everything is provided, a search for knowledge, dawning sexual awareness and the need for clothes, the sexual symbol of a snake, the loss of childlike innocence, a child's discovery that his thinking is separate from the parent's and that he can keep secrets, and then the obligation to work in the real world after leaving the protection of home. Even more specifically, this is a story about verbal development. Symbolically speaking, Smith has used the Tower of Babel to represent the time when he was developing language out of the confusing noises made by surrounding adults—his "time of babbling." Smith is placing this story then under the sign of his very earliest development, perhaps as early as toddlerhood.

This admittedly speculative interpretation receives support from the intense and extreme fantasies. In the Genesis stories, men lived hundreds of years. The flood destroyed humankind, although an ark preserved one family and all of the animals. Lot's wife turned into a pillar of salt. "The sons of God saw the daughters of men that they were fair; and they took them wives of all which they chose. ... There were giants in the earth in those days; and also after that, when the sons of God came in unto the daughters of men, and they bare children to them, the same became mighty men which were of old, men of renown" (Gen. 6: 1-6). From a psychiatric perspective, this tale emphasizes the size disparity between adults and children and implies that only grown-ups can have sex. Nimrod, the "mighty hunter before the Lord" (Gen. 10:8-10), is the traditional founder of Nineveh.

This aura of biblical magic extends into Ether. In Helaman it had seemed extreme when God had promised Nephi that he could move mountains if he wanted to. In Ether "the brother of Jared said unto the mountain Zerin, Remove—and it was removed" (BM 565; Ether 12:30). There are no unicorns and dragons in Ether's fantasy world, but there are "cureloms and cumons; all of which were useful unto man, and more especially the elephants and the cureloms and cumons" (BM 556; Ether 9:19). We are dealing with the most regressed, the most fantastic book in the Book of Mormon. This book tells us of Smith's most basic units of personality.

3. The difference between this story and the later, less regressed, Nephite-Lamanite story is the relative absence of any struggle against evil. The Jaredites are evil, filled with hatred, without redeeming qualities. And that is the final message from the book of Ether. At the deepest layers of Smith's personality and from the earliest time of his existence, he lacked the resources for a fully constructive life. It is his followers' exemplary lives that counterbalance his miraculous story and make it believable. In my professional judgement, their lives are the sole "objective" evidence for the validity of the Book of Mormon.

The subtext of the Mulekite story confirms this desolate view. Without the five books of Moses, they had lost their literacy, religion, and civilization, suggesting Smith's bare escape from, and alternative to, the raw violence of savagery. Smith held on to the brass plates of Laban and the genealogy of his fathers, and (most importantly) the scriptures of his own time as the final tools to keep him from violence. They did not save him, for deceit, manipulation, and coercion were more effective than raw violence in injuring his people.

I am profoundly aware of how offensive this interpretation may be to devout Mormons. This very dark view of Joseph Smith's early infancy and childhood is admittedly extreme speculation, and there is no historical documentation of such emotional deprivation from his mother's history that would justify such furious hatred in the story. (Reports of the family's economic and social inferiority and dysfunction do come from later outside antagonistic testimonies which are rejected by devout Mormonism.) But with our present state of naturalistic (psychological) knowledge, this reading from the Book of Mormon back into Joseph's life may be the closest we can get to what happened.

The Book of Moroni

But the Book of Mormon does not end on this bleak note. Smith's past has been told completely, ending with the deaths of two civilizations. His final surrogate is Moroni, a new and future prophet. He speaks directly and authoritatively to Smith's contemporaries:

> Now I, Moroni, after having made an end of abridging the account of the people of Jared, I had supposed not to have written more, but I have not as yet perished; and I make not myself known to the Lamanites, lest they should destroy me. For behold, the wars are exceeding fierce among themselves; and because of their hatred, they put to death every Nephite who will not deny the Christ. ... Wherefore, I wander whithersoever I can, for the safety of mine own life. Wherefore, I write a few more things ... (BM 574; Moro. 1:1-4)

In these verses Smith confirms that his internal warfare will continue and he will go into hiding. We are reminded of the first Nephi who put on the disguise of Laban. Fifteen years later at the end of his last great teaching sermon, Smith will confirm that he keeps his secrets well: "You don't know me—you never will[.] I don't blame you for not believing my history[. H]ad I not experienced it [I] could not believe it myself."[10]

In the message from Moroni, we see Smith turning his attention toward the church he will soon found. The first five brief chapters contain basic rituals of baptism and the sacrament that are still part of Mormon practice. These final chapters also include sermons, ostensibly from Moroni's father Mormon. A language of faith, hope, and charity (quoting and elaborating on Paul's famous verses to the Corinthians) contrasts sharply with the language of death and destruction which had become familiar in the narrative during the downfall of the Nephites and Jaredites. It is as though the narrative wants to erase the memory of that world of evil and hate. It is a conundrum that Smith erects a message of goodness on top of coercion, deceit, destruction, and hatred. I, no doubt like many readers, see the goodness as superficial. Mormon preaches that good is discernible and powerful:

> The way to judge is as plain, that ye may know with a perfect knowledge, as the day light is from the dark night— For behold, the spirit of Christ is given to every-man, that ye may know good from evil ... for everything which inviteth to do good, and to persuade to believe in Christ, is sent forth by the power and gift of Christ; Wherefore ye may know with a perfect knowledge it is of God. (BM 578; Moro. 7:15-16)

A sense that such hopeful religious language is implicated in another effort at compensation and reversal is only underscored by the specific content of Mormon's teachings. I hear another attempt from Smith to work through the trauma and possible grief at the death of his malformed son: "Little children cannot repent; wherefore it is awful wickedness to deny the pure mercies of God unto them, for they are all alive in him because of his mercy. And he that saith that little children need baptism ... are in danger of death, hell, and an endless torment. I speak it boldly, God hath commanded me" (BM 582; Moro. 8). By God's decree, Smith has found another resolution and compensation for his loss and despair. Thus, though the language is further and further removed from any direct connection to Smith's life story, the language of the prophet is still articulated through the concerns and burdens of that life story.

This hopeful, forward-looking image is followed by the last letter Moroni had received from Mormon before his death. In it Smith directly expresses the oral rage of a child raised in deprivation, deception, and trauma:

> And the husbands and fathers of those women and children they have slain; and they feed the women upon the flesh of their husbands, and the children upon the flesh of their fathers; and no water, save a little do they give unto them. And notwithstanding this great abomination of the Lamanites, it doth not exceed that of our people in Moriantum. For behold, many of the daughters of the Lamanites have they taken prisoners; and after depriving them of that which was most dear and precious above all things, which is chastity and virtue;[11] and after that they had done this thing, they did murder them in a most cruel manner, torturing their bodies even unto death; and after that they have done this, they devour their flesh like unto wild beasts, because of the hardness of their hearts; and they do it for a token of bravery. (BM 584; Moro. 9:8-10)

The images here are the most extreme in the Book of Mormon. As I read this passage, I hear oral rage behind narcissism, mixed with the fever, thirst, and torture of childhood surgery. It is as though, even as his "grandiose self" forms into a prophet and church president, the dangerous underside of his psychological world erupts to the surface one final time.

And finally the concluding image of Moroni is troubling. For over two decades Moroni will wander alone over the American continent, hiding so he will not be killed, separated and alienated from humankind. Moroni's final words are again addressed to Smith's contemporaries: "And now I bid unto all, farewell. I soon go to rest in the paradise of God, until my spirit and body shall again reunite, and I am brought forth triumphant through the air, to meet you before the pleasing bar of the great Jehovah, the Eternal Judge of both quick and dead. Amen" (BM 588; Moro. 10).

The time is 421 C.E. It is this Moroni who "returned" to earth in 1823 as the angel telling Smith where he had buried the gold plates. It is fitting that there is confusion in the original manuscripts whether Nephi, the first prophet/alter ego for Smith, or Moroni, the last one, made this return. The first one put on a disguise, the last one remained in hiding.

Notes

1. Otto Kernberg, *Borderline Conditions and Pathological Narcissism* (New York: Jason Aronson, 1975), 17. Oral rage is unrefined, global, all-encompassing anger of a primitive kind, frequently containing images of raw violence. If consciously suppressed or unconsciously repressed, it may reappear in a variety of forms in interactions with other people, from direct explosive violence to more subtle ongoing psychological attacks.

2. Phyllis Greenacre, "The Family Romance of the Artist," *The Psychoanalytic Study of the Child* (New York: International Universities Press, Inc., 1958), 13:10.

3. Dan Vogel, *Indian Origins and the Book of Mormon* (Salt Lake City: Signature Books, 1986), 43-44.

4. B. H. Roberts, *Studies of the Book of Mormon* (Urbana: University of Illinois Press, 1985), 186.

5. Smith was dictating this story of the carved stone in 1829. In 1799 Napoleon had discovered the Rosetta Stone at the mouth of the Nile, and Champollion

deciphered the code that made it possible to translate Egyptian in 1824. The news was reported in U.S. newspapers by 1825.

6. Sidney B. Sperry, *Problems of the Book of Mormon* (Salt Lake City: Bookcraft, 1964), 203, believed this slip was a result of "human error" and blames it on Mormon. Almost 4,000 changes have been made in the Book of Mormon since it was first published, most of them grammatical. See Jerald and Sandra Tanner, *3,913 Changes in the Book of Mormon* (Salt Lake City: Modern Microfilm, 1965).

7. I think William D. Morain in *Joseph Smith and the Dissociated Mind* (Washington, D.C.: American Psychiatric Press, 1998) 129-66, contributes toward understanding the various layers in the Book of Mormon by his suggestion that the book of Ether may have been dictated by Smith as a memorial to his dead brother, Alvin (the "brother of Jared"). However, if my interpretation that the book of Ether is an expanded version of the whole Book of Mormon, angel story, and dictation period, I think that we may also have observed the major step toward his "first vision" story of the visit of God and Jesus. The angel with magic spectacles at the start of the Book of Mormon creation period has been expanded into the pre-mortal Jesus, providing "interpreters" with which Joseph Smith could translate ancient records. From here, the story is divided into two parts: the angel with the breastplate and stone spectacles ("interpreters"), and the visitation of God and Jesus.

8. Brent Lee Metcalfe, "Apologetic and Critical Assumptions about Book of Mormon Historicity," *Dialogue: A Journal of Mormon Thought* 26 (Fall 1993): 153-84, esp. 169-70.

9. Roberts, *Studies of the Book of Mormon*, 164.

10. Andrew F. Ehat and Lyndon W. Cook, eds., *The Words of Joseph Smith* (Provo, UT: Religious Studies Center, Brigham Young University, 1980), 343.

11. In these verses Smith fails to make an important distinction. Chastity and virtue are qualities of the mind that cannot be destroyed by rape.

CHAPTER 7

Diagnosis and Commentary

A brief discussion in chapter 2 summarized the advent of Mormonism as a product of the dying subculture of magic. But Mormonism emerged at the crossroads of magic and Christianity. The first part of this chapter describes how the Age of Enlightenment promoted acceptance of the Book of Mormon. While scholars have ably located Mormonism within the U.S. political, economic, and social milieu,[1] surprisingly little has been written about the Age of Enlightenment; and the only significant study I am aware of, written by a Lutheran minister, takes what I consider to be an overly charitable position toward Joseph Smith.[2]

The second part of this chapter provides a psychological diagnosis of Smith,[3] focusing on the psychological forces within him, their possible origins in his childhood and background, and his fit into known psychiatric categories. Examples already discussed from the Book of Mormon will be mentioned, as well as biographical examples to age twenty-four with occasionally references to his last fourteen years of life. My main diagnostic category is that of the narcissistic personality, but four modifications will better approximate Smith's personality: (1) combining this personality with the anti-social personality; (2) the proximity of the narcissistic personality to imposture in origins and characteristics; (3) the ability of the impostor to believe his fantasy (pseudologica fantastica); and (4) the enhancement of all of these characteristics by the "groupthink" of his followers who abandon critical assessment as they strive to touch the eternal world of omnipotent perfection (or "projective identification"). Projective identification, an important psychological defense for narcissists and some other personality types, is the psychological basis for charisma. I will discuss it last because it will serve as both a foundation and introduction to any assessment of Smith's last fourteen years.

Historical Context: The Treason of the Clergy

Christianity has now been in decline for 900 years. That decrease has taken the form of a teeter-totter response to the slow rise of rationalism. The Western European opposition to Christianity coalesced during the Age of Enlightenment, the century between the beginning of the Commonwealth in England (1689) to the end of the French Revolution (1789). It was a century of practical and philosophical writings attacking theology. It spanned three generations, but closely overlaps Voltaire's life (1694-1778), and this witty French philosopher became its major spokesman.[4] The Mormon story, beginning with the marriage of Joseph's parents in 1796, started only a few years later.

Some fifteen to twenty philosophers formed an international group, centered in France, but international in composition, known as the "little flock." Their active debates, in person and by widespread correspondence, had a common goal: to enthrone reason rather than authoritarianism or "superstition." Some of its participants became household names: Jean-Jacques Rousseau, who wrote on the noble savage; Edward Gibbon who authored the multi-volume and magisterial *Decline and Fall of Rome;* encyclopedist Denis Diderot, and metaphysician Immanuel Kant. In America, Enlightenment thinkers included Thomas Jefferson, Benjamin Franklin, and Thomas Paine.

Voltaire issued the group's battle-cry in 1759, repeating it in letters, booklets, and in place of his signature: *Ecrasez l'infame!* [Crush the infamy!][5] of bigotry, intolerance and superstition, particularly as embodied in Catholicism. But behind this popular movement mounted against ecclesiastical injustice, those who read the basic writings of the *philosophes* knew they were not just attacking Catholic control, but Protestant belief as well. Their intent was to dismantle the whole Christian edifice—book, beliefs, and organization. Voltaire wrote, "I hate priests, I hate them, I shall hate them till doomsday. ... I have two hundred volumes [on Christianity], and, what is worse, I have read them. It is like going the rounds of a lunatic asylum."[6] Instead he advanced Deism—a belief in a creator who did not interact with human beings. People worshipped this creator by honoring his creations, including humankind and the human ability to reason. But if Voltaire represented Deism, the even more heretical Scotsman David Hume represented atheism and anticipated a day free of "Stupidity, Christianity, and Ignorance."[7]

These men had no weapons but reason and a close affinity with classical philosophy; Charles Darwin's scientific observations would come a generation later. Their extensive literature relentlessly challenges unreasonable elements in the doctrine of original sin, the fall of Adam, the Flood, etc. They brought technical criticism of the Bible home to every educated man, enhanced skepticism, liberated many, and also increased insecurity for many.

The end of the eighteenth century saw "the Treason of the Clergy"—substantial numbers of the ministry who became agnostic, atheistic, and skeptical about their own life's work. The growth of critical rationalism in the minds of educated Christians during this period was enormous. As early as 1720, Cardinal de Bernis said, "It was no longer considered well-bred to believe the gospels."[8] It was a significant victory for rationalism, but a signal defeat, not so much for religious institutions, but ordinary people whose hopes of compensation in the next life to make up for misery in this one were shrinking. In England, beginning at Oxford, and then in the American colonies, the first response to this religious devastation was the Great Awakening of the 1740s. It sprang from the emotional message of John Wesley (1703-91), the founder of Methodism and evangelical fundamentalism.[9] He returned the people to orthodox beliefs, with simplicity in worship, intensity of emotion, and clarity of doctrine. The Second Great Awakening, which began in 1799, lit a blaze of revivalist fervor that swept back and forth over western New York for thirty-five years until the area was termed the Burned-Over District.[10] In this emotional maelstrom, Joseph Smith grew to manhood.

Voltaire's writings had been in French; his English counterpart was Thomas Paine. Paine, born in England in 1737, had endured terrible poverty and government injustice. He ran away from home, served at sea, worked at varied jobs, educated himself, barely escaped debtors prison, and saw injustice everywhere, partly fostered by the Church of England. He had already written some pamphlets and met Benjamin Franklin before he immigrated to America in late 1774 to work at a Philadelphia printing shop. In December 1775 he showed a manuscript of a book to Benjamin Rush who named it *Common Sense.* A half million copies were published in January 1776, and its simple, plain, direct message catalyzed the people. Some of America's leaders desired compromise with Britain, and not revolution. Paine argued that America's purpose must be "complete independence, to break all ties with corrupt and tyrannical Britain." George Washington stated that it was filled with "sound doctrine and unanswerable reasoning." "No learned treatise, no lawyer's brief, no philosophical discourse, *Common Sense* was a blunt and direct argument written in a language that could be understood by any ... simple farmer" with an effect that was instant. The pamphlet gathers "momentum with an attack on the English constitution in particular and on aristocratic institutions in general," then talks "of the messianic mission of America ... [with] the triumph of radical Republican principles. ... O ye that love mankind! Ye that dare oppose, not only tyranny, but the tyrant, stand forth! ... and prepare in time an asylum for mankind."[11] Its dramatic call for political independence prompted the formation of a five-man committee (June 1776) in the Continental Congress to write the Declaration of Independence. Paine vigorously supported the American Revolutionary War and, later, France's revolution. He opposed the beheading of Louis XV, got caught in the political infighting, was imprisoned, and barely escaped death. Immediately before entering prison, he gave a manuscript to a friend for safekeeping. It was the first part of his greatest work, *The Age of Reason.*[12] James Monroe, U.S. ambassador to France, facilitated his release, then gave him asylum in his own home where Paine convalesced and finished the manuscript. President Thomas Jefferson invited him to return to the United States in 1802, which he did. Meanwhile both parts of the book had been published in 1794 with dramatic effect. The publisher of the book was convicted of blasphemy and Paine of seditious libel in England (he escaped to France); he was hanged in effigy; anyone who read the book was officially persecuted; and some were arrested for displaying a portrait of Paine. In the United States, Jefferson stood by him, but Rush and most of his friends abandoned him. A hundred years later Theodore Roosevelt called him a "filthy little atheist."[13]

He was not an atheist but a Deist; and this campaign of slander and vilification resulted from his success in carrying the message of Deism to the people at the expense of Christianity and belief in the Bible. He respected Christ but condemned Christianity. He described his book as going "through the Bible, as a man would go through a wood with an axe on his shoulder and fell trees. Here they lie; and the priests, if they can may replant them. They may, perhaps, stick them in the ground, but they will never make them grow."[14]

The Age of Reason was similar to *Common Sense,* but directed against religious belief, not governments. Paine argued effectively that the Gospels were not "written by the apostles and that they appeared centuries after the death of Christ." The Immaculate Conception was a pure piece of fiction and the resurrection doubtful. Christianity was too "absurd for belief, too impossible to convince and too inconsistent to practice."[15] The book is noted for its witty irony and stunning clarity in translating the arguments of the *philosophes,* as well as the higher criticism and internal inconsistencies of the Bible, to a level that every man with an eighth-grade education could understand. It is still effective.

As a result of Paine's work, the Bible desperately needed support; a second witness for Christ was necessary for those who needed, in a psychological sense, a future life better than this one. *The Age of Reason* was a major precipitant of the Second Great Awakening. When Joseph Smith, Sr., attended the Methodist church with Lucy, his father and brother were so appalled that his father "came to the door one day and threw Tom Pain's age of reason into the house and angrily bade him read that untill he believed it."[16]

But where was the proof necessary to continue believing in supernatural Christianity? Prior to the Age of Enlightenment, the proof had partly come from the European trials for witchcraft. The existence of devils implied the existence of angels and God. Even after the Age of Enlightenment, John Wesley linked the two. "To give up belief in witchcraft, one might as well give up belief in the Bible," he lamented in 1768, adding two years later, "The infidels have hooted witchcraft out of the world."[17] But without torture, there would be no confessions of witchcraft. Proof of a supernatural world now came in the dramatic effects of the Holy Spirit in the revival and conversion meetings, but these emotional reactions were not the longed-for solid evidence needed psychologically to buttress belief in the Bible. In psychological terms, the Book of Mormon led converts back from the edge of existential despair by sanctioning Wesley's emotional proofs, adding another budget of miraculous conversions, the "falling exercise," and angelic visions. Its existence is adduced as proof that God exists. "How do you explain the Book of Mormon?" is a question still put to doubters. The Book of Mormon is termed both a "second" and a "new" witness for Jesus Christ.

Joseph Smith rode the backlash to the Age of Enlightenment. Mormonism still continues, psychologically, to provide security while rapid change and scientific development demolish social myths. The Book of Mormon anti-Christ episodes dealing with the challenge of the Age of Enlightenment—"Believest thou in God?"— assume the existence of God, engage in sectarian doctrinal squabbles, but concentrate on the secondary argument of proofs for and against the coming of Christ. I see influence from the Age of Enlightenment in the Book of Mormon's more reasonable versions of the doctrines of original sin, the Fall, etc. The Book of Mormon's view of original sin is: "Adam fell that men might be; and men are, that they might have joy. And the Messiah cometh in the fullness of time" (BM 65; 2 Ne. 2:25-26). The Fall is no longer the cause of humankind's miserable condition, but an ambivalent necessity to enter the joy of life; it answers the *philosophes* who pointed out God's unreasonableness and injustice for the forced choice in Eden.

The Book of Mormon could also provide definitive attacks on such specific doctrines as the necessity of infant baptism (BM 581-82; Moro. 8:11-21). It still can. What it was not prepared for was science. Darwin, a child of the Enlightenment, was born the year Paine died (1809), and published *The Origin of Species* fifty years later. It challenges the concept of a literal man and woman in a literal garden and talking with a literal God who prohibited them from eating a literal apple. The Fall necessitates the Atonement, a literal death balancing that literal sin.[18] The Book of Mormon does not have an argument for Darwinism. Today, as Mormonism entrenches itself in fundamentalism against scientific advance, the church finds itself facing the arguments of the *philosophes* with increasing frequency.[19] From my perspective, Mormonism today finds itself where general Christianity was 200 years ago.[20]

The Age of Enlightenment was much more than an attack on Christian religion. The *philosophes* examined politics, education, taste, science, and

Erases separation of Church & state

art—arguing against authoritarianism and for individual freedom. Their influence can be seen in the U.S. Constitution and Bill of Rights.[21] These documents created the pluralism that allowed Joseph Smith's church to flourish, yet he wanted to obliterate that pluralism by erasing the separation of church and state.

Under the anxiety of pluralism and individual freedom, Joseph Smith's religion spoke to those who desired the apparent clarity and simplicity of authoritarianism, which promised certainty, power over nature and one's enemies, explanations for misfortunes, the conquest of death, and meaning in life. In psychological terms, however, such individuals have regressed from both democratic individual responsibility and from pluralism. Mormonism combines the claimed divinity of the British monarchy and the authority of Roman Catholicism in which decisions are made by one for all.[22] Sigmund Freud (1856-1939), a grandson of the Enlightenment and an atheist, acknowledged the comforts of religious illusion but still attacked them as wasteful and stunting. "Science is no illusion," he stated. "But an illusion it would be to suppose that what science cannot give us we can get elsewhere."[23]

Joseph Smith and Narcissism

It is important to recognize that this discussion from this point on is speculative theory. In both science and general life, we want to encourage imagination, but it is either foolish or arrogant to treat ideas that have no outside confirmation as fact. Accepting either sexual abuse from "recovered memories" leading to multiple personality disorder or alien invasion as fact, without external evidence, are current examples of unsupported ideas that can cause great mischief. Accepting psychodynamic theory as fact can also cause damage. For example, forty years ago psychiatrists speculated that schizophrenia was caused by a "schizophrenogenic mother," not genetics; and families in general and mothers in particular had to deal not only with a terrible illness in the family, but unnecessary guilt, and sometimes very expensive unproductive psychoanalytic treatment. Similarly, psychoanalytic explanations of major depression, obsessive-compulsive rituals, and manic-depressive illness are of questionable merit, probably delayed the widespread use of lithium and other chemical treatments, and contributed to unnecessary emotional turmoil and suicide. Let us therefore be cautious and willing to face ambiguity.

The characteristics of a narcissistic personality, described in the introduction and quoted from American Psychiatric Association guidelines throughout the text, do not define a factual illness in an absolute sense. Rather, they gather "symptoms" that are believed to have a common origin into a "syndrome." As statistics and studies about the role of biologic illness accumulate, however, that description will almost certainly be altered.[24] My elimination of bipolar affective disorder as a diagnosis for Joseph Smith is based on present knowledge and may have to be rewritten if a percentage of narcissistic personalities responds favorably to specific medications such as lithium. It would be unwise to close the door to any possibility, including the idea that a more subtle form of bipolar disorder may have provided Smith with energy.

The cause and source of the narcissistic personality are not known.[25] We will not conclusively determine a source for Joseph Smith's either, given our limited information about his formative years. His mother's biography, our best source, at times seems defensive and self-serving. And others who come from depriving and dysfunctional families do not become narcissists or prophets.

Psychoanalytic theoreticians do not have statistics. The individual cases psychiatrists encounter seek treatment because of pain or dissatisfaction. Some do not respond to intervention despite strong energy and lengthy time. We cannot be certain in every case that the treating physician has made a correct diagnosis or is not imagining improvement. Many "narcissistic personalities" are "successful" and are never seen in evaluation or treatment, although I suspect that we frequently see their spouses and children.

Despite these caveats, the psychodynamic setting provides an unusual laboratory. Many hours of quiet listening to free association occur nowhere else in life. Finally, some individual narcissists do seem to respond to prolonged intensive psychotherapy. Both patient and doctor, supported by comments from family and friends, see a clear difference over time, supporting the hypothesis that at least some narcissistic personalities are psychological in origin. I draw on the body of literature produced by observation, experiment, theory, and psychiatric experience in my attempt to understand the Book of Mormon and Joseph Smith.

Splitting is a major defense demonstrated in the Book of Mormon; psychologically it requires less mental energy than more mature defenses such as repression. Because it is a fundamental cause of personality weakness and because the weakness and the splitting reinforce each other, progress is difficult. Its most obvious manifestation is the division of the world into polar opposites, and the lack of integration of various parts of the patient's psyche. The individual may oscillate between two opposite positions. This "all-or-nothing" splitting can be seen in the polarized opposites of the Nephites and Lamanites. I would argue that splitting best describes Joseph Smith's ability to present one face in public (such as denying polygamy) while simultaneously converting associates and new plural wives to the principle in private.

splitting

Besides polarization, another manifestation of splitting is reversal. The individual may reverse attitudes toward a particular person, switching instantly from compliments to vilification. He or she may oscillate in moral positions, yet not be troubled by the contradiction. Individuals who reverse in the Book of Mormon are the instantaneous conversions of Alma Jr., Zeezrom, and the whole Lamanite population in 30 B.C.E. Joseph Smith also reversed, opposing Masonry as a young man, yet later becoming a Mason himself and drawing on Masonic ritual, in part, for Mormon temple ceremonies.

Most psychiatrists believe that small children exhibit splitting because of lack of neurological development but that psychotic, narcissistic, and borderline patients retain it as a defense against disturbing emotional states, frequently rage.[26] In my professional judgment, its excessive use in the Book of Mormon establishes that Smith's basic emotional age was pre-Oedipal, that is, somewhere before the age of four. I also argue that he experienced Oedipal fears of castration as a result of his surgery (at some point between five and seven), and also had to deal with the demasculizing effects of a weak father. On a psychological level, he oscillated between the deprivation of an unstable childhood and the psychological trauma of his surgery. Consequently, he regressed, drawing on the magic and omnipotent defenses of very early childhood to resolve the later Oedipal fears and being locked in at a childhood stage characterized by magic, fantasy, splitting, omnipotence, devaluation, projection, and denial. In my view, this earlier emotional age was a fixation point that he had only tenuously left before. Later in life, I believe, he applied this omnipotent privilege and counterphobic defense to his sexual life, at which point he most closely fit the unofficial subclassification of "phallic narcissist," whose prototype in the Book of Mormon was Ammon. These attempts, in my opinion, account for the Book of Mormon's compensating and conquering fantasies of invincibility and conquest by the sword. They also suggest the rather gloomy prognosis that he would never escape from extreme fantasy compensation for his real life.

Recognizing splitting as a defense points a direction toward the general diagnosis. It is considered a "primitive" defense used in psychotic states and by borderline or narcissistic personalities. It is believed that personalities develop from genetic givens, very early emotional experiences, and also, partly, as patterns of thinking and manners ("character armor") in attempts to modify these genetic and early experiences favorably. Thus a personality, in addition to being "given" also has an adaptive purpose, not only with society, but with itself. The purpose of the borderline personality is to block disintegration. These individuals lead turbulent, destructive, and sometimes suicidal lives, always attempting to ward off psychosis and reacting violently to breakups of important relationships. Their lives are "stable in their instability," and they would not be capable of the regular functioning necessary to found a church. In contrast, the day-to-day purpose of the more stable narcissistic personality is to block shame, avoid humiliation, and maintain self-esteem.[27] Smith could not avoid the shame and humiliation of his 1826 trial and never mentioned it in any of his public writings. Yet I have argued that this trial appears in the Book of Mormon under three narrative guises: first, as a gigantic geophysical holocaust that destroyed almost everyone; second, as a literal court trial, after which, the jail, guards, lawyers, and whole town were destroyed by the Lamanites acting as instruments of God's vengeance; and third, as a supernal ministry of angels in a literal prison that converted the whole Lamanite nation, restored the Nephite lands, and ended thirty-two years of war. When Smith experienced the more personal humiliation of boasting about the supposed powers of his unborn child to hostile relatives and then having the child not only stillborn but badly malformed, he converted the experience into an angel-attended scene of Jesus blessing many children who received spiritual gifts denied the adults, later reversed the humiliation into hypomania, and then followed it by thirty-two years of intense war, suggesting his rage. Indeed, from a psychoanalytic perspective, Smith was trying to compensate for shame and humiliation, and his retaliation was intense.

The narcissistic personality may present himself[28] attractively and competently, can function well socially, and may have good impulse control. In relationships, the narcissist has a marked degree of self-reference and a strong need for "love" and admiration; these traits may appear normal or they may manifest themselves more disquietingly as an inflated view of their own importance and as a need for tribute from others. The Book of Mormon is filled with Smith's heroic alter egos, valiant, dazzlingly faith-filled, literally special to God. "I, Nephi" appears eighty-six times, for instance. Smith dictated a prophecy of himself as part of the Book of Mormon text in which he appears as "one mighty ... which shall do much good, both in word and in deed, being an instrument in the hands of God, with exceeding faith, to work mighty wonders, and do that which is great in the eyes of God" (BM 67-68; 2 Ne. 3:5-21).

Despite narcissists' superficial appearance of mental health, their emotional life is shallow; they live for the admiration of others or for their own ego-massaging fantasies. Boredom is their nemesis; during too-peaceful times, they create agitation. Because their self-esteem is fragile, no accomplishment is adequate, and they must agitate for more admiration from others. In the Book of Mormon, the two centuries of peace after Jesus' mission take only two and a half pages. The rest of the book is filled with agitated conflict. During Smith's last fourteen years after the Book of Mormon was published, he moved from one self-made crisis to another. Historian

Richard Van Wagoner commented, "Perhaps the greatest ambiguity in Smith's thorny persona was his proclivity to test conventions, to live on the edge of his impulses. ... Smith's career, in many respects, was the equivalent of a held breath."[29] In an 1843 statement that is wholly characteristic of the narcissistic personality's need for perpetual energy to sustain the grandiose self, Smith commented revealingly: "Excitement has almost become the essence of my life. When that dies away, I feel almost lost."[30]

Narcissists envy others. As a result, they tend to idealize those from whom they expect admiration and gifts—perhaps explaining why Smith developed such sudden and extreme attachments to individuals like John C. Bennett—yet may treat with contempt previous idols whom they have "used up," perhaps accounting for the deep and permanent estrangements that developed with David Whitmer, Oliver Cowdery, and Martin Harris. When a follower "repented" and again submitted to Smith's authority, thereby reinforcing his narcissism, he could be very forgiving. But Smith's demand for submission could be total, and only conditionally forgiving. Apostle Orson Hyde testified against the church and its vigilantism in Missouri in 1838, left the church, repented, and was reinstated to his apostleship in 1839. In 1842 Smith sent him to Palestine to dedicate that land for the return of the Jews. While away, Smith pressed Hyde's wife, Marinda Nancy Johnson Pratt, into becoming his plural wife.[31] "Is somebody who always has to walk on stilts not bound to be constantly envious of those who can walk on their own legs, even if they seem to him to be smaller[?]," queries psychologist Alice Miller. Narcissists' envy includes others who "do not have to make a constant effort to earn admiration ... [and] are free to be 'average.'"[32] In Book of Mormon terms, envy drives the consistently immature Nephites relentlessly toward materialism. They routinely forsake God, who punishes them harshly, forcing them to worship him in humble submission. Nephi Jr. avoids the conflicts of envy by becoming so omnipotent that his word brings famines and destruction.

Narcissists exploit others and may be parasitic at times. Nephi, the son of Lehi, gained access to Laban's treasury by murder, disguise, and deceit. Ammon won over Lamoni by "guile." Historically, Smith practiced deception in money-digging and later. From my perspective, his later life evinces such extreme examples that an item of orthodox belief is that all Smith's behavior was in obedience to God's commandment, thus exonerating him from otherwise reprehensible behavior. I would include here his secret polygamy, the establishment of secret intimidating societies bound by secret "Masonic"-like oaths, dictating to the members how to vote, the attempt to establish a secret theocratic government that superseded democracy, etc.[33]

Despite superficial warmth, on a deep emotional level, narcissists cannot trust or depend on anyone else. Beneath their controlling behavior lies oral rage that may appear in violent fantasies or in paranoid suspiciousness during interactions with others. Examples of oral rage in the Book of Mormon increase in frequency as the book progresses, including Moroni's fury at Pahoran when his troops are deprived of supplies, descriptions of cannibalism, and the destruction of the Nephites by the Lamanites. Ether, which may represent Smith's earliest experiences, develops a chronology in which all goodness disappears and total destruction ensues. (See chapter 6.) Smith, in Nauvoo, accused Emma of trying to poison him.

The present state of psychological theory concerning the formation of the narcissistic personality goes something like this: In response to very early frustrations too great for the child to handle, internal mental images of violence and destruction emerge that interfere with normal development and function, accompanied by unrealistic images of himself as perfect and wished-for images of perfection in his caretakers, usually his parents. These become fused into an idealized picture of himself which is superimposed over the destructive images and have a quality of grandiosity. This superimposed idealized image, the "false self," becomes the basis for the socially functioning personality of the narcissist and, because of its grandiosity, has been labeled, in the narcissist, the "grandiose self." This personality compensates for the feelings of helpless rage experienced in childhood and presents to the world what sometimes appears to be successful functioning.[34]

However, the origins of, and responses to, frustration never fully disappear and demonstrate themselves in the fantasies of violence and conquest that the psychiatrist hears in therapy and uncovers in works of fantasy. Further, the personality of the narcissist may appear warm and charming but will demonstrate the characteristics of splitting, devaluing others, idealizing relationships until they falter, making grandiose claims of specialness and special abilities, feeling constant threats to his self-esteem, needing perpetual admiration, and overreacting to shame and humiliation. These techniques of faulty personality interactions are necessary, it is believed, to help keep away the original feelings of helplessness and fury: "oral rage." Full maturation and integration of personality require moving past splitting and facing the underlying fury and helplessness, which is difficult, if not impossible, for the narcissist to do; as a consequence, full maturation is not possible.

Is there a possible genetic predisposition to narcissism? Kernberg believes that it is an "open question"; but the strongest suggestions come from family statisticians who suggest that an obscure form of bipolar affective disorder ("manic-depressive illness") might be at play. At this point in time, these are only theoretical considerations. I have previously discussed the difficulties with this suggestion, for it changes an episodic illness into a steady-state condition, and narcissists do not necessarily show mania or hypomania.[35] As already noted, Jungian analyst C. Jess Groesbeck has communicated to me (August 1993) his belief that he has found evidence of bipolar affective disorder in five generations of the Smith family.

Viewed from the psychological side, it is frequently believed by those who do intense psychodynamic psychotherapy that, under optimal conditions, we begin life in a relatively blissful situation, with a vague feeling of omnipotence and perfect union with the universe, represented by the mother. While no one knows, perhaps some of this initial state is a residual memory of the womb where the infant is warm, comfortable, and never hungry. Even after birth, all needs are quickly gratified with no special effort on the infant's part. According to Arnold Cooper, "The experience of satisfactory unity with the caretaking environment, usually the mother, builds in the young psyche a sense of omnipotence, a fantasy of total bliss and power."[36] At about six or seven months of age, the child realizes that the mother is a separate person, and separation anxiety develops. In normal development the child experiences hunger, discomfort, loneliness, fear, and anger in small episodes that are not overwhelming; the child reacts with disappointment and rage, but, again, in episodes short enough and sufficiently infrequent that he or she can handle them without being overwhelmed. The normal child delegates his own sense of omnipotence to a parent for whom he has loving feelings; as a result, he slowly develops a feeling of greater effectiveness and takes pride in his abilities to crawl, walk, and talk. If the parent is unreliable or inadequate, the jolts are traumatic, the child reacts with prolonged and intensive rage, and he becomes a source of stress for his mother, thus worsening his chances for receiving comfort. This failure to get another to meet his needs makes the child feel inadequate. He returns to the previous feelings of omnipotence (which, needless to say, are fantasies) that compensate for this insufficient world. Rather than relinquishing his primitive memory of a world of power and perfection, he absorbs it into his view of himself.[37]

While the day-to-day superficial functioning of the narcissist is directed at maintaining self-esteem and avoiding shame, his ultimate, underlying goal is to return to that initial stage of bliss he has now lost. In his thinking and feeling, he dares not fully rely on anyone else but himself. If this self were able to articulate its need for self-sufficiency, it would be as Kernberg summarized: "I do not need to fear that I will be rejected for not living up to the ideal of myself which alone makes it possible for me to be loved by the ideal person I imagine would love me. That ideal person and my ideal image of that person and my real self are all one and better than the ideal person whom I wanted to love me, so that I do not need anybody else anymore."[38]

In contrast, a child at about age two who is developing normally transfers the characteristic of omnipotence from himself to his parents, who seem godlike, giant, omniscient, and omnipotent. Through the years he learns that his parents are imperfect humans, but this potentially terrifying knowledge becomes tolerable as the child learns his own abilities. "Typically, the child's 'I am perfect and you admire me,' gradually changes into 'you are perfect and I am part of you,'"[39] perhaps seen most strongly between the ages of two and six. Eventually, this idealism will coalesce into the "ego ideal" (residual images of perfection) and, through the years, will mellow and attenuate into a reasonable conscience by the late teens. The ideal never fully disappears but remains in the average adult as an unobtainable goal—the search for perfection. Because healthy people know that ideal perfection is unobtainable, they use their ideals as guiding stars in their development and enjoy the process, not demanding perfection in themselves or others. In other words, the normal healthy person is clearly aware that the ego ideal for himself—his imagination of how he would be if he were perfect—is not who he is nor ever will be; he is accepting of this fact and comfortable with progressing in the direction of his ideal.

In contrast, the narcissistic personality must see himself as perfect or almost perfect to feel contentment. No matter how self-sufficient he believes himself to be, however, he knows that he cannot return to this ideal paradise without also returning to the fused state with someone else that he once dimly experienced as an infant. "The main task of the narcissistic personality," comments Burstein, "is to achieve the bliss and contentment characteristic of the primary narcissistic state, and this implies the reunion of the self which must be very grand with an object which must be nourishing and powerful. ... Self-esteem, the approval of others and the confirmation of one's sense of worth by the ability to use others are ... derivatives of the earliest narcissistic state."[40] In short, the narcissist needs no one but must have someone. This drive in Joseph Smith may explain why he attached himself to other grandiose figures, including Sidney Rigdon, a charismatic preacher, and John C. Bennett, a dynamic lobbyist and promoter, whose underlying corruption Smith overlooked. While narcissists seem "dependent" because of their need for admiration, their deep distrust prevents them from developing real attachments or interdependencies with anyone.

Because of their previous helplessness, their difficulty in truly trusting anyone, and their fear of shame and humiliation, their relationships with others tend to be controlling, usually by manipulation and coercion. The technique most commonly used is their attitude of superior abilities and confidence which draws less secure people to them.

First Modification: Combining the Narcissistic Personality with the Antisocial Personality

In mental health work, the primary diagnosis is the specific problem that brings the patient to treatment—for example, depression, anxiety, obsessive-compulsive behavior, or psychosis. The psychiatrist also tries to define the underlying enduring personality pattern from a separate list which is divided into three categories: the odd or eccentric (paranoid, schizoid, and schizotypal types), the anxious or fearful (avoidant, dependent, and obsessive-compulsive), and the dramatic, emotional, or erratic (borderline, histrionic, narcissistic, and antisocial).

The last-named diagnosis in the third category consists of a pervasive pattern of disregard for and violation of the rights of others. Clients in this category break the law, repeatedly lie, con and exploit others, act impulsively, ignore consequences, are aggressive, get into fights, show reckless disregard for their own safety or that of others, are generally irresponsible, and lack remorse when others are injured.

Many crimes in this country occur simply as "survival" behavior on the part of individuals who lack the resources to make better choices. The most frightening criminal, however, is someone who commits terrible crimes without remorse and gets enraged at being arrested or punished. Some of these individuals can be considered an extension of narcissism, with their arrogant assumption of right and control, complicated by faults or gaps in their "superego" or conscience. Characteristics of narcissism that might overlap with antisocial attributes include feelings of special entitlement, exploitation, lack of empathy, and arrogance. When these two personality types combine, the unofficial term is "malignant narcissism," an intermediary group of patients between the two diagnoses.

Such patients may be physically aggressive, paranoid, sadistic, and/or triumphantly self-mutilating or suicidal. But the combination of antisocial and narcissistic personality should be seen as a sliding scale, with some patients closer to one end than another. Less severe forms might manifest moral behavior in some areas and exploitive behavior in others. Some individuals may experience some forms of guilt, concern, and loyalty to others. They may be able to plan for the future. These lesser forms of malignant narcissism may be characterized by sexual promiscuity and/or financial exploitation of followers, yet be honest and consistent in other dealings. They may blame others for their problems and offer rationalizations for troubles.[41]

In the case of Joseph Smith, the theme of deceiving self and others is not a thread, but a steel cable. Seldom has such a characteristic been so well documented. It began with money-digging and seer stone peeping (see chapter 3); after the Book of Mormon was published, it continued with his sexual conquests under the guise of religious practice.[42] So consistent is his deceit that believers must see the dictation of the Book of Mormon as an exception to his dishonesty, and excuse Smith's behavior at other times as "expedient" because of special circumstances, as obedience to God's commandment, or, in the case of seer-stone peeping, as "preparatory" to his later "divine" calling. In the Book of Mormon, all the religious leaders are above reproach. Those who failed were always the congregations of ordinary Nephites. Nephi rationalized his murder of Laban; Joseph Smith was prepared to blame imaginary enemies for "forging" mistakes into the lost 116 pages. When the very first Mormon deaths occurred from cholera during an ill-fated military march a few years after the Book of Mormon was published, he blamed the sufferers, attributing the disease to their disobedience. He also blamed others for the collapse of his banking venture.

Placing Smith's basic personality somewhere between the narcissistic and antisocial, yet tending toward the former, allows us to proceed with other modifiers to his style. One modification is the symptom of pseudologica fantastica.

Second Modification: Pseudologica Fantastica

> The basic inner conflict in Joseph Smith's life was not, I believe, a conflict between his telling the truth or not telling the truth, but rather between what he really was and what he most desperately wanted to be.[43]

Pseudologica fantastica is defined as pathological misrepresentation, which varies from ordinary lying and daydreams in that the person intermittently believes in his fantasies or holds them for intervals long enough that he acts on them. It is a symptom found in a variety of personalities; but when combined with either the narcissistic or antisocial personality, it bodes a poor therapeutic outcome, for without honesty, the basic foundation of trust cannot develop.

> These patients tend to outrage the moral sensibilities of their victims and commonly provoke punishment. When confronted with damning evidence, the patient usually acknowledges the falsehoods readily. However, these patients have compulsive need to act out their fantasies repeatedly. It is often difficult to ascertain whether the truths are expressed with conscious or unconscious intent to deceive or as part of an actual delusional distortion of reality.[44]

A textbook example occurred in the summer of 1827 when Isaac Hale confronted Smith about his seer stone claims. (See chapter 3.) Reportedly, Smith readily acknowledged that he could not see anything in his magic stone and never had been able to. He promised he would give up money-digging. According to Peter Ingersoll, Smith knew that his family would press him to continue his supernatural claims and seemed "much perplexed." His forebodings were fulfilled; rather than following Hale's advice, he allowed himself to be swayed by his family and soon returned to his stories of magic, the gold book, and the guardian angel.

Third Modification: The Impostor

This discussion of narcissistic and antisocial personalities using the symptom of pseudological fantastica allows us to move to the next modification—the impostor.

The pure narcissistic personality behaves as if he is special, unique, or has special qualities, but without making a factually dishonest claim. His acts are not illegal. It is his attitude that draws people to him. The impostor differs from him in at least one critical way by making a factually fraudulent claim—that he has earned a diploma which he has not, that he performed a heroic action on the battlefield, that he has made certain financial achievements, that he has suffered a particular illness, that he has a particular kind of authority, or that he has a close relationship with a distinguished person. Joseph Smith claimed to receive visits from angels (among other heavenly beings) and that he could translate ancient documents. Although believers accept these claims, I see him *imposing* a false, grandiose self on others, demanding their regard and consideration for qualities and/or achievements that he does not, in fact, possess. If, for a period, he believed his own fantasies, he simply added pseudological fantastica to the picture. "Such persons are often quite gifted and capable of authentic success in the real world," observes Linn.[45] Underneath the façade lies a severe identity problem, which we have already discussed as the incomplete personality of the narcissist.

Phyllis Greenacre, an American psychoanalyst who wrote widely and deeply on a wide range of human behavior, wrote the defining paper on "the imposter" in 1958, before the delineation of the narcissistic personality, yet prescient in its similarity.[46] I find its depiction of symptoms that Smith may have possessed to be striking. Greenacre noted that, with impostors, a quality of showmanship is involved, interacting with the wishes of the andience, believers or followers. The desire of the believer, and willingness to accept the trickery, is an important part of this dynamic.

The impostor "flourishes" in his success, enjoying the limelight and experiencing an inner triumph at "putting something over," while delighting in being admired and observed as a spectacle. Greenacre believed that the impostor has a "malformation of the superego" (the conscious and unconscious conscience), and a pressure to live out his fantasy that "has the force of a delusion ... but is ordinarily associated with 'formal' awareness that the claims are false." The impostor may be sharp and perceptive, have immediate keenness and quick responses in the area of his imposturing, but may appear foolish, brazen, or stupid in other areas; these paradoxes make them puzzling and fascinating. Did Smith believe that American archaeology would find evidences of the Nephites? Did he foresee that his translation of the Egyptian papyrus would be eventually compared with its scientific translation?

Greenacre believed that the impostor grows up in a family of parental conflict, with the mother demeaning and reproaching the father who often responds by detaching himself emotionally, or even by leaving. It must be admitted that, writing after the death of her husband and four adult sons, Lucy nowhere hints at such attitudes. Instead she speaks with the utmost affection for her husband, consistently describes him as industrious and hard-working until his health was broken by the shock of Joseph's and Hyrum's arrests in Missouri, and, after bringing her family safely from New Hampshire to Palmyra (an example widely cited of her own competence), reports: "The joy I felt in ... throwing myself and My children upon the care and affection of a tender Husband and Father doubly paid me for all I had suffered. ... The children surrounded their Father clinging to his neck ... covering his face with tears and kisses that were heartily reciprocated by him."[47] However, we might wonder how she had earlier felt about her husband's business misjudgements, loss of their farm, periods of poverty, many moves, many children, his developing drinking, and preoccupation with money-digging. Was Lucy, who supported and believed in money-digging, and then encouraged her son's claim about angels and gold plates, capable of realistically evaluating and reporting the emotional states in her family? In the courtroom her husband was described as "poorly dressed ... lank and haggard ... indicating a wandering vagabond"[48] and also as reinforcing the flagrant deceptions of his son. The specific and general testimonies of the Palmyra townspeople (rejected as biased muckraking by devout Mormonism) present an unattractive family picture. After this trial occurred, Joseph's father-in-law described Joseph's behavior toward his father as "very saucy and insolent."[49] I wonder if Joseph had behaved in a similar way in his home of origin.

Greenacre believes that the impostor is singled out in the family and receives an inappropriate degree, or abnormal form, of intense attachment from the mother which may come in the form of extreme possessiveness, ambivalent concern, constant watchfulness, and marked anxiety and guilt or great pride. If such attitudes existed, they would have been intensified as a result of Joseph's surgery.

Kernberg, writing on the narcissistic personality, agreed with Greenacre: "These patients often occupy a pivotal point in the family structure, such as being the only child, or the only 'brilliant' child, or the one who is supposed to fulfill the family aspirations; a good number of them have a history of having played the role of 'genius' in their family during childhood."[50] Smith's paternal grandfather had "long ago predicted that there would be a prophet raised up in his family."[51] This Smith family statement receives some support from much later third-hand statements by unfriendly non-Mormons. In 1884 Clark Braden quoted Mrs. Horace Eaton (wife of a Presbyterian pastor in Palmyra for almost forty years and an acquaintance of the Smiths), who stated, "Even in Vermont, before moving to New York, while Joe was a child, Mrs. Smith's mind was made up that he should be a prophet. The weak father agreed that Joe was the 'genus' of the family and would be a prophet."[52] Braden also stated that "The minister employed by the Home Missionary Society, to labor in Vermont 1809-10-11-12-13, says, in his autobiography, that in 1812 a religious impostor created an excitement in the neighborhood of the Smith's. ... [Joseph Smith's mother] prophesied, at the time, that Joe, then seven years old, would be a prophet, and give to the world a new religion. Joe was raised with this idea before him. All the family used to speak of Joe as the 'genus,' as he termed it, of the family."[53]

Such abnormal mental attachment to the mother forms a type of fusion between the two, interferes with the development of a separate self, and nudges the boy into a position of superiority to the father. This repositioning adds to possible troubling outcomes of the developing Oedipal conflict, for the child has "won" in the competition with his father: "There is set a potentially serious imbalance of the oedipal relationship, the child being able to assume an uncontested supersedence over its [his] father."[54]

Here, both the Book of Mormon and Smith's life story provide firm correspondences. Nephi superseded Lehi as a prophet, even while the family was wandering in the wilderness; as a teenager, Joseph acquired a facility with his seer stone that made him the central figure in the accounts of Vermont money-digging activity. Smith later acted out his precedence over the legal husbands of numerous female followers in a very remarkable way.

The inevitable intensification of infantile narcissism favors a reliance on omnipotent fantasy in other aspects of self-evaluation to the exclusion of reality testing. The child is thus impaired before he gets to the Oedipal conflict and impaired by having a view of himself as superior as he passes through that critical time. This period of extreme importance may contain "the exhilaration of seeming independence with the great pleasure in and capacity to win admiration for the recently developed skills of walking and talking, but without real responsibility." The child is rewarded and praised for the *appearance* of accomplishment.

> Indeed, the behavior of the impostor utilizes exactly these characteristics with a very great dependence on ... gestures which are acted out with plausible and astounding mimicry. It is also conspicuous that impostors utilize

words in a similar way, with punning variations and substitutions, especially in names through which nuances of change in identity may be implied.

This pattern is used throughout the Book of Mormon in its mimicry of the nineteenth-century revivalist language, phrases, and fantasy of the Methodist camp meetings, as Baptist minister Lamb and historian Michael Walton have demonstrated.[55] The pseudo-biblical wording style of the Book of Mormon may be important in this regard. Jesus spoke and Paul wrote in the ordinary language of their day. The elevation of day-to-day language occurred as a result of translations and the King James Version around the time of Shakespeare. There is no reason for the literary style of the Book of Mormon except to mimic the Bible and make it appear "spiritual" in origin—to give it the *appearance* of something not really there. And, if Walter Prince was correct, then the "anti-Masonic" upheaval after William Morgan's death is found throughout the names in the Book of Mormon, in fourteen "anti" place names and the twenty-five uses of the syllable, "Mor[gan]," in proper names.[56] Symbolic "gestures" would become part of the sacred rituals of his secret temple ceremonies. To continue quoting Greenacre:

> The impostor seems to be repeatedly seeking confirmation of his assumed identity to overcome his sense of helplessness or incompleteness. It is my impression that this is the secret of his appeal to others, and that often especially conscientious people are "taken in" and other impostors as well attracted because of the longing to return to that happy state of omnipotence which adults have had to relinquish.
>
> ... Sustained imposture [thus] serves two important functions in the lives of the pretenders. It is the living out of an oedipal conflict through revival of the earliest definite image of the father. In so far as *the imposture* is accomplished, *it is the killing of the father through the complete displacement of him. It further serves to give a temporary feeling of completion of identity* (sense of self) that can be more nearly achieved in this way than in the ordinary life of an individual so impaired from having been psychologically incorporated by his mother. As part of this imposturous impersonation[,] there is a seemingly paradoxical heightening of his feeling of integrity and reality. This is certainly re-inforced and sustained by the sense of being believed in by others and, with the intoxication of being in the limelight (which reproduces the infantile situation with the general public taking the place of the mother), furnishes a most powerful incentive for endless repetition of this special type of gratification.[57]

I consider that the Smith family provided this setting for the teenage Joseph when, according to Lucy, they gathered around Joseph nightly listening "in breathless anxiety to the religious teachings of a boy 18 years of age."[58]

Many of Greenacre's points reappear in the later psychoanalytic literature on the narcissistic personality. To summarize both and apply them to Joseph Smith's creation of the Book of Mormon, I would say: (1) Joseph's warfare with the surgeon, presented again and again throughout the Book of Mormon represents, on a deeper level, his symbolic murder and replacement of his father (in his mother's eyes) in the home. So the story that began the Book of Mormon—of Joseph/Nephi murdering the inebriated surgeon/Laban—also represents Joseph "destroying" his father, who had a weakness for drink, and who had bankrupted the family. Smith repeated the pattern in his description of the final Jaredite battle in which the people were "drunken with anger, even as a man which is drunken with wine" (BM 572; Ether 15:22). The replacement of the father by the son may be represented in the Book of Mormon when evil Amalickiah murdered the Lamanite king and married the queen, thus suggesting superiority. I also argue that Smith's life after 1829 shows that he increasingly became who his followers wanted him to be; he presented himself as their prophet, and then took their belief back into himself as his most secure self-image.

Greenacre deals insightfully with the symbiotic relationship between charismatic leader and supportive followers by pinpointing the leader's "secret": he is able to activate their deep and even unconscious "longing to return to that happy state of omnipotence which adults have had to relinquish."[59]

Projective Identification

> It was emotionally impossible for the Saints to challenge the integrity of their prophet, in the matter of his early life or anything he chose to tell them. If deceived in anything, it might be they were deceived in everything. The whole power and discipline of their faith conditioned them to belief. Yet their own responsibility in the make of their prophet, in the proliferation of his legend, is not to be dismissed. Their hunger for miracle, their thirst for the marvelous, their lust for assurance that they were God's chosen people, to be preserved on the great and terrible day, made them hardly less than Joseph, the authors of his history. His questionable responsibility is the faithful image of their own.[60]

> [A]ll leaders—especially charismatic leaders—are at heart the creation of their followers.[61]

To summarize the psychological points made thus far: If the psychiatric hypothesis is true that human beings begin life in blissful fusion with the mother, all needs being rapidly and almost effortlessly satisfied, then the experiences of those days may be programmed into our autonomic nervous system. In our culture the legend of Adam and Eve in the Garden of Eden represents this period. Later fantasies may draw upon and symbolically reflect these primordial memories.

The narcissistic personality spends his life desperately trying to return to that "eternal world of omnipotent perfection," without limitations and problems. He has been so hurt by his confrontation with reality—either out of extraordinary need or extraordinary frustration and deprivation—that he will never again truly trust anyone. Still, he desperately needs to fuse with someone because only then can he replicate the most necessary condition of that state. He therefore creates an artificial and omnipotent self, whose fantasies compensate for the failures of the real world. In a vicious circle, he consoles himself for his failures by retreating into his fantasies; but his fantasies, while providing comfort, assure continued failure by preventing him from finding more effective ways to seek success. This pattern continues as a technique through life. If the child narcissist's family responds deferentially to this false self, it will be enhanced and give the impression of partially returning to that blissful state of omnipotence and unity. This false or grandiose self is enhanced when the mother turns from a weak husband to make her son her special companion. Already emotionally crippled, the son passes through the Oedipal period, knowing that he is the most important person for his mother and that his father can be disdained. But such processes are not unalloyed, and such overt attachments to the mother become increasingly awkward and must be disguised or suppressed. Joseph may have turned to his father during his surgery because he was "too old" to turn to his mother; he also may have wished to reassure his father.

Subject that child to a lengthy and painful illness, punctuated by three agonizing surgeries, and the prognosis is excellent that the boy will be fixated on compensatory fantasies of omnipotence, both for dealing with the pain and for dealing with the castrating effect of having a weak father. The mother's attention reinforces the child's fantasies of greatness. Compensation as a style—the child's constant need to be strengthened against the underlying fears of incompleteness, emptiness, and fear—may create a phallic narcissist. Repeated conquests, including sexual victories, will reinforce the omnipotent fantasies that diminish the feelings of being small and helpless. Add training in deception, such as from a weak, drinking father who subscribes to a silly outdated belief in magic, and an impostor, who intermittently and increasingly believes his own fantasies as fact, becomes possible.

It is not easy to describe the psychological methods used by narcissistic personalities because they are so primitive. The major technique is "projective identification," or, more accurately, "interactional projection." Ordinary projection, in comparison, is always an intrapsychic phenomenon. It occurs and is completed within one person and consists of mentally ascribing to someone else qualities that the person does not want to see in himself or herself. Those individuals or groups to whom the feelings, thoughts, or behavior are placed or projected don't know, don't care, or quickly disagree and leave. Projective identification, however, is part of an ongoing relationship between the first person and second (or group) in which the second person or group accepts the emotional assignment from the first person.[62] The process is not necessarily unhealthy. A small child whose diaper pin is jabbing him wants to project his distress immediately into his mother so that she will urgently seek out the cause. Throughout childhood, the child will do things to evoke and provoke feelings, such as frustration and anger, in the mother. The mother will experience the frustration, but then usually process it, and turn it into a modulated, educating, and growth-producing response. In symbolic terms, the mother returns the child's feelings to him in modified form. The child is comforted and learns. The process goes on daily. It is not growth producing when the mother responds to the screaming child by screaming back or spanking the child to "really give him something to cry about." For growth to occur, the second person must experience the feeling that has been projected, hold it and evaluate it, then elevate it to a higher plane of emotional and mental functioning before returning it to the child in modified form.

This pattern is the major mode of emotional growth in the child and continues into adulthood in a much diminished form in most of us. However, with some personality types, including narcissists and their followers, it continues as a major method of relating, but with two important differences. The narcissist not only assigns feelings and roles to other(s) but also coerces and manipulates others into taking the assignment. A common technique is the implied threat: "If you don't accept the position, feeling, or role in relationship to me, I will leave or send you away." The second party—individual or group—accepts the role, abandons critical evaluation, and remains locked in a primitive form of fused function with the narcissist.

"Projective identification," a variation of the defense of splitting, occurs when an individual symbolically places part of himself into a person he has to control to manage the projected part.[63] The narcissist first denies some feeling or thought within himself (such as feelings of guilt, inferiority, or helplessness), then, by persuasion, coercion, intimidation, denigration, or frank deceit, evokes those feelings in others. The narcissist maintains some sense of contact with the feelings he has injected in the individual or group, continues to control it, and reidentifies with it. "Fusion" is a reasonably accurate term for this interaction. The other(s) accepts the interactional manipulation by acceptance and/or may offer a counter response. For example, fearful of overvaluing himself, he may assign to the narcissist whatever feelings of omnipotence he himself feels. To compensate for his feelings of inadequacy, he must remain attached to the charismatic leader who radiates value to him, as long as he does the leader's bidding. He accepts blame for any failures of the leader and finds forgiveness only when the narcissist reaccepts and forgives him. The fantasies acted out by the impostor, then cycled through the colluding beliefs of his followers, return to the impostor as fact instead of fantasy and create pseudologia fantastica.[64]

As Greenacre notes, the followers "are not only victims but unconscious conspirators." Both the leader—in this case, the religiously charismatic Joseph Smith—and his followers are seeking that blissful state of infant fusion with the mother or, in religious terms, contact with the "eternal world of omnipotent perfection." If Greenacre and other scholars of narcissism are correct, the followers bask in the leader's radiant charisma and then, in endless cycles, reflect it back to the charismatic leader.

Jerrold Post, who has studied the narcissistic personality in leadership roles, describes "mirror-hungry" leaders and "ideal-hungry" followers:

> The "mirror-hungry" leader requires a continuing flow of admiration from his audience in order to nourish his famished self. Central to his ability to elicit that admiration is his ability to convey a sense of grandeur, omnipotence, and strength. These individuals who have had feelings of grandiose omnipotence awakened within them are particularly attractive to individuals seeking idealized sources of strength. They convey a sense of conviction and certainty to those who are consumed by doubt and uncertainty. This mask of certainty is no mere pose. In truth, so profound is the inner doubt that a wall of dogmatic certainty is necessary to ward it off. For them, preserving grandiose feelings of strength and omniscience does not allow of weakness and doubt.
>
> What are the characteristics of the *ideal-hungry followers?* ... Incomplete unto themselves, such individuals can only feel whole when in relationship with, when attached to, when merged with this idealized other. The charismatic leader comes to the psychological rescue of the ideal-hungry followers. Taking on heroic proportions and representing what the followers wish to be, he protects them from confronting themselves and their fundamental inadequacy and alienation. ... The leader's success becomes the follower's success, a succor to his self-esteem. ... [W]hen they come together in a group they behave as if they are acting on the basis of shared basic assumptions. ... The identity of follower becomes a badge of honor, a statement of membership in a collective self. ... In a figurative manner, we can speak of the development of a group mind or group ego.[65]

Early Mormons achieved the illusion of returning to the "eternal world of omnipotent perfection" through personal contact with Smith, through the omnipotent stories in the Book of Mormon, and through attachment to the priesthood and group activities. In reading the history of the church during the remainder of Smith's life, it seemed to me that he could not claim enough miracles for his followers. In the theoretical framework of projective identification, the congregation failed to respond to the assignment by critical evaluation, then elevation to a higher plane of thinking. Instead, when Smith injected an omnipotent view of himself into their psyches, they remained dissatisfied and asked for more.

An example how Smith's followers encouraged Smith's grandioseness occurred within a year or two after the Book of Mormon was published. Thirteen-year-old Mary Elizabeth Rollins, an early convert and later one of

Smith's plural wives, recalled his speaking to a gathering of friends and neighbors in her home:

> Joseph began talking. Suddenly he stopped and seemed almost transfixed, he was looking ahead and his face outshone the candle which was on a shelf just behind him. I thought I could almost see the cheek bones, he looked as though a searchlight was inside his face and shining through every pore. I could not take my eyes from his face. After a short time he looked at us very solemnly and said: "Brothers and Sisters do you know who has been in your midst this night?" One of the Smith family said, "An angel of the Lord." Joseph did not answer.
>
> Martin Harris was sitting at the Prophet's feet on a box, he slid to his knees, clasped his arms around the Prophet's knees and said: "I know, it was our Lord and Saviour, Jesus Christ." Joseph put his hand on Martin's head and answered: "Martin, God revealed that to you. Brothers and sisters, the Saviour has been in your midst. I want you to remember it. He cast a veil over your eyes for you could not endure to look upon Him, you must be fed with milk and honey, not meat. I want you to remember this as if it were the last thing that escapes my lips. ... He knelt and prayed. ... I felt he was talking to the Lord.[66]

From a psychoanalytic perspective, Smith here instilled his grand image into his followers, and they reinjected it back into him in even greater form—basically communicating that no miracle can be too great for them to believe and accept. They respond without critical evaluation or maturity. While this reaction may be understandable in ideal-hungry thirteen-year-old Mary Elizabeth, in Martin Harris it creates a scene filled with pathos.

At the Kirtland temple dedication in Ohio on 27 March 1836, many members of the congregation experienced ecstatic states. Those in attendance described the experience: "a shock on the house [temple] like the sound of a mightily rushing wind ... hundreds of [men] speaking in tongues, prophesying or declaring visions, almost with one voice." "[Many] beheld the angels of God; they heard the voice of the Lord ..." "Angels appeared to some, while a sense of divine presence was realized by all present, and each heart was filled with 'joy inexpressible and full of glory.'"

> Others testified to divine manifestations during various portions of the dedicatory program. During [the] first prayer President Frederick G. Williams saw an angel enter a window, take a seat beside Joseph Smith, Sr., and remain throughout most of the service. Heber C. Kimball described the individual: "He was tall, had black eyes and white hair, and stooped shoulders, and his garment was whole, extending to near his ankles on his feet he had sandals. He was sent to accept of the dedication." Lydia Knight remembered that Smith arose during the service and told the congregation "the personage was Jesus, as the dress described was that of our Savior, it being in some respects different to the clothing of the angels."[67]

Hysterical psychosis, whether stimulated by hypnosis or group psychology, can in fact produce specific images, but it can also be blocked by critical evaluation. There was none, and the experiences of his followers encouraged Smith to expand the magnificence of his miracles. In this scene, as I interpret it, the mirror-hungry leader has fused with ideal-hungry followers.

Their barriers between reality and the wished-for fantasy of fusion with the omnipotent world steadily faded. Yet the consequences for them were serious. According to Kets de Vries, the continued use of projective identification as a major defense into adulthood is usually considered mutually destructive:

> [When the] "positive responses from the [leader's] direct subordinates for even his most erratic actions [are continuous, they] may be responsible for a gradual deterioration of reality testing." The irony is that the leader who succeeds in pushing his movement toward the realization of their fantasies may well be on the way to his own self-destruction.[68]

What was Joseph Smith like to those who did not idealize him—to the ordinary non-Mormon? Charlotte Haven, a young woman of Portsmouth, New Hampshire, arrived in the Mormon town of Nauvoo, Illinois, in December 1842 to visit her brother and his wife. She stayed a year, and her letters to her family and friends were published forty-eight years later. Her letters are pleasant, literate, and observant. She observed Smith up close on three occasions:

> Joseph Smith is a large, stout man, youthful in his appearance, with light complexion and hair, and blue eyes set far back in the head, and expressing great shrewdness, or I should say, cunning. ... He is also very round[-]shouldered. ... I, who had expected to be overwhelmed by his eloquence, was never more disappointed than when he commenced his discourse by relating all the incidents of his journey. This he did in a loud voice, and his language and manner were the coarsest possible. His object seemed to be to amuse and excite laughter in his audience. He is evidently a great egotist and boaster, for he frequently remarked that at every place he stopped going to and from Springfield people crowded around him, and expressed surprise that he was so "handsome and good looking." He also exclaimed at the close of almost every sentence, "That's the idea!" ... [N]ot one sentence did that man utter calculated to create devotional feelings, to impress upon his people the great object of life.

Less than a month later she heard that Emma Smith wished her to visit, which she did in the company of a judge.

> Sister Emma, for by that name Mrs. S. is known, is very plain in her personal appearance, though we hear she is very intelligent and benevolent, has great influence with her husband, and is generally beloved. She said very little to us, her whole attention being absorbed in what Joseph was saying. He talked incessantly about himself, what he had done and could do more than other mortals, and remarked that he was "a giant, physically and mentally."

In fact, he seemed to forget that he was a man. I did not change my opinion about him, but suppose he has good traits. They say he is very kindhearted, and always ready to give shelter and help to the needy.

Charlotte and her brother's family had a number of visitors that summer, among them Joseph and Emma Smith.

> Mrs. Smith was pleasant and social, more so than we had ever seen her before, and we were quite pleased with her; while her husband is the greatest egotist I ever met.
>
> In the course of the afternoon he touched as usual on his peculiar doctrines, and [my] Brother asked him on what he founded his belief. He replied: "Upon the Bible."
>
> "All denominations do the same," said Brother, very innocently.
>
> At this Joseph became much excited; there was "no dubiety" about his religion, for he had more light directly from God, he said, and seemed to consider it an insult for any one to have the audacity to compare his doctrine with others. Finding him so dogmatical and so unable to reason, Brother let the Seer monopolize—as he always does—the conversation; or rather, glorify himself and his wonderful supernatural powers. However, the afternoon passed pleasantly.[69]

Joseph Smith was murdered a year later, after he destroyed a printing press that had published the *Nauvoo Expositor* which spoke negatively about him, polygamy, and a theocratic monarchy. His charismatic image would have faded quickly after his death, but his truly unique and permanent contribution was his literature. He created a permanent touchstone to the infinite—a written supernatural history filled with superheroes and miracles, capable of touching the heart of every person who has felt small, helpless, and alone. Allowing themselves to believe his autobiography as history because of its Christian veneer, members of his church are now known by the name of his book. Mormonism has become the only truly successful American religion, now international in scope and capable of wielding social and political power.

Notes

1. Klaus J. Hansen, *Mormonism and the American Experience* (Chicago: University of Chicago Press, 1981); Leonard J. Arrington and Davis Bitton, *The Mormon Experience* (New York: Alfred A. Knopf, 1979); Jan Shipps, *Mormonism: The Story of New Religious Tradition* (Urbana: University of Illinois Press, 1985); D. Michael Quinn, *The Mormon Hierarchy: Extensions of Power* (Salt Lake City: Signature Books, 1994); D. Michael Quinn, ed., *The New Mormon History: Revisionist Essays on the Past* (Salt Lake City: Signature Books, 1992); George D. Smith, ed., *Faithful History: Essays on Writing Mormon History* (Salt Lake City: Signature Books, 1992).

2. Robert N. Hullinger, *Joseph Smith's Response to Skepticism* (Salt Lake City: Signature Books, 1992), 1-5, 156. Hullinger sees Smith as much more consciously intentional in countering the Age of Enlightenment than I and, in fact, defines this goal as the Book of Mormon's main purpose: Smith "intended to inspire faith and encourage faithfulness ... and provide proof: of God, of Jesus Christ, of the

Bible, of itself. ... the Book of Mormon was intended to save people. ... Smith wanted them to look to the Messiah, obey him, be faithful to him. ... The stories and theology in the Book of Mormon constitute a defense of Jesus," while Smith intended "to bring doctrinal peace to Christendom." Hullinger thus sees Smith as working toward an honorable goal, even if his methods were questionable. In contrast, I believe that Smith had multiple goals in writing the Book of Mormon, some of them personal and self-serving. I see him using the conflict over religious skepticism opportunistically as well as a natural part of telling his life story.

3. Lawrence Foster, "The Psychology of Religious Genius: Joseph Smith and the Origins of New Religious Movements," *Dialogue: A Journal of Mormon Thought* 26 (Winter 1993): 1-22, has suggested a diagnosis of bipolar affective disorder (manic-depressive illness), following the suggestion of C. Jess Groesbeck, a devout Mormon Jungian analyst. In personal communication with me in 1993, Groesbeck stated that he believed he had found evidence of lesser forms of bipolar affective disorder in five generations of the Smith family. However, I find this diagnosis insufficient. Smith's personality was not episodic, and its main characteristic was self-centeredness, not excessive energy or profound depression. With the exception of Ammon's exultant cry of joy over the murdered Lamanite converts, assured salvation by martyrdom (BM 295-299; Alma 26) and perhaps one or two other episodes, the Book of Mormon does not contain examples of hypomania. See chapter 4 for my discussion of this event as an example of the psychological defense of compensating reaction-formation, stemming, I would argue, from Smith's humiliation when the firstborn son about whom he had boasted was born malformed and dead. See also Robert D. Anderson, "Toward an Introduction to a Psychobiography of Joseph Smith," *Dialogue: A Journal of Mormon Thought* 27 (Fall 1994): 249-74, esp. 268-72.

4. See Will Durant, *The Age of Voltaire. Vol 9 of The Story of Civilization* (New York: Simon and Schuster, 1965), 116-61, 361-96, 605-786; Peter Gay, *The Enlightenment: An Interpretation* (New York: W. W. Norton, 1977), Vol. 1: *The Rise of Modern Paganism.*

5. Durant, *The Age of Voltaire,* 736-43, esp. 738.

6. Qtd. in ibid., 744, 745.

7. Letter to Hugh Blair, 6 Apr. 1765, qtd. in Gay, *The Enlightenment,* 20, 401-19. See also Durant, *The Age of Voltaire,* 116-61.

8. Gay, *The Enlightenment,* 336-58, 339.

9. Durant, *The Age of Voltaire,* 128-37.

10. Arrington and Bitton, *The Mormon Experience,* 3-12; Jan Shipps, "The Prophet Puzzle: Suggestions Leading Toward a More Comprehensive Interpretation of Joseph Smith," *Journal of Mormon History* 1 (1974): 3-20; Whitney R. Cross, *The Burned-Over District* (Ithaca, NY: Cornell University Press, 1950), 3-13.

11. George Washington quote in Isaac Kramnick, "Introduction," to Thomas Paine, *Common Sense* (New York: Penguin Classics, 1986 [1776]), 29; "simple farmer," ibid., 9; quotes from *Common Sense* in ibid., 38, 43.

12. Thomas Paine, *The Age of Reason,* introduction by Philip S. Foner (1794; Secaucus, NY: Citadel Press, 1974).

13. Ibid., 48.

14. Ibid., 36, 156.

15. Ibid., 47-48.

16. Lucy Smith History, 1845, in *Early Mormon Documents,* Vol. 1, ed. Dan Vogel (Salt Lake City: Signature Books, 1996), 250.

17. Wesley, as qtd. in Rossell H. Robbins, *The Encyclopedia of Witchcraft and Demonology* (New York: Crown Publishers, 1965), 170. See also Robert D. Anderson, "The History of Witchcraft: A Review with Some Psychiatric Comments," *American Journal of Psychiatry* 126 (June 1970): 1727-35; H. R. Trevor-Roper, *The European Witch-Craze of the Sixteenth and Seventeenth Centuries and Other Essays* (New York: Harper Torchbooks, 1969), 168ff; and Norman Cohn, *Europe's Inner Demons* (New York: Basic Books, 1975). Cohn critically evaluates the evidence for witch cults and convincingly demonstrates that it is without merit and that the witch craze was a cultural delusion. Trevor-Roper comes to the same conclusion using other arguments.

18. Thomas Paine, *Age of Reason,* 67-68, excoriated the atonement of Christ as "an idea of pecuniary justice and not that of moral justice." He used this analogy:

> If I owe a person money and cannot pay him, and he threatens to put me in prison, another person can take the debt upon himself and pay it for me; but if I have committed a crime, every circumstance of the case is changed; moral justice cannot take the innocent for the guilty, even if the innocent would offer itself. To suppose justice to do this is to destroy the principle of its existence, which is the thing itself; it is then no longer justice, it is indiscriminate revenge. This single reflection will show that the doctrine of redemption is founded on a mere pecuniary idea corresponding to that of a debt which another person might pay. . .
>
> Let him believe this, and [the believer will] contemplate himself as an outlaw, as an outcast, as a beggar, as a mumper, as one thrown, as it were, on a dunghill an immense distance from his Creator, and who must make his approaches by creeping and cringing to intermediate beings, that he conceives either a contemptuous disregard for everything under the name of religion, or becomes indifferent, or turns what he calls devout.
>
> In the latter case, he consumes his life in grief, or the affectation of it; his prayers are reproaches; his humility is ingratitude; he calls himself a worm, and the fertile earth a dunghill; and all the blessings of life by the thankless name of vanities; he despises the choicest gift of God to man, the GIFT OF REASON.

19. See the essays recounting the struggle between Mormon fundamentalism and science in Gene A. Sessions and Craig J. Oberg, eds., *The Search for Harmony: Essays on Science and Mormonism* (Salt Lake City: Signature Books, 1993).

20. Brigham Young carried scriptural literalism a step farther by insisting that "our Father and our God—the only God with which we have to do" left heaven and came to earth as Adam (his position as god over this earth being temporarily assumed by his own Heavenly Father and God) to father the human race with one of his plural wives, later returning to father Jesus by another plural wife who had been sent ahead to be born as Mary. See David John Buerger, "The Adam-God Doctrine," *Dialogue: A Journal of Mormon Thought* 15 (Spring 1982): 14-58; Boyd Kirkland, "The Development of the Mormon Doctrine of God," and "Eternal Progression and the Second Death of the Theology of Brigham Young," both in *Line Upon Line: Essays on Mormon Doctrine,* ed. Gary James Bergera (Salt Lake City: Signature Books, 1989), 35-52, 171-82; Gary James Bergera, "The Orson

Pratt—Brigham Young Controversies: Conflict within the Quorums, 1853 to 1868," *Dialogue: A Journal of Mormon Thought* 13 (Summer 1980): 7-49.

21. Peter Gay, *The Enlightenment: An Interpretation* (New York: W. W. Norton, 1969) 2; *The Science of Freedom*, 555-68.

22. Mario S. De Pillis, "The Quest for Religious Authority and the Rise of Mormonism," *Dialogue: A Journal of Mormon Thought* 1 (Spring 1966): 68-88.

23. Sigmund Freud, "The Future of an Illusion," (1927) in *Complete Psychological Works of Sigmund Freud*, 23 vols. (hereafter *Standard Edition)* (London: Hogarth Press, 1951), 21:56; see also "Civilization and Its Discontents" (1930), 21:57-145.

24. H. S. Akiskal, "Characterologic Manifestations of Affective Disorders: Toward a New Conceptualization," *Integrative Psychiatry*, May-June 1984, 83-96. My discussion of narcissism throughout this section relies heavily on Otto Kernberg, *Borderline Conditions and Pathological Narcissism* (New York: Jason Aronson, 1975), 16-44.

25. The two leading psychoanalytic theoreticians on narcissism disagree about its origins. Kohut believed narcissism had its own biological developmental line, passing through various phases toward maturity, and can therefore be forced offtrack to aberrant behavior or fixated at a certain immature point. Kernberg, on the other hand, believes that there is no biologic line for narcissism and defines it as always a pathology that develops in response to a destructive environment in childhood. Heinz Kohut, *The Analysis of the Self* (New York: International Universities Press, 1971), passim, esp. 3; Kernberg, *Borderline Conditions*, passim, 279; Manfred F. R. Kets de Vries and Danny Miller, "Narcissism and Leadership: An Object Relations Perspective," *Human Relations* 38 (1985): 583-601, esp. 587.

26. Psychosis is a mental disorder in which a person's mental capacity, emotional response, and capacity to recognize reality are impaired enough to interfere with the ordinary demands of life. The borderline personality is considered to be more dysfunctional than the narcissistic personality and uses the defense of splitting extensively. They demonstrate a pervasive pattern of instability in interpersonal relationships, self-image, and emotions, along with impulsivity. They become frantic with real or imagined abandonment, and suicide attempts and brief episodes of psychosis may occur. The term *borderline* was first used to describe these patients "on the border" between more normal "neurotics" and the more severely disturbed psychotic patients. See Alfred M. Freedman, Harold I. Kaplan, and Benjamin J. Sadock, *Comprehensive Textbook of Psychiatry*, 2d ed. (Baltimore: Williams and Wilkins, 1975), under references to borderline personality (847-49) and glossary (2577, 2601).

27. W. W. Meissner, "Narcissistic Personalities and Borderline Conditions: A Differential Diagnosis," in *Essential Papers on Narcissism*, ed. Andrew P. Morrison (New York: New York Universities Press, 1986), 403-37.

28. Because half to three-fourths of narcissists are male, and the focus of this work is a male, I will refer to the narcissist as male.

29. Richard S. Van Wagoner, *Sidney Rigdon: A Portrait of Religious Excess* (Salt Lake City: Signature Books, 1994), 290-92.

30. In a sermon delivered 14 May 1843, Joseph Smith, Jr., et al., *History of the Church of Jesus Christ of Latter-day Saints*, 2d ed. rev., 7 vols., ed. B. H. Roberts (Salt Lake City: Deseret Book Co., 1951), 5:389.

31. Marvin Hill, *Quest for Refuge: The Mormon Flight from American Pluralism*

(Salt Lake City: Signature Books, 1989), 96-98; Richard S. Van Wagoner, *Mormon Polygamy: A History* (Salt Lake City: Signature Books, 1986), 224-25.

32. Alice Miller, "Depression and Grandiosity as Related Forms of Narcissistic Disturbances," in Morrison, *Essential Papers on Narcissism*, 323-37, on 330.

33. Klaus J. Hansen, *Quest for Empire: The Political Kingdom of God and the Council of Fifty in Mormon History* (East Lansing: Michigan State University Press, 1967), 24-88.

34. Kernberg, *Borderline Conditions*, 231, believes that the narcissistic personality forms from "a fusion of ideal self, ideal object, and actual self images as a defense against an intolerable reality in the interpersonal realm." He describes five admittedly subjective differences between the normal narcissism of childhood and pathological narcissism: (1) The normal child's grandiose fantasies—angry effects to control mother and to keep himself as the center of her attention—have a far more realistic quality than those of the narcissistic personalities. (2) The normal child's overreaction to criticism and failure, along with his excessive need for love, coexist with simultaneous expressions of love and gratitude, interest in, and capacity to trust and depend on his parents. (3) Normal infantile narcissism and the child's demandingness relate to real needs, while the demands of the pathological narcissist are excessive and can never be fulfilled. (4) The normal child's self-centeredness has a warm quality, while the narcissist, when not exercising his social charm, is cold, aloof, contemptuous, dismissive, and devaluing of others. (5) The pre-Oedipal fantasies of power, wealth, and beauty of the normal child do not imply an exclusive possession of all that is valuable, and he does not need admiration for being the sole owner of such treasures, while narcissistic personalities do. Ibid., 272-73.

35. Ibid., 276; see also Anderson, "A Psychobiography of Joseph Smith," n3; Hagop S. Akiskal, "Dysthymic and Cyclothymic Depressions: Therapeutic Considerations," *Journal of Clinical Psychiatry* 55, suppl. (Apr. 1994): 46-52, and "The Prevalent Clinical Spectrum of Bipolar Disorders: Beyond DSM-IV," *Journal of Clinical Psychopharmacology* 16 (1996): supplement 1, 4s-14s.

36. Arnold M. Cooper, "Narcissism," in Morrison, *Essential Papers on Narcissism*, 132-33.

37. Ibid., 139-40.

38. Kernberg, *Borderline Conditions and Pathological Narcissism*, 231.

39. Kets de Vries and Miller, "Narcissism and Leadership," 590.

40. Ben Burstein, "Some Narcissistic Personality Types," in Morrison, *Essential Papers on Narcissism*, 381-82; see also 377-401.

41. Otto Kernberg, "The Narcissistic Personality Disorder and the Differential Diagnosis of Antisocial Behavior," *Psychiatric Clinics of North America* 1 (Sept. 1989): 553-70.

42. Examples of this to his wife, friends, the general church membership, the state, and the nation are documented in Linda King Newell and Valeen Tippetts Avery, *Mormon Enigma: Emma Hale Smith* (Garden City, NY: Doubleday & Co., 1984), 52-198, and in George D. Smith, ed., *An Intimate Chronicle: The Journals of William Clayton* (Salt Lake City: Signature Books in association with Smith Research Associates, 1995), 93-197.

43. Fawn M. Brodie, *No Man Knows My History: The Life of Joseph Smith*, 2d ed. (New York: Alfred A. Knopf, 1971), 417.

44. Louis Linn, "Clinical Manifestations of Psychiatric Disorders," in *Compre-*

hensive Textbook of Psychiatry, eds. Alfred M. Freedman, Harold I. Kaplan, and Benjamin J. Sadock, 2d ed. (Baltimore: Williams and Williams Co., 1975), 790.

45. Linn, "Clinical Manifestations of Psychiatric Disorders," 790.

46. Phyllis Greenacre, "The Imposter," *Psychoanalytic Quarterly* 27 (1958): 359-82.

47. Vogel, Lucy Smith History, 276.

48. W. D. Purple, "Joseph Smith, The Originator of Mormonism," *Chenango Union,* 3 May 1877, qtd. in Francis W. Kirkham, *A New Witness for Christ in America* (Independence, MO: Zion's Publishing, 1951), 2:362-68, on 366.

49. Testimony of Isaac Hale, in E. D. Howe, *Mormonism Unvailed* (Painesville, OH: Author, 1834), 262-66.

50. Kernberg, *Borderline Conditions,* 23.

51. Statement by Joseph Smith's grandmother, Mary Duty Smith, in Kirtland, Ohio, on 17 May 1836, in Smith, *History of the Church,* 2:442-43.

52. Mrs. Horace Eaton, "The Origin of Mormonism" (1881), as quoted in Clark Braden, *The Braden-Kelley Debates: Public Discussion of the Issues Between the Reorganized Church of Jesus Christ of Latter Day Saints and the Church of Christ (Disciples) held in Kirkland, Ohio beginning February 12 and closing March 8, 1884* (St. Louis: Christian Publishing Co., 1884, and Kansas City: J. H. Smart and Co., 1884), 348.

53. Ibid., 46.

54. Greenacre, "The Imposter," 369.

55. M. T. Lamb, *The Golden Bible* (New York: Ward and Drummond, 1887), 222-28; Michael T. Walton, "Joseph Smith and Science: The Methodist Connection. A Case Study in Mormonism as a Response to Nineteenth-Century American Revivalism," Sunstone Symposium, Aug. 1984; see also Brigham H. Roberts, *Studies of the Book of Mormon* (Urbana: University of Illinois Press, 1985), 284-318. See discussion in chapter 3.

56. Walter F. Prince, "Authorship of the Book of Mormon," *American Journal of Psychology* 28 (July 1917): 379-80.

57. Greenacre, "The Imposter," 370-71.

58. Vogel, Lucy Smith History, 296.

59. Greenacre, "The Imposter," 370.

60. Dale Morgan, "Chapter three of A[n Incomplete] History," in *Dale Morgan on Early Mormonism: Correspondence and a New History,* ed. John Phillip Walker (Salt Lake City: Signature Books, 1986), 260.

61. Jerrold M. Post, "Narcissism and the Charismatic Leader-Follower Relationship," *Political Psychology* 7 (1986): 676.

62. Projective identification is "the most intensely studied type of explicitly interactional defensive activity ... and was first described by Melanie Klein [in] 1946." Theo. L. Dorpat and Michael L. Miller, *Clinical Interaction and the Analysis of Meaning* (Hillsdale, NJ: Analytic Press, 1992), 259. From the voluminous literature on this method of relating, I also selected Robert Langs, *The Therapeutic Interaction* (New York: Jason Aronson, Inc., 1976), 521-22, 575-78; Joseph Sandler, "Countertransference and Role-Responsiveness," *International Review of Psycho-Analysis* 3 (1976): 43-47; Margaret S. Mahler, "On Child Psychosis and Schizophrenia," *Psychoanalytic Study of the Child* (New York: International Universities Press, 1952), 7:292-300; Martin Wangh, "The 'Evocation of a Proxy,'" *Psychoanalytic Study of the Child* (New York: International Universities Press, 1962), 17:451-69; Warren M.

Brodey, "On the Dynamics of Narcissism: Externalization and Early Ego Development," *Psychoanalytic Study of the Child* (New York: International Universities Press, 1965), 20:165-92.

63. Gerald Adler, "Correctional (Prison) Psychiatry," in Harold I. Kaplan and Benjamin J. Sadock, *Comprehensive Textbook of Psychiatry IV* (Baltimore: Williams and Wilkins, 1989), 1993.

64. One of my patients, a registered nurse, told me in the presence of her physician husband that she had been diagnosed with an unusual form of cancer five years earlier and given an estimated four years to live. She asked her husband to let her deal privately with her physicians and medical therapists. He honored her request. She had been seeing a psychiatrist colleague for some time to deal with her illness, and he had referred her husband to me because of his stress over his wife's illness. Husband, children, friends, and Catholic congregation gave added attentiveness to this dying woman and planned a group trip before her health deteriorated too far. She remained remarkably healthy. When she reported that her physician had suggested minor surgery, the husband called her physicians. They had never heard of her. She admitted, "They all believed it, and then I began to believe I really did have cancer." She deceived her psychotherapist as well.

65. Post, "Narcissism and the Charismatic Leader-Follower Relationship," 679-80, 683-85; emphasis his.

66. Mary Elizabeth Rollins Lightner, manuscript autobiography, qtd. in Brodie, *No Man Knows My History*, 85-86.

67. Van Wagoner, *Sidney Rigdon*, 172-74, quoting Orson Pratt, Eliza R. Snow, Heber C. Kimball, and Lydia Knight.

68. Gary James Bergera, "Joseph Smith and the Hazards of Charismatic Leadership," *John Whitmer Historical Association Journal* 6 (1986): 33-42, quoting Kets de Vries, "Crisis Leadership and the Paranoid Potential," *Bulletin of the Menninger Clinic* (July 1977): 358.

69. Charlotte Haven, "A Girl's Letters from Nauvoo," *Overland Monthly*, Dec. 1890, 621, 623, 631.

Index